# Urbane and
# rustic England

MANCHESTER
UNIVERSITY PRESS

Politics, culture and society in early modern Britain

General Editors

PROFESSOR ANN HUGHES
DR ANTHONY MILTON
PROFESSOR PETER LAKE

This important new series publishes monographs that take a fresh and challenging look at the interactions between politics, culture and society in Britain between 1500 and the mid-eighteenth century. It seeks to counteract the fragmentation of current historiography through encouraging a variety of approaches which attempt to redefine the political, social and cultural worlds, and to explore their interconnection in a flexible and creative fashion.

All the volumes in the series will question and transcend traditional interdisciplinary boundaries, such as those between political history and literary studies, social history and divinity, urban history and anthropology. They will thus contribute to a broader understanding of crucial developments in early modern Britain.

Already published in the series

*The idea of property in seventeenth-century England:*
*tithes and the individual*   LAURA BRACE

*Home Divisions: aristocracy, the state and provincial*
*conflict*   THOMAS COGSWELL

*Inventing a Republic: the political culture of the English*
*Commonwealth 1649–1653*   SEAN KELSEY

Forthcoming

*The Earl of Leicester and the politics of*
*Elizabethan England*   SIMON ADAMS

*Ambition and failure in Stuart England: the career of John,*
*1st Viscount Scudamore, 1602–43*   IAN ATHERTON

*Betting on lives: the culture of insurance*
*in early modern England*   GEOFFREY CLARK

*Cromwell's Major Generals*   CHRIS DURSTON

*Reading Ireland*   RAY GILLESPIE

*Londinopolis*   MARK JENNER AND PAUL GRIFFITHS

*A courtly community?*   JOHN MERRITT

*Sixteenth century courtship*   DIANA O'HARA

*The public sphere in early modern England: public persons*
*and popular spirits*   STEVE PINCUS AND PETER LAKE

# Urbane and rustic England

## Cultural ties and social spheres in the provinces 1660–1780

CARL B. ESTABROOK

Manchester
University Press

*Published by* Manchester University Press
Oxford Road, Manchester M13 9NR, UK
http://www.man.ac.uk/mup

*British Library Cataloguing-in-Publication Data*
A catalogue record is avalaible from the British Library

ISBN 0 7190 5319 6 *hardback*

First published 1998

05   04   03   02   01   00   99   98        10   9   8   7   6   5   4   3   2   1

Typeset in Scala with Pastonchi display
by Koinonia Ltd, Manchester

Printed in Great Britain
by Bookcraft (Bath) Ltd, Midsomer Norton

TO B.,
WHO WAS THERE,
WITH LOVE

# Contents

—◆—

# List of tables

Note: Bold figures indicate contingencies that are significant in statistical terms, that is to say surprisingly common (+) or rare (−) given the distribution of cases. Noteworthy contingencies are indicated as common (+) or rare (−). For example, in Table 7.1 the cross-tabulation of the rural setting with a book ownership level of 'no books' for the period 1660–99 has a computed significance level of 0·041, which is considered statistically significant. The computer analyses of contingency tables exclude columns or rows with no entries. For the method of computer analysis applied to contingency tables in this book, see: C. B. Estabrook and G. F. Estabrook, 'ACTUS: a solution to the problem of small samples in the analysis of two-way contingency tables', *Historical Methods* 22 no. 1 (1989), pp. 5–8.

# Abbreviations

B.C.L.      Bristol Central Library MSS and Collections
B.L.        British Library
B.R.O.     Bristol Record Office
G.R.O.     Gloucestershire Record Office
P.I.         Probate Inventories and Cause Papers
P.R.O.     Public Record Office
Q/SR      Somerset Quarter Sessions Records
S.R.O.     Somerset Record Office

# Acknowledgements

Along the path leading to the completion of this book, I was helped by numerous people and institutions. It is my pleasure to thank them here. The good will and expert assistance extended to me by archivists and staff at the Bristol, Somerset and Gloucestershire record offices, and by the librarians at the Bristol City Library, never failed to impress me. Robin Bush, Sheila Lang, James Skeggs and John Williams in the city and county record offices, and Anne Crawford of the Public Record Office, were especially helpful. The good work of librarians and special collections curators at Bristol, Brown, Dartmouth, Oxford and Yale universities was instrumental to the completion of the research on which this book is based. The Kingsley Trust of Yale University, the Burke Award of Dartmouth College, and the Mellon Foundation provided generous grant support. I am grateful to the Institute of Historical Research in London and to Ronald Hutton at the University of Bristol for including me in the collegial life of those places during my research visits in England. I should like to thank those local historians, Edwin and Stella George in particular, who so generously showed me their own work. It was my pleasure and privilege to sing in the choir of Bristol's beautiful St Mary, Redcliffe church. The rector and vestry of that justly famous church graciously admitted me to their parish, one that proudly curates copies of its own early modern records.

A number of fellow English historians were kind enough to comment on all or part of this work as it went through various stages. Susan Amussen, Jonathan Barry, Laura Corballis, Perry Curtis, Mary Fissell, Tim Harris, Ann Hughes, Ben Klein, Peter Lake and David Underdown must not go unmentioned by name. Paul Fideler, Paul Halliday, Mark Kishlansky, John Morrill, Catherine Patterson, Steven Pincus and many other participants in the British Studies Workshop at Harvard provided a forum for discussions contributing to the completion of the book, as did the Conference on British Studies. I owe an intellectual debt to people working outside my field as well. Phil Benedict kept me alert to the possibilites of continental comparisons. George Estabrook introduced me to new ways of reasoning with quantifiable evidence. Very early on, Joan Scott encouraged me to explore the theoretical implications of my work. I very much hope that the debts I owe many other scholars, on both sides of the Atlantic, will be obvious to all readers, including those scholars themselves. I should like to thank Vanessa Graham, Carolyn

## Acknowledgements

Hand and all others at Manchester University Press who worked on the publication of the book. I am continually grateful to my colleagues at Dartmouth College who have provided a truly supportive and nurturing environment in which to be scholars, teachers and friends.

C.B.E.
Hanover, N.H.

# Introduction

◆

# Culture and the urban sphere of influence

> Where in the world is Stanton Drew?
> A mile from Pensford, another from Chew.
>
> Old Somerset rhyme

At some point in the late seventeenth century, a clever person identifying himself as Ned composed a ribald poem narrating his trip to London from a Somerset village near Taunton and Glastonbury.[1] The poem comes to us on a tattered piece of paper in cramped, but tidy, handwriting. It is barely fifty lines long, so our rustic hero moves suddenly from his opening escapade in the West Country to his impressions of the metropolis as if he were instantly drawn across the intervening landscape. Thus the transition is as abrupt for the reader as it was for Ned.

> Thorn goeing on, London's city z' did view
> And when z' did zeet schor a ready to spew
> What with the neeze and what with the smoake
> Twas Death in my ears and schor a ready to choake.
> But oh how the coaches did vlee up and down
> Iz thought the whole world had a bee in ye Town.
> The stones did spet vire, the horzes did vly
> Like thunder and lightning drough the sky.
> But o mee thoughts how my moth did water
> At theire floeth cream and whott pudding pies.
> But the slutts are zoe nasty, it can never be clean.
> Schad rather eat wittpott in Taunton Dean.

The parody of Somerset dialect and rustic speech patterns is so extreme here as to suggest that Ned was the creation of another commentator whose origins will be forever unknown. The identity of the poet, however, matters less than the poem's barbed quality and its normative message. The point of the poem is not to ridicule Ned, but to identify him as an alien in the urban setting where, as Ned and his creator would have agreed, people of a rustic disposition do not belong.

Rural visitors to cities and towns in early modern England often suffered unpleasant experiences. This was so much the case that even a surprising degree of geographical mobility and ample scope for urban–rural interaction did little to nurture more lasting social ties or cultural affinity between people of urban and rural origin until the last decades of the early modern period. The persistence of such an urban–rural divide is puzzling given the conspicuous, even dazzling, changes in urban society and culture, especially after the Restoration in 1660 'symbolised the recovery of civic harmony and order after twenty years of conflict and confusion'.[2] Nevertheless, it is unsafe to assume that villagers in early modern England felt at home in the urban setting or were dazzled enough by cities to have stayed in one of them for very long.

An affluent minority of urban dwellers occasionally removed themselves from the cities to comfortable country retreats. But these people energetically maintained their principal social and cultural ties with the urban network. Indeed, from the point of view of many local villagers, these amphibious creatures adversely transformed the rural setting to suit their urbane tastes. For their own part, successful merchants, professionals and other upwardly mobile members of urban society, drawn to the reputed beauty and salubrity of the rural setting, found that once they were actually there work was impossible, discomfort was probable, and villagers were inhospitable. One urban developer, on a tour through the West Country in the early eighteenth century, found rural accommodation so alien that he could hardly bring himself to move his bowels there.[3] Daniel Defoe referred to a place he called Evil (rather than Yeovil), Somerset, where he remarked that:

> the country way of expressing themselves is not easily understood, it is so strangely altered ... This way of boorish country speech, as in Ireland, it is called the brogue upon the tongue; so here 'tis called jouring and 'tis certain, that though the tongue be all mere natural English, yet those that are but a little acquainted with them, cannot understand one half of what they say.[4]

The world of villagers was like a foreign land, a strange setting, for members of urban society in early modern England; indeed, the cultural and social gulf between urbane and rustic England was reflected in the land itself. We get the unmistakable sense from the letters and travel journals of urbane commentators that life would have been splendid if the social spheres and culture forms in the rural setting had only followed the urban example.

It is tempting for historians of English cities and towns to adopt this view. The early modern period is an exciting one for students of English urban history. It was a period in which England showed clear signs of urban growth, a process which had an enormous impact on virtually every aspect of the urban experience: social structure, physical environment, economics, politics, and cultural life. One historian has identified the period following the Restoration of the monarchy in 1660 as an 'English urban renaissance' and has gone so far as to attribute England's overall social and economic modernisation to the cultural revival of cities which in turn sparked imitative patterns of consumption, display, and sociability in rural areas surrounding cities and towns.[5]

> It might be imagined that the Urban Renaissance, with its emphasis on the cultural identity of the town, intensified the divide between the urban and rural spheres. The contrasts between the two types of environment, and the contribution of leisure to accentuating these, are certainly evident in the literature of the period. However, it would be dangerous to assume that such accounts reflected a general or deepening alienation between town and country. In reality, the two worlds were inextricably bound together, particularly at the provincial level.[6]

According to this view, a revived city or town was the centre of an expanding sphere of influence which promoted more widespread interaction between urban dwellers and nearby villagers.

The view that an immediate consequence of the urban renaissance was the emergence of the urban dynamic as the dominant force shaping social and cultural life in England as a whole has achieved the status of an axiom without the benefit of much critical discussion.[7] There is the assertion that rural dwellers could not develop 'a truly regional culture', a sense of community beyond the confines of the village, 'without an urban focus of some kind'.[8] Two of the most influential historians in this field state plainly that 'towns were the essential cogs in the machinery of rural society' and that 'towns were also the social and cultural centres of the country'.[9] The implication that rural life was rapidly transformed in some imitative fashion – that cities served as the principal cultural resources and social foci for nearby villages – is a notion worth testing. Although the English urban renaissance of the late seventeenth and early eighteenth centuries is a celebrated phenomenon, little has been said about the impact of this early modern urban revival on villages, village life, and people of rural origin. Through direct urban–rural comparisons, we can examine systematically the notion of an urban sphere of influence. The evidence for the city of Bristol and the villages in its rural environs points to the persistence of a gulf between urban and rural society for nearly a century following the Restoration. A study of cultural forms and practices also prompts us to consider that the durability of this urban–rural gulf may have owed less to impersonal economic and demographic forces than to the causal agency of cultural affinity and personal volition linked with an awareness of topographical setting. When social and cultural expressions of urban–rural convergence became more widespread, as they did by the middle of the eighteenth century, these too reflected changes in conscious practices, attitudes, and values.

It is important to point out that an English urban revival did, in fact, take place, at least in the larger and more economically diverse cities and towns. Furthermore, the second half of the seventeenth century, closely associated with the conspicuous aspects of the revival, is rightly identified as a watershed in English urban development in contrast to the preceding period, which concluded in the violence, destruction, instability, and austerity of civil war and revolution. It is widely accepted that the spectacular rate of English population growth from roughly 3 million in 1500 to nearly 6 million by 1650[10] was a major source of social polarisation and economic hardship. The century after 1660 is regarded as a period of recovery associated with the redistribution of population and the rejuvenation of English cities and towns.[11] During the century following 1650, one out of every six English adults actually resided in London at some point in his or her life, despite the frightening rate of mortality there.[12] Although the characterisation of the early eighteenth-century English population as predominantly rural is entirely valid,[13] something approaching 25 per cent of the entire English population resided in urban areas by the 1670s.[14] Moreover, the second half of the seventeenth century was a turning point in the nature of urban migration. English cities had been flooded with paupers, vagrants, and dependants during the century preceding 1650, but capable workers and married adults with more promising claims to settlement rights migrated to cities in increasing numbers after the Restoration.[15] Whereas the wealthy fled cities and towns in order to avoid supporting the influx of poor migrants between 1550 and 1650,[16] affluent people began to return to urban areas during the century after the Restoration. Commercial centres and port cities profited greatly from the late seventeenth-century expansion of international trade, a source of wealth and upward mobility associated almost entirely with urban activity and what we might call an urban ethos.[17] A perceived decline in the profitability of agriculture and a tapering off of the population explosion prompted the wealthy to return to cities and towns after 1650 or so. These social and economic incentives were accompanied by the rise of the urban professional classes, a development which fostered a new association of urban life with prosperity and the enhancement of status.[18]

The urban revival assumed conspicuous forms. New urban affluence sponsored a lively programme of building featuring schools, churches, monuments, elaborate town houses, and other visible signs of personal success and civic pride.[19] After the Restoration, the beautified and renovated urban setting became the stage on which formal celebrations of art and recreation were more frequently performed. Bristol created public walks and gardens along the banks of the river Avon by 1673. Theatres were erected in both Bath and Bristol before 1710. Between 1668 and 1704, musical societies and concert festivals sprang up in the cities of Salisbury, Wells, Oxford, Winchester, and York. Assembly dances and assize balls became lively events in provincial cities and towns that formerly lacked the attractive cultural scene of university or cathedral cities. Preston began regular assembly dances in 1682. In some cities long known as ecclesiastical centres, civic events rose to take a place of prominence on the public stage. Assembly dances were held in Norwich by 1688. In 1711 and 1722 Chester and Bristol built ballrooms for the social events accompanying the sessions of the assize courts. The assizes were of possible use to people in the surrounding countryside but the occasions surrounding them signified the vitality of the cities in which the assizes and assemblies were held.[20]

A recurring aspect of the urban historical perspective is its tendency to suggest that early modern urban growth and vitality 'urbanised' rural life and placed all villages and rural dwellers within the sphere of influence of some city or town along the lines of a model suggested by early nineteenth-century theorists.[21] According to the old view, as cities and towns rose to prominence, more clearly unified regional spheres formed around urban centres, thereby diminishing the relative significance of the urban network and blurring old distinctions between urban and rural society and culture. In her important study of late seventeenth-century Norwich, Penelope Corfield observes the formation of a regional culture and society focused on the concerts, plays, and balls held in that city. Norwich's influence was sustained by the size and diversity of its population. Its growing service sector provided amenities for the expanding ranks of urban professionals. An increasingly active assize brought the gentry into closer contact with Norwich. In view of all this, Corfield offers Norwich as one example of a 'provincial capital'.[22] Other historians have invoked the concept of the urban sphere of influence more cautiously, limiting its rural participants to the gentry. Nevertheless, gentry 'power, as well as wealth, still rested in tenurial relationships in the countryside' and the 'elite were unlikely to abandon their rural estates completely for the pleasures of civil society'.[23] Thus any cultural hegemony exercised by the gentry in the villages was mediated through the context of the rural setting and its social conventions. That members of a rural elite appeared in urban centres for litigation or occasional celebrations of high culture does not demonstrate a more widely felt merger of urban and rural society – or the transformation of the rustic by the urbane – during the late seventeenth and early eighteenth centuries. The notion that united regional communities, or even widespread signs of 'material conformity', were achieved in the generations following the Restoration as a product of renewed urban vitality is worthy of reconsideration.

A principal aim here is to assess the social and cultural influences of a major English city upon villagers in its rural environs as these influences and environs changed during the century or so after 1660. The large and lively port of Bristol and the villages of southern Gloucestershire and northern Somerset provide an excellent case on which to base a study of this period associated with the urban revival and its influence. Bristol was a location of county, municipal, judicial, and ecclesiastical administration. Bristol was certainly among the most prosperous and influential of English provincial cities. Its citizens were impressively engaged in medical, artistic, scientific, and educational pursuits, especially after a period of severe sectarian animosity came to a close in the late seventeenth century.[24] Bristol's population, which grew from 12,000 to just over 19,000 during the seventeenth century, swelled to 50,000 by 1750.[25] That is to say, while the English population as a whole was beginning to level off in the late seventeenth and early eighteenth centuries, the number of Bristol's inhabitants roughly tripled. After the Restoration, Bristol was second only to London among English ports, and remained so until Liverpool emerged as a busier maritime centre in the 1750s.[26] Bristol was the site of several weekly markets and major annual fairs. A cathedral city, Bristol was the centre of a diocesan administration. At the same time, it was a provincial centre of religious nonconformity, home to George Fox after the late 1650s and consequently a hub of Quaker activity. Bristol, where Charles Wesley came to make his home, was the urban centre of Methodism for the West Country if not all of provincial England by the 1740s.[27] And in 1695, through an act of no small significance on the part of the corporation, Bristol became the first provincial community, apart from Oxford or Cambridge, with its own printing press after the lapsing of the Licensing Act.

The countryside surrounding Bristol, nestling between the Mendips and the Cotswolds and bordering on the Severn Channel to the west, formed an area recognised by contemporary cartographers as Bristol's natural 'environs'.[28] This area was more or less within a twelve-mile radius of the symbolic high cross, or heart of the city, where Wine, Corn, Broad, and High Streets converged at the city's commercial and geographical centre one mile from the outer edges of the city. The environs or vicinity of Bristol therefore excluded Bath, the nearest urban rival. Margaret Spufford has suggested that the 'ideal basis' for a comparative study of villages would be to select a 'social area' within an eight-mile radius of a focal settlement. The most thorough study of apprentice migration in this period recognises 'the vicinity of Bristol' to be within a twelve-mile radius of the city.[29] All the villages within eleven miles of Bristol's own outer parishes are considered here to have been within the city's rural environs. There were examples of nucleated manorial villages as well as more dispersed settlements among the villages in Bristol's rural environs. There were arable villages that were mainly under cultivation, but many rural folk engaged in textile work as an alternative source of income. The rural area of Kingswood, bordering directly on Bristol, had a significant collier population. The seat of the powerful Smyth family, Ashton Court, was in the Somerset countryside just across the Avon from the city. There were gentry homes in the nearby villages of Henbury, Stapleton, and Abson. Thus the region not only had clear topographical definition, it had considerable social, economic, and cultural diversity. As we will see, some of the settlements in Bristol's rural environs were transformed, near the end of the early modern period, into pockets of a more modern form of suburbia. In short, the city of Bristol and its rural environs did not present a highly specialised case. Rather, they appear to have been excellent candidates for the representation of the urban sphere of influence, if this was in fact a common aspect of the English urban renaissance and its impact on society and culture.

Applying the concept of culture to urban–rural comparisons raises complicated questions concerning the relationship between cultural ties and social spheres. One of the aims of articulating an applied theory of culture here is to promote a careful reconsideration of analytical categories in general, for the related purposes of faithfully representing the past and interrogating the historical evidence itself. Until relatively recently, historians have invoked the concept of culture rather broadly or, at worst, uncritically. The use of conventional social categories to characterise culture has been recognised as problematic, even by historians who continue to speak in terms of 'popular' culture, for example.[30] Under pressure to identify the nature of their discipline, champions of cultural history have placed new emphasis on the effects imposed on the historical process by the production, transmission, appropriation, and reception of symbols.[31] Although such an approach assigns to culture the quality of agency (as opposed to immutable and passive objectivity), it still does not explain how culture is distinct from all other agents of continuity and change.

Perhaps we should understand culture in functional terms as the conduit through which values and affinities are expressed, and characterise culture in terms of the forms it takes. Understood in this way, as an analytical category embracing many expressive forms, culture is not defined subordinately in terms of the social groups that make use of those forms. Culture assumes a variety of forms all of which can be used by any social group to establish and regulate its membership by communicating shared values, identities and affinities. In early modern England, cultural ties assumed three dominant forms: personal culture (direct and deliberate face-to-face interaction); material culture (artificial surroundings and tangible possessions); and print culture (the complex merger of ideas and the technology whereby words and images are recorded in a replicated and widely disseminated form). It is important to remember that print culture has both material and abstract components. The proposed distinctions among personal, material, and print culture provide many of the organisational schemes for urban and rural comparisons. It is clear that until the later years of the early modern period the dominant cultural forms, and the most widely observed practices involving their use, varied significantly with topographical setting. This helps to explain the maintenance of largely separate urban and rural social spheres for much of this period despite the urban renaissance. This functional understanding of culture avoids the use of social groups to identify cultural forms. It also points to the fascinating relationship between social spheres and the cultural forms which were used, often in conscious ways, to include some people in a community while excluding others from it.

In order to understand fully the interaction among messages, cultural forms, and social groups, it is essential to recognise these as three distinct analytical categories. This approach is meant to avoid the assumption that cultural forms, expressed values, and social groups interact in inextricably linked, fixed, or exclusive combinations. It would be misleading to speak categorically of 'the oral transmission of superstition in peasant culture', for example. To supply a highly specific concept of culture based on its function is not to diminish the importance of the messages conveyed through culture. On the contrary, the understanding of ideas, tastes, expectations, prohibitions, and affinities expressed in value-laden messages, symbols, artefacts, possessions, languages, utterances, gestures, customs, rituals, conventions, and laws, all in their social and historical contexts, is among the central aims of cultural history. The conceptual framework applied here does not narrow the inquiry; it opens it to a consideration of the possibilities presented by the entire constellation of cultural forms, messages, and social groups in all their complexity.

Cultural categories and social categories are not strictly coterminous. Cultural categories are extremely useful as conceptual and analytical devices for the study of the past. Historians widely accept that language, dress, ritual, law, and other codified normative conventions are artificial constructs and products of historical change. We no longer need to be reminded by anthropologists that a village charivari, for example, is more than a colourful piece of theatre;[32] it is the expression of a powerful social sanction that must be studied from the participants' point of view, rather than that of the modern audience, in order to appreciate its true significance. Social categories, like cultural categories, are useful conventions. They are analytical devices by which we can construe groups according to gender, occupation, wealth, age, family, race, legal status, ethnicity, religious affiliation, or place of origin, to name a few possibilities. But it is problematic to use social terms to modify or specify cultural forms. Should we juxtapose, with unreserved confidence, popular and elite culture? There were, for example, learned labourers of extremely modest means in early modern England.[33] Peter Burke's well known characterisation of the early modern period as one in which elites came to distance themselves from the beliefs and customs of their social inferiors has come under reconsideration. Heightened concern over the use of popular culture as an analytical category has given rise to some scholarly claims for cultural divisions within social strata, the persistence of cultural uniformity over time, or both.[34]

It is no less problematic to speak of urban and rural culture than it is to speak of popular and elite culture. Precise terminology, a virtue in the abstract, becomes inflexible language in practice and can pose problems in telling the story of real villagers and citizens. Cultural forms and practices predominant in one setting – examples of what we might call urbane or rustic culture – were present to some degree in the other setting. Nevertheless, for nearly a century after the Restoration, the dominant forms and conventions of personal, material, and print cultural ties varied significantly with setting while most of the social spheres formed by those cultural ties were rooted in one setting or the other. As it turns out, however, we typically dismiss setting as purely descriptive. To be sure, early modern English people acted upon distinctions based on gender, wealth, occupation, age, status, religious affiliation, political allegiance, ethnicity, and other categories conventionally recognised by social historians. Setting was also a major organising principle of early modern English society. The influence of localism and topographical affinity in early modern English society was so great that the most comprehensive and compelling distinction maintained by members of that society was often between urban and rural social spheres and their values. Cultural ties in early modern England eventually effected a widespread mediation of the urban–rural divide during the middle decades of the eighteenth century, when the rise of extraparochial religious nonconformity and the transformation of villages into extramural suburbia, a new kind of community, permitted the freer application of all cultural forms across eroding institutional, ideological, and topographical barriers. Thus 'urban' and 'rural' are not only descriptive terms but analytical terms with explanatory powers grounded in the urbane and rustic sensibilities of historical actors themselves.

Some urban historians have moved beyond the invocation of setting for purely descriptive purposes to investigate how the urban setting imparted values and a sense of shared identity expressed by urbane people themselves in former times. Jonathan Barry and David Sacks have both centred on Bristol as a subject of study. Sacks has demonstrated that the development of a capitalist society in an early modern city should not be understood 'cliometrically' as the historical by-product of incremental economic forces beyond the control of that society. Rather, it should be understood 'paradigmatically' as the concious adoption of an ethos by people responding to the exigencies of a particular time and place; as a paradigm, early modern Bristol serves as an example of a general type – an ascendant commercial city – but for its very own reasons and as a result of volition and culture, 'a continuously altering arrangement of beliefs and practices governing the whole of social life'.[35] Jonathan Barry has shown that residents of a provincial town would cultivate a life identifiable not only with urbanity but with the specific town in which they lived.[36] Other early modern cities have been read as texts, unveiled as theatrical backdrops, surveyed as environments, decoded as anthropological case studies, gendered and dissected as corporeal entities. We can see how the urban setting itself supported conspicuous consumption by providing a captive audience; gave rise to public buildings as signs of power; and induced the rapid pulse of people and goods though its congested innards.[37]

Early modern village life has been the subject of numerous studies, but in a separate vein for the most part, while urban history has emerged as a distinct school of research. By keeping the study of urban and rural history artificially separate, the typical uses of setting as a category have had the effect of obscuring an historically grounded dynamic while urban–rural interaction and the causes and consequences of a persistent urban–rural gulf have been explored far too rarely. How did rustic people respond to the urban setting? How did urbane people respond to the rural setting? How did urban and rural people interact? How did this change over time? All of these theories and questions will be kept in mind as we go about analysing the configurations of urban and rural ties and boundaries within the context of urbanisation and renewed urban vigour.

As urban and rural dwellers all knew in early modern England, one's place of origin was such a defining ingredient of personal identity that it followed one indelibly through the record of one's life. Place of origin identified infants at the time of baptism, children at the time of indenturing, spouses at the time of marriage, deponents at the time of testimony, and nearly all migrants at crucial times when they moved in search of assistance or employment. When they arrived in cities, people of rural origin, whose lives were likely to involve a series of occupational changes,[38] lacked affiliation with a guild and the occupational identity this could bestow. But villagers who met as migrants in a city could form rustic social spheres in an alien urban setting. Villagers raised in an agricultural world actively rooted their identities in a plot of ground. The nobility derived their titles from place names. Characters populating the mental world of chapbooks and traditional stories were unfailingly identified by their place, or at the very least setting, of origin.[39]

Arguments attributing the dynamics of community formation to class relations, uneven distribution of wealth, political allegiance, religious sectarianism, national or ethnic identity, racial tension, and gender construction have all achieved conventional status, some more recently than others. Wealth, occupation, and class are so routinely invoked as causal forces in society, and as organising principles in historical scholarship, that a campaign has been launched to rescue this important approach from devolving, through uncritical use, into an antiquated truism.[40] The categories of class, wealth, and occupation have earned their prominent role in our understanding of the processes of continuity and change in early modern England. We invoke, with justifiable confidence, the vicissitudes of an aristocracy at first declining and then resurgent; the adaptive strategies and endurance of the ubiquitous gentry; the emerging capitalist ethos and dynamic prosperity of the ascendant urban classes; the conservative corporatism – or the devout radicalism – of artisans; and, ultimately, the self-determination of a 'nascent' working class.[41] On the other hand, the powerful notions that people in former times actually organised their normative and descriptive views of social experience around concepts of race, ethnicity and gender have won well deserved general acceptance relatively recently.[42] Considerations of wealth, occupation, gender, age, sexuality, religion, ethnicity, status, and power will all play a part here in assessing the relative importance of setting to the formation of cultural ties and social spheres in provincial England during the urban renaissance. And yet the conceptual frameworks of historical scholarship and analyses of continuity and change over time largely relegate the categories 'urban' and 'rural' to descriptive roles. Conscious affinity for – or aversion to – setting, a fundamental aspect of experience, has rarely been acknowledged as a causal force in the historical process.

Powerful distinctions between traditionally festive and austerely reformed forms of expression, each identified with two competing concepts of order, have been explained with reference to topographical setting. This notion that culture is a means of expressing concepts of social order, and maintaining orderly social groups, has been applied to questions of divided political allegiance in early modern England without the need to characterise culture itself in terms of class or some other social category. In the generations leading up to the civil war, villages with nucleated settlement patterns, supervision from resident lords, and co-operative use of arable land tended to promote harmonious relations and discourage transgressions through traditionally festive means: maypoles, ball games, church ales, wakes, dances and skimmingtons. Villages on marginal land suitable for mixed husbandry, with dispersed settlement patterns, individualised holdings and no resident squire tended to be under the reforming supervision of ardent Protestants, the village elect whose programme of godliness assaulted what they saw as the disorderly festivities of the reprobate.[43] Although distinctions between nucleated and dispersed settlements are very useful for understanding the social underpinnings of festive and reformed expressions of communal life in early modern English villages, it would be misleading to apply this model to the urban–rural gulf. We might expect urban areas to be like nucleated settlements in which traditional notions of order and deference embraced festive ritual as a means of dissipating social tensions and preserving harmonious relations within a hierarchical society. On the other hand, cities and towns could have a strong, and often dominant, reforming contingent before the Restoration and a continuing association with religious dissent after the Restoration.[44] There is also the possibility that all villages – as well as all urban communities, for that matter – were sites of unresolved cultural contention; it was this very contention at the level of intimate social interaction that produced the surviving record of complaints and testimonials about reformed and festive practices. In any event, we should not see the distinction between reformed and festive cultures as a distinction between the urban and rural settings. The dominance of festive or reformed culture varied from place to place and changed over time, but these variations neither caused nor bridged the urban–rural gulf.

Although an urban–rural divide persisted for much of the century or so following the Restoration, urban–rural interaction was an essential ingredient of a dynamic, not a static, world. Villagers near the revived and growing cities actively and consciously resisted the encroachment of urban society and culture in ways that shaped family formation, apprenticeship migration, the consumption of goods, the regulation of community boundaries, the development of printing and the spread of information in the provinces, acts of collective protest, and the evolution of religious groups, among other trends. The active defence of exclusive privilege by civic bodies and the persistence of the Anglican parochial system, featuring highly localised institutions sustained by the established church in both settings, actually formed a remarkably durable wedge between urban and rural communities. The analytical category of setting points to changes by which periodisation itself, including the transition from early modern to modern, can be determined. Early modern England is properly characterised as a religiously divided society; the ultimate bridging of the urban–rural divide by the extraparochialism of religious nonconformity itself was among the most conspicuous harbingers of a new era. Urbane communities that settled outside cities, the seeds of extramural suburbia planted after 1740 or so, anticipated a distinct feature of modern life in England: the appropriation of rural space for the expression of urbane taste, values, and cultural conventions. Apart from the aesthetic considerations involved,[45] those distinctions that contemporaries themselves drew between the urban and rural settings, and the importance of these for mentality, community formation, and collective action are appreciated as incidental in retrospect. Contemporaries, however, were clearly aware of the abrupt contrast between cities and villages, and their actions and choices reflected this awareness.

An abrupt topographical transition between city and country was a visual reminder of the social and cultural differences between the two worlds. Formal complaints were lodged in the 1680s that on 'solemn occasions of rejoicing' guns were fired in the meadows near enough to Bristol neighbourhoods to disturb the sleeping residents or break their windows.[46] By the 1720s, a large portion of Stapleton, Gloucestershire, a rural parish near the Bristol parishes of St James and St Philip and Jacob, was secured by the powerful Southwell family and preserved as a hunting ground slightly over a mile from the heart of the city.[47] Domesticated as well as wild animals roamed just beyond the city. Thomas Garland, one of significantly few villagers to be identified as a mariner residing in the coutryside near Bristol, owned sixty sheep valued at £60 in 1680.[48] He kept this large flock at his homestead in what was then the rural settlement of Clifton, less than a five-minute walk along the gorge of the river Avon from the Bristol quays in the city's parish of St Augustine. The village of Clifton, wedged between the city of Bristol and the Avon gorge, would become known as one of Bristol's 'suburbs' by the middle decades of the eighteenth century, but before that time 'suburbs' were the outer parishes of the city itself.[49] The size, relative density, and general commotion of cities made them conspicuous, but we should not assume that these qualities placed them at the centre of rural experience, even during the urban renaissance which Bristol and other urban areas enjoyed in the late seventeenth and early eighteenth centuries. Where in the world is Stanton Drew? 'A mile from Pensford and another from Chew', was the answer provided by the Somerset rhyme.[50] All three of these Somerset villages were within a few miles of the Bristol High Street, but in the rustic consciousness they were identified in relation to each other, not in reference to the region's largest city, despite its proximity, prosperity, and fame.

## NOTES

1   S.R.O. DD/SF/1343, Manuscript poem in Somerset dialect (*c.* late seventeenth century).

2   D. Underdown, *Revel, Riot, and Rebellion: Popular Politics and Culture in England 1603–1660* (Oxford, 1985), p. 272.

3   S.R.O. DD/DN/230, Caleb Dickinson's Travel Diary (1740).

4   D. Defoe, *A Tour through the whole Island of Great Britain* (1724–26), ed. P. Rogers (Harmondsworth, 1971), pp. 215–16.

5   P. Borsay, 'The English urban renaissance: the development of provincial urban culture *c.* 1680–*c.* 1760', *Social History* 5 (1977), pp. 581–603, and *The English Urban Renaissance: Culture and Society in the Provincial Town 1660–1770* (Oxford, 1989).

6   Borsay, *The English Urban Renaissance*, p. 315.

7   A. McInnes, 'The emergence of a leisure town: Shrewsbury 1660–1760', *Past and Present* 120 (1988), pp. 53–87, argues that the period following the Restoration was marked not so much by a widespread urban renaissance as by the transformation of a few of the more prosperous urban areas into 'leisure towns'. This issue is debated in P. Borsay and A. McInnes, 'The emergence of a leisure town: or an urban renaissance?', *Past and Present* 126 (1990), pp. 189–202.

8   A. Everitt, 'Country, county and town: patterns of regional evolution in England', in P. Borsay (ed.), *The Eighteenth-Century Town: A Reader in English Urban History 1688–1820* (London and New York, 1990), p. 95.

9   P. Clark and P. Slack, *English Towns in Transition 1500–1700* (Oxford, 1976), p. 1.

10  E. A. Wrigley and R. S. Schofield, *The Population History of England 1541–1871: A Reconstruction* (Cambridge, 1981; 2nd ed. 1989).

11 M. Daunton, 'Towns and economic growth in eighteenth-century England', in P. Abrams and E. A. Wrigley (eds), *Towns in Societies: Essays in Economic History and Historical Sociology* (Cambridge, 1978), pp. 245–78.

12 E. A. Wrigley, 'A simple model of London's importance in changing English society and economy 1650–1750', *Past and Present* 37 (1967), pp. 44–70.

13 C. W. Chalklin, *The Provincial Towns of Georgian England: A Study of the Building Process 1740–1820* (London, 1974), p. 3. According to Chalklin's conservative estimate (p. 17), the portion of the entire country's population residing in cities and towns grew only about 6 per cent between 1670 and 1750. Nevertheless, the absolute rate of growth was probably greater than that experienced by most urban areas on the European continent. See J. de Vries, *European Urbanization 1500–1800* (Cambridge, Mass., 1984), pp. 69–77. For France's early modern urban growth see: P. Benedict, 'French cities from the sixteenth century to the revolution', in P. Benedict (ed.), *Cities and Social Change in Early Modern France* (London, 1989), pp. 7–64.

14 J. Patten, *English Towns 1500–1700* (Folkestone, 1978), pp. 110–14.

15 P. Slack, 'Vagrants and vagrancy in England 1598–1664', *Economic History Review*, 2nd ser. 27 no. 3 (1974), pp. 360–79; D. Souden, 'Migrants and the population structure of later seventeenth-century provincial cities and market towns', in P. Clark (ed.), *The Transformation of English Provincial Towns 1600–1800* (London, 1984), pp. 133–68. It should be mentioned that just prior to the urban revival there was a decline in the migration of apprentices to London. See R. Finlay, *Population and Metropolis: The Demography of London 1580–1650* (Cambridge, 1981), pp. 140–2.

16 The trend continued in Bristol into the 1680s. See the presentment of the grand jury in B.R.O. #04452(1), Bristol Quarter Sessions: Presentments and Convictions (Easter Term 1685).

17 D. H. Sacks, *The Widening Gate: Bristol and the Atlantic Economy 1450–1700* (Berkeley, Cal., 1991), pp. 331–53; K. Morgan, *Bristol and the Atlantic Trade in the Eighteenth Century* (Cambridge, 1993), which emphasises competition among Atlantic ports; K. N. Chaudhuri, *The Trading World of Asia and the East India Company 1660–1760* (Cambridge, 1978); R. Davis, *The Rise of the Atlantic Economies* (Ithaca, N.Y., 1973); W. E. Minchinton, *The Trade of Bristol in the Eighteenth Century* (Bristol, 1957).

18 G. S. Holmes, *Augustan England: Professions, State and Society 1680–1730* (London, 1982).

19 M. Laithwaite,'The buildings of Burford: a Cotswold town in the fourteenth to the nineteenth centuries', in A. Everitt (ed.), *Perspectives in English Urban History* (London, 1973), pp. 60–90; M. Reed, *The Georgian Triumph 1700–1830* (London, 1983), pp. 104–28; Chalklin, *The Provincial Towns of Georgian England* and 'The financing of church building in the provincial towns of eighteenth-century England', in Clark, *The Transformation of English Provincial Towns*, pp. 284–310.

20 Borsay, *The English Urban Renaissance*, pp. 323–67.

21 J. von Thunen, *Die isolierte Staat* (1826); P. Hall (ed.), *Von Thunen's Isolated State*, trans. C. M. Wartenberg (London, 1966).

22 P. J. Corfield, 'A provincial capital in the late seventeenth century: the case of Norwich', in P. Clark and P. Slack (eds), *Crisis and Order in English Towns 1500–1700* (London, 1972), pp. 263–310. The urban sphere of influence model has also been applied to Bristol. See W. E. Minchinton, 'Bristol: metropolis of the west in the eighteenth century', in P. Clark (ed.), *The Early Modern Town: A Reader* (London, 1976).

23 F. Heal and C. Holmes, *The Gentry in England and Wales 1500–1700* (Stanford, Cal., 1994), pp. 317–18.

24 J. Barry, 'The Cultural Life of Bristol 1640–1775' (D.Phil. thesis, Oxford, 1985). I should like to thank Dr Barry for allowing me early and extensive use of his personal copy of this very helpful dissertation.

25 Clark and Slack, *English Towns in Transition*, p. 83; P. J. Corfield, *The Impact of English Towns 1700–1800* (Oxford, 1982), p. 15. Sacks, *The Widening Gate*, p. 353, says of seventeenth-century Bristol, 'No longer was its population essentially stable in size.' Although emphasising rapid growth here, Sacks seems to place Bristol's late eighteenth-century population closer to 40,000 than to 50,000.

26 C. B. Estabrook, '*Bristol and the Atlantic Trade in the Eighteenth Century*: a review', *Albion* 27 no. 2 (1995), pp. 312–13; Morgan, *Bristol and the Atlantic Trade*.

27 H. Abelove, *The Evangelist of Desire: John Wesley and the Methodists* (Stanford, Cal., 1990), p. 69; M. Watts, *The Dissenters: From the Reformation to the French Revolution* (Oxford, 1978), pp. 403–90.

28 *Jacobus Millerd's Plan of Bristol* (1673), Bristol City Museum; Benjamin Donne, *Map of the Country Eleven Miles round the City of Bristol* (1769); *Donne's Map of Bristol* (1773), Bristol City Museum, Braikenridge Bequest, Reg. No. M745.

29 M. Spufford, *Contrasting Communities: English Villagers in the Sixteenth and Seventeenth Centuries* (Cambridge, 1974), p. 57; I. K. Ben-Amos, *Adolescence and Youth in Early Modern England* (New Haven, Conn., 1994), p. 80.

30 See especially S. L. Kaplan (ed.), *Understanding Popular Culture: Europe from the Middle Ages to the Nineteenth Century* (Berlin, 1984); B. Reay (ed.), *Popular Culture in Seventeenth-Century England* (London, 1985); S. Desan, 'Crowds, community, and ritual in the work of E. P. Thompson and Natalie Davis', in L. Hunt (ed.), *The New Cultural History* (Berkeley, 1989), pp. 47–71; B. Scribner, 'Is a history of popular culture possible?', *History of European Ideas* 10 (1989), pp. 175–91; T. Harris, 'The problem of "popular political culture" in seventeenth-century London', *History of European Ideas* 10 (1989), pp. 43–58, and 'Problematising popular culture', in T. Harris (ed.), *Popular Culture in England* c. 1500–1850 (New York, 1995), pp. 1–27.

31 R. Darnton, 'Intellectual and cultural history' in M. Kammen (ed.), *The Past before Us: Contemporary Historical Writing in the United States* (Ithaca, N.Y., 1980) and 'The symbolic element in history', *Journal of Modern History* 58 (1986), pp. 218–34; R. Chartier, 'Intellectual history or sociocultural history? The French trajectories', in D. LaCapra and S. L. Kaplan (eds), *Modern European Intellectual History: Reappraisals and New Perspectives* (Ithaca, N.Y., 1982), pp. 13–46; *The Cultural Uses of Print in Early Modern France* (Princeton, N.J., 1987), and 'Texts, printing, readings', in Hunt, *The New Cultural History*, pp. 154–75; S. Archer, *Culture and Agency: The Place of Culture in Social Theory* (Cambridge, 1988); A. Grafton and A. Blair (eds), *The Transmission of Culture in Early Modern Europe* (Philadelphia, 1990).

32 The influence of anthropology on the study of social and cultural history is old enough to be taken for granted. Nevertheless, some contributions are worth reviewing, such as C. Geertz, 'Thick description: toward the interpretive theory of culture', in his *The Interpretation of Cultures* (New York, 1973), pp. 3–30.

33 For the story of John Clare, a poor labourer and autobiographer from rural Northamptonshire, see M. Spufford, *Small Books and Pleasant Histories: Popular Fiction and its*

*Readership in Seventeenth-Century England* (Cambridge, 1985), pp. 3–9.

34 P. Burke, *Popular Culture in Early Modern Europe* (London, 1978). More recent discussions emphasise continuity but are still cautious. Arguments that the notion of popular culture is inherently problematic appear in Reay, *Popular Culture in Seventeenth-Century England*; Scribner, 'Is a history of popular culture possible?'; T. Watt, *Cheap Print and Popular Piety 1550–1640* (Cambridge, 1991); Harris, 'Problematising popular culture'.

35 Sacks, *The Widening Gate*, pp. xx and 12–15.

36 J. Barry, 'Provincial town culture 1640–80: urbane or civic?', in J. H. Pittock and A. Wear (eds), *Interpretation and Cultural History* (London, 1991), pp. 198–234.

37 D. Roche, *The People of Paris: An Essay in Popular Culture in the Eighteenth Century* (Leamington Spa, 1987); R. Darnton, 'A bourgeois puts his world in order: the city as text', in R. Darnton, *The Great Cat Massacre and other Episodes in French Cultural History* (New York, 1984), pp. 107–43; P. Borsay, 'Culture, status, and the English urban landscape', *History* 67 no. 219 (1982), pp. 1–12, and '"All the town's a stage": urban ritual and ceremony 1660–1800', in Clark, *The Transformation of English Provincial Towns*, pp. 228–58; E. Jones, 'London in the early seventeenth century: an ecological approach', *London Journal* 6 no. 2 (1980), pp. 123–33; D. M. Palliser, 'Civic mentality and the environment in Tudor York', *Northern History* 18 (1982), pp. 78–115; R. Tittler, *Architecture and Power: The Town Hall and the English Urban Community* c. 1500–1640 (Oxford, 1991); L. Manley, 'From matron to monster: Tudor-Stuart London and the languages of urban description', in H. Dubrow and R. Strier (eds), *The Historical Renaissance: New Essays on Tudor and Stuart Literature and Culture* (Chicago, 1988), pp. 347–74; R. Sennett, *Flesh and Stone: The Body and the City in Western Civilization* (New York, 1994).

38 H. Cunningham, 'The employment and unemployment of children in England c. 1680–1851', *Past and Present* 126 (1990), pp. 113–50; K. D. M. Snell, *Annals of the Labouring Poor: Social Change and Agrarian England 1660–1900* (Cambridge, 1985); A. Kussmaul, *Servants in Husbandry in Early Modern England* (Cambridge, 1981).

39 The examples are too numerous to mention. For an example of an author whose works of cheap fiction were practically a tribute to the convention, consider Thomas Deloney, whose chapbooks, including *Thomas of Reading* and *Jack of Newbury*, came into print between 1597 and 1600. They were still being printed when Pepys formed his library and well into the late eighteenth century. Spufford, *Small Books and Pleasant Histories*, p. 238–44; J. Ashton (ed.), *Chapbooks of the Eighteenth Century* (London, 1882), pp. 384–6.

40 P. Joyce (ed.), *Class* (Oxford, 1995); G. Stedman Jones, 'The Rise and Fall of Class Struggle', keynote address, North-east Conference on British Studies (September 1994); N. Rogers, 'Writing History from the Left: an Appreciation of Edward Thompson and George Rudé', plenary address, North-east Conference on British Studies (October 1994).

41 The very point I wish to make is that the body of scholarship in which categories of class, wealth and occupation are considered primary is vast. But some prominent examples of the positions characterised here should be supplied: L. Stone, *The Crisis of the Aristocracy 1558–1641* (Oxford, 1965; abridged ed., 1967); J. C. D. Clark, *English Society 1688–1832: Ideology, Social Structure and Political Practice during the Ancien Régime* (Cambridge, 1985), especially, chs 1–3; Heal and Holmes, *The Gentry in England and Wales*; Sacks, *The Widening Gate*; N. Rogers, 'Money, land and lineage: the big bourgeoisie of Hanoverian London', *Social History* 4 (1979), pp. 437–54; P. Earle, *The*

*Making of the English Middle Class: Business, Society and Family Life in London 1660–1730* (London, 1989); P. Seaver, *Wallington's World: A Puritan Artisan in Seventeenth-Century London* (Stanford, Cal., 1985); E. P. Thompson, *The Making of the English Working Class* (New York, 1963) and *Customs in Common* (Harmondsworth, 1993).

42 J. W. Scott, 'Gender: a useful category of historical analysis', *American Historical Review* 91 (1986), pp. 1053–75. The contribution of women's and gender studies to our understanding of early modern England is significant and growing, but only recently has the first synthetic scholarly survey even been attempted: A. Fletcher, *Gender, Sex and Subordination in England 1500–1800* (New Haven, Conn., 1995). For the relation of gender to other analytical categories in the study of early modern England, see especially: S. D. Amussen, *An Ordered Society: Gender and Class in Early Modern England* (Oxford, 1988), and K. F. Hall, *Things of Darkness: Economies of Race and Gender in Early Modern England* (Ithaca, N.Y., 1995). For an overview of race relations in early modern England, with an emphasis on people of Asian and African descent, see especially: P. Fryer, *Staying Power: The History of Black People in Britain* (London, 1984), chs 1–7. Ethnicity in early modern England is an area in even greater need of attention, and is addressed briefly below in the context of anti-Welsh and anti-Catholic (especially anti-Irish and anti-continental) xenophobia in provincial England. The subject of early modern English Judaism has received some treatment elsewhere. See especially F. Felsenstein, *Anti-semitic Stereotypes: A Paradigm of Otherness in English Popular Culture 1660–1830* (Baltimore, Md., 1995); D. S. Katz, *The Jews in the History of England 1485–1850* (Oxford, 1994); B. Williams, *The Making of Manchester Jewry 1740–1875* (Manchester, 1976).

43 Underdown, *Revel, Riot, and Rebellion*. See also, on the competition between festive and austere programmes of order, R. Hutton, *The Rise and Fall of Merry England: The Ritual Year 1400–1700* (Oxford, 1994); M. Spufford, 'Puritanism and social control?', in A. Fletcher and J. Stevenson (eds), *Order and Disorder in Early Modern England* (Cambridge, 1985), pp. 41–57; K. Wrightson, 'Two concepts of order: justices, constables and jurymen in seventeenth-century England', in J. Brewer and J. Styles (eds), *An Ungovernable People: The English and their Law in the Seventeenth and Eighteenth Centuries* (New Brunswick, N.J., 1980), pp. 21–46.

44 P. Clark, '"The Ramoth-Gilead of the good": urban change and political radicalism at Gloucester 1540–1640', in P. Clark *et al.* (eds), *The English Commonwealth 1547–1640* (Leicester, 1982); G. S. De Krey, *A Fractured Society: The Politics of London in the First Age of Party 1688–1715* (Oxford, 1985), pp. 74–6; T. Harris, *London Crowds in the Reign of Charles II: Propaganda and Politics from the Restoration to the Exclusion Crisis* (Cambridge, 1987), pp. 62–95, and *Politics under the later Stuarts: Party Conflict in a Divided Society 1660–1715* (London, 1993), pp. 9–12; Sacks, *The Widening Gate*, pp. 238, 294–303, 307–14; D. Underdown, *Fire from Heaven: Life in an English Town in the Seventeenth Century* (New Haven, Conn., 1992).

45 S. Schama, *Landscape and Memory* (New York, 1995).

46 B.R.O. #04452(1), Bristol Quarter Sessions: Presentments and Conviction (Easter Session 1685).

47 B.R.O. #12964(76), Somerset MSS, 1672–1741, Letter of J. Henley, Bristol Merchant, to Edward Southwell (5 November 1720).

48 B.R.O. Probate Inventories (T. Garland, 1680). Garland was worth £579 3s 10d at the time of his death and was clearly more than just a deckhand. Garland's assessor, who provides what appears to be a grossly inflated valuation of sheep, probably knew more

about the seafaring life than the pastoral one. In 1679 the assessor of Elizabeth Grumwell's goods and chattels out in Westbury-on-Trym valued her flock of sixty sheep at £14. The value of sheep in other inventories is generally around 4s, not £1, per head.

49 *Jacobus Millerd's Plan of Bristol* (1673); B.R.O. #33044, J. Rocque, *A Geometrical Plan of the City and Suburbs of Bristol with Vignettes of Brandon Hill* (c. 1740s).

50 R. Adams, J. Arlott *et al.*, *Book of British Villages* (London, 1980), p. 113. This is identified as an 'old Somerset rhyme'.

# Part I

Settings and the
topographical divide

# Chapter 1

## Communal institutions and localism

> The greatest inconveniences of Bristol are its situation and the tenacious folly of its inhabitants who by the general infatuation, the pretense of freedoms and privileges, that corporation-tyranny, which prevents the flourishing and increase of many a good town in England, continue obstinately to forbid any, who are not subjects of their city sovereignty (that is to say, freemen) to trade within the chain of their own liberties.
>
> Daniel Defoe, *A Tour through the Whole Island of Great Britain* (1724–26)

An affinity for a particular setting or place was so much a part of human experience in former times that it played a major role in the social and cultural dynamics of England right through the early modern period. An appreciation of this will help us understand the fundamental aspects of life as experienced by the thousands of relatively obscure people whose range of experience provides the subject matter discussed throughout this book. It makes sense, however, to begin with the formal institutions governing communal life in villages, towns, and cities. The institutional differences between urban and rural communities provide some useful preliminary explanations for the divisions between urban and rural social spheres.

Authorities and institutions in both settings aimed to adjudicate disputes, keep order, enforce regulations, and protect local interests, but these common ends were addressed in ways that tended to police the very boundaries and membership of the city or village itself. So the separateness of urban and rural social spheres was maintained in large part by conscious strategies to that effect. Indeed, the greater extent to which formal institutions were to be found in cities and towns was a distinguishing characteristic of the urban setting. Communal institutions in the urban setting included governing corporations, guilds, extraparochial corporations of the poor, and special judicial bodies, to name a few. In most villages formal communal institutions were limited to parochial bodies, although there were examples of village almshouses and manorial leet courts. Many cities and towns grew up on manorial lands, but urban communities strove to remove any manorial restrictions and obligations imposed on their activities contrary to the privileges and powers citizens claimed for themselves. Rural manor courts, where they survived, served to perpetuate, in secular form, an idealised and traditional notion of community linked with direct personal interaction undertaken in shared space of which the parish church was only the most conspicuous example. Village leet courts had aims and conventions unlike those of Bristol's Piepoudre Court, for example, which evolved to address market disputes without reference to royal or manorial authority.[1] The parish was an official expression of communal life in the urban and rural settings alike. Early modern English parishioners appear to have been highly xenophobic in both settings, and their definition and treatment of outsiders – or strangers, as they were called – was shaped, in large part, by affinity for locality. Thus parochial mentality, which influenced communal life in both settings, contributed significantly to the persistent divisions between urban and rural social spheres.

The claim that early modern cities, by virtue of the corporate nature of urban polity and economic organisation, also stood apart from the state has been challenged convincingly. This familiar claim was made by no less a political commentator than Thomas Hobbes, who observed in the mid-seventeenth century that an urban community, whose powers and privileges could command the primary loyalty of its members, was a community necessarily detached from the state whose claims to loyalty were obviously weak. The idea of organically separate cities has an antiquarian appeal for some local historians. We must now accept, however, that larger cities, ports in particular, did become increasingly outward-looking with the rising importance of international trade. In this long process cities came to be envisaged as gateways to broader horizons as much as enclosed states unto themselves. In this evolving role, cities were hardly excused from royal taxes or exempt from the laws of the realm.[2] Some have argued that the offices of mayor and town clerk became especially powerful in provincial cities after the Restoration because Charles II used these urban officials as agents of royal policy,[3] a development consistent with the steps taken by the crown to install royalist candidates in corporate offices at the Restoration.[4]

The close relationship between city and state did not necessarily promote a close relationship between cities and villages, however. On the contrary, the evolving relationship between urban communities and remote central authorities promoted the special interests of cities as distinct from those of villages or regions as a whole. As early as 1543, the crown granted the citizens of Bristol the right to claim for their own markets all 'wheat, malt, beans or any other kind of grain or corn' carried along the Severn, the main route of transport for the entire agricultural region. This right was invoked by 'the King's customers of the town of Bristol' as late as 1791 and, as we will see, it was an incendiary cause of division between Bristol and its surrounding villages well into the eighteenth century.[5] The borough community, as it was conceived in the Middle Ages, 'was a bounded world, a communion of interests and purposes separating the townsmen and their life of trade from the agrarian existence of the rest of England'.[6] Bristol's early modern charters confirmed the city's county status; Bristol's members of Parliament represented the city, not the villages of Somerset and Gloucestershire. In short, the evolving relationship between the state at the centre and the institutions governing economic, political, and judicial affairs in cities hardly diminished the gulf between urban and rural communities in the localities.

At the heart of institutionalised localism was the parish. Authority in the parish derived from the established church as exercised by clergy presiding over vestries, overseers, wardens, and other local elites. By the seventeenth century, long-standing practices had become laws empowering parish officials to exact rates, or property taxes, from parishioners to provide aid for the parish poor and subsidies for those apprentices who met with parish approval. Parish authorities were empowered to remove relief applicants who lacked settlement rights within the parish; the prospect of a parish community supporting any strangers or their illegitimate offspring was a source of considerable anxiety.[7] Records of removal and settlement in Bristol and the surrounding villages indicate that rural parish overseers, who vigorously combated any influx of poor migrants, were far less lenient towards applicants for settlement whose travels included any history of urban residence.[8] In some cases villagers who wished to return to the countryside after a difficult stint in the city were officially denied assistance and legally removed to the urban parishes where they had worked long enough to be assigned settlement.[9] By contrast, in 1728 the overseers in the village of Dyrham, Gloucestershire, arranged an apprenticeship in their parish for a poor boy from Westerleigh, another village in Bristol's rural environs.[10] Bristol migrants were conspicuously absent from all applicants for settlement or aid in the nearby rural parishes. All cities, and many towns, had several contiguous parishes subject to strongly binding civic institutions and traditions, but it was not entirely the case that life in a city obscured parochialism while life in rural areas, where parishes were scattered from one village to the next, reinforced it. Participants in the public celebrations of early modern English cities, including London, assembled according to highly localised neighbourhood ties. Even outdoor festivities, such as maypoles, were not city-wide attractions.[11] In the outer parishes of sixteenth-century Canterbury, 'neighbourhoods' criss-crossed parish boundaries, but high levels of in-migration in urban Kent undermined neighbourliness and promoted even greater reliance on parochial institutions.[12]

The notion that the parish was more clearly an instrument of local authority in villages than in towns is a mistaken one. There were a few examples of villages where the squires still appointed their parish rectors in Victorian times,[13] but there was a strong and long-standing connection between parochial authority and civic localism as well. By 1627 the corporation of Bristol had acquired advowsons for seven, or nearly half, of that city's parishes.[14] Urban borough corporations exerted influence on almshouse admissions and expulsions as well as on decisions to ban strangers from the city altogether in times of special hardship or epidemic disease.[15] The vital importance of parishes as administrative units in cities survived the creation of corporations of the poor in fifteen English cities between 1696 and 1711. The Bristol Corporation of the Poor, established in 1696, did not eliminate the influence of parish churchwardens; on the contrary, with the recovery of high church politics, culminating in 1714 with a Tory victory, the senior parish wardens' places among the governors of the city's corporation of the poor were assured. This consolidation of parish agencies addressing the problems of poverty, vagrancy and illness actually enhanced the moral influence of civic elites in urban parishes. The 1,916 urban workhouses established by English corporations of the poor after 1696 were still attached to parishes in the 1770s.[16] In cities as well as villages parochial authority was maintained and expressed through a highly localised relationship between the minister and his own parishioners who, after the disappearance of tithes, exercised even more control over parish expenditures, including clerical livings. Despite the measure of toleration and open popularity achieved by religious nonconformity and ecumenicalism during the early eighteenth century, parishes remained an organising force in civic life, particularly as party politics began to take a more pronounced role in urban factionalism.[17] Even the most urban setting in England, the metropolis of London, was clearly atomised by parochial localism.[18] Any tiny children who wandered from one London parish into another would be lucky to be identified and returned to their parents.[19] In short, urban parishes were as prone to localism and as susceptible to the influence of local authorities and their interests as rural parishes were. Any simple equation of parochialism and rural mentality is therefore suspect.

Attempts to characterise urban polity as distinctly collective and electoral[20] are also unconvincing ultimately. Manorial lords did enjoy hereditary power, but their arbitrary exploitation of estates, like their paternalism, actually diminished in the late seventeenth century, when agricultural market stagnation sapped gentry interest in manorial enterprise.[21] Resident lords became thinner on the ground in the eighteenth century while those who did remain on their estates realised that their own economic welfare was tied to the interests of their tenants.[22] Village leet courts were collectives involving tenants and land holders of all ranks. In many cases city councillors and aldermen were elected by constituencies so highly restricted that they amounted to oligarchies.

The parish vestry was also an elected body. It consisted of a council of at least two churchwardens and four or five other men serving as overseers and other lay officials. In villages members of the parish vestry served in the most exalted roles of local government and were likely to have been selected by a wider body of adult male parishioners. In cities and towns, on the other hand, mayors and other ruling members of urban oligarchies were likely to usurp the functions of the parish vestry,[23] although this did not change the localist tendencies of parochial authority, as we have seen. In the seventeenth century Bristol burgesses repeatedly, but unsuccessfully, petitioned the Common Council for the right to vote in parliamentary elections controlled by members of the city's corporation.[24] The perpetuation and protection of privileged sub-groups was a major function of urban communal institutions.[25] Women were largely excluded from holding office or casting a vote in either setting. To the extent that communal institutions varied qualitatively according to setting, this reinforced their exclusionary tendencies as well as the topographical affinities of the people subject to them.

Incorporated cities, such as Bristol, were immediately distinguishable in legal and political terms from the village communities in the surrounding countryside. The crown granted corporate charters to Bristol in 1373 and within four years of the Restoration.[26] The second of these affirmed that the city's governing body, or corporation, was entitled to an assembly of common councillors, aldermen and a mayor elected by, and from among, these forty-three citizens. During the Restoration these were joined by a recorder (a chief legal officer) and a city chamberlain, assisted by a town clerk, sheriffs, sergeants-at-mace, and guild representatives. Corporations represented the special and collective interests of city burgesses, those citizens allowed to conduct their business or trade within their city, while preventing outsiders from enjoying these benefits.

Urban magistrates and civic officials widely used their own powers to fine individuals, spend tax revenues, sell licences, and lease public property for personal gain.[27] Corporate expenditures, unlike those of parishes, were met not through rates but through the management of chartered property and the private resources of corporation members themselves, whose priorities were understandably coloured by corporate, even personal, concerns.[28] In 1685 Judge Jeffreys of the assizes reprimanded the mayor and council of Bristol for their corrupt practice of arresting migrants and poor folk on minor charges in order to transport them as free convict labour to the West Indian plantations privately owned by members of the corporation. Jeffreys publicly condemned one Bristol mayor, Sir William Hayman, as a 'kidnapping knave'.[29] Market bailiffs and inspectors, water bailiffs and customs officials, reeves, watchmen, market appraisers, and scavengers, were a few of the officials who often paid themselves out of the fines they exacted.[30] Civic officials presided over the regulation of nearly every aspect of public activity and the institutionalisation of supervisory self-interest was another defining characteristic of urban life that rural migrants could expect to find intense.

People with an urbane sensibility, however, delighted in urban communal institutions. With no small measure of arrogant self-satisfaction, urbane commentators compared a civic corporation to a divine creation:

> The best of polities is that invention whereby men have been framed into corporations ... Although art alone cannot altogether arrive at the perfection of Nature, yet has it in this showed a fair adumbration, and given to man the nearest resemblance of his maker, that is, to be in a sort immortal.[31]

According to this view, incorporated cities reflected the sacred power of their royal creator just as humans reflected the divine countenance of the supreme being. Unlike villagers, freemen of an incorporated city enjoyed embodiment in an immortal collective with spiritual as well as legal, political, and economic significance. Corporations did more than protect the special interests and exclusive rights of citizens; corporations, and their proprietorial ethos, provided a cultural tie for members of the same urban community.

This community excluded migrants and those urban dwellers whose transience, age, gender, or lack of guild affiliation made their status ambiguous at best. Apprenticeship, guild membership and other means of gaining economic and political rights within the urban setting were strictly regulated.[32] Guilds largely excluded women from decision making. Indeed, women almost certainly exercised more economic authority in the rural setting, over the production and marketing of dairy goods in particular. Even urban widows who inherited the trades and free status of their husbands found it very difficult to take on apprentices except in times of depression when fewer apprentices could afford the higher indentureship fees demanded by male members of the skilled trades. Regardless of their gender or age (successful apprentices stayed in training well into their twenties), apprentices themselves were given little or no legitimate power under guild regulation.[33] The corporate community did embrace merchants, artisans, professionals and other members of the urban propertied classes whose celebration of this collective identity, some argue, produced the urban renaissance during the generations following 1660.[34] The very nature of the urban renaissance, therefore, may have been to exclude rustic society rather than transform it.

One view is that the collective operation of these urban middle classes, more effectively and politically engaged after 1689 or so, prompted the central authorities to devise and apply uniform solutions to social and economic problems in the localities. There is ample evidence to support this view as it applies to cities and towns,[35] but little to suggest that the reinvigoration of urban corporations prompted them to defend the interests of their rural neighbours. Indeed, corporate charters after 1660 provided cities with more of their own JPs in addition to their mayors, who had traditionally served in that capacity. Royal appointees, taken from among the urban elites, aldermen as a rule, became more numerous in urban communal institutions. These corporation JPs, 'the clearest and strongest link between crown and locality', represented 'private bodies with public functions'. They actually confronted country dwellers in disputes over jurisdiction, assessments, and civic projects that encroached on extramural space, particularly along rivers and roads.[36] Developments in urban political institutions during the urban renaissance may have intensified links between urban representatives of special interests and a remote authority, but these did little to introduce positive connections between cities and the villages near by.

Urban charitable institutions established for health care, poor relief, and occupational training in cities tended not to embrace people of rural origin. The primary aim of the urban middle-class patrons of these institutions was to exert moral influence on their own urban work force in order to keep it fit and submissive. Far from promoting urban–rural co-operation in this regard, these urban institutions were fraught with divisions within the urban community itself along sectarian and political lines.[37] Acts of Parliament establishing what we might call social service institutions in the urban setting – workhouses, corporations of the poor, hospitals, and houses of correction – represented little departure from the principles espoused by sixteenth-century moralists long before the urban renaissance and hardly diminished the gulf between urban and rural communities.[38] In the city of Gloucester, corporation funds were used to assure places for apprentices approved by the city.[39] The poor showing of adolescents and young adults admitted to Bristol's trained work force from villages was linked, in part, with the recruitment and sponsorship preferences of Bristol masters and philanthropists. The case of Brislington, a large village within two miles of the city, provides a clear illustration of preferential aid – or topographical discrimination – at work.[40] By the mid-eighteenth century plenty of financial support was available for the humbler apprentices of Bristol masters. In 1740 alone, fifty-two of 128 apprentices whose masters' fees were recorded by the corporation of Bristol were completely supported in their careers by the city's private donors and charitable organisations to the total of £501, an impressive amount. Three apprentices received generous £20 donations. In the 1730s not one of the poor apprentices from the village of Brislington went to Bristol. In 1740 thirty-seven apprentices whose fees were paid by Bristol donors came from Bristol or, more significantly, from other cities and towns; by contrast, of all Bristol apprentices receiving aid, only two came from any village in the city's rural environs.

As residents of Bristol became more philanthropic toward needy, job-seeking adolescents as a whole, the percentage of rural children who took their apprenticeships in Bristol actually declined. The resources existed, but Bristolians chose overwhelmingly to share with other urban dwellers and there was no apparent effort to recruit local rural apprentices into urban social spheres. This was so obviously the case that migrants in Bristol formed the Wiltshire, Gloucestershire, and Somerset county societies of their own to redress the balance. In effect, however, the loyalties and practices of these societies reinforced the established divisions along topographical and geographical lines. There were some exceptions, of course. In 1740, of the six donations made by the Somerset Society for Bristol apprenticeships, four did in fact go to Somerset children of urban and rural origin. But one went to a boy from Wiltshire and the other went to a native Bristol child, perhaps the son of migrants.[41]

As well as accentuating hierarchical and exclusionary distinctions within urban society, guilds also accentuated localism. Guilds were communal institutions that perpetuated local privileges without extending rights beyond the local polity. Freemen in one city could not expect to practise their trades freely in other cities. The guilds of a city had their own courts to punish encroachers and to adjudicate disputes among guild members; migrants could expect none of the benefits enjoyed by the latter and all the scrutiny given the former.[42] The chance that a rural migrant of ordinary means would gain admission to one of the more lucrative and powerful of the urban guilds was very slim indeed. Fewer than 7 per cent of Bristol apprentices registered in the last three decades of the seventeenth century were children of farming husbandmen from any village.[43] The exclusionary powers of urban guilds did erode between 1756, with legislation against restricted trades, and 1814, with the final repeal of the apprenticeship clauses of the Tudor statute of artificers.[44] During most of the early modern period, however, guilds and apprenticeships were dominant institutions designed to keep city and village separate.

Villages were not without occupational diversity and apprenticeships. Representatives of each occupational category represented in small towns could be found somewhere in the villages near Bristol by the middle of the sixteenth century. By the early eighteenth century, roughly 10 per cent of the residents in villages south of London were skilled in a craft or trade. In the sixteenth and seventeenth centuries between a quarter and a third of all rural households included someone 'in service' and one-fifth of the rural population consisted of unmarried people residing away from home as servants. Villagers did not need to apply to apprenticeship in urban guilds to locate work outside agriculture. Other rural migrants who failed to complete apprenticeships in cities and towns brought crafts and trades back home to their villages,[45] provided their parishes of origin did not rescind their settlement rights. An artisan's workshop costing £100 to set up in an incorporated city would cost £30 to set up in a village.[46] As early as the 1340s, most of the operations in woollen textile production (combing, spinning, weaving, fulling and finishing) were carried out separately in various villages sprinkled throughout the Cotswolds and the Mendips, despite laws prohibiting this, as well as in the city of Bristol.[47] As we will see, feltmakers in the villages near Bristol were among the most popular masters for rural apprentices, especially those of modest means who tended to be apprenticed within their own parishes. Not only did artisans exist in the rural setting, they were seen as an affront by members of nearby urban communities.[48] In short, it was the localism of communal economic institutions, more than the occupational profiles of villages and towns, that divided urban and rural spheres.

Even apprentices, who migrated to cities with the prospect of training and freeman status, could be bitterly disappointed.[49] During the generation before the civil war, two-thirds of all apprentices who ventured to Bristol fell short of completion, often fleeing indentured service, their masters, and the city altogether. At all times single women and girls who migrated to Bristol mainly fell into housewifery, unskilled domestic service in which the risk of sexual abuse was great.[50] As one educator observed in the late seventeenth century, 'of all the youth that yearly come up to London, to be apprentices ... there is not one in twenty that serves his time out, or lives on his trade'.[51] In the second half of the eighteenth century, although guilds were in decline, local papers were still filled with grim stories of the abusive conduct of urban masters. In less than a year the *Exeter Mercury* reported the murder of an apprentice 'barbarously' beaten by her master, the branding of the buttock of another apprentice who was kept chained to a tree, and the castrating of two young apprentices by their master.[52] The ranks of urban casual criminals were expanded by distressed apprentices and other alienated migrants. Hogarth's 1747 series depicting a pair of hopeful London apprentices suggested that the alternative to guild admission was a brief career in the city's criminal underworld brought to a fatal close at the Tyburn gallows.[53] The emotional and physical abuse of migrant apprentices was an old problem and the urban renaissance did little to alleviate it.

In socially isolated situations away from home, needy migrants were weeded out by the xenophobic practices of local institutions. People who wandered and applied for parish relief were either removed to what was regarded as their proper parish of settlement or subjected to forced labour and corporal punishment as vagrants. One could claim settlement rights in the parish of one's birth, in the parish of one's legitimate parents, or in the parish of one's legitimate spouse. One could earn settlement in a parish by renting property there for the substantial sum of £10 per annum, by paying rates there, or by holding a job or an apprenticeship there for a year or more, but employers of migrant labour were careful to limit terms of employment to less than a year in most cases. Parish overseers anxiously removed those migrants who failed to qualify for settlement within forty days of their appearance.[54] A single woman who became pregnant outside her parish of origin was usually doomed to expulsion by the overseers, although imprisonment was a possibility in cities and towns. Among migrants to cities in the late seventeenth and early eighteenth centuries, roughly twice as many women as men were incarcerated. Most of these imprisoned migrants to cities were single, unskilled women thrust out of work as domestic servants who were then charged with petty crimes, prostitution, or 'lewd' behaviour.[55] If caring for an illegitimate child conceived and born in the city, a needy single woman of rural origin almost certainly faced rejection by her own village, whose overseers would invoke the child's urban settlement rights. This pattern was typical in the lives of rural women reduced to vagrancy; their stories are told in parish removal examinations all across the land. By the same token, unemployed migrants of urban origin fared no better in the villages, where parish overseers guarded against demographic encroachment with vigilance.

After the Restoration, when the long-standing removal practices were given the additional weight of statute, the spectre of urban bureaucratic corruption intensified xenophobic localism. Parish overseers in villages near cities had reason to be increasingly suspicious of urban migrants in general, and mariners in particular. As early as 1668, counterfeiters in Bristol and Plymouth were doing a brisk business in bogus mayor's certificates testifying to the worthiness of settlement applicants. Mariners bearing counterfeit certificates did their best to swindle settlement rights, and then relief, from villages near port cities.[56] Some villagers, with no intention of staying in the city, went to Bristol, to the Green Dragon in Redcliffe Street or a notorious house near the bridge in Tucker Street, to buy counterfeit 'passes to travel' which they used to wander unmolested through the countryside as licensed beggars. A vagrant detained in Somerset in 1674 testified that with one of these certificates a man could 'leave his work and travaile [and] have £3 in his pocket' within a month.[57] Local authorities regarded with immediate suspicion all 'strangers', people with whom they did not share resources and spaces within the confines of the parish.

Major provincial cities maintained broad judicial systems, but the extent to which this fact undermined localism before the second half of the eighteenth century is questionable. In communities of all sizes the fellow locals of jurors were far less likely than 'outsiders' to be convicted, or even indicted, for theft in early modern England. One man appeared in a Wiltshire court and refused to testify against a local thief 'for neighbourhood sake'.[58] The grand jury of Bristol declared in the late seventeenth century that rural migrants were prone to 'many abuses'. So, after a series of unsolved burglaries in the city, the jury instituted a special registration of any unmarried adult who came into Bristol from 'out of the country'.[59] Three or four times each year, Liverpool's mayor selected citizens to sit in judgement of misdemeanour offenders in that city's own court of Portmoot. The offences with which this court was concerned amounted to violations committed by any stranger encroaching on local privileges, any citizen encroaching on a neighbour's property, or any persons obstructing city streets and civic spaces.[60] By virtue of its chartered rights, like those of other incorporated cities, Bristol operated as its own county, apart from the counties in which the surrounding villages were located. Bristol had its own court of gaol delivery in which the city's mayor presided over the trials of felons. Lesser offences and the presentments of the grand juries were dealt with in Bristol's own quarter sessions, in which the mayor was a justice of the peace. Bristol's charter of 1499 had added a city recorder to the corporation. Although the aldermen and mayors were drawn from Bristol's wealthiest residents, the city recorder was often a London lawyer.[61] The administration of a city's own legal institutions was more closely tied to the urban network than to nearby villages.

Some have identified the presence of courts in a 'county town' as evidence that the administrative activity of an individual urban centre unified various settlements under a shared focus upon that urban centre.[62] The view that county communities revolved around urban centres of court activity is not without its complications. To begin with, assizes and quarter sessions were held in a number of different towns in each county. Villagers in the counties outside Bristol were likely to appear in sessions at Gloucester, Wells, Taunton and other towns, if they appeared in court at all. Even if we set aside the argument that English society did not become broadly litigious below the ranks of the elite until the dramatic legislative increases of the mid to late eighteenth century,[63] the most common private disputes before the Restoration, those involving slander and moral conduct, had been adjudicated in ecclesiastical, not county, courts and these were still concerned with 'controlling the parish' after the decline of church courts in the late seventeenth century.[64] Inheritance disputes, which were on the rise after the 1740s or so, were, like other probate matters, diocesan business. The most popular secular disputes in early modern England, involving indebtedness and land tenure, were dealt with in a 'confusing' system in which 'manorial customs in the countryside and borough customs in the towns varied locally'.[65] Whether serving as county justices or representing their own interests, gentry who resided in the countryside did appear at court sessions and related social assemblies that assize towns established.[66] To be sure, apart from the royal circuit judges presiding over assizes, amateurs drawn from among even lesser 'men of property' did play the largest role in legal prosecution and judgement.[67] But litigation was inconvenient and burdensome for people of modest means who circulated outside a wealthy minority. Arthur Lodge spent £45 13s 2d – close to a shopkeeper's or artisan's annual income – in litigation, travel and boarding expenses during the March 1737 assizes held in Taunton. In fact, this included £8 15s spent on coach hire, not from some village to Bristol but from Bristol to Taunton.[68]

Those villagers who resided in rural manors were likely to be familiar with another system of highly localised adjudication: their manor court. A manor court neither articulated nor administered broadly abstracted notions of justice. Rather, it was the focus of activities which affirmed social relations within a very closed sphere attached to a specific place. Abson and Wick, a manorial village seven miles east of Bristol, operated leet and manor courts throughout the entire period. The records of the proceedings survive for all but forty-two of the years from 1665, when the Haynes family acquired the manor, until well after 1780.[69] The overwhelming discovery to be made in reviewing generations of manor court activity is that as an agency of legal disputation, adjudication, and enforcement the institution had largely atrophied. This was the case with most manor courts after the mid-seventeenth century with the general rise of petty sessions where jurors sometimes had leet court experience, and face-to-face adjudication was still observed, but rarely with the effect of involving neighbours.[70] At the same time, the manor court continued to be very busy as a local forum, its participants were prominent and energetic, and its clerk and lord were actively involved. In short, regardless of the theoretical justification of the manor court, its function in practice was to affirm the closed social boundaries of the manor. Participation in a manor court, even as an offender, signified membership of an esteemed social sphere based on shared space and resources – on having a residence and a visible presence in the manor.

The same presentments were repeated, and the same offenders identified, year after year in Abson and Wick. The offenders appeared before the court, held at popular gathering places, such as the house of innkeeper Richard Mansell or the Sign of the Rose in Wick,[71] rather than in the manor house. The proceedings, a kind of manorial convocation, identified prominent actors in the court – presenters, jurors, and offenders – all of whom were residents of the manorial village. Because the court rendered no effective judgement, minor but persistent offences, the very concern of the manor court, were left uncorrected with impunity year after year.[72] In 1677, of the twenty-five presentments, twenty-two were reiterations from at least the previous two years. Thomas Rodburn was presented without punishment for every session for thirteen years between 1657 and 1669 for his failure to build a bridge connecting a common pathway on either side of a brook which ran through his property. The disposition of the court cannot be blamed on the influence of lax individuals because positions of responsibility rotated among all the manor's freeholders and every Haynes generation presided over the manor in a similar fashion. In 1681 Thomas Haynes's son, Richard, succeeded him and remained resident lord of the manor until 1726. Unpunished repetition of presented offences was the rule under Richard as well. Edward Hale was presented in every session between 1697 and 1702 and never complied with the manor's requirement that he should build a communal bridge over a stream running across his property. The situation remained the same under every squire and steward. In 1746 all thirteen presentments were repetitions. In sum, offenders blithely ignored the stipulations of the court but appeared religiously in its social setting to participate in the proceedings, often serving as jurors themselves.[73]

The functional, social, geographical, and even ideological distance that separated the judge from the judged in assize courts and other urban courts hardly typified relations among the actors in the Abson and Wick manor court. The lord of a manor would refer serious criminal matters to the assizes and reserved the prerogative of administering summary justice in all other cases concerning his tenants. But any freeholder, as 'homager', could present a fellow villager in manor court. At Abson and Wick, between twelve and fourteen jurors approved by the lord sat before the manor court in any given session and registered presentments. In 1657 the lord of the manor himself was presented by his own leet court for failure to repair his kennel. In October 1676 Thomas Haynes was presented for failure to maintain his hedges and failure to provide and maintain two bridges for communal access to a mill. That lords were subject to their own manor courts and not exempt was by no means in violation of a tacit code of deference. On the contrary, the inclusion of the lord in all capacities spoke to the high level of personal involvement identified by villagers as the basis of respectability, acceptance, and authority. It was highly significant that offenders, presenters, and jurors were virtually indistinguishable in the Abson and Wick manor court, the purpose of which was to convene the community, not to marginalise individuals.

In a manor court the most frequently presented members of the community were prominent freeholders, who took turns presenting, judging, and petitioning one another without enforcing any punitive measures.[74] Of course, presentments did not require convictions. In 1673 Tom Smalcom and Tom Seymor continued their annual squabble over Smalcom's refusal to share his gate with Seymor despite the fact that their lands were adjoining. Tom Seymor had the upper hand that year because he happened to be serving as a juror. In that very same year, John Geebe was both a juror and a defendant. Those villagers who were never presented were those who lacked influence. The only woman presented in Abson and Wick between 1657 and 1664 was a prominent widow who hired a surrogate to serve her term as the tithe officer, a position of local significance. Most women must have been regarded as having had insufficient status to be recognised and identified through manor court activity. By contrast, a jury might even present itself, as it did in 1662, for 'giving alms at the door' contrary to statute.

The primary emphasis on the sharing of space as the means of affirming membership and status in village circles was reinforced by the customs of the manor court. As a result of the manor court's own devising, the parish offices were assigned in Abson and Wick according to a rotation not among persons but among places of residence within the confines of the settlement. The offices of constable and tithe officer were passed from one house to the next according to proximity. The lord's tenement 'near lower green' was followed by a 'tenement at the bottom of Hormaple Hill' which immediately preceded the 'house near Sisford's bridge' and so on. In a practice consistent with the spatial awareness behind the court's organising principle, new houses were inserted in the rotation according to their physical location rather than the timing of their appearance or the social status of their occupant. The same rotation, involving more than fifty houses, was observed until 1772 regardless of the fact that the houses changed occupants over time.[75]

Significantly, an offence for which punishments were enforced was a housing violation, a violation of shared space. Beginning in 1675 the manor court, under the authority of the Haynes family, conducted a thorough campaign against cottages encroaching on common or demesne land. In October 1675 the manor court levied the monumental fine of £10 on such an offender and gave him until Christmas to demolish the cottage which had been allowed to stand, it should be mentioned, for the previous five years. The manor court remained vigilant in this particular regard until the middle of the eighteenth century.[76] By then, cottages against which the manor took action were fewer in number, and, given the success of manorial enclosure in the eighteenth century, this would indicate that fewer cottagers were able to encroach. Thus, in obstructing the development of additional cottages, villagers protected the rural quality of their chosen environment and effectively limited membership of their social sphere to the existing residents with whom they shared space and resources.

The only other presentments that were routinely and effectively enforced were those against the failure to serve as a juror, an offence for which a fine was levied. The language in such presentments barely concealed the notion that failure to participate was not so much regarded as a violation of code or duty as seen by the jurors as antisocial and personally insulting.

> But being called to take his oath to join with the rest of us in the presentment, he peremptorily refused to do so, but continued drinking in the house all the rest of the day. And at last, whilst we were perfecting the presentment, rudely thrust himself into the room, he being drunk.[77]

The ready availability of intoxicating drink in or near the court's gathering place, an inn or tavern in all likelihood, is worth noting. In the final analysis, the principal functions of the manor court were to convene the active members of a social sphere based on shared space, to identify and limit the occupants of that space, and to enforce personal participation in a highly localised forum.

Civic ritual served much the same function. Civic pageantry in Tudor Bristol trotted out the figure of King Bremmius, the legendary founder of the city, to assert that the ancient origins of the city's autonomy antedated the royal charter of 1373. In such ceremonies 'the city presented itself to the larger world as a single, integrated whole, existing independently of its surroundings'. Lively guild processions, which wove symbolic strands throughout the city on the feast days of special saints, eventually died out in Bristol and other cities in the sixteenth century.[78] In the early seventeenth century, ritual expressions of civic unity and autonomy either developed less festive forms acceptable to ardent Protestants or temporarily lost their place in formal institutional life. Sharper distinctions between civic and hagiographic iconography developed during the urban renaissance. After the Restoration, civic rituals with religious origins were revived as secular celebrations, but this did not undermine localism, as each town had its own calendar of events. Old Snap, the dragon who had appeared in Norwich's St George's Day pageants, survived the secularisation of communal ritual after the urban renaissance because he became associated with the mayor and the annual event celebrating the filling of that corporate office.[79]

Whether the revival of festive practices by communal institutions contributed to urban–rural divisions or urban–rural convergence may be difficult to determine. Most analyses emphasise a widening gulf between the collective aims and expressions of the wealthy elite and their social subordinates; the latter were either politically manipulated by self-interested sponsors of festivities or targeted by the 'reformation of manners' whereby commercial capitalists could exploit a more sober and docile labour force. Thus, in the last century or so of the early modern period, defiant reactions and radical protests as well as traditional institutions revived festive, even theatrical, expressions of communal identity.[80] Perhaps a distinction existed between urbane and rustic elites such that the former manipulated festivity and austerity to exploit subordinates while the latter observed cultural practices that tied them more closely to their village neighbours. As for the disposition of the elites who subsidised village festivities, until the middle of the eighteenth century:

> Most of the country houses were not yet principally seasonal extensions of a polite and increasingly self-conscious urban culture, and many of their occupants remained relatively uncitified. They still retained some of the characteristics of rusticity, traits which they shared with the common people ... there actually were a large number of gentlemen whose modes of thought and behaviour were deeply embedded in the experiences of rural life.[81]

Squire Booby, a stereotype invoked derisively by urbane commentators, makes sense as a product of the urban renaissance, when a self-consciously distinct urban identity became even more pronounced. In the late seventeenth century Aubrey was mocked by other antiquarians because he was 'steeped in rural society' and uncritically fascinated by the rustic, even pagan, customs of village communities.[82]

A more meaningful way to distinguish urban and rural patterns of communal culture, therefore, might be to recognise the continuing role of seasonal rhythms in village ritual observance and the ascendant role of the political, administrative, and judicial events – elections, inaugurations, market fairs, royal visits, quarter and assize sessions – dominating the civic calendar after the Restoration. Football matches, wakes, revels, church-sponsored booze-ups, transvestite parades, Shrovetide antics, Whitsuntide pageants, May games and all the other community festivities were just as likely to be denounced by reforming authorities in rural parish vestries as in civic corporations before and after the Restoration. Communal rituals of a festive nature did not vanish in either setting after the Restoration, they became parish expenses as opposed to parish fund raisers. Civic ceremony during the urban renaissance generated a variety of calendars shaped less by universal cycles, seasonal rhythms, and religious observances than by local celebrations of individual cities and towns. To be sure, the administrative and judicial calendars were still organised around quarter days linked with saints' festivals. But civic ceremonies lost the liturgical significance that had been obvious in pre-Reformation civic events such as processions on local saints' days and on Corpus Christi, when members of the body politic, in mystic communion, flowed through their city's streets like blood in the veins of the eucharistic body. Diocesan articles of visitation still required Rogationtide perambulations of parish boundaries after the Restoration and it was in the observance of such seasonal rituals linked with natural surroundings that the rustic quality of communal ceremony in villages could be detected. Easter, the springtime festival of rebirth, is not a fixed holy day but a movable feast tied to the lunar cycle. It was the central event of the Anglican liturgical year and yet, during the last forty years of the seventeenth century, those parish churches where the celebration of communion at Easter was revived were almost exclusively rural. Not one of Bristol's parish churches revived the custom in this period and only one parish church in all London did so.[83]

Despite the visible distinctions between them, urban and rural communal institutions had in common the tendency to reinforce xenophobia and exclusionary localism. The institutions took a variety of forms – ecclesiastical, judicial, occupational, philanthropic – and were subject to the competing influences of festive and reformed styles of expression. Nevertheless, communal institutions consistently upheld a normative construction of community based narrowly on the sharing of limited resources and confined spaces within a single settlement. At the centre of this was the parish, the model of the highly localised community. The parish was endowed with the sacred communal space of its own church and legally empowered to exclude outsiders who shared neither space nor resources with members of the parish social sphere. This Anglican parochialism exerted a powerful influence in both topographical settings until religious non-conformity effectively undermined it by the middle decades of the eighteenth century. Until villages were transformed into a modern form of suburbia around this same time, the divide between urban and rural communities, spaces, and resources persisted.

## NOTES

1  B.R.O. #04411 and #04412, Bristol Piepoudre Court Records (1655–96).

2  D. H. Sacks, *The Widening Gate: Bristol and the Atlantic Economy, 1450–1700* (Berkeley, Cal., 1991), especially pp. 5–15.

3  B. Little, *The City and County of Bristol: A Study in Atlantic Civilization* (London, 1954), p. 138.

4  R. Hutton, *The Restoration: A Political and Religious History of England and Wales 1658–67* (Oxford, 1985), pp. 130–1.

5  34 and 35 Henry VIII, ch. 9, s. iii (1543); B.R.O. #04101(2)(b), Act for the Preservation of the River Severn, and B.R.O. #04101(2)(a), Corn Sheds on the Back (1791–1839). For evidence to suggest that, before the 1790s, Bristolians regarded all riots in the city as invasions of outsiders, see P. D. Jones, 'The Bristol Bridge riot and its antecedents: eighteenth-century perception of the crowd', *Journal of British Studies* 19 no. 2 (1980), pp. 74–92.

6  Sacks, *The Widening Gate*, p. 143.

7  P. Slack, *Poverty and Policy in Tudor and Stuart England* (London, 1988) and *The English Poor Law 1531–1782* (Cambridge, 1995).

8  B.R.O. P/StS/OP, Overseers of the Poor of St Stephen, Bristol: Settlement Papers (1695–1712); B.R.O. P/B/OP/6/g(1–160), Bitton, Gloucestershire, Overseers of the Poor: Settlement Examinations (1723–75); B.R.O. P/B/OP/6c(1–20), Removal Orders to Bitton, Gloucestershire (1713–79); B.R.O. P/StLB/OP/11d(1–36), Removal Orders to Brislington, Somerset (1694–1801); B.R.O. P/W/OP/4(1–42), Removal Orders to Westerleigh (1677–1779); B.R.O. P/FC/3(1–15), Removal Orders to Frampton Cotterell, Gloucestershire (1743–78). Some urban parishes also required liability bonds from the original parishes of rural migrants. See B.R.O. P/StJB/OP(1–28) (Settlement Papers of the Overseers of the Poor for the Parish of St John the Baptist, Bristol, 1656–96).

9  B.R.O. P/B/OP/6/g(1–36), Bitton, Gloucestershire, Overseers of the Poor: Settlement Examinations (1723–49); B.R.O. P/StLB/OP/10/(1–15), St Luke, Brislington, Somerset, Overseers of the Poor: Settlement Examinations (1695–1780); B.R.O. P/FC/OP/4/(1–14), Frampton Cotterell, Gloucestershire, Overseers of the Poor: Settlement Examinations (1733–79).

10  B.R.O. P/Dy/OP3(1). For similar expressions of parish localism see P. Sharpe, 'Poor children as apprentices in Colyton 1598–1830', *Continuity and Change* 6 (1991), pp. 253–69.

11  C. Phythian-Adams, *Desolation of a City: Coventry and the Urban Crisis of the Later Middle Ages* (Cambridge, 1979), pp. 158–69; M. J. Power, 'Shadwell: the development of a London suburb community in the seventeenth century', *London Journal* 4 (1978), pp. 29–46; P. Burke, 'Popular culture in seventeenth-century London', *London Journal* 3 (1977), pp. 143–62.

12  P. and J. Clark, 'The social economy of Canterbury suburbs', in A. Detsicas and N. Yates (eds), *Studies in Modern Kentish History* (Maidstone, 1983), pp. 80–1, and P. Clark, 'The migrant in Kentish towns 1580–1640', in P. Clark and P. Slack (eds), *Crisis and Order in English Towns 1500–1800* (London, 1972), p. 153.

13  O. Chadwick, *Victorian Miniature* (Cambridge, 1991), pp. 9–15.

14  B.R.O. #01075(1), as cited in Sacks, *The Widening Gate*, p. 162. As Sacks points out, the Bristol corporation already appointed the Mayor's Chapel chaplain, the minister of Temple Church, and public lecturers in theology who appeared weekly in the city.

15  P. D. Halliday, 'Partisan Conflict and the Law in the English Borough Corporation 1660–1727' (University of Chicago, Ph.D. thesis, 1993), pp. 63–7.

16  M. E. Fissell, *Patients, Power and the Poor in Eighteenth-Century Bristol* (Cambridge, 1991) and 'Charity universal? Institutions and moral reform in eighteenth-century Bristol', in L. Davison, T. Hitchcock, T. Keirn, and R. B. Shoemaker (eds), *Stilling the Grumbling Hive: The Response to Social and Economic Problems in England 1689–1750* (New York, 1992), pp. 121–44; T. Hitchcock, 'Paupers and preachers: the SPCK and the parochial workhouse movement', in Davison *et al.*, *Stilling the Grumbling Hive*, pp. 145–66; E. E. Butcher (ed.), *Bristol Corporation of the Poor 1696–1834* (Bristol, 1932). The Bristol Corporation of the Poor, as proposed by John Cary in 1695, came into being in 1696 through an Act of Parliament, 7 and 8 William III, ch. 32. For Cary's own promotional remarks about the plan see British Library 816.m.54–5.

17  J. Barry, 'The parish in civic life: Bristol and its churches 1640–1750', in S. J. Wright (ed.), *Parish, Church and People: Local Studies in Lay Religion 1350–1750* (London, 1988), pp. 152–78.

18  C. R. Friedrichs, *The Early Modern City 1450–1750* (London, 1995), pp. 266–71 and 329–30; I. Archer, *The Pursuit of Stability: Social Relations in Elizabethan London* (Cambridge, 1991); S. Rappaport, *Worlds within Worlds: Structures of Life in Sixteenth-Century London* (Cambridge, 1989); P. Earle, *The Making of the English Middle Class: Business, Society and Family Life in London 1660–1730* (London, 1989), pp. 240–50; J. Boulton, *Neighbourhood and Society: A London Suburb in the Seventeenth Century* (Cambridge, 1987); M. D. George, *London Life in the Eighteenth Century* (London, 1925; 3rd ed. 1984).

19  P. S. Seaver, *Wallington's World: A Puritan Artisan in Seventeenth-Century London* (Stanford, Cal., 1985), pp. 90–1.

20  Friedrichs, *The Early Modern City*, pp. 43–60.

21  F. Heal and C. Holmes, *The Gentry in England and Wales 1500–1700* (Stanford, Cal., 1994), pp. 112–19.

22  C. Clay, 'Landlords and estate management in England 1640–1750', in C. Clay (ed.), *Rural Society: Landowners, Peasants and Labourers 1500–1750* (Cambridge, 1990), pp. 357–78.

23  R. Whiting, *The Blind Devotion of the People: Popular Religion and the English Reformation* (Cambridge, 1989), p. 91.

24 Sacks, *The Widening Gate*, pp. 230–1.

25 Friedrichs, *The Early Modern City*, pp. 43–60.

26 R. C. Latham (ed.), *Bristol Charters 1509–1899* (Bristol, 1947); Sacks, *The Widening Gate*, p. 161.

27 P. Clark and P. Slack, *English Towns in Transition 1500–1700* (Oxford, 1976), pp. 131–3; P. J. Corfield, *The Impact of English Towns 1700–1800* (Oxford, 1982), pp. 153–6.

28 Halliday, 'Partisan Conflict and the Law', pp. 49, 54, and 63–7.

29 Little, *The City and County of Bristol*, p. 148.

30 Friedrichs, *The Early Modern City*, pp. 267–71; Sacks, *The Widening Gate*, p. 161.

31 William Sheppard, *Of Corporations, Fraternities and Guilds* (London, 1659), preface, cited in Halliday, 'Partisan Conflict and the Law', p. 34.

32 I. K. Ben-Amos, *Adolescence and Youth in Early Modern England* (New Haven, Conn., 1994); Sacks, *The Widening Gate*, pp. 87–127; D. Woodward, 'The background to the Statute of Artificers: the genesis of labour policy 1558–63', *Economic History Review*, 2nd ser. 33 (1980), pp. 32–44; D. M. Palliser, *Tudor York* (Oxford, 1979); D. M. Palliser, 'The trade gilds of Tudor York', in Clark and Slack, *Crisis and Order in English Towns*, pp. 86–116.

33 M. Prior, 'Women and the urban economy: Oxford 1500–1800', in M. Prior (ed.), *Women in English Society 1500–1800* (London, 1985), pp. 93–117, especially pp. 104–10; I. K. Ben-Amos, 'Women apprentices in the trades and crafts of early modern Bristol', *Continuity and Change 6* (1991), pp. 228–38; Friedrichs, *The Early Modern City*, pp. 161–3. For women's economic authority in the rural setting see A. Clark, *The Working Life of Women in the Seventeenth Century* (London, 1919, repr. 1982), pp. 46–63; S. D. Amussen, *An Ordered Society: Gender and Class in Early Modern England* (Oxford, 1988), pp. 67–9, in which Amussen also cites John Fitzherbert, *Booke of Husbandrie* (London, 1598), pp. 177–8. On the subject of hierarchical divisions within guilds based on age, craft, or mastery see C. Phythian-Adams, 'Ceremony and the citizen: the communal year at Coventry 1450–1550', in Clark and Slack, *Crisis and Order in English Towns*, pp. 57–85, at pp. 60–2; Ben-Amos, *Adolescence and Youth in Early Modern England*, pp. 193–6 and 226.

34 See especially Earle, *The Making of the English Middle Class*; G. S. Holmes, *Augustan England: Professions, State and Society 1680–1730* (London, 1982).

35 Davison *et al.*, *Stilling the Grumbling Hive*.

36 Halliday, 'Partisan Conflict and the Law', pp. 49 and 54.

37 Fissell, 'Charity universal?', especially pp. 122–4; J. Barry, 'The politics of religion in Restoration Bristol', in T. Harris, P. Seaward, and M. Goldie (eds), *The Politics of Religion in Restoration England* (Oxford, 1990), pp. 163–89.

38 C. B. Estabrook, '*Stilling the Grumbling Hive*: a review', *Albion* 25 no. 3 (1993), pp. 500–2.

39 G.R.O. GBR B3/4, fo. 2, 20, 121, and 199 are examples.

40 B.R.O. P/StLB/OP/15(h)i and ii.

41 B.R.O. #04353(5) and #04353(6).

42 Rappaport, *Worlds within Worlds*, pp. 201–14; Friedrichs, *The Early Modern City*, pp. 271–72.

43  Ben-Amos, *Adolescence and Youth in Early Modern England*, pp. 221 and 299. In early seventeenth-century London, only one of the city's 140 wealthiest members of the merchant companies was the son of rural parents below gentry status. See R. G. Lang, 'Social origins and social aspirations of Jacobean London merchants', *Ecomonic History Review*, 2nd ser. 27 (1974), p. 36.

44  Corfield, *The Impact of English Towns*, pp. 86–8; J. G. Rule, *The Experience of Labour in Eighteenth-Century Industry* (London, 1981), pp. 95–119, and *The Vital Century: England's Developing Economy 1714–1815* (London, 1992), p. 314.

45  A. Kussmaul, *Servants in Husbandry in Early Modern England* (Cambridge, 1981), p. 11; M. K. McIntosh, 'Servants and the household unit in an Elizabethan English community', *Journal of Family History* 9 (1984), pp. 13–15; R. M. Smith, 'Some issues concerning families and their property in rural England 1250–1800', in R. M. Smith (ed.), *Land, Kinship and Life-Cycle* (Cambridge, 1984), p. 34; K. D. M. Snell, *Annals of the Labouring Poor: Social Change and Agrarian England 1660–1900* (Cambridge, 1985), pp. 232–3; H. Cunningham, 'The employment and unemployment of children in England c. 1680–1851', *Past and Present* 126 (1990), pp. 113–50; I. K. Ben-Amos, 'The failure to become freemen: urban apprentices in early modern England', *Social History* 16 no. 2 (1991), pp. 171–2, and *Adolescence and Youth in Early Modern England*, pp. 69, 77–80, 241, and 301.

46  Earle, *The Making of the English Middle Class*, pp. 106–8; Ben-Amos, *Adolescence and Youth in Early Modern England*, p. 220.

47  Sacks, *The Widening Gate*, pp. 55–6.

48  Friedrichs, *The Early Modern City*, p. 97.

49  Ben-Amos, *Adolescence and Youth in Early Modern England*, pp. 101–8; S. R. Smith, 'The ideal and reality: apprentice–master relationships in seventeenth-century London', *History of Education Quarterly* 21 (1981), pp. 449–59.

50  Ben-Amos, 'The failure to become freemen' and 'Women apprentices in the trades and crafts of early modern Bristol'. For emphasis on the ability of migrants to develop coping strategies see P. Clark, 'Migrants in the city: the process of social adaptation in English towns 1500–1800', in P. Clark and D. Souden (eds), *Migration and Society in Early Modern England* (London, 1987), pp. 267–91.

51  T. Tryon, *A New Method of Educating Children* (1695), p. 83.

52  *Exeter Mercury* (9 March 1764, 23 March 1764, 4 January 1765) as cited in: Rule, *The Vital Century*, p. 202.

53  D. Jarrett, *England in the Age of Hogarth* (London, 1974), pp. 97–8; Friedrichs, *The Early Modern City*, p. 234.

54  Slack, *The English Poor Law*, especially pp. 9–13 and 28–30.

55  B. Hill, *Women, Work, and Sexual Politics in Eighteenth-Century England* (Oxford, 1989), p. 173; R. B. Shoemaker, *Prosecution and Punishment: Petty Crime and the Law in London and Rural Middlesex c. 1660–1725* (Cambridge, 1991), pp. 180–6 and 212–13.

56  S.R.O. Q/SR/111(30–31), Somerset Quarter Sessions (Easter, 1668).

57  S.R.O. Q/SR/121(21), Somerset Quarter Sessions (Michaelmas, 1674).

58  M. J. Ingram, 'Communities and courts: law and order in early seventeenth-century Wiltshire', in J. S. Cockburn (ed.), *Crime in England 1550–1800* (Princeton, N.J., 1977), pp. 128 and 132–3.

59  B.R.O. #04452(1), Bristol Quarter Sessions: Presentments (Michaelmas, 1691). A registration of the places of origin of extramural lodgers in the city was demanded by the grand jury at the Epiphany Session of 1699–1700.

60  Friedrichs, *The Early Modern City*, pp. 256–7.

61  Sacks, *The Widening Gate*, pp. 149–60.

62  P. Borsay, *The English Urban Renaissance: Culture and Society in the Provincial Town 1660–1770* (Oxford, 1989), pp. 6–7 and 155–6. The evidence that litigation in urban centres became a sign of community formation at the county level for people other than urban and rural elites dates from the second half of the eighteenth century. See, for example, *The History and Antiquities of the County of Essex* (London, 1768), cited in Borsay, in which Morant describes one county town 'much frequented' because of the 'conveniency' of its 'public business' including assizes, quarter sessions, and petty sessions.

63  D. Hay, P. Linebaugh, J. G. Rule, E. P. Thompson, and C. Winslow (eds), *Albion's Fatal Tree: Crime and Society in Eighteenth-Century England* (New York, 1975). The observation that litigation became an increasingly common experience among the propertied classes during the late sixteenth and early sventeenth centuries has been made in J. A. Sharpe, *Crime in Early Modern England 1550–1750* (London, 1984), p. 145.

64  Sharpe, *Crime in Early Modern England*, pp. 73–93.

65  A. L. Erickson, *Women and Property in Early Modern England* (London, 1993), p. 23.

66  N. Landau, *The Justices of the Peace, 1679–1760* (Berkeley, Cal., 1984); Heal and Holmes, *The Gentry in England and Wales*, pp. 166–87 and 307–8. Again, it was not until the mid to late eighteenth century that active involvement in the magistracy extended to include a broader section of county society. The number of appointed JPs doubled between the early eighteenth century and 1760, but the numbers of the traditional ruling elite among the justices fell, especially after about 1740.

67  Sharpe, *Crime in Early Modern England*, pp. 21–40; C. B. Herrup, *The Common Peace: Participation and the Criminal Law in Seventeenth-Century England* (Cambridge, 1987).

68  B.R.O. #00154(8) Temple Ah8, An Account of Expenses paid by Mr Arthur Lodge in going to Taunton Assizes (March 1737).

69  B.R.O. #14581 HA/M.4, Haynes Manor Court Records (1657–77); HA/M.5, Haynes Manor Court Records (1697–1726); HA/M.6, Haynes Manor Court Records (1746–68); HA/M.7, Haynes Manor Court Records (1770–92).

70  Sharpe, *Crime in Early Modern England*, pp. 25–6, 83–5, and 171–2; Herrup, *The Common Peace*, pp. 131–40.

71  B.R.O. #14581, see Abson and Wick Manor Court records of 1701 and 1750.

72  The most common offences concerned the maintenance of hedges, ditches, roads, and bridges, the management of livestock, littering and dumping, encroachment on land, and failure to serve in a manorial office.

73  This was true as late as 1752, when, out of twenty-one villagers presented, nine had utterly ignored the orders of the court from previous sessions, but five of the nine served as jurors in that very same session.

74  See the sessions of 1704, 1726, and 1750 for a few of the examples of juries consisting of more than one offender from the very same year.

75  B.R.O. #14581 HA/M.4–7, Haynes Manor Court Records (1657–77; 1697–1726; 1746–68; 1770–92).

76  Between 1746 and 1748 Thomas King was presented for enclosure of the common. He was never fined and after 1748 was pressed no further. His case seems to have been an exception.

77  B.R.O. #14581 HA/M.4, Haynes Manor Court Records (16 April 1660).

78  Phythian-Adams, 'Ceremony and the citizen'; D. M. Palliser, 'Civic mentality and the environment in Tudor York', *Northern History* 18 (1982), pp. 78–115; Sacks, *The Widening Gate*, pp. 177–80 and 136–45.

79  R. Hutton, *The Rise and Fall of Merry England: The Ritual Year 1400–1700* (Oxford, 1994), p. 30.

80  R. W. Malcolmson, *Popular Recreations in English Society 1700–1850* (Cambridge, 1973), pp. 68–74 and 158–71; E. P. Thompson, 'Patrician society, plebeian culture', *Journal of Social History* 7 (1974), pp. 382–405; N. Rogers, 'Popular protest in early Hanoverian London', *Past and Present* 79 (1978), pp. 76–9; J. Brewer, 'Theatre and counter-theatre in Georgian politics', *Radical History Review* 22 (1979–80), pp. 7–40; P. Borsay, '"All the town's a stage": urban ritual and ceremony 1660–1800', in P. Clark (ed.), *The Transformation of English Provincial Towns 1600–1800* (London, 1984), pp. 228–58; D. Underdown, *Revel, Riot, and Rebellion: Popular Politics and Culture in England 1603–1660* (Oxford, 1985), pp. 280–84.

81  Malcolmson, *Popular Recreations in English Society*, p. 68.

82  Hutton, *The Rise and Fall of Merry England*, pp. 236–40.

83  *Ibid.*, pp. 118–23, 229–33, and 246. On the distinct qualities of urban communal ritual, see also M. Berlin, 'Civic ceremony in early modern London', *Urban History Yearbook* (1986), pp. 15–27. For the sacred aspects of civic and guild processions before the Stuart period, see M. E. James, 'Ritual, drama and social body in the late medieval English town', *Past and Present* 98 (1983), pp. 3–29; Sacks, *The Widening Gate*, pp. 132–53; M. Rubin, *Corpus Christi: The Eucharist in Late Medieval Culture* (Cambridge, 1991), pp. 243–71.

# Chapter 2

## Urban and rural spaces

> As for the city itself, there is hardly room to set another house in it, 'tis so close built,
> except the great square, the ground about which is a little too subject to the hazard
> of inundations.
>
> Daniel Defoe, *A Tour through the Whole Island of Great Britain* (1724)

Upon entering an early modern city, villagers experienced an abrupt environmental transition. Although the civil war took its toll on the walls, fortifications and gates of English provincial cities, entering urban space still moved the traveller through imposing channels as if by design.[1] Arriving at Bristol, one passed through Lawford's Gate, with an almshouse on one side and an alehouse on the other, making the first impressions of the city a mixture of intoxication and destitution.[2] Rural migrants, passing into unfamiliar urban surroundings, might fail to recognise in the city their idealised notion of that setting. Edward Barlow, who left the north country in the late seventeenth century to become a seaman's apprentice in London (despite his mother's fears), was genuinely perplexed upon first crossing the Thames to see strange objects 'with long poles standing up in them and a great deal of ropes about them'.[3] A popular chapbook of the same period tells the story of a 'country-man' who, after his first sight of the London docks, rushed home to the farm, where he tied bedclothes to his plough, 'thinking the plough would go with the wind, but it removed not'.[4] Apart from making a jest at the expense of a rustic stereotype, the story carries the larger message that the realities of one setting did not apply to the other.

It is well established that the psychology of affinity and orientation is powerfully shaped by spatial awareness. Diverse ways of handling social space indicate that urban and rural dwellers experience attraction or repulsion, depending on their learned tolerance of the closeness of other people and their buildings. Urban dwellers construct mental images of their surroundings organised around the entire cityscape of fixed objects, while rural visitors to cities orientate themselves subjectively along the selected pathways they have taken.[5] Recalling the urban street scene of the 1760s, one London merchant noted that clever shopkeepers used imagery to guide visitors through the otherwise labyrinthine streets:

> Instead of houses being distinguished by numbers ... every one had its *sign* ... Some of the signs were very large and with them Whitechapel was so crowded that ... it was a dark street. Before many tradesmen's doors there stood square posts about eight or ten feet high and on the top were emblems of the occupation of the owners, thus John Fry's had a ruddy milkmaid with a pile of cheese below, and a milk pail on her head, our next door neighbour, John Adams, a cooper, had on its top a bathing-tub ... Tavern doors were decorated with branches of the vine crowned with a jolly Bacchus.[6]

Given the complexity of the urban setting, the importance of negotiating shared space for the nurturing of social relations was as important in the city as it was in the country, a fact which contributed to the maintenance of the urban–rural gulf for most of the early modern period. In describing his first reaction to the city as a young apprentice of rural origin, Thomas Raymond came right to the point; it was 'a very dreadful sight to a young country boy'.[7]

While the urban–rural topographical divide remained stark, those villagers whose housing fell under the control of urban landlords were, perhaps, likely to be distressed and surprised by urban practices. On an April morning in 1662 a brickmaker named John Painter strolled from his cottage in the Somerset village of Bedminster to Long Ashton, near Bristol, to 'buy some victuals'. When Painter returned he found his friend Thomas Gough, a currier from the neighbouring Bristol parish of St Mary Redcliffe, fending off a gang of men. Painter scurried inside his cottage, only to discover that the men, whom he later learned had been sent from Bristol by his landlord, James West, were in the process of pulling his cottage down around him as he huddled beneath the falling timbers. The next day, inside the walled garden of West's house in the Bristol parish of St James, Painter discovered some of his belongings that had been taken from the rubble of his cottage. Despite the dramatic assault and the evidence of theft, West was excused by the justices when he plainly testified that the lease on Painter's 'hovel' included a clause permitting West's 're-entry for non-payment of rent', a strikingly urban practice which even the most intensely vigilant of the manorial estate managers in the nearby villages did not deploy against their cottagers and other tenants.[8]

Early modern cities were enclosed and congested settlements with strictly enforced regulations of their own concerning the use of private, as well as public, space. It was not just poor vagrants for whom housing was a problem; all rural migrants to the city could expect to settle for housing that was darker, more cramped, and less private than what they had left behind in the villages.

A large house built for a single occupant, a Mr Fry of St James, Bristol, orginally had gardens and coach houses, but after 1720 or so its subsequent owners subdivided it to such an extent that three separate occupants of one-room lodging spaces resorted to drawing up a deed formalising access rights, and routes, to the house's only 'necessary room' or privy.[9] Urban landlords thought nothing of demolishing houses if it was in their material interest, especially if their occupants were socially or physically removed from them. Even in the centre of Bristol, hundreds of homes were destroyed, with the authority of the corporation itself, to make room for the new Exchange in the 1740s. So the grim picture of urban proprietorial space is further complicated by urban uses of space that were, because of the exigencies of spatial limita-tions, less individual and more communal than practices deemed acceptable in the rural setting, where such encroachments on dwelling spaces were rare.

Poor John Painter's cottage was demolished roughly a century before Bristol's absorption of neighbouring villages at least partly mediated these cultural differences. Because Bristol's settled area intensified rather than sprawled for most of the early modern period, the contrasts between the spaces in which urban and rural dwellers lived became increasingly pronounced until nearby villages were transformed into a modern form of suburbia in the second half of the eighteenth century. Until the close of the early modern period, the perceived immiscibility of the urban and rural settings had the conservative effect of a cultural imperative. Given the economic and demographic forces of the urban renaissance, the preservation of distinctly urban and rural spaces, even at the very boundaries between cities and villages, cannot be explained without reference to choices and affinities rooted in spatial and topographical awareness.

The significant abruptness of the transition between provincial cities and their rural environs during the early modern period, the prolonged confine-ment of urban built-up areas despite powerful urban demographic pressures, and the persistence of the rural quality of the landscape close to cities was remarkable. For most of the early modern period cartographers used the term 'suburbs' to refer to the more thinly settled urban parishes just within a city's boundaries. Since its incorporation in 1373 Bristol had enjoyed the status of a city.[10] Its boundaries enclosed an area of nearly 738 acres. By 1696 something approaching 285 of these acres were built-up, that is to say, devoted to build-ings and the small yards fully enclosed by them.[11] Until the parish of St George was added in 1756, Bristol had seventeen parishes (and a residential area known as the Castle Precincts). By 1696, despite the long-term saturation of the city's centre, there remained within the so-called City and County of Bristol over 450 acres of virtually rural, unsettled land insulating the nucleated urban settlement from the surrounding villages. Superimposing scaled projections of seventeenth-century and eighteenth-century surveyors' plans produces a

Table 2.1 Built-up acres in the city of Bristol, by parish

| Parish | Total acres | Built-up in 1673 | % built-up in 1673 |
|---|---|---|---|
| *Central* | | | |
| St. Ewen | 0·7 | 0·7 | 100 |
| All Saints | 1·9 | 1·9 | 100 |
| St. Mary-le-Port | 2·5 | 2·5 | 100 |
| St. Werburgh | 3·4 | 3·4 | 100 |
| Christchurch | 4·8 | 4·8 | 100 |
| St. Leonard | 5·1 | 5·1 | 100 |
| St. John | 9·5 | 9·5 | 100 |
| *Interior* | | | |
| St. Peter | 11·5 | 9·1 | 79 |
| Castle Precincts[a] | 13·4 | 13·4 | 100 |
| St. Thomas | 15·7 | 15·7 | 100 |
| St. Nicholas | 21·1 | 11·2 | 53 |
| St. Stephen | 25·3 | 18·3 | 72 |
| *Peripheral* | | | |
| SS. Philip and Jacob | 29·2 | 27·6 | 95 |
| St. Mary, Redcliffe | 68·5 | 28·7 | 42 |
| Temple | 77·9 | 21·6 | 28 |
| St. Michael | 100·0 | 23·3 | 23 |
| St. Augustine | 154·1 | 43·9 | 28 |
| St. James | 193·1 | 44·1 | 23 |

*Note:* (a) Not ecclesiastical.
*Source:* E. Ralph and M. Williams (eds), Bristol Record Society, 25 (1968).

graphic demonstration of how limited Bristol's physical expansion was be-tween the 1670s and the 1770s.[12] Among all of Bristol's own parishes only the peripheral one of St Philip and Jacob in the east had spilled out of Bristol's county limits, established in the city's fourteenth-century corporate charter. (Table 2.1.)

The relative population densities of city and village maintained the abrupt-ness of the urban–rural transition. Most of the Somerset and Gloucestershire villages within eleven miles of Bristol still had between 5·5 and 15 acres per person at the very end of the eighteenth century. The village of Compton Greenfield, Gloucestershire, still had 27·5 acres per person in 1801. By contrast, the city of Bristol in 1696 had fewer than 0·04 acre per person, even when the 450 open acres of unoccupied land in Bristol's peripheral parishes are included in the calculation. By 1750, the figure had dropped to 0·015 acre per person – over sixty-six people per acre – even if the entire area granted by Bristol's charter is used in the calculation. That is to say, in the middle of the eighteenth century, Bristol was of the order of 360 times more crowded than Frampton Cotterell, one of the most densely settled parishes in the rural environs at that time.[13] Between 1695 and 1750 Bristol's population, which had increased by over 60 per cent during the seventeenth century, roughly tripled, to reach 50,000 by the mid-eighteenth century,[14] but the sprawl of urban population into neighbouring villages was remarkably delayed.

During most of the eighteenth century Bristol responded instead with a period of intense building, subdividing, and rebuilding within the urban space as it was already defined. There was a pronounced increase in the portion of the skilled labour force devoted to the non-maritime building trades.[15] The fact that the density of Bristol's built-up portion, more than its acreage, increased during the century following the Restoration is striking.[16] The newly developed areas of peripheral urban parishes were more, rather than less, densely constructed than these neighbourhoods, to which Jacobus Millerd had referred as 'suburbs' on his 1673 map of the 'famous City of Bristol'.[17] During the eighteenth century Bristol's growth did not expand suburbia into the countryside, it formed an increasingly dense architectural rim within the city. In 1696 there was 0·16 acre per house, on average, for the built-up area of Bristol as a whole. Bristol's peripheral parish of St James had an average only of 0·11 acre per house in 1773. There is some appeal in the notion that a developing urban settlement assumes the shape of a sand pile which, when more sand is poured on to it, develops a taller central portion which in turn sheds on to a steadily widening shallow base. After its great fire was doused, London did sprawl like a puddle.[18] During the same period, however, Bristol moulded into an architectural enclosure like a clay vessel rising from the potter's wheel.

The city presented a dramatically abrupt environmental transition from the rural setting. On average, each of Bristol's 285 built-up acres had between six and seven houses on it in the late seventeenth century.[19] The level of building density in St Nicholas and the other interior parishes was probably closer to twenty-six houses per acre at that time. The city was roughly forty times more densely constructed than the neighbouring village of Stoke Gifford. With its 2,323 acres, Stoke Gifford had over 54 acres per house in the 1670s.[20] Kingswood Chase, a rural area bordering directly on the Bristol parish of St Philip and Jacob, contained settlements that were nucleated by local rural standards because they were established by colliers, for the most part, who lived together in close proximity to highly localised mining sites. Nevertheless, even the most densely settled of the Kingswood colliers moved about in an environment approximately twenty-five times less densely built-up than Bristol's interior parishes and fifty-five times less densely built-up than the central parishes. (Table 2.2.) At one-tenth the settlement density of Bristol, the thirty-five Creswick cottages clustered along the road leading out of Lawford's Gate away from the city represented the least abrupt transition from Bristol to its rural environs prior to the late eighteenth century.

A great deal more representative of the abrupt urban–rural transition was the one which took place between the extensive Bristol parish of St James and the neighbouring village of Horfield, Gloucestershire. The Horfield parish church was little more than two miles up the Stokes Croft Road, via St James, from the Bristol Market Exchange, the heart of the city. Wooded areas divided the parish and separated residents from one another.[21] A local historian in the eighteenth century described Horfield as a 'pastureland' parish, meaning, no doubt, that it lacked the consolidated arable tracts associated with more nucleated settlements. Despite the immediate proximity of the city, when eighteenth-century travellers along the Stokes Croft road entered St James, Bristol, from Horfield, they passed directly from rural environs into a compact and populous urban environment which was 150 times more densely constructed than the nearest village.[22]

A definitive aspect of urban life is the concentration of several homes in a confined space. We can see for Bristol in the seventeenth and eighteenth centuries, high concentrations of soapmakers and distillers in the parish of St Thomas, weavers in Temple, butchers in St Nicholas, where the shambles were located, and mariners and maritime artisans in St Stephen, along the quay.[23] Nevertheless, these patterns may have been related more closely to the location of resources than to gregariousness within certain trades. A study of 109 London parishes shows that the metropolitan parishes had evolved into

Table 2.2 Acres per cottage in Kingswood Chase, 1672

| Owner | Acreage | Cottages | Acres/cottage |
|---|---|---|---|
| Berkley | 720 | 14 | 51·4 |
| Player | 571 | 23 | 24·8 |
| Newton | 604 | 42 | 14·4 |
| Chesier | 880 | 71 | 12·4 |
| Creswick | 60 | 35 | 1·7 |
| Totals | 2,835 | 185 | 15·3 |

*Note:* Each of the five liberties tabulated is a consolidation of contiguous plots.
*Source:* B.R.O. #38016, a Map of Kingswood Chase (1672).

socially stratified and occupationally diverse 'microcosms' by the seventeenth century.[24] As guild influence waned in eighteenth-century Bristol, parishes there became more occupationally diverse. In 1767 the residents along Prince Eugene Lane in the Bristol parish of Temple were ordered by the city to clean and repair their sewer, which had become a 'common nuisance'.[25] The neighbours who co-operated in compliance with the order were two victuallers, a maltster, a schoolmaster, a tiler, an engraver, a potter, a glassmaker, a glazier, a carpenter, a tobacco cutter, a customs officer, a mariner, and a linen draper. These people, who saw one another daily in their home environment, acted in concert in order to protect their shared interests not as an occupational group but as a residential group. In view of the fact that throughout the late seventeenth and early eighteenth centuries parts of all Bristol parishes were periodically coerced by law into chores of routine maintenance, it seems unlikely that the more occupationally homogeneous neighbourhoods in the city had ever been more industrious in this regard. Residential life involved responsibility for the maintenance of shared space, an important locus of social spheres, and this normative value was expressed and enforced in the law itself.

Added to the picture of considerable occupational diversity at the parish level is some good evidence that closely cultivated personal ties were based on life nearer to home than to work. In seventeenth-century Southwark 'occupational solidarity was unusual' between a will's testator and its overseer; 'a far more powerful determinant, influencing choice of overseer, appears to have been close residential proximity'.[26] It has been argued for early modern Worcester that urban social groups formed along residential lines in areas confined to particular streets and alleys.[27] The similar tendency to identify immediate neighbours, rather than fellow workers, as trusted friends was also strong in rural England.[28] Apparently the nature of English home life in the early modern period was such that it cultivated extended social contacts more than it served as a shelter or retreat from the intense interaction associated with the modern work day. The maintenance of social spheres operating in shared space may have owed more to the hospitable mingling of neighbours in leisure time than to collaboration in the workplace.

The importance of conviviality in familiar shared spaces for both formal and informal interaction gave rise to the proliferation of pubs and their emergence as centres of political and intellectual as well as social activity.[29] The pub or tavern was a communal extension of every neighbour's home. Indeed, some Bristol parishes may have had nearly as many pubs, inns and alehouses as domestic kitchens. Kitchens were far more widely used as gathering spaces in the rural setting, but the shared spaces on which social spheres were based in the city were rather more intimate in scale than we might suppose. By 1760 on average a Bristol parish could be expected to have thirty-two alehouses or pubs, a conservative estimate based on the 573 pubs that were actually licensed.[30] In Bristol's seven central parishes, this amounted to something like eight of these communal gathering spots per acre. It is difficult to know how often the faces of unfamiliar, or even rural, folk were seen by the Bristolians who frequented the pubs sprinkled among their houses. The London and Bath waggons, which did not develop schedules until the eighteenth century brought passengers bound for Bristol to only one or two of the city's larger inns. In the first half of the eighteenth century the rural surveyors of highways for the countryside near Oldbury, Gloucestershire, routinely met their JPs at the White Hart in Pucklechurch, over a dozen miles away on the other side of Bristol.[31] Local villagers actually circumvented the city, with all its gathering places, in favour of a rural pub farther away.

Residential mobility resulting in anonymity and loose personal relations has been stressed as an aspect of life in early modern cities and towns.[32] In the Boroughside area of Southwark between 1609 and 1641, about a quarter of the residents did not move for a period of ten years or more, but nearly as many Boroughside residents lived there for less than a year.[33] This raises questions about the extent to which transient people entered the established social spheres of the urban setting. Rural areas may have had slightly higher levels of residential persistence. In pre-industrial villages of Nottinghamshire and Northamptonshire half the householders resided in their parishes for at least ten years.[34] Manor rosters of Abson and Wick, seven miles east of Bristol in the county of Gloucestershire, contain 131 different family names for the years 1660, 1720, and 1780 divided by intervals of roughly a life span.[35] Of these family names, thirty (23 per cent) appeared in all three successive generations. The persistence of thirty families, not only over ten-year spans but over entire generations, indicates that very deep roots were established by a substantial core of the village population.

It may be worth reconsidering the blanket association of wealth with geographically extended social spheres. The wealthier villagers in Abson and Wick exhibited a higher degree of residential continuity and may have relied more on personal culture, direct and prolonged social interaction with their immediate neighbours, as a basis of their social sphere. The families rooted in that village were identified on the manor rosters as yeomen and freeholders rather than as cottagers, labourers, or non-agricultural workers. It seems likely that those families whose source of wealth was land (especially if they flourished by it), rather than labour or manufacture, had an incentive to stay put. The primary allegiance of wealthier villagers, who were more likely to have cultivated and managed their own land, was surely bound up in a shared reverence for a particular space. The Haynes family, the manor lords who were in continuous residence for the 123 years recorded in the manor rosters, were perhaps the most persistent of all.

Until the late eighteenth century landowners below the level of the gentry, whether they lived in the city or the countryside, held property where they resided or in spaces topographically similar to their own place of residence. Samuel Seager of Almondsbury left an estate valued over £1,023, making him one of the wealthiest farmers in Bristol's rural environs at the end of the seventeenth century. He had leases on four separate plots and three houses, but all these were situated in his own village.[36] Some of the most prominent Bristol families of the late seventeenth century did have tenants in the local villages.[37] But significantly few members of Bristol's urban middle classes invested in the countryside, or established alternative residence there, until the growth of extramural suburbia in the later eighteenth century. John Finney, one of the wealthiest Bristolians of the late seventeenth century, confined his holdings to the urban landscape. In addition to his house in Tucker Street, he owned property and storage or retail space in the city of Exeter and the Cheshire town of Macclesfield. Despite his impressive wealth, he had no real estate in the countryside,[38] a form of topographical selectivity that his descendants may not have observed by the middle of the next century.

The more general tendency to identify with a highly localised space was an expression of parochialism. The established church provided ample reminders of how closely confined space had the power to include and exclude: the required attendance at services within the parish church; the spatial arrangement of parishioners in pews according to social station; the ritual of rogation and annual perambulations of parish boundaries; the recorded ceremonies of baptism, marriage, and burial within the parish on which settlement rights themselves were based.[39] St Augustine, a Bristol parish in the heart of the port, and St James, which bordered the countryside, virtually ignored the new Corporation of the Poor's wider jurisdiction over such matters when they pursued an unnecessary dispute in which responsibility for an unwanted male child was thrust by each parish upon the other.[40] Even parochial space was not highly localised enough for the residents of St Philip and Jacob, who, after the Restoration, divided that Bristol parish into two parts, one 'within' and the other 'without' Lawford's Gate. A rift in the vestry produced rivalling administrations within this single urban parish and effected an uneven dispersal of poor relief along residential lines well into the mid-eighteenth century.[41] Space was more congested in cities than in villages, but the ubiquity of the Anglican church meant that parochialism was hardly confined to one setting or the other.

Parochial justifications of formalised assault and ritual violence perpetuated popular and official xenophobia alike. Parochial notions of community were so closely linked with the policing and regulation of space that if churchwardens forcibly whisked a strange and unwed woman in labour into the next parish, they might avoid having to grant any settlement claims to her needy bastard. In 1722 the annual stick fight between the London parishes of St

Anne and St Giles resulted in the death of a chimney sweep who was blud-geoned by a sixteen-year-old boy from the next parish. The incident was ruled in court not as murder but as an unfortunate manslaughter, the result of natural, voluntary, and traditional forms of parochial allegiance.[42] After all, authority figures observed a long tradition of brandishing staves, like those of shepherds, in symbolic defence of highly localised territorial interests. In 1690 constables of Bristol parishes demanded that the wardens should provide them with staves, emblems of their office, authority, and parish affiliation. The constables of St James in Bristol successfully presented their own church-wardens before the magistrates, who upheld the significance of staves and the importance of symbolic parochial distinctions.[43] One London authority remarked derisively, as late as 1791, that 'every little dirty parish in the environs of London must have a law for itself'.[44]

Market spaces were such frequent theatres of contention that, even before the urban renaissance, incorporated cities were granted courts devoted to the adjudication of disputes involving extramural merchants and rival parishes.[45] Urban parishes were proprietorial about their own market spaces, which were sources of revenue for them. The proceeds from St Paul's Fair in Bristol were as valuable as the parish rates to the maintenance of Temple, the parish in which the fair was held.[46] The same could be said of the market in St James. That parish mounted handsome profits on stall rental fees exacted from hundreds of vendors per year, all on parish premises.[47] After 1746 or so, when the creation of the Bristol Exchange placed centrally located market space directly under municipal supervision, the distinction between citizens and extramurals became clearer. The clerk of the Bristol corporation took 'dues' for 'every sack of wheat, flour, barley, malt, oats, peas, beans, clover seed, etc.' that needed to be stored in the municipal corn sheds prior to market day.[48] Grain or any goods left about the market or on the streets constituted a violation of space and were subject to confiscation and fines. Clearly, this presented a problem for non-residents who lacked local storage in homes, shops or warehouses of their own. Vessels piloted into Bristol from outside the port paid steep fees to the corporation for space at the quays. The strict regulation of shared space in the urban setting was a major component of judicial business in general throughout the entire period. Among the quarter sessions presentments of Bristolians in the late seventeenth century, those regarding the violation of shared space were twice as numerous as the com-plaints about the violation of private space and the destruction or theft of private property.[49]

In both settings the conspicuous and collective use of shared space was often used as a fitting corrective whereby a transgressor could be reintroduced to the communal fold. The public parading of offenders could involve violence, as in the case of Eleanor Knight of Isleworth, who, for 'keeping a bawdy house' in 1725, was flogged in public. Her humiliation was acted out within the context of a parade along a route prescribed in explicit terms by the magistrate: 'from Brentford Bridge to the market place, round the market place and back again to the said bridge, on a market day'.[50] The route was a circuit defining an enclosed space in the offender's own neighbourhood, and the sentence was carried out at a time when that space was most congested with those people who frequented it. A prison was as much an affirmation of the socialising power of enclosures as a means of isolating the antisocial. As late as 1762 a tap room was installed in Bristol's Newgate jail as a means of promoting visitations from lawful members of society.[51] The line between a skimmington procession and a church rogation, whereby the bounds of a parish were ceremoniously traced around its inhabitants and their animals, was very fine. Although they may have contained some folk elements denounced as pagan by the established church, these popular shaming rituals of enforcement, such as charivari and rough music, still made plain the identification of social spheres with shared, highly localised spaces, be they village greens or urban market places.[52]

In addition to spatial considerations, varying attitudes towards time complicated the regulation of public and private space. These cultural differences presented visitors to cities with sets of rules that may not have applied in the rural setting. Annually, in late July and early August, the parish of St James erected what amounted to a small colony of stalls and shops on its premises. All these spaces were for the proprietorial and commercial use of the extra-parochial vendors who held leases on them, occasionally for life. But every October the stalls themselves were demolished and the space reverted to communal use. Similar shifts took place almost daily in the city, and the reversion of the market space to non-commercial uses at a precise hour was strictly enforced, but there must have been some ambiguity surrounding the public or private nature of the space itself. In 1694 extramural vendors at market were in one instance successful in denouncing Bristol street performers as nuisances who drew a 'multitude' of 'idle people' to Tucker Street at a time and on a day designated as for 'trading people or people of business, both of the city and the country'. In the same court session John Sheppard was cited as a 'huckster' because he was an outsider who attempted to set up a shop that was permanent rather than temporary.[53] In the early seventeenth century the town of Godalming, Surrey, had required citizens to pay a tax for a municipal clock to order the activities of apprentices, servants and workers in the town. In view of the importance of time to the definition of shared space in the urban landscape, it is not surprising that large clocks were more often visible on the exterior of churches and public buildings in towns than they were in villages.[54]

The use of space at the level of settlement patterns, and the level of private dwellings, varied considerably with setting. As we will see in subsequent chapters, the differences between urban and rural dwellings were conspicuous and the uses of living space constituted cultural differences which sustained distinctly urban or rural settings and customs of sociability. Urban dwellers had long-standing reasons for constructing tall, narrow buildings in which walls, rather than floors and ceilings, separated neighbouring houses and their occupants from one another. Such chimney-like arrangements helped confine fires to the dwellings of the careless persons who kindled them. The destruction of urban homes by fire underscored a general aspect of life in urban space, the tension between private impulses and communal restraints.[55] A widespread commitment to vertically organised dwelling spaces persisted in Bristol throughout the urban renaissance. In the early decades of the eighteenth century Thomas Westell, a Bristol brazier and broker worth the considerable sum of £706 17s 1d, occupied a house with only five rooms on three floors and an attached shop on the ground floor.[56] Seven desirable dwellings valued at £300 and bringing in annual rents of £5 apiece in 1728 stood in an area of Bristol identified on Millerd's 1673 map as an open pasture or orchard outside the urban development. Despite having been fairly new dwellings in an urban peripheral parish, each of the houses had dividing walls in common with houses on either side. None of the seven dwellings was more than a single room in width. Five of the seven were only one room in depth; they were column dwellings. One house, which was two rooms deep, had no exterior space whatsoever, illustrating that the practical trade-off between interior and exterior space in the city was observed regardless of its proximity to rural land.[57] Court sessions were enlivened by the colourful complaints of urban dwellers concerning the real or potential consequences of living beneath someone else's privy or furnace.[58]

As cities clung to their urban quality, residents resorted to other socially significant housing strategies: subdivision, sub-letting, and lodging.[59] In 1680 John Comberbatch, a Bristol horner, was found to have a combmaker and his entire family living with him. In two nearby dwellings he housed four more families all under one roof and three widows with children all under the other.[60] In 1696 the largest group of lodgers occupying parts of a single Bristol dwelling (eight) lived in the peripheral parish of St Philip and Jacob, not in one of the more affluent inner parishes.[61] Urban dwellers took in lodgers or sub-let portions of their homes out of need. Mary Thomas, a Bristol spinster, was worth only £15 8s 2d at the time of her death in 1735. She certainly did not own a house; her assets consisted of her clothes, £6 10s in cash, a 5s personal debt owed to her, and £2 2s 6d owed to her from her three boarders with whom she must have shared a rather cramped dwelling space. It is possible that a widow of an artisan, merchant, or more substantial freeman could keep her accustomed residence by converting it into a boarding house under her management after her husband's death.[62] Assessors of urban dwellings often described the contents and location of the rooms occupied by the principal tenant in a vertical house but skipped an entire storey or intervening room occupied by someone else. Some time before 1776 a Bristol writing master agreed to pay two house carpenters a sum approaching £132 to fashion a comfortable detached house for him in the peripheral parish of St James. By 1780, when the house was conveyed to a new owner, it had been subdivided into three dwellings.[63]

The dwellings inhabited by the city's wealthiest residents were set apart from most urban houses by virtue of the very fact that the most desirable urban houses actually resembled, in the configuration of their rooms and exterior spaces, rural dwellings. These configurations featured interior walls and passageways that were private and not held in common with another dwelling. They featured greater width, which gave scope for larger private yards, and more windows to permit light and air into the house. They provided greater interior and exterior barriers against the ravages of fire and the disturbances of street life. Put metaphorically, wealthier urban residents occupied houses that resembled fields more than they resembled fence posts. John Finney, a Bristol merchant worth over £5,060 at his death in 1700, had a house with six rooms on the ground floor and four rooms on one storey above that on Tucker Street, near St James's Church. The most valuable estate assessed in Bristol between 1700 and 1739 was valued at £3,112 and belonged to a wine cooper named Matthew Adean. Until his death in 1738 Adean resided in the central parish of St Leonard in a house of no fewer than nine rooms on exactly two floors. As late as 1766 a wealthy sexton named Thomas Bolt lived in a fourteen-room, two-level house near the Frome docks in the middle of the city. Bolt paid an impressive window tax of £1 7s per annum, so, despite its central location, the house was exposed to open space on many sides, not bound by exterior walls held in common with other houses. Bolt lived comfortably with the aid of a servant. He entertained in his dining room and three parlours, which were decorated with sixty-two pictures, stocked with tea and chocolate service, clocks, silver, and sixty-four printed volumes. He left an estate of £327.[64] Long before prosperous members of urban society left the city altogether in numbers large enough to transform the rural environs into suburbia, they replicated, as closely as possible, rural dwelling space within the familiar and stimulating urban setting they preferred.

A bitter irony, of course, was that most rural migrants to cities wound up in the vertical and attached dwellings typical of the urban setting. They left behind, in their villages, dwellings whose spatial configuration signalled, in the city, a quality of life that few migrants could afford in the urban setting. On the other hand, urban dwellers opted to live in subdivided spaces before they would move out of their urban environment altogether. This tendency to preserve one's familiar setting almost certainly contributed to the vigilance of villagers who prevented the urban poor from settling into rural dwelling space.

Despite the availability of rural space there were absolutely and proportionately far fewer examples of large houses in the villages near Bristol than in the city itself. Outside the country seats and great houses of the gentry, the greatest number of rooms to be found in a single rural home at any time during the entire period was nine, and the probate record gives evidence of only one dwelling that large in the villages near Bristol: the rectory of Winterbourne.[65] In 1720 a surgeon named Potter, whose estate was valued at £608 17s 9d, lived in a twenty-four-room house in Bristol. Out of the fifty-five Bristol inventories from which definite room totals can be taken, twelve (22 per cent) describe homes with ten or more rooms, a surprisingly large portion of an urban sample that also includes small dwellings. The occupants of these twelve very large houses in Bristol lived between 1684 and 1766 and included two widows, two merchants, two victuallers, a sailmaker, a surgeon, a clerk, an ordinary cooper and a wine cooper. The clerk was worth only £59 1s and the poorer merchant was worth a modest £62 19s 10d. Five members of this palatially housed urban group had total assets valued under £200. This would make them less wealthy than most yeomen farmers, all of whom lived in smaller houses of four to six rooms in the villages.

Just as urban dwellers found ways to reside within urban confines for as long as possible, villagers were loath to put any more buildings or any larger dwellings on the rural landscape than was necessary. The construction of new cottages was legally and socially discouraged in rural parishes, especially those still under manorial supervision. Indeed, all the villagers of Wick, not only the lord of the manor of Abson and Wick, appeared in the leet court throughout the entire period to demand the destruction of cottages if they encroached 'upon the waste'.[66] By act of Parliament in 1589, in response to the rural building explosion of the sixteenth century, the erection of a new house on a plot of fewer than four acres became prohibited. The act was not repealed until 1775. One architectural historian has noted that housing subdivision became fairly common in rural areas of the West Country. In fact, in one instance dating from 1631, the manor house itself in Wylye, Wiltshire, was subdivided into eight lodgings of only two or three rooms apiece. Some barns and stables were converted into rural dwellings.[67] But Elizabethan law, which confronted the problem of new houses built on inadequate parcels of land, in no way placed a size limit on proposed or existing houses. Rural yeoman had the financial wherewithal to build larger houses for themselves. There was certainly more available space surrounding houses in the countryside than there was in Bristol neighbourhoods. Why, then, were the largest houses in the region – apart from a handful of the gentry's country houses – in the city of Bristol rather than in the surrounding countryside?

We must recognise the possibility that the curious persistence of this pattern reflected powerful differences between urbane and rustic customs and practices. The upper and lower systems of rooms maintained in larger urban houses imitated manor house power strategies[68] far more closely than village houses imitated any urban dwelling space. An additional room might have made a farmhouse slightly more comfortable for its occupants, but it is not clear that it would have conferred any social or economic advantage upon them. Thus, in the rural setting, where the uneven distribution of land reflected social stratification, the range of house sizes was narrow. Contrasted against this rural housing pattern of comfortable moderation with little variation from house to house was the urban situation, in which a wide spectrum of dwelling sizes was exhibited in close formation. One historian has identified social ambition and public display as the creative forces behind the revival of cities as centres of production, distribution and cultural influence.[69]

The types of images on display within a dwelling conformed closely to patterns associated with the setting of the dwelling as well as the spatial awareness and topographical affinity of the people who lived there. The most common images on display in Bristol and the nearby villages were those of landscapes and specific places. In 1742 a Bristol cordwainer named Richard Sanders had a picture of the city's High Cross, a familiar urban landmark which any of his neighbours could have identified. Maps visible in urban homes depicted cities and foreign places. In 1736 John Mansell, a wealthy Bristol haulier, owned scriptural maps depicting the Holy Land. Bristol innkeepers and victuallers, playing upon the far-flung origins or musings of their customers, displayed world maps in their establishments.[70] Even Bristol's mariners owned maps with urban, and not simply nautical, themes. By 1685 a Bristol seaman by the name of Bartholomew Jefford revealed his attachment to other great cities and ports when he hung maps of London and Amsterdam in his rooms. Several Bristol residents expressed, through the maps displayed in their homes, a similar affinity for the urban landscape in general. George Stearte, a Bristol surgeon, had a map of London in his house in 1671. A year later a map of Hamburg was found in the hall of a Bristol cooper named Jonas Neason. James Dickinson, a Bristol tiler of modest means, had a framed map of Venice on display in his house in 1708. A poor Bristol barber, in the spirit of urban localism, had a map which his assessor readily identified in 1717 as a map of the city of Bristol itself. Despite the widespread ownership in Bristol of urban maps (both English and foreign), maps of the world, and maps of foreign locations, there were no maps of the nearby villages or counties identified in any urban households. Why was this so?

A map could be a navigational device in a figurative sense, a substitute for travel, a decorative reminder of its owner's preferred surroundings. Clergy, for example, were prominent among the few map owners in the rural setting, but those members of the clergy who actually lived in the city of Bristol had no maps at all in their household inventories. This odd contrast invites the speculation that the university-trained occupants of village rectories, deprived of urban surroundings, displayed maps depicting remote and urban subjects more familiar to them but unknown to their parishioners. Maps in the possession of the rural clergy were mentioned among their 'pictures', evocative windows into the imagination. William Manning, the clerk and vicar of Bedminster, Somerset, was an avid collector of books, maps and pictures until his death in 1702.[71] He had no fewer than twenty pictures. A clerk or vicar in a rural parish was almost certainly educated, if not raised, in some urbane setting removed from the village he served. It is not unreasonable to imagine that he might have preserved his fond recollection of a distant urban setting, such as Oxford, Cambridge, or London, in the pictures and maps on display in his house. The Bristol clergy maintained loyalty to their university towns in other ways. Bishop John Conybeare's sermon preached on 5 September 1751 at the annual meeting of the Sons of Clergy in Bristol Cathedral was sent to be printed at Oxford, while the sermons for ordinary audiences by this time were routinely printed locally.[72]

Perspectives of the extended community and its shape, which varied from the rural to the urban point of view, also varied from one medium to another. In the later eighteenth century, Donne's printed map of Bristol, a carefully measured representation of the city, actually featured a superimposed grid complete with numbered and lettered coordinates.[73] Manuscript maps, especially rural ones, provided the idiosyncratic details of a specific natural setting. The trees in hand-drawn surveys were particular individual trees known to the mapmakers and their neighbours. This emphasis on the natural depiction of individual objects was consistent with the particular, as opposed to semiotic, nature of rustic expression. To be sure, urban dwellers lived in close familiarity with their environment, but the printed maps which urbane surveyors produced, and the owners of printed materials saw, provided a representation of the world built upon conventional symbols – a generalised, rather than localised, frame of reference. Rural maps were often in aid of proprietorial claims which rustic draughters of hand-drawn maps took obvious pains to reinforce with a kind of subjective specificity. Hence rustic manuscript maps featured landmark trees cleft by lightning, landmark stones with facial features, and other landmarks with individual traits.[74] By the latter part of the eighteenth century, the urbane surveyors in the employment of the gentry and their estate managers produced elegant manuscript maps, but these adopted the printed symbols for trees, buildings, and hedges. In keeping with printing conventions, Isaac Taylor, the professional surveyor of Edward Southwell's vast estates in Henbury, Shirehampton, and Lawrence Weston, placed tree-like figures on the parts of his maps representing the location and extent of

Southwell's orchards and forests by the 1770s. But any farmer's child would have queried what Taylor accepted; even in those maps which placed the eastern horizon along the top of the page, the shadows cast by the standard symbolic trees all fell to the right, according to printing conventions, contrary to the observed ways of the natural world readily observable in one's own immediate surroundings.[75]

Urban dwellers were far more likely to own printed maps than villagers were. For the entire period between 1660 and 1780 there exist for Bristol and the surrounding villages sixty-four inventories which include references to printed maps. Of these sixty-four map owners, fifty-seven (89 per cent) resided in the city of Bristol. All seven of the map owners whose inventories date from the period after 1740 lived in the city. The overall incidence of map ownership in the period between 1700 and 1740 was 50 per cent greater than it had been during the previous forty-year period at the end of the seventeenth century, but rural representation among map owners actually declined to a ninth of the total in the later period, despite the advent of local printing in the city. The handful of map owners living in the rural villages was made up of one gentleman, two Westbury mariners, a wealthy Westbury widow who owned a one-sixth share of the merchant ship Robert, a clergyman in Stapleton, Gloucestershire and one of his successors (the earlier of whom had a 'small boat'), and the vicar of Bedminster in Somerset. Thus the few rural homes containing printed maps between 1660 and 1780 all had strong clerical or maritime connections.

Before the mid-eighteenth century, there was nothing in Bristol's early printed maps to supply the viewer with a picture of a local community consisting of a city and the nearby villages combined. Millerd's *Exact Delineation of the Famous City of Bristol* of 1673 barely included the outer parishes of Bristol itself; these Millerd regarded as 'suburbs'. Some time after 1749 a newspaper presented a map of Somersetshire which had been printed in September 1741. This simply included Bristol along a small portion of its border because, as the paper explained, a good portion of Bristol was once considered part of Somerset; this was clearly a county map rather than an expression of regional identity centred upon a city.[76] One Bristol newspaper ran an advertisement in 1742 for *Rocque's New Plan of Bristol*. The notice pointed out that the plan confined its scope to the city limits and, at a scale of 1 in. to 200 ft, could show Bristol residents the exact locations of their individual houses and the precise boundaries of their parishes. The advertisement appealed not only to a sense of extreme urban localism but to a sense of civic pride based on the observation that Bristol was larger in surface area than intramural London.[77] It was not until 1769 that Benjamin Donne published a truly regional map centred on the city but providing rural details. It should be noted that Donne took as his definition of Bristol's rural environs all the villages within an eleven-mile radius of the city centre.[78]

The contrast between the reticular world of the urban dweller and the spatial world of the rural dweller provides a conceptual framework in which to analyse some crucial distinctions between urbane and rustic attitudes towards community. In the late seventeenth century, a Bristol butcher had among his four maps a 'long map',[79] quite probably of the kind made popular by the cartographer and surveyor John Ogilby.[80] A copy of Ogilby's Survey was found among the other books, pamphlets, and prints in the home of a Bristol couple in the 1770s.[81] Every one of these long maps, or strip maps, depicted one route connecting some city with another and confined its scope to the towns and strips of land which lined the side of that road. (Figure 1.) Strip maps did not show a collection of towns and villages scattered across a particular area; they were strictly concerned with urban origins, urban destinations, and the most direct routes between them. This printed idealised representation of an urban network ought to be seen in contrast to hand-drawn maps of the same period. 'A Mapp of Kingswood Chase' was drawn up by hand in 1672, presumably for the sake of estate management.[82] (Figure 2.) It is concerned with depicting a local area of land, situating its contiguous parcels in relation to one another in the landscape, recording their acreages, and identifying the general expanse and the spaces within it by name or by the names of the principal land holders. In reality, Kingswood had a border in common with the city of Bristol, but clearly the maker of the Kingswood Chase map perceived the city as a symbolically different, compact, removed, and detached place.

In the middle decades of the eighteenth century, when rural defences against urban encroachment were challenged on a grander scale, confrontations over the arteries of urban expansion were frequent and erupted into urban–rural violence. In 1733 200 Kingswood colliers signed a petition against turnpikes and demanded the release of villagers arrested in turnpike riots.[83] From the 1730s to the 1770s local villagers tore down turnstiles on new roads leading from the city and protested that turnpike roads were urban tentacles disrupting consolidated rural space. Turnpikes traversed the rural landscape but, in the view of villagers, only in the interests of maintaining the network of urban commercial centres and their residents. In the 1770s the jurors of the Abson and Wick manor court complained that the new turnpike which was being extended through their village was a source of danger and a lamentable violation of their customary way of life; the turnpike had turned an 'ancient footway into a miry tract offensive to all'.[84] Urban dwellings were situated on streets. By contrast, rural deeds and land surveys made it clear that villagers observed the practice of placing farm houses in the middle of fields and meadows, often bound by hedges and fences, to insulate their dwellings from public roads.[85]

An abrupt transition between city and country was part of the early modern mental picture of an ordered world, even for the more influential or well

Figure 1: 'Ogilby's strip map of the road from London to Bristol' (1698).
*Source:* B.R.O. AC/PL2(a–c).

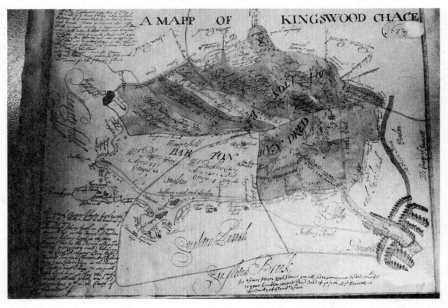

Figure 2: A map of Kingswood Chase (1672). *Source:* B.R.O. MS #38016,
C.T. 47.

informed members of provincial English society. The enforcement of such separateness and the prevention of expansion or violation of observed confines was a practical function of maps. As late as 1762 a manuscript map, 'Plan of encroachment on waste in Westerleigh Manor ... contrary to the survey of 1671', was produced to invoke territorial claims established three generations earlier.[86] The concept of encroachment applied not only to the offensive presence of cottagers upon parochial or manorial holdings, it also held larger meaning for villagers who regarded the city and its population as potential violators of rural space. A 1772 parish map, drawn up in the same manor of Westerleigh, labelled all the roads 'to' other villages, but labelled other roads 'from Bristol', a subtle expression of the perception that, rather than beckoning the members of the rural community, the urban network and its members had begun flowing into rural space.[87]

## NOTES

1 P. Clark, 'The civic leaders of Gloucester 1580–1800', in P. Clark (ed.), *The Transformation of English Provincial Towns 1600–1800* (London, 1984), p. 322; C. R. Friedrichs, *The Early Modern City 1450–1750* (London, 1995), pp. 22.

2 B.R.O. #4312(42), Plans of Trinity Alms House and Lawford's Gate.

3 Edward Barlow, *Barlow's Journal of his Life at Sea from 1659 to 1703*, ed. B. Lubbock (1934), I, p. 23, as cited in I. K. Ben-Amos, *Adolescence and Youth in Early Modern England* (New Haven, Conn., 1994), p. 98.

4 H.B., *Sackfull of News* (London, 1685).

5 D. Appleyard, 'Styles and methods of structuring a city', in S. and R. Kaplan (eds), *Humanscape: Environments for People* (Ann Arbor, Mich., 1982), pp. 70–81; H. Kummer, 'Spacing mechanisms in social behavior', in Kaplan and Kaplan, *Humanscape*, pp. 321–4; A. Rapoport, *The Mutual Interaction of People and their Built Environment* (The Hague, 1976) and *The Meaning of the Built Environment: A Nonverbal Communication Approach* (London, 1982).

6 J. W. Frost (ed.), *The Records and Recollections of James Jenkins* (Lewiston, N.Y., 1984), pp. 10–11.

7 Thomas Raymond, *Autobiography*, ed. G. Davies, Camden Society, 3rd ser. 28 (1917), pp. 22–23, as cited in Ben-Amos, *Adolescence and Youth in Early Modern England*, p. 98.

8 S.R.O. Q/SR/102, Somerset Quarter Sessions (Easter Term, 1662, #66 and #67). Rural landlords, and villagers themselves, opposed the building of cottages in congestion or upon communal ground. But in all the manor court records extant for Abson and Wick, for our entire period, there is not a single case of a rural landlord confiscating household property or even threatening to demolish housing as a means of collecting rent. See B.R.O. #14581 bundles HA/M.4–7, Haynes Manor Court Records (1657–77, 1697–1726, 1746–68, 1770–92).

9 B.R.O. #29571(2), Plan of Property on a Deed, Charles Street.

10 Any settlement having a charter, an official market, a cathedral, at least 2,500 inhabit-

ants, or any combination of these, is considered urban. Bristol's charter also granted county status.

11  E. Ralph and M. Williams (eds), *The Inhabitants of Bristol in 1696* (Bristol, 1968), pp. xx–xxv; Benjamin Donne's printed survey and map of Bristol (1773), Bristol City Museum, Braikenridge Bequest, 1908 Reg. No. M745 (repr. 1979).

12  *Jacobus Millerd's Plan of Bristol 1673*, Bristol City Museum, 1923 (repr. 1979); *Donne's Map of Bristol 1773*, Bristol City Museum, Braikenridge Bequest, 1908 Reg. No. M745 (reprinted, 1979). See E. George's frontispiece of Ralph and Williams, *The Inhabitants of Bristol in 1696*, for a representation of Millerd's survey to which parish boundaries, rather than comparisons with Donne's 1773 survey, have been added.

13  G. S. Minchon, 'Table of population 1801–1901', in W. Page (ed.), *The Victoria History of the County of Somerset* II (London, 1911), pp. 338–52, and W. Page (ed.), *The Victoria History of the County of Gloucestershire* II (London, 1907), pp. 175–87.

14  P. J. Corfield, *The Impact of English Towns 1700–1800* (Oxford, 1982), p. 15.

15  In seven sample years taken at twenty-year intervals, annual percentages of all apprentices registering with the Bristol corporation who were apprenticed under Bristol tilers, plasterers, brickmakers or bricklayers, carpenters, joiners, turners, glaziers or glassmakers, and masons are as follows: 1660, 9·3 per cent (11/118); 1680, 7·7 per cent (20/260); 1700, 17·5 per cent (49/280); 1720, 15·3 per cent (34/222); 1740, 12·0 per cent (24/200); 1760, 17·0 per cent (30/176); 1780, 7·1 per cent (13/183). B.R.O. #04357(2), #04353(1)b, #04353(3), #04353(4), #04353(6), #04353(7), #04356(15), Corporation of Bristol Apprenticeship Registers.

16  S. J. Jones, 'The historical geography of Bristol', *Geography* 16 (1931), pp. 180–9, and 'The growth of Bristol', *Transactions of British Geographers* 2 (1946), pp. 57–83, show that the containment of Bristol was persistent.

17  The portion of St James land under developmment rose from 23 per cent (44·1/193·1 acres) in 1696 to no more than 51 per cent (114/223 acres) in 1773. According to window tax records of 1773, the parish of St James had 1,016 – only 730 fewer than had been reported in similar records for the entire city in 1696 – including houses listed as exempt because their occupants were judged to be poor. B.R.O. St James's window rate (25 March 1773 to 25 March 1774). Hearth taxes produce conservative estimates because hearths judged to be used by artisans or in manufacturing were exempt despite the frequent combination of home and workplace. In the period 1660 to 1780 Bristol and southern Gloucestershire assessors recorded exemptions and taxations alike. As for the St James window tax of 1773, there is corroborating evidence in B.R.O. #07785(11), Ashmead's Map of Bristol (1828).

18  The transformation and absorption of greater London has been treated in G. R. Williams, *London in the Country: The Growth of Suburbia* (London, 1975).

19  With 21.1 acres, St Nicholas was the second largest of the interior parishes. It contained 296 assessed houses (more than any other Bristol parish in 1696), or fourteen houses per acre overall. But in the late seventeenth century only 11·1 of St Nicholas's 21·1 acres were built-up.

20  P.R.O. E.179/247/13–4, Hearth Tax of 1672. These particular hearth tax records also listed exempt buildings and are therefore unusually informative. In the village of Stoke Gifford forty-two houses were taxed for hearths and one was listed as exempt in 1672.

21 B.R.O. P/Hor/X/la, The Reverend Samuel Sayer's Notes on Horfield (1813). A manuscript map of Horfield, probably dating from the eighteenth century, shows the scattered, dispersed pattern of housing plots in the parish. See B.R.O. P/Hor/P/8.

22 Samuel Rudder, *A New History of Gloucestershire* (1779), p. 501. This contemporary observer also determined that Horfield had only twenty-six houses and 100 occupants in the early 1700s, and only 125 residents by 1779.

23 B.R.O. Diocese of Bristol Probate Inventories and Cause Papers 1660–1780. For the entire collection of probate records, organised by names, parishes, occupations, and total assessments, see E. and S. George (eds), *Guide to the Probate Inventories of the Bristol Deanery of the Diocese of Bristol 1542–1804* (Bristol, 1988).

24 E. Jones, 'London in the early seventeenth century: an ecological approach', *London Journal* 6 no. 2 (1980), pp. 123–33; V. Pearl, 'Change and stability in seventeenth-century London', *London Journal* 5 no. 1 (1979), pp. 3–34.

25 B.R.O. Bristol Quarter Sessions: Papers, 1763–68 box, bundle 1 (Epiphany, 1767).

26 J. Boulton, *Neighbourhood and Society: A London Suburb in the Seventeenth Century* (Cambridge, 1987), p. 239.

27 A. Dyer, *The City of Worcester in the Sixteenth Century* (Leicester, 1973).

28 K. Wrightson and D. Levine, *Poverty and Piety in an English Village: Terling 1525–1700* (London, 1979), pp. 100–2.

29 P. Clark, *The English Alehouse: A Social History 1200–1830* (London, 1983); A. Everitt, 'The English urban inn 1560–1760', in A. Everitt (ed.), *Perspectives in English Urban History* (London, 1973); J. Money, 'Taverns, coffee houses, and clubs: local politics and popular articulacy', *Historical Journal* 14 no. 1 (1971), pp. 15–47.

30 B.R.O. Bristol Quarter Sessions papers (1760). There were also thirty–nine unlicensed Bristol alehouses presented in 1760 alone.

31 B.R.O. #14581 HA/P/6, Haynes Collection: Miscellaneous, letter (1747).

32 Boulton, *Neighbourhood and Society*, pp. 202–27; M. Reed, 'Economic structure and change in seventeenth-century Ipswich', in P. Clark (ed.), *Country Towns in Pre-industrial England* (Leicester, 1981), pp. 93–5; and P. Clark, 'The migrant in Kentish towns 1580–1640', in P. Clark and P. Slack (eds), *Crisis and Order in English Towns 1500–1700* (London, 1972), pp. 125–6.

33 Boulton, *Neighbourhood and Society*, pp. 211 and 216.

34 P. Laslett, 'Clayworth and Cogenhoe', in P. Laslett (ed.), *Family Life and Illicit Love in Earlier Generations* (Cambridge, 1977), pp. 50–101.

35 B.R.O. #14581 HA/M.4; HA/M.5; HA/M.7, Haynes Manor Court Records (1657–77, 1697–1726, 1770–92).

36 B.R.O. Probate Inventories (Samuel Seager, 1699). For examples of similarly localised, but substantial, holdings in the rural setting, see the inventories of John Jayne, who in 1752 had seven occupied parcels, six of which were in Almondsbury and one in Compton Dando, Somerset; Elizabeth Cox, whose 'several' holdings were all in Almondsbury in 1713; T. Collins, a yeoman with several cultivated and occupied holdings in Elberton and only one in Littleton in 1767. Thus, even in the middle of the eighteenth century, real estate in the hands of the sturdier proprietors was confined to their own parishes or to the countryside.

37  See, for example, B.R.O. #9728(2), Diary and Accounts of Francis Creswicke (1674).

38  B.R.O. Probate Inventories (John Finney, 1700). After the settlement of his estate, Finney, a merchant, was worth £5,060. It is not clear why his inventory was not proved in the archdiocese, given his holdings in multiple dioceses.

39  R. Hutton, *The Rise and Fall of Merry England: The Ritual Year 1400–1700* (Oxford, 1994), pp. 175–6 and 217–18, argues that parish rogation observances even survived Puritanical attacks on festive culture. For illustrations of how church pew assignments reflected the association of spatial arrangements and social hierarchy in urban as well as rural parishes, see R. Gough, *The History of Myddle* (1702, ed. D. Hey, Harmondsworth, 1981), pp. 77–249, and P. Earle, *The Making of the English Middle Class: Business, Society and Family Life in London 1660–1730* (London, 1989), pp. 244–7. On the subject of settlement laws, which have received extensive treatment, see D. Souden, 'Migrants and the population structure of later seventeenth-century provincial cities and market towns', in Clark, *The Transformation of English Provincial Towns*, pp. 133–68; N. Landau, 'The laws of settlement and the surveillance of immigration in eighteenth-century Kent', *Continuity and Change* 3 (1988), pp. 391–420; P. Slack, *Poverty and Policy in Tudor and Stuart England* (London, 1988) and *The English Poor Law 1531–1782* (Cambridge, 1995).

40  B.R.O. #0449(1), Bristol Quarter Sessions: Docket (1695–1703).

41  B.R.O. P/StP&J/V/1, St Philip and Jacob Vestry Minutes (1649–1722) and P/StP&J/V/2, St Philip and Jacob Vestry Minutes (1722–1832).

42  D. M. George, *London Life in the Eighteenth Century* (London, 1925; repr. Chicago 1984), p. 272. George cites London Sessions Papers, Case of Elias Dyer (May 1722).

43  B.R.O. #04452(1), Bristol Quarter Sessions (Michaelmas, 1690).

44  George, *London Life in the Eighteenth Century*, pp. 21–3 and 58.

45  B.R.O. #04411 and #04412. Two volumes of Piepoudre Court records, amounting to roughly 173 pages of depositions and rulings, survive for the period 1655–96.

46  The records of parish markets and fairs are plentiful and detailed. For alms and charities of Temple entirely subsidised by St Paul's Fair revenues see B.R.O. #00156(1023), St Paul's Fair: Alms and Charities (1623–1743); B.R.O. #00066(22), St Paul's Fair: Gifts (1708); B.R.O. #0066(19), St Paul's Fair: Gifts (1707). For general revenues of the St Paul's Fair see B.R.O. #00120, Agreements for Stands (1673); B.R.O. #00147, Agreements for Stands (1705); B.R.O. #00148–9 and #00044, Agreements for Stands (1719–20, 1723); B.R.O. #00127, Tolls for Stands (1750); B.R.O. #00132, Tolls and Distresses for Stands (1753); B.R.O. #00113(1–32), Miscellaneous: St Paul's Fair, Temple.

47  B.R.O. P/StJ/F/2–17 and 21, St James Fair Stall Rentals (1721–1830); B.R.O. #04287, St James Market Accounts (1721–74); B.R.O. #04094, St James Market Accounts (1774–1800).

48  B.R.O. #04101(1), Bristol Corn Sheds (1747–91).

49  See, for example: B.R.O. #04452(1), Bristol Quarter Sessions: Presentments and Convictions (1676–1700). From Trinity 1676 to Trinity 1700 141 presentments were made, seven of which dealt with theft, destruction, or endangerment (usually by fire) of private space or property, and thirteen of which dealt with the use of public space, for storage, vending, or the like, by unauthorised persons. In addition there were twenty-seven

presentments for objectionable disposal of waste on the street, docks, churchyards, or some other public space. The two most frequent presentments were for dangerous or poorly maintained buildings or grounds which threatened public thoroughfares (forty-two cases), and for the unlicensed sale of ale (fifty cases).

50 *Farley's Bristol Newspaper*, No. 24 (16 October 1725), p. 4, concerning the 'news from London'.

51 J. Latimer, *The Annals of Bristol in the Eighteenth Century* (Bristol, 1893), p. 355. Quaker and Methodist enthusiasts would even visit condemned prisoners in order to restore them to the community of souls. For an example of this dating from roughly the period of the Newgate tap room see B.C.L. #20095, Diary of William Dyer (entry of 23 April 1752).

52 Hutton, *The Rise and Fall of Merry England*, pp. 46–47; D. Underdown, *Revel, Riot, and Rebellion: Popular Politics and Culture in England 1603–1660* (Oxford, 1985), chs 4–5, 8–10, and 'The taming of the scold: the enforcement of patriarchal authority in early modern England', in A. Fletcher and J. Stevenson (eds), *Order and Disorder in Early Modern England* (Cambridge, 1985), pp. 127–34; M. Ingram, 'Ridings, rough music and "the reform of popular culture" in early modern England', *Past and Present* 105 (1984), pp. 79–113; E. P. Thompson, '"Rough music": le charivari anglais', *Annales E.S.C.* 27 no. 2 (1972), pp. 285–312.

53 B.R.O. #04452(1), Bristol Quarter Sessions: Presentments and Convictions (Michaelmas, 1694).

54 R. Tittler, *Architecture and Power: The Town Hall and the English Urban Community c. 1500–1640* (Oxford, 1991), p. 137; C. M. Cipolla, *Clocks and Culture 1300–1700* (New York, 1978), pp. 40–3.

55 E. L. Jones, S. Porter, and M. A. Turner, *A Gazetteer of English Urban Fire Disasters 1500–1900* (Norwich, 1984); Friedrichs, *The Early Modern City*, pp. 276–9.

56 B.R.O. Probate Inventories (Thomas Westell, 1743).

57 B.R.O. #32009, Plan of Seven Properties on a Deed, Bread Street (1728).

58 There were already examples of this by the late seventeenth century. See the cases of the 'above ground necessary rooms' and large-scale soapboiling and brewing operations in action above neighbours' dwellings in B.R.O. #04452(1), Bristol Quarter Sessions: Presentments and Convictions 1676–1700 (Easter and Michaelmas Sessions, 1676).

59 Boulton, *Neighbourhood and Society*, pp. 172–4; Reed, 'Economic structure and change in seventeenth-century Ipswich', pp. 118–19.

60 B.R.O. #04452(1), Bristol Quarter Sessions (Epiphany, 1680/81).

61 Ralph and Williams, *The Inhabitants of Bristol in 1696*, p. xxiv.

62 For example, see B.R.O. Probate Inventories (B. Gagg, 1714). Barbara Gagg was the widow of a soapboiler. She was worth only £41 2s 3d at her death, but she had occupied a ten-room house in which she had, according to her assessor's accocunt, fee-paying lodgers.

63 B.R.O. #29571(2), Plan of a Property on a Deed in Charles Street, St James (1780). Charles Street was renamed Brickhouse Lane in 1780 as explained on the deed.

64 B.R.O. Probate Inventories (Thomas Bolt, 1766).

65 B.R.O. Probate Inventories (John Griffyth, 1698).

66 B.R.O. #14581 HA/M.4–M.7, Haynes Manor Court Records (1657–1790).

67 R. J. Brown, *The English Country Cottage* (London, 1979), pp. 28–30.

68 M. Girouard, *Life in the English Country House: A Social and Architectural History* (New Haven, Conn., 1978), chs 1 and 5–8.

69 P. Borsay, 'Culture, status, and the English urban landscape', *History* 67 no. 219 (1982) and 'The English urban renaissance: the development of provincial urban culture, *c.* 1680–*c.* 1760', *Social History* 5 (1977), pp. 581–603.

70 See, for example, B.R.O Probate Inventories (John Gwillim, 1705) and (Thomas Hopper, 1717 bundle).

71 His probate inventory values his 'study of books' at £20. Manning's inventory is in the B.R.O. despite the fact that he was probably an incumbent in the Diocese of Bath and Wells.

72 B.C.L. pamphlet #6127.

73 A copy of the 1773 edition of Donne's printed map of Bristol is among the holdings of the Bristol City Museum, listed in the Braikenridge Bequest as Reg. No. M745.

74 See, for example, B.R.O. AC/PL 17(a–b), a map of two Bedminster, Somerset, fields, on which the surveyor drew no fewer than forty-two individual trees and labelled them 'shrowded elm', 'ash', 'a lime tree', 'the young elm', or 'the tall elm'. Even in the eighteenth century, manuscript maps mainly depicted patchworks of fields identified by name. See, for example, in B.R.O. AC/PL 5, Survey of a dairy farm in Chew Magna (1737), or B.R.O. AC/E 3, Survey of Smythe Henbury Estates.

75 B.R.O. #26570, Clack Mill Farm and Bowdown Field surveyed by Isaac Taylor (1772), drawn map.

76 B.C.L. #6420(1277, 88b), Somerset Gleanings: Descriptions of Somerset extracted from Newspapers (1749–1871).

77 *Bristol Oracle: or, Bristol Weekly Miscellany* 1 no. 3 (17 April 1742), p. 4.

78 An original printing of Donne's *Map of the Country Eleven Miles round the City of Bristol* is held by the Bristol University Library. B.R.O. #247 BP210 and Non-archival #64 are photocopies.

79 B.R.O. Probate Inventories (John Hurtnoll, 1686).

80 *Ogilby's Strip Map of the Road from London to Bristol* (1698 ed.). B.R.O. as AC/PL 2(a–c) is a copy of this printed edition.

81 B.R.O. Probate Inventories (Samuel and Mary Smith, 1776).

82 B.R.O. #38016, A Mapp of Kingswood Chace (1672), drawn map.

83 B.R.O. #09701(26), Letter of R. Holland to T. Haynes regarding Colliers' Petition against Turnpikes (4 April 1733).

84 B.R.O. #14581 HA/M.7, Haynes Manor Court Records (October 1770).

85 B.R.O. #AC/PL 89(1) and 89(2), R. Hall's Plan of the Parish and Manor of Westerleigh (1772).

86 B.R.O. AC/PL 7.

87 B.R.O. AC/PL 89(1–2), Plan of the Parish and Manor of Westerleigh (1772), drawn map.

# Chapter 3

—◆—

# Urban and rural resources

Iz put ane my bootes, zword by my zide
Vor up to London Iz mean'd vor to ride.

'Ned' (late seventeenth century)[1]

I n October 1728 Arthur Peters and John Jenkins, both weavers in the Somerset village of Chew Magna, located in the Mendip Hills six miles south of Bristol, watched in horror as:

> there came into the parish of Chew Magna a great company of lewd, idle and disorderly persons to the number of four or five hundred persons from Bristol, from without Lawford's Gate, Bedminster and other places pretending to be weavers but among them were butchers, ropers, tilers, carpenters and other disorderly, idle fellows and presently entered the houses ... of several ... persons, and took from them not only the looms and harness thereto, and burnt the same in a great fire they had made in the churchyard, but likewise in a violent manner assaulted the houses ... broke windows, cut their beds, destroyed their goods, eat [sic] or carried away all their victuals, so that they left them destitute either of tools and materials to work or any other means of maintaining their families.[2]

Jenkins, whose house was nearly ruined, complained that John Gamerell, of St Philip and Jacob in the city of Bristol, and four accomplices were 'all amongst the rioters and acted, assisted, and encouraged them in the violent and tumultuous proceedings to the pain ... and horror of all the [village] inhabitants', regardless of occupation. Clearly, Bristol weavers wished to prevent any nearby village from developing into a centre of their craft, and the villagers readily identified Bristolians as the motivating force behind the horde of plunderers, the size of an entire rural community, that descended on their village. In the sixteenth century, Chew Magna had been a prosperous link in the West Country wool trade. But during the urban renaissance Bristol artisans took punitive measures to enforce the distinctions between their great city and a village in its shadows. The villagers knew their assailants by sight, if not by name, thus any prior urban–rural interaction had hardly mollified tensions. Moreover, the Bristol weavers, as the villagers noted, had no trouble enlisting the support of similarly 'lewd, idle and disorderly' urban dwellers from a variety of trades. Three years earlier 1,500 rural weavers near Taunton 'three or four miles around' had attacked that town and 'plundered' it. The combers of Taunton, despite an occupational tie with weavers, actually had a prominent role among their fellow townspeople in the defence of Taunton against those village weavers.[3]

During the third week of May in 1753, at a time of high grain prices, villagers from the countryside near Bristol descended upon the city and rioted there for several days. Bristol had a history of redistributing grain and dairy products to other coastal, or even foreign, trading cities in times of shortage in the interest of urban merchants.[4] But the city's newspaper reports emphasised the 'idleness and drunkenness' of the rural mob while it argued that the scarcity of food was an act of God for which the city should not be held responsible.[5] The newspaper employed the conventional editorial device of speaking through an anonymous letter,[6] in this case one purported to be written by a local collier who wished to be dissociated from his 'brethren' who were prominent among the rioters. The author of the letter noted that farmers were as much to blame as merchants for the price of grain and pleaded with his 'countrymen':

> If you must rise up in mobs and riots, rise up against alehouses, against playing ball, kettle allies, and what is commonly, though falsely, called holidays. For these are your worst enemies who cheat you out of time and money, which would more than make amends for the present dearness.

The newspaper argued, 'supposing the corn were stopped from going abroad, the farmers would not think it worth their while to raise it'. Once the Bristol newspaper denigrated the economic and moral position of the rioters, it went on to identify the rioters themselves as outsiders and intruders:

> Thursday morning there was a fresh alarm of their approach to the city; about noon a great mob consisting of colliers, country people, weavers, assembled at Lawford's Gate ... Several of the city guard were dangerously wounded and divers are yet missing who were carried off by the rioters into Kingswood.

Clearly the two camps were divided along topographical lines, with the rioters withdrawing into the forest. Despite the importance of grain for everyone, none of the rioters was identified as an urban resident. From an urban point of view, the rioters were identifiable as immoral, dangerous, unsophisticated and rural.

An eye-witness account, written privately by a Bristol resident with rural connections, makes it clear that the rioters identified themselves in opposition to the city itself and its special interests.[7] The rioters assembled at the Bristol Council House and attacked that civic building. They marched upon the quays and scuffled with the city constables who stood guard over merchant ships filled with grain for export. By 25 May the citizens of Bristol, including 'tradesmen and others', took up guns, cutlasses, and clubs in defence of their Council House. John Clement, the mayor himself, 'though a very nervous man, and unavoidably agitated', marshalled the city's forces 'with constable's staff in hand'. The rioters even made an attempt to release convicts from the city jail, but were repelled by 'the townspeople'. Then, having assaulted symbols of civic pride and insularity – and provoked a display of the same on the part of the citizens – the rural rioters fled:

> no other weapons than stones with which their pockets were loaded, and even the wives of some of those deluded men were seen in St James church yard with a supply of stones in their aprons, which made a mighty clatter as they ran through the church yard ... The armed citizens in their indiscreet zeal pursued the rioters even to West Street without Lawford's Gate.

This was not an occupational conflict, a rebellion of apprentices against masters, tenants against landlords, or some religious dispute. It was an urban–rural conflict taking place nearly a century after the Restoration. Until the 1790s, Bristolians themselves regarded all riots there as attacks upon the city by outsiders.[8] The attack of the Kingswood colliers and other local villagers upon Bristol was so concerted and on such a scale that, as the eye witness stressed, the city shut its gates and barred its bridges, evoking a strikingly medieval picture of a topographical divide between the city within and the rural environs without.

The existence of a topographical divide was clear to contemporaries and they organised their understanding of the use and distribution of resources around the perception of distinctly urban and rural social spheres. We can safely assume that regardless of its duration most of the routine interaction between villagers and urban dwellers was not confrontational. Collective action and highly charged confrontations such as grain riots, house demolitions, village sackings, and the storming of civic buildings were only more dramatic, if recurring, expressions of the basic connection that both urban and rural contemporaries drew between resources and localities. The link between shared access to resources and shared spaces was reinforced through routine and ritual in early modern England. Since the fifteenth century the Bristol corporation had dispensed wine in the streets, on festive occasions, mainly through the guilds. In 1449 ninety-six gallons of wine flowed freely in one celebration, ten gallons distributed by the weavers' guild alone.[9] The celebration of the eucharist in the cosier confines of the parish church throughout the early modern period conveyed in ritual an idealisation of community based on the provision of essentials within shared space. In this most confined and confining sense, The Book of Common Prayer codified the ideal when it bade 'all sorts and conditions of men' to draw close to their communion table.[10] The levying of poor rates and the granting of relief by parish overseers is a clear illustration that resources were shared at a highly localised level as a matter of course; in some cities special poor relief funds were further restricted to local freemen and their families.[11] Until the later decades of the eighteenth century, most social spheres based on the regulation and distribution of resources still formed on either side of an abrupt topographical divide. The contrasts between urban and rural practices in the management of financial networks and the organisation and use of the market place sent strong messages about social relations and played a significant role in what we might call the logistics of community formation.

The conventions of charity and credit, important links in social networks, were not purely expressions of neighbourliness. They were also key elements of commercial relations and power relations. Edward Colston, in his munificence, gave something approaching £80,000 of his personal wealth to institutions and individuals in Bristol.[12] But like much charity in the urban setting it was channelled through the corporation or dispersed through bureaucratic societies and hardly represented a face-to-face relationship between donor and recipient. It has also been argued for the rural setting that the extension of hospitality by the powerful – in the practice of providing dinners, for example – was mainly a means of identifying and recruiting subservient social clients, despite the fact that such dinners tended to be larger affairs – less intimate and less selective – in the countryside.[13] Credit was also the means by which artisans and merchants, albeit in good faith, attracted customers. Or, in some instances, lending was a business in itself. By the mid-seventeenth century London had 500 pawnbrokers who typically loaned sums of 40s or less while exacting illegal rates of interest up to 50 per cent per annum.[14] The management of credit did indicate certain kinds of generosity associated with direct personal relations, rather than transient, remote, or divisive ones. We can know quite a bit about who lent money to whom, how widely or heavily they lent, and what effective measures they took, if any, to recover their money. As we will see in another chapter, the charitable support given to apprentices reflected very strong topographical allegiances. The distribution of resources and access to them as managed through credit networks and in the market place were similarly informed by the separation of urban and rural spheres.

The lending and borrowing of money was a common practice in early modern English society. Credit was readily available in the rural setting, so villagers had access to credit without having to approach the city. In fact, the portion of the population engaged in lending was even higher in the villages near Bristol than in the city itself during the first forty years of the eighteenth century.[15] But the conventions of credit networks varied conspicuously from one setting to another.[16] In the city, credit networks revolved around a wider variety of social relations, including many based on reciprocity and complex roles, whereas practices in the villages reinforced the power that a few creditors exercised over a few debtors. Credit relations in the city were more likely to be products of social relations formed inside the workplace, but were not necessarily coterminous with occupational groups. Widows in both settings were active lenders who extended credit to members of all sorts of occupations, but urban merchants of both sexes, seeking more means of promoting sales and customer relations, appeared as willing to extend credit to women as to men. One enterprising collarmaker in Bristol borrowed £1 some time before 1772 'for ale to treat customers'.[17] Although urban artisans, small merchants, and food preparers and vendors were particularly well represented among lenders, they were also extensive borrowers whose credit networks were hardly restricted to channels of commercial activity. Lack of purchasing power was by no means a barrier to membership of the urban credit network, and the poor were even included among lenders in the city. In 1672 Thomas Maszon of St Stephen, Bristol, was worth £14 15s 6d, of which £11 was in the form of credit he had extended.[18] Maszon's occupation is unknown, but if he was a mariner – and there were many in St Stephen – his 'credit' may have been ships' wages in arrears and therefore evidence of powerlessness rather than gregarious generosity. In any event, there were several examples of poor lenders in the city, and they may have had a credit network of their own that did not require profitable transactions in goods or services between borrower and lender.[19] In the city, one's role in the credit network was less likely to be limited to either borrowing or lending, less likely to diminish or elevate social status, and less likely to be gender-specific.

Women were especially active borrowers and lenders in the city, where some men went heavily into debt to single women as well as widows. Ann Phillips, a poor spinster who had only two debtors and was hardly a professional creditor, was owed £13 in 1700 by a fellow Bristolian named Andrew Gifford. Hester Sissell, a spinster living in Bristol in 1718, was owed £41 from a Mr Dickson, her only debtor.[20] Unmarried women in the city could also get substantial loans, not only from widows but from men. Margaret Phelps of Bristol owed a Bristol weaver, Robert Ford, £40 which Ford had not gone to the trouble to collect by the time of his death in 1697.[21] There is no doubt that some urban women operated their own businesses[22] and controlled reserves of cash and collateral goods.[23] Elizabeth Flemming, a widow who died in Bristol in 1763, was worth £67 and owned no tools or stock in trade. Nevertheless, ten years earlier, perhaps at the time of her husband's death, she had extended a single loan of £50 on which she succeeded in collecting £2 10s in interest per annum. Her estate recovered the entire remaining principal at the end of her life.[24] The law complicated the attempts of married women to convert their property into investment capital while their husbands were still alive, no matter where they lived.[25] On the other hand, some urban widows were not just lenders to individuals but were very serious investors in going concerns. Ann Green, a Bristol widow who lived in the parish of St James in the 1660s, owned six small tenement dwellings from which she collected rents. At much the same time, Ann Love, a widow in St Stephen, had £22 10s worth of shares, or 'adventures', in 'Barbados ships'. Margaret Blackmore, a Bristol widow with more than £297 in total assets, listed the 'Chamber of the City of Bristol' among her debtors.[26] Widows at extreme ends of the adult age spectrum were less likely to have sons at home of the intermediate age at which they contended for their fathers' businesses. Urban widows, if advanced in age or quite young, were more likely to have inherited trades, if their husbands had them, and thus enjoy the status of other burgesses and the infusion of cash and capital. So many urban widows maintained high portions of their assets in the form of cash and credit that the liquidation of inherited businesses was surely common practice among widows of all ages in the city.

Arrangements whereby men were heavily in debt to women were mainly confined to the urban network and appear to have rankled those men who were accustomed to the more traditional sexual politics of rural credit practices. To be sure, according to the law, husbands were liable for their wives' debts, and this led some men to assume as a corollary that married women should not be creditors. Elizabeth Harvey, a small textile merchant from the town of Taunton at the turn of the century, met with considerable resistance from some men who insisted on dealing, as creditors or debtors, with Elizabeth's husband, William Harvey. This was awkward because William, who was employed primarily as a lawyer, acted as Elizabeth's subordinate agent when she was away on routine trips to London. For the most part Elizabeth had amicable credit ties with men in the urban network, while other men who owed her money insisted on settling their accounts only through Elizabeth's husband in her absence. Few women contested their accounts with Elizabeth, but when Joan Jermin discovered that the value of goods she had returned to the Harveys had not been deducted from her bonded debt she addressed her complaint, complete with explicated figures, directly to Elizabeth. Apparently only one of the men with whom Elizabeth did business in London, a serge dealer named Christopher Blower, used her husband to circumvent her, but this was a fearful response to legal action brought by Elizabeth against Blower for the settlement of accounts in April of 1700.[27]

Generally speaking, merchants and pawnbrokers lending at interest for gain should not be seen as the urban standard against which some ideal of rural charity and neighbourliness can be contrasted. Indeed, quite the reverse seems to have been the case. Most lenders in the city were active artisans and smaller merchants who extended what appears to have been interest-free credit on goods for the sake of attracting customers. William Elliatt, a Bristol draper, was worth £384 12s 1d at the time of his death in 1680.[28] Nearly 90 per cent of his wealth was in the form of credit extended to a variety of people. All these debts were described in Elliatt's account as 'desperate'; that is, to say, he was prepared never to collect them. One man had owed Elliatt over £104 for twenty-seven years and there were others who had owed him large sums since the late 1650s or early 1660s. Bristol sellers of staple items dealt heavily and extensively in credit and undoubtedly saw the same customers on a frequent and regular basis. George Phipps, a Bristol meal seller, was owed £140, or 32 per cent of his total worth, at the time of his death in 1679. In 1710 Walter Landen, a mealman in Bristol's St Michael, was owed £660 6s by 106 people, of whom sixty-eight were not expected ever to pay.[29] Rural artisans and merchants, despite the nature of their occupations, were far more reserved in their treatment of credit. In 1683, three years after the death of William Elliatt of Bristol, a clothier by the name of Thomas Smith in the nearby village of Almondsbury had amassed an estate valued at £655 3s 9d. None of this was in the form of debts owed to him. Apart from nineteen acres under cultivation and some livestock, Smith's business and means were similar to Elliatt's, but Smith was typical of rural artisans and merchants in his credit record. Villagers in trade either extended no credit or were far more serious and determined than their urban counterparts in the collection of debts.[30]

Rural social spheres based on financial ties were characterised by the power of the lender to monitor, in some respect, the circumstances of a closed circle of familiar people.[31] In villages, lenders were not likely to be borrowers, and borrowing was generally an indication of subordinate status. This was not so in the city. By 1692 Robert Nelson, a Bristol ship's carpenter, had loaned £20 (over 25 per cent of his total wealth) to the ship's captain, who was clearly his superior.[32] In rural practice, a creditor would have only one or two debtors and those debtors operated under considerable pressure to repay, typically under the terms of a formal bond, often at some rate of interest. Rural lenders exacted rigid terms from their own relatives, who were reluctant, apparently, to look beyond a very intimate social sphere for assistance.[33] Villagers dispersed wealth to heirs in advance in order to assure the execution of their wishes and promote the early economic independence of their children, but required bonds in order to retain control of their resources and exact more deference from close relations and neighbours.[34] In the city widows were less likely to be protected by this rural convention. In 1696 Margaret Tyler, a poor old widow in Bristol, had to sue her own son, Benjamin, in order to wheedle support out of him. The court awarded her the modest rate of 3s per week.[35] Prior to the mid-eighteenth century, rural lenders who held bonds from their personal debtors far outnumbered rural lenders with 'desperate' debtors. Quite the reverse was true in Bristol, where lenders who did not collect at least some of their debts were roughly three times more common than Bristolians holding bonds. (Table 3.1.) In fact, the ratio of forgiving lenders (or unsuccessful collectors) to bond holders was between fifteen and twenty times greater in the city than in the countryside during the eighty years following 1660.[36] The popular publication *The Countryman's Counsellor, or Everyman his own Lawyer* referred specifically to the rural lender whose tendency to exact interest, collect aggressively, and require a written bond or collateral was widely recognised by contemporaries beginning in the seventeenth century.

Urban neighbourliness, in the form of apparent generosity and material forgiveness, was a product of localism. One Margaret Neady, a very aptly named Bristol widow, was worth only £1 16s at the time of her death in 1748.[37] Her accounts show that she succeeded in borrowing £24 8s 6d, all from her fellow citizens. Neady certainly benefited from the neighbourliness of a Bristol merchant, John Angier, who appears to have subsidised her funeral up to the alarming sum of £15 19s 4d. The ability of widow Neady to borrow nearly fourteen times beyond her ability to pay says a great deal in general about the generous, forgiving, and even charitable nature of urban lenders, even in the middle of the eighteenth century, if lender and borrower were residents of the same city.

In general, Bristol's lenders left more evidence of exotic contacts than of rural contacts. Richard Jones, a Bristol gunsmith in the early eighteenth

Table 3.1 Creditors in the city of Bristol and the nearby villages who required bonds for loans or extended loans to'desperate' debtors (% in parentheses)

|  | 1660–99 | | 1700–39 | |
|---|---|---|---|---|
|  | Urban | Rural | Urban | Rural |
| Total creditors | 261 | 116 | 169 | 67 |
| Lenders to desperate debtors | 54 (20·7) | 6 (5·2) | 65 (38·5) | 8 (11·9) |
| Lenders whose credit was mostly desperate | 20 (7·7) | 4 (3·4) | 30 (17·8) | 2 (3·0) |
| Lenders requiring bonds from debtors | 20 (7·7) | 44 (37·9) | 18 (10·7) | 34 (50·7) |
| Lenders whose credit was mostly bonded | 6 (2·3) | 40[a] (34·5) | 12 (7·1) | 29[a] (43·3) |

*Note:* (a) Entirely bonded.
*Source:* B.R.O. Probate Inventories and Cause Papers.

century, had no fewer than sixty thoroughly identified debtors, none of whom was a rural dweller. Thirty-two, however, were mariners, captains, or other seafaring travellers. These debtors almost certainly included customers. One of the contacts was from Denmark and another was a merchant from New-foundland. Thomas Waters, a poor Bristol mariner, was owed £7, a hefty loan under his circumstances, from a Mr Whidler of Newfoundland. Matthew Adean of St Leonard extended loans to contacts in Cork and Waterford in Ireland and Barbados and Jamaica in the West Indies. His circle of credit included residents of Bath, Milford, Worcester, London, Taunton, and other English urban areas, but excluded English villagers.[38] The urban credit net-work reached across the ocean but hardly penetrated the local countryside at all.

In view of the fact that villagers came to major markets to buy and sell, the lengths to which urban and rural people went to avoid financial dealings on one another's terms must have involved an element of choice. Jonathan Fisher, a Bristol joiner who was worth only £13 1s at the time of his death in 1719, was owed two debts, one from John Codrington, Esq., also of Bristol. The other was extended to William Humpheries, who lived in the next county, Somerset, but in the cathedral city of Wells, not in a village. Thus Fisher, a poor urban artisan, extended loans above his social station, and to residents of other cities, but not to villagers.[39] At the same time, rural dwellers who extended loans beyond their residential spheres confined their contacts to borrowers who also lived in the countryside. A man by the name of Maggs who lived in the village of Winterbourne, Gloucestershire, lent in the rural fashion, intensively and under a binding agreement, in this case a profitable annuity. His sole debtor resided in a Somerset village farther from Winterbourne than from any Bristol parish, but the context in which one dealt with Maggs was far more similar in size, topography, and cultural practices to that debtor's own physical and social environment.[40] The clerical credit net-work did operate across topographical lines and therefore represents the exception to more widely observed practices governing the sharing of material resources. In the late seventeenth century, the curate in the Gloucestershire village of Ovelston, a man by the name of Humphreys, borrowed the large sum of £16 from George Williamson, a Bristol parish clerk. In Williamson, Humphreys had an urbane contact, a like-minded student of scripture who had among his possessions a 'study of books' valued at £60.[41] In approaching a fellow professional Humphreys avoided the embarrassment of entering into the subordinate role that borrowing from one of his own village parishioners would have required him to adopt according to rural cultural practices. Urban and rural attitudes toward lending, borrowing, collecting, and repaying differed so much that the separation of urban and rural spheres on the basis of financial resources was nothing less than perfectly understandable to all involved.

Some urban conventions of lending could place the uninitiated migrant at considerable personal risk. Eighteenth-century social commentators were well aware of a trick tavern proprietors played upon young migrants, inexperienced mariners, and others who came from outside the city or had been excluded from urban credit networks. Proprietors, operating in collusion with sea captains, would encourage dupes (usually young men) to drink themselves into a state of addiction and indebtedness. After extending credit to support their victims' habits, publicans acting as notorious 'crimps' would sell to captains the letters of debt signed or marked by the inebriated 'carcasses' (as they became known in Bristol). These unsuspecting debtors could be forced, by a corruption of the law, to labour at sea for meagre wages until their debt was erased. Urban masters were also known to invoke fees owed by their indentured apprentices to sell them into maritime servitude or drive them, though cruelty, into the hands of naval press gangs.[42] In the final analysis, it seems likely that the maintenance of largely separate urban and rural credit networks was another expression of village resistance to urban influence.

There was one notable exception, the credit network revolving around Walter Landen in the early eighteenth century. Landen was a maltman in the Bristol parish of St Michael just inside the city limits. Like other urban dealers in grain, he was an extensive lender. At one time he was owed £660 6s, roughly 84 per cent of his total wealth, from 106 different borrowers, most of whom were customers.[43] Fellow parishioners who had borrowed from Landen were among the sixty-eight debtors from whom he did not expect to collect. Four of these were on bond, suggesting that bonds represented closer familiarity between lender and borrower, as they did in the countryside, but that even the treatment of bonded debtors could be lax in the city. A weaver, a glazier, and a wheelwright were among the good customers who bought on credit. But not all Landen's debtors were customers or even artisans of comparable social station. A surgeon and an attorney owed Landen money. Three of the debtors were identified as 'Mrs' and were possibly of higher social status than Landen himself. All told, only fifteen women were in debt to Landen, suggesting that not all the shopping for household necessities, such as basic foodstuffs, was carried out by women. Landen recorded the Bristol street addresses of many borrowers, four of whom were close neighbours in St Augustine. The vast majority of the borrowers probably saw one another on the street near one another's homes or *en route* to market.

Of special interest are Landen's rural debtors. There were only thirteen of them, a small fraction of the whole circle, but they were by far the largest group of rural borrowers connected with any Bristol creditor. Five of the thirteen lived in Clifton, which bordered directly on St Michael's to the north-west, and three came from Redland, which bordered directly to the north. One came from Horfield, a parish bordering directly on Bristol at St James. The only country folk who travelled through other rural settlements to reach Landen in Bristol were four villagers from Westbury. In rural circles, borrowers were expected to pay all their debts, and neither Landen nor his accountants identified any of the villagers as a bad credit risk.

It is beyond dispute that rural dwellers visited market towns to provision themselves and to sell goods. Bristol had busy open markets in St James and along the quays in its Welsh Back section. St Paul's Fair, in the Bristol parish of Temple, attracted hundreds of vendors every season. In the 1740s the corporation erected the Market Exchange in the heart of the city. These markets and fairs scattered across Bristol's urban landscape were reliably held and plentiful enough to permit urban and rural consumers a degree of selectivity in their commercial dealings. But who were the established vendors and familiar dealers? With whom could customers, vendors, artisans, and dealers expect to interact? Rural goods may have appeared in urban markets in ways that did not necessarily promote personal contacts between villagers and urban dwellers. In the 1720s Thomas Hort, from the village of Kingsweston, six miles north-east of Bristol, regularly put his cheese up for sale in the city, but Hort paid a haulier to come and get his goods rather than go into the city himself.[44]

The mechanisms of distribution, including the activities of coastal and river traders, travelling chapmen and grander middlemen, were complex enough to allow additional factors, beyond supply, to shape the behaviour of vendors and consumers in the urban market place. By the late seventeenth century, Bristol had long enjoyed the power of first refusal of any grain shipped down the Severn as far as the river Avon.[45] This meant that a hefty portion of Monmouthshire's, Herefordshire's, and northern Gloucestershire's surplus grain found its way to Bristol markets. Contemporary experts monitoring the city's food supply as late as the 1760s still identified the hinterland well beyond the nearby villages as the city's principal source of grain.[46] Many of the staples sold at all ports arrived at market through coastal traders and dealers and not in the hands of farmers attending the markets themselves. Even inland market towns could be supplied by middlemen of urban origin. The farmers who did bring grain to Bristol markets were governed by their fellow villagers and were not in co-operation with Bristol's own dealers. In 1658 the manor court presiding over the local hamlets of Abson and Wick set the price at which manor farmers were to sell grain at 5s per bushel for that year.[47] Surely such locally determined prices, coupled with the careful monitoring of distribution and supply from scattered sources, made consumers and vendors at Bristol markets keenly aware of their places of origin. This awareness, on the part of urban and rural people alike, was a factor shaping behaviour and relations in the early modern market place.

The sale of grain, typically negotiated in bulk quantities, involved preliminary interaction between wholesalers and retailers. Even at the end of the early modern period, Bristol's grain supplies were handled by a remarkably small group of merchants.[48] In the year 1780 no more than thirteen and as few as three wholesalers appeared at the Welsh Back corn market on any given delivery day. Only sixteen different wholesalers conducted business in that market place that entire year. They dealt with a total of nineteen grain vendors. A tiny group of thirty-five people, made up of travelling wholesalers and Bristol dealers, provided the city with all the grain supplied by domestic shipping. Despite the cosy dimensions of this grain traders' coterie, no firm associations or exclusive trading arrangements developed between any wholesalers and retailers; these commercial dealings were guided by market forces, not by personal ties. Not one wholesaler sold routinely to the same retailer during an entire year of twice-weekly transactions. The largest retailer of 1780, Messrs Young & Co., frequently bought up more than half the shipment on any given day, which was more than even the largest wholesaler, James Weaver, could ever supply on his own. Thus the single most important staple commodity of domestic origin involved fewer than twenty wholesalers from outside Bristol, and these extramural dealers failed to cultivate special ties with the urban retailers.

Bristol's port, which was actually a series of quays on two confluent rivers, gave the city direct access to imported commodities of every imaginable type. The city was hardly economically dependent on nearby villages.[49] Bristol artisans and vendors were by no means dependent upon local villagers for meat, hides and other animal products. Cattle grazed in St James and St Philip and Jacob. Bristolians butchered their own animals, judging from some of the ancillary economic activities of urban dwellers.[50] Inner-city residents complained of pig tending going on in their neighbourhoods where Bristol artisans and their wives hawked their own bacon and pork in the streets and kept pigs in their cellars.[51] A tanner in St Peter, Bristol, had a considerable inventory of raw materials in the late seventeenth century. But, of his 921 hides, not a single hide came off the back of an animal raised in a nearby village; 105 were from Virginia and the rest were 'Irish calf skins'.[52] On the other hand, a winter storm in 1725 deprived Bristol of basic provisions for a week because it caused the destruction of vessels *en route* from Wales.[53] As late as 1789, of all British coastal trading ports sending ships directly to Bristol, only Minehead in Somerset, Exeter, London and, perhaps, Gloucester, surpassed the Welsh port of Carmarthen.[54]

At Bristol the Welsh Back quay was reserved by the port deputy for the landing of coastal trading vessels. Foreign vessels or ships carrying overseas cargo landed and departed from the river Frome docks. As the name Welsh Back suggests, most of the poultry, fruit, and vegetables sold there were sailed across the Severn Channel from Wales.[55] A weekly account of stall rentals at the Welsh Back between November 1776 and September 1778 shows that 85 per cent of the vendors were women.[56] On any given Wednesday there were as many as thirty women, but never more than four men, vending on the Welsh Back. No stalls were rented on the Welsh Back between April and late September. It is possible that Bristol residents harvested their own small garden plots during the summer months. There seems to have been enough local production in the city to compensate for lulls at the Welsh Back and justify a competing market location.

St James market in the north-west corner of the city was the place where local villagers could be found selling goods in Bristol.[57] The parish market, held every Wednesday and Saturday year round, featured the sale of vegetables and poultry. It was in direct competition with the Welsh Back. By contrast, at the very same time, all greengrocers vending at the popular St James parish market were from the city of Bristol. St James market was not restricted to the sale of agricultural and farm products, but for some reason Bristol residents, with the notable exception of greengrocers, were poorly represented among the vendors there. The St James market appears to have been treated as Bristol's rustic market place. Of seventy-eight vendors renting stalls at the end of our period, the places of origin of seventy-five are known for certain. Three came from rural areas farther than ten miles from Bristol. At least fifty-nine came from nearby villages. Only twelve were Bristol residents. One came to Bristol from another urban area. Of the seventy-eight vendors, only five were women, all of them from the local villages. In short, there had developed in Bristol at least two produce and poultry markets held on exactly the same days: one operated by Welsh women in the middle of the port and another operated by nearby villagers, mainly men, on the outskirts of town.

St James also held a butchers' market. Between 1778 and 1780 inclusive, twenty-nine different butchers rented shambles in St James meat market, located on the northern periphery of the city. Of the twenty-eight butchers whose places of origin are known, nineteen were from nearby villages, five were from remote villages, and only four were Bristol residents. Overall, Bristol butchers heavily outnumbered butchers from the local villages during the early modern period.[58] The vast majority of Bristol's resident butchers met their customers at the arcade located in Corn and High Streets in the middle of the city; eighty-three different butchers rented stalls there in April and May 1745.[59] Moreover, arcade officials segregated vendors according to their place of origin and separate areas of the arcade were designated 'Somerset Arcade' and 'Gloucester Arcade'. It was also customary in Liverpool's markets to segregate rural grain sellers according to their place of origin. Those from the Lancashire countryside lined up on the east side of the main street and those from the Cheshire countryside lined up on the west side.[60] Butchers were further divided in the Bristol market according to the types of meat they sold.

The nine women who were butchers were sprinkled among the seventy-four men, so gender segregation was far less carefully observed here than geographical segregation, which was the more compelling basis of the observance of separate market locations overall in the city.

Bristol's meat, fruit, vegetable, and poultry markets were hardly places where vendors of various origins mingled on equal terms. The most basic provisions were vended on the same market days at competing locations. The topographical origins of the vending groups varied from one market place to the next, as did the predominant gender in those groups according to what appeared to be the customs observed in each setting. And, remarkably, rural consumers could interact with rural venders without going into the heart of the city. In view of these arrangements, we can picture how consumers consciously divided themselves according to their preferences for female or male, centrally located or peripheral, urban or rural vendors.

In addition to weekly markets, Bristol held important seasonal fairs. Unlike the weekly markets, which mainly supplied food, the fairs gave customers an opportunity to buy finished goods from local or well travelled artisans. During the 1650s there were relatively few extramural vendors at these fairs. The only travelling vendors at the St Paul's fair in 1652 were 'Manchester men' selling nails.[61] Like the markets, these fairs produced revenue for the parishes from which the vendors rented temporary stall space. From 1550 St Paul's fair was held in the Bristol parish of Temple (Holy Cross) during the last week of January. The stalls at St Paul's, like those at all other fairs, stood for only a week or so each year at fair time, after which the ground reverted to the parish. But the extramural vendors assigned real importance to the location of their stalls. In 1723 a hosier from London negotiated a twenty-year lease, at £1 1s per annum, to secure the same 12 ft of vending frontage at St Paul's fair.[62] In 1673 John Bower, a London needlemaker, rented a stall at St Paul's fair, or the annual right to it, for life.[63]

Travelling vendors of urban origin made a point of reuniting in the same stalls from one year to the next. In 1720 a Surrey feltmaker and a Middlesex combmaker agreed to travel, every year for twenty years, from different locations on the outskirts of London, to share the same 20 ft standing at St Paul's fair. Their predecessor on the spot was a whipmaker from London.[64] Until 1723 a widow who made musical instruments and a man who sold books travelled from separate London shops on a yearly basis to share a single booth at St Paul's fair.[65] During the 1660s the same group of London fishmongers rented an entire house in the Pithay section of All Saints' parish each year, but only for late July and early August, when they gathered in Bristol for the St James fair.[66] Bristol vendors and vendors from other cities and towns reunited year after year in neighbouring stalls, and within shared stalls, at Bristol fairs, where temporary colonies of gregarious urban dwellers formed on a regular basis. By contrast, there is no similar evidence to suggest that local villagers rented vending space at Bristol fairs at all, much less in association with people of urban origin.

The eighteenth-century development of permanent shops almost certainly undermined the direct personal interaction that took place between travelling vendors and customers at open, seasonal fairs.[67] There is evidence that permanent shops began to control a major portion of Bristol's market place in the seventeenth century,[68] but those shops that evolved as an opportunistic outgrowth of parish fairs met with official resistance and were presented in court as unseasonable encroachments.[69] Thus the growth of urban shops, which accompanied the urban revival, not only diminished the importance of fairs, it promoted a means of distribution from which rural vendors could be excluded.

Local villagers and Bristolians shared the streets on crowded market days and during seasonal fairs, but these interactions were incidental, fleeting, and, at times, seriously acrimonious. The summertime fair in St James Bristol, held where the city met the countryside, was famous for its popularity with country folk. In the early nineteenth century the fair was brought to a permanent close because of a history of crowd disturbances.[70] The verbal abuse of country folk by quick-tongued citizens was a staple ingredient of chapbook and pamphlet dialogue in our period. As one city woman snapped to a country 'whore' visiting her market: 'Away thou impudent Welch Runt ... thou mealfac'd Bawd thou, dost thou think to forestall me in the market place, that was bred and born in the parish and you come to eat the bread out of my mouth with a pox on you.'[71] A subtle connection between occupying a market stall and forestalling someone in the market may have been implied here, along with proprietorial claims suggested by the pun on 'bred' in the parish and 'bread' of the parish. In early modern Bristol, market segregation provided one solution for situations such as those in which Bristol vendors, competing for space with rural vendors 'in the high street', grievously 'annoyed country people and hinder [them] in standing and exposing to sale provisions'.[72] Some urban merchants showed a strong reluctance to venture into the countryside at all. In 1662 one Bristol barge pilot dumped a boatload of pigs overboard into the Avon to let them swim ashore rather than make his delivery to a village.[73]

Villagers had their own reasons for regarding the city as the repository of ill-gotten goods and the home of shady dealers. When some sheep went missing from the village of Blagdon, Somerset, in the winter of 1674, the Gallop family immediately came under suspicion in the village on the grounds that they were known to a 'dealer in mutton at the Three Tuns on the quay in Bristol'. When they were later discovered in possession of another villager's saddle, the Gallops claimed, to their discredit, as it turned out, to have got the saddle from a man in Bristol.[74] George Pinny of the village of Henbury, Gloucestershire, elected to travel some distance to the smaller markets of

Somerset, in places like Crewkerne and Somerton, rather than do business in nearby Bristol. He came to grief anyway in 1675 when he sold three 'bullocks' at Crewkerne to John Coles, a travelling cattle dealer from Bristol. Pinny took a grey mare as partial payment in good faith, but 'had taken the man's word for £5 of the money' owed him, a loss about which he ranted so adamantly that he was finally arrested, at the White Horse in Glastonbury, for creating a disturbance.[75] Even though villagers realised that their neighbours stole from them they identified urban markets as the motive for theft. Villagers near Bristol typically assumed in testimony that stolen livestock always wound up in the hands of Bristol dealers and not in any of the smaller livestock markets in the countryside. In the summer of 1661 one woman from the Somerset village of North Petherton swore up and down in court that she not only recognised a particular bundle of carrots at a Bristol market but knew the very field in her parish from which they had been stolen.[76]

In many ways the distribution of resources, through private management of credit networks and interaction in the market place, mediated social relations essential to community formation. Although urban and rural dwellers both appeared in the market centres of cities, they maintained largely separate social spheres even in that context. The practices of credit management varied so significantly with setting that the extension of credit, although increasingly widespread, did little to combine urban and rural spheres. Moreover, just as urban dwellers, who occasionally gave freely without concern for intramural parish boundaries, withheld aid from the poor of rural origin, members of rural society rarely shared charitable resources with urban dwellers. By the eighteenth century, parish boundaries meant much less to Bristolians; they accepted the notion of civic, as opposed to parish, poor relief and attended parish churches other than their own.[77] But topographical affinity and geographical proximity were persistent influences in the voluntary sharing of resources in early modern cities and villages alike. In 1725 one Bristol newspaper reported in approving tones that the 'gentlemen' of St Olive's, Southwark, had donated over £1,755 to forty-eight heads of households whose homes in the neighbouring parishes had been destroyed by a fire near London Bridge.[78] By contrast, in that very same week, in rural Hampshire, a woman 'big with child' collapsed and died beside the road in the village of Gosport 'purely through want and inhumanity' because 'it seems she came from London nobody cared to take her in'.[79]

## NOTES

1 S.R.O. DD/SF/1343, A manuscript poem in the Somerset dialect.

2 S.R.O. Q/SR/296, Somerset Quarter Sessions (Michaelmas Term, 1728), #23.

3 *Farley's Bristol Newspaper* (23 October 1725).

4 In 1673 the pilot of a corn barge plying between Herefordshire and Bristol testified that 'country men and women' attacked grain boats as they tried to pass along the waterways connecting Bristol with its coastal trading partners. See B.R.O. #04440, Bristol Depositions: Deposition of David Morris (27 February 1673).

5 *Felix Farley's Bristol Journal* (19–26 May 1753), p. 4.

6 The use of letters to convey editorial opinion is treated in R. M. Wiles, *Freshest Advices: Early Provincial Newspapers in England* (Columbus, Oh., 1965), p. 322.

7 B.C.L. #20095, Diary of William Dyer (entries of 21 and 25 May 1753). Dyer had relatives whom he visited regularly in their villages. (See his 31 May 1757 entry, for example.) He was also involved with Methodists and Quakers in Bristol's rural environs.

8 P. D. Jones, 'The Bristol Bridge riot and its antecedents: eighteenth-century perception of the crowd', *Journal of British Studies* 19 no. 2 (1980), pp. 74–92.

9 B. Little, *The City and County of Bristol: A Study in Atlantic Civilization* (London, 1954), p. 82.

10 N. Alldridge, 'Loyalty and identity in Chester parishes 1540–1640', in S. J. Wright (ed.), *Parish, Church and People: Local Studies in Lay Religion 1350–1750* (London, 1988), p. 88.

11 P. Ripley, 'Poverty in Gloucester and its alleviation 1690–1740', *Transactions of the Bristol and Gloucestershire Archaeological Society* 103 (1985), pp. 185–99, especially pp. 193–4; J. Boulton, *Neighbourhood and Society: A London Suburb in the Seventeenth Century* (Cambridge, 1987), pp. 92–5. R. W. Herlan, 'Poor relief in London during the English revolution', *Journal of British Studies* 18 (1979), is useful for the consideration of the possible effects of undermined established parish institutions upon poor relief. For the eighteenth century the subject is less widely discussed, but see A. W. Coats, 'The relief of poverty: attitudes to labour and economic change in England 1660–1782', *International Review of Social History* 21 (1976), pp. 98–115. For the Tudor-Stuart period the subject of poor relief is widely addressed in works by Slack, Beier, Pound, Wrightson, and Levine.

12 This estimate is provided by Bryan Little in *The City and County of Bristol*, p. 183.

13 F. Heal, 'The idea of hospitality in early modern England', *Past and Present* 102 (1984), pp. 66–93.

14 Boulton, *Neighbourhood and Society*, pp. 87–92.

15 B.R.O. Probate Inventories and Cause Papers, Diocese of Bristol. For Bristol and its rural environs, inventories showing credit can be expressed as a percentage of all extant inventories as follows: 1660–99, 20·1 per cent (261/1300) of the urban inventories and 14·9 per cent (116/776) of the rural ones; 1700–39, 12·6 per cent (169/1337) of the urban inventories and 17·9 per cent (67/374) of the rural ones. The death of many Bristol sailors at sea during the eighteenth century may have contributed to the number of urban inventories lacking credit in that period.

16 B.R.O. Probate Inventories and Cause Papers indentify the debtors, creditors, terms, and sums involved.

17  B.R.O. Probate Inventories and Cause Papers (Samuel Westcott, 1772).

18  B.R.O. Probate Inventories and Cause papers (Thomas Maszon, 1672).

19  B.R.O. Probate Inventories and Cause Papers. The following Bristol residents, all of whom died within the same ten-year period, were all worth between £3 and £19, with anywhere from 17 per cent to 64 per cent of their total wealth in the form of credit: John Kimble, 1709; Elizabeth Cock, 1709; William Frances, 1710; Bridget Thomas, 1711; James Cornish, 1713; Henry Evans, 1715; Francis Dunn, 1715; John Morgan, 1718. Some of these lenders were owed money 'from several people'.

20  B.R.O. Probate Inventories (Ann Phillips, 1700; Hester Sissell, 1718).

21  B.R.O. Probate Inventories (Robert Ford, 1697).

22  M. Prior, 'Women and the urban economy: Oxford 1500–1800', in M. Prior (ed.), *Women in English Society 1500–1800* (London, 1985), pp. 93–117.

23  B.R.O. Probate Inventories of the following: Ann Fisher, 1691, who had a shop; Ann Kimber, 1683, who ran an inn; Hester Northall, 1681, who owned a house in Broadmead and who may have been whitawer; Joan Thomlinson, 1674 (1679 bundle), who had a large shop inventory of worsteds, woollens, and serge; Sarah Browne, 1684, who had a shop inventory of watches and clocks; Mary Jones, 1727, who had £152 worth of 'stock in trade'; Susannah Hopper, 1731, an apothecary; Priscilla Fry, 1706, had a grocer's inventory including 20 lb of 'Barbados sugar'; and Nancy Bastable, 1768, who was a cheese vendor with thirty-two 'hundred' (101 lb equal 1 cwt) of cheese at her death.

24  B.R.O. Probate Inventories and Cause Papers (Elizabeth Flemming, 1763).

25  A. L. Erickson, *Women and Property in Early Modern England* (London, 1993), pp. 102–55; S. Staves, *Married Women's Separate Property in England 1660–1833* (Cambridge, Mass., 1990), pp. 131–61.

26  B.R.O. Probate Inventories and Cause Papers (Ann Green, 1667; Ann Love, 1662).

27  S.R.O. DD/X/WHI/1(a)&(f), Letters of Mrs Elizabeth Harvey (1697–1706).

28  B.R.O. Probate Inventories and Cause Papers (William Elliatt, 1680).

29  B.R.O. Probate Inventories and Cause Papers (George Phipps, 1679; Walter Landen, 1710).

30  B.R.O. Probate Inventories and Cause Papers (Thomas Smith, 1683).

31  An argument for a slightly different characterisation of rural credit arrangements in which friendlier relations are stressed can be found in B. A. Holderness, 'Credit in a rural community 1660–1800', *Midland History* 3 (1975), pp. 94–115.

32  B.R.O. Probate Inventories (Robert Nelson, 1692).

33  See, for example, B.R.O. Probate Inventories of John Griffiths, Winterbourne yeoman, in 1750, whose one debtor was Joshua Griffiths, also of Winterbourne; Isaac Russell, of Alveston, whose one debtor, N. Russell, of Alveston, owed him £20 on bond in 1694; Hannah Hollester, a Henbury spinster, who was owed £250 by Stephen Hollester in 1700; John Baker, a Henbury yeoman, who was owed £100 on bond from his son, Ralph Baker; N. Brookes, a Stoke Gifford yeoman, who owed over £52 to his own mother, the 'Widow' Brookes.

34  M. Spufford, *Contrasting Communities: English Villagers in the Sixteenth and Seventeenth Centuries* (Cambridge, 1974), pp. 80–90, 104–5, and 159–60.

35  B.R.O. #04449(1), Bristol Quarter Sessions: Docket Book (1695–1703).

36  The ratios of inventories showing 'desperate' debts to inventories showing bonds were as follows: 1660–99, urban 54:20 (2·7), rural 6:44 (0·14); 1700–39, urban 65:18 (3·6), rural 8:34 (0·24). 1660–99 urban ratio: rural ratio = 2·7/0·14 = 19·3; 1700–39 urban ratio: rural ratio = 3·6/0·24 = 15·0.

37  B.R.O. Probate Inventories (Margaret Neady, 1748). There are several other examples of Bristolians lending to fellow citizens who clearly unable to pay. See, for example, the probate inventory of S. Parrelt, a tinplate maker in St James, who was worth only £11 10s 9d in 1713 but had been loaned a total of £14 by nine different people.

38  B.R.O. Probate Inventories (Richard Jones, 1714; Thomas Waters, 1736; Matthew Adean, 1739).

39  B.R.O. Probate Inventories (Johnathan Fisher, 1719).

40  B.R.O. Probate Inventories (S. Maggs, 1695 bundle).

41  B.R.O. Probate Inventories (George Williamson, 1685).

42  P.R.O. ADM 36/6554, Admiralty Musters and Paybooks as cited in N. A. M. Rodger, *The Wooden World: An Anatomy of the Georgian Navy* (Glasgow, 1990), p. 173, and for 'crimps' see pp. 109 and 184; M. Rediker, *Between the Devil and the Deep Blue Sea: Merchant Seamen, Pirates, and the Anglo-American Maritime World 1700–50* (Cambridge, 1987), p. 43; Clarkson, *History of the Abolition of the Slave Trade* I, p. 294, cited in M. D. George, *London Life in the Eighteenth Century* (Chicago, 1925; 3rd ed. 1984), p. 302.

43  B.R.O. Probate Inventories (Walter Landen, 1710). Landen kept excellent accounts, of which his assessors made good use. A list providing the names, indebtedness, places of residence, and, in some cases, occupations of his debtors was presented with his inventory of 1710.

44  B.R.O. Diocese of Bristol Probate Inventories (Thomas Hort, 1792).

45  34 and 35 Henry VIII, ch. 9, sec. 3 (1543). This right to first refusal on 'wheat, malt, beans or any other kind of grain or corn' was invoked by 'the King's customers of the town of Bristol' as late as 1791. B.R.O. #04101(2)(b), Act for the Preservation of the River Severn, and B.R.O. #04101(2)(a), Corn Sheds on the Back (1791–1839).

46  B.R.O. Bristol Quarter Sessions: Papers (1763–68), bundle 4, Report of Charles Welsh to the mayor's attorney (August 1767).

47  B.R.O. #14581 HA/M.4, Haynes Manor Court Records.

48  B.R.O. #04100(1), Market Day on the Back.

49  P. McGrath (ed.), *Merchants and Merchandise in Seventeenth-Century Bristol* (Bristol, 1995), pp. 288–93.

50  See, for example: B.R.O. Probate Inventories (Grace Sims, 1678; George Jocelin, 1681; Edward Summers, 1682; Nicholas Willis, 1694).

51  B.R.O. #04452(1), Bristol Quarter Sessions: Presentments and Convictions (1676–1700), especially Trinity terms, 1673 and 1689. From probate inventories we know that Joseph Mills, a Bristol baker, kept a pig in his cellar in 1729, as did Katherine Burd of Bristol in 1678.

52  B.R.O. Probate Inventories (P. Pontyn, 1688).

53  *Farley's Bristol Newspaper* (11 December 1725).

54  B.R.O. #04060, Coasters: Vessels arrived Coastwise, commencing 29 September 1789 and ending 28 November 1807. Coastal arrivals from the city of Gloucester and the Welsh ports of Newport and Chepstow were so common that they were recorded in a separate ledger.

55  J. Latimer, *The Annals of Bristol in the Eighteenth Century* (Bristol, 1893), p. 422.

56  B.R.O. #04096, The Collection of Messrs James Matthews and Edward Ward from the Market on the Back. The names of the vendors are recorded here, and many of the women had Welsh names as well as Welsh produce and poultry. Three of the most active vendors were Jane Williams, Ann Llewellin, and Mary Griffiths.

57  B.R.O. #04084, Accounts of Rents received for Stalls at St James Market (1776–82).

58  E. and S. George (eds), *Guide to the Probate Inventories of the Bristol Deanery of the Diocese of Bristol 1542–1804* (Bristol, 1988), p. 277. Of fifty-five butchers whose origins are identified on their inventories, forty-three (78 per cent) were from Bristol and twelve (22 per cent) were from nearby villages.

59  B.R.O. #04070(1), Account Book for Butcher's Market, beginning 30 March, 1745.

60  P. Clark and P. Slack, *English Towns in Transition 1500–1700* (Oxford, 1976), p. 27.

61  B.R.O. #00065(2) Temple Ca17, Accounts of Richard Crabb, Churchwarden of Temple, for the Rents and Profits of St Paul's Fair for the Year 1652.

62  B.R.O. #00149(18) Temple Ae16, Mr. Gery's Lease (7 February 1723).

63  B.R.O. #00120 Temple Ae7, Agreement for a Standing on St Paul's Fair, Parish of Temple, Bristol (1673).

64  B.R.O. #00149(1) Temple Ae14, The Lease of Mr. Cooper and Mr. Greenwood for Twenty-one Years (3 February 1720).

65  B.R.O. #00044 Temple Ae15, Articles of the Lease of Mrs. Miller (25 July 1723).

66  B.R.O. P/AS/D/L/222, All Saints, Bristol: Deeds and Leases. The St James Fair should not be confused with the St James Market. I owe Dr Jonathan Barry thanks for the information that the St James Fair was rescheduled for a different season after 1769, although this was discussed in Bristol as early as 1731.

67  The growth of shops and shopkeeping in England is stressed in N. McKendrick, J. Brewer, and J. H. Plumb, *The Birth of a Consumer Society: The Commercialization of Eighteenth-Century England* (Bloomington, Ind., 1982).

68  D. H. Stacks, 'Bristol's "little business" 1625–41', Past and Present 110 (1986), pp. 69–105.

69  B.R.O. #04452(1), Bristol Quarter Sessions (Trinity term, 1676/77).

70  Latimer, *The Annals of Bristol in the Nineteenth Century*, p. 242.

71  *Vinegar and Mustard; or, Wormwood Lectures for Every Day of the Week* (London, 1686); R. Thompson (ed.), *Samuel Pepys' Penny Merriments: Being a Collection of Chapbooks* (New York, 1977), p. 292.

72  B.R.O. #04452(1), Bristol Quarter Sessions (Easter term, 1685).

73  B.R.O. #04439(4), Bristol Depositions (30 October 1662).

74  S.R.O. Q/SR/120(32) and 121(26), Somerset Quarter Sessions (Epiphany, 1673/74, and Michaelmas, 1674).

75  S.R.O. Q/SR/126(31–3), Somerset Quarter Sessions (May 1675).

76  S.R.O. Q/SR/114(16–17), 122(13), and 125(6–10), Somerset Quarter Sessions (Michaelmas, 1670; Easter, 1674, and Easter, 1675). The case of the familiar carrots is recorded in Q/SR/100(39), Somerset Quarter Sessions (Midsummer, 1661).

77  B.C.L. MS #20095, Diary of William Dyer.

78  *Farley's Bristol Newspaper* (23 October 1725).

79  *Ibid.* Gosport was not among the settlements with a population of 2,500 or more, not even by 1750, according to P. J. Corfield, *The Impact of English Towns 1700–1800* (Oxford, 1982), pp. 12–13. It was directly across the harbour from Portsmouth, another major port, and therefore is comparable, in many respects, to some of the larger villages near Bristol.

# Part II

---

# Cultural forms
# and affinities

# Chapter 4

---

# Personal culture:
# marriage and sex

If the sexual experiences of villagers and citizens were any indication, for most of the century or so associated with the urban renaissance it was uncommon for two people from different settings to form a lasting or intimate bond. In the late seventeenth century, John Day managed to have two wives for twenty-five years without either one knowing about it despite the fact that one wife lived in the city of Bristol and the other lived in the nearby village of Pensford, Somerset. Day's Pensford wife knew of another woman in her village with whom Day had had five children, but when she learned of his city wife, it was said to have driven her mad.[1] Around that same time, a woman from the Somerset village of East Pennard did not know the name of her sister's husband of five years, but knew that the couple lived in his house somewhere in the city of Bristol.[2] Some villagers who fled to Bristol to escape from unhappy marriages found they liked the city even less and returned to their spouses in the countryside.[3] In 1701 a woman by the name of Freke would have married her own grandfather in order to stay at home in the Somerset village of Corton Denham if only the bishop's authorities in Wells had not got wind of it.[4]

The levels of geographical mobility exhibited in early modern England suggest that ample opportunity existed for urban and rural dwellers to interact in a close, direct and personal manner with one another beyond the confines of the village, city or parish.[5] Indeed, until the late eighteenth century, young villagers at work in the countryside may have moved more frequently than urban dwellers of comparable age.[6] Nevertheless, when we retrace the important contacts achieved by several thousand individuals moving in and around a provincial city and its rural environs during the century or so following 1660, we notice that where long-term associations were concerned, the social spheres of urban residents and those of people dwelling in nearby villages tended to be separate rather than convergent. This situation persisted for a surprisingly long time. Patterns of highly localised social interaction were neither especially urban nor especially rural. Even migrants, in their new places of residence, tended to interact most closely with people whose places of origin were, in terms of setting, like their own. In other cases, migration into cities was transient; cities surely drew rural as well as urban migrants, but many of these did not stay in the urban setting long enough to establish enduring relationships with urban dwellers. Alienated or disappointed migrants withdrew from apprenticeships at a very high rate. Other migrants without affiliation to the city's guilds were employed transiently or perhaps not at all. In the case of Bristol, as with other ports, many of the migrants drawn from within twenty miles were making their way to some destination overseas and had no intention of staying in the city.[7] Despite the urban revival associated with the late seventeenth and early eighteenth centuries, a major provincial city and its surrounding countryside were the distinct settings of surprisingly separate urban and rural social spheres for roughly a century after the Restoration.

Nearly all of life's routine activities involve direct personal interaction of some sort, but relatively few face-to-face encounters develop into enduring relationships that influence life-altering decisions, shape personal allegiances, and provide compelling experiences. These sorts of relationships arise from some of the more binding forms of direct personal interaction – what we might call personal culture – through which shared beliefs, values, knowledge, and sentiment are mediated. In early modern villages and towns, all face-to-face dealings, recurring personal encounters and enduring relationships took place in the context of topographical setting. Sexual intimacy, marriage, apprenticeship, and co-operation in the workplace – types of personal culture that were highly influential in the formation of social spheres – all conformed to patterns shaped by setting. This chapter will consider the extent to which sexual activity and marriage may have brought urban and rural dwellers into deliberate, close, personal associations.

Caricatures of rural courtship were a staple of abusive comedy, burlesque theatre and chapbooks of the late seventeenth and early eighteenth centuries. Samuel Pepys had in his vast chapbook collection *A Merry Dialogue between Andrew and his Sweetheart Joan*.[8] It opens with an ardent country suitor addressing the object of his desire as 'my poor sweetheart Joan, the flower of all shitten-heels'. In a single ironic phrase the author has ridiculed Andrew's awkward vulgarity and Joan's farmyard appearance. Superstitious customs associated with rural courtship reflected the assumption that fate intended rustic maids and rustic suitors to be together. A popular chapbook tutored the country girl in the ways of divining the identity of her intended husband. These involved, appropriately, an agricultural test.

> Take hemp seed and go into what place you will by yourself, carry the seed in your apron and with your right hand throw it over your shoulder, saying, 'Hemp seed I sow, hemp seed I sow, and he that must be my true love, come after me and mow.'[9]

That women, not men, were cast as the sowers of seeds in the agricultural imagery of early modern sexual discourse is worth noting, as is the invocation of the groom reaper rather than the grim one. In any case, the normative view was that mowers and sowers, companions in the rural setting, were meant to court and wed one another.

As for rural impressions of urban sexual encounters, we already know that Ned, the rustic Somerset traveller, formed the striking opinion that in town 'the slutts are zoe nasty'.

> Than's went to the 'change to the zigne of the Spurs
> And they cry'd, 'What lack you good zurs?'
> And I said 'a wanch if' s' that Iz could meete',
> And they zhewed mee the way to Turnbold Streete.
> Iz went to a houze, and Iz zate mee downe.
> Come in a vine lasse in a zilken gowne.
> Touch pott and touch penny if that th' one comst here.
> 'Thou shalt pay ready money or not mell with my ware.'
> 'Why missus,' coth mee, 'won't Love gain your coney?'
> Then Iz keepe my ware and thou's keepe thy coney.
> For I can have one at hoame vor a pint of wine
> That's zweeter, and zounder, and better than thine.'[10]

This hardly suggests that a vulgar rube in the city is inherently blameless or that his etiquette is flawless. Ned's creator, despite his own obscurity, was almost certainly aware of this, but his poem goes beyond caricature to a compelling observation. It asserts frankly that a rustic person actually prefers people of rural origin or, at the very least, their customs. This seems to have been the case.

In the city of Bristol and the nearby villages a wedding uniting an urbanite and a local villager was a significantly rare occasion before 1760 or so. Bristol inhabitants had a very strong tendency to marry one another. In the surrounding countryside, local villagers tended to marry people from their own parish or from other rural settlements. There is evidence to suggest that, despite a widespread tendency to take spouses of rural origin, English villagers were less endogamous than urban dwellers in the early modern period and well into the nineteenth century.[11] Local villagers appeared in Bristol marriage registers only rarely and in tiny numbers. Villagers living in the shadow of Bristol virtually circumvented the city in their courtship and rarely, if ever, married people of urban origin, regardless of the general population's geographical mobility. The persistence of this urban–rural gulf is astonishing. Of those mobile villagers who did marry in Bristol, significant numbers had courted fellow migrants of rural origin, quite often people from their own villages. A closer examination of marriages registered in two Bristol parishes, two rural parishes within ten miles of the city, and religious nonconformists registered outside the parochial system will reveal that endogamy and the pairing of people of similar topographical origin was the rule rather than the exception in both settings. It was not until the second half of the eighteenth century that marriages of religious nonconformists reflected a significant convergence of urban families and families from the villages. In this regard, as in others, the transcendence of the topographical divide by extraparochial nonconformists was ahead of the patterns to which most villagers, citizens, and migrants had long conformed.

The urban parish of St Philip and Jacob, Bristol, was a large, poor, and peripheral one. It was a sprawling parish with more inhabitants than its vestry could monitor easily. Local vigilance indicates that the influx of non-parishioners was a matter of concern in St Philip and Jacob.[12] The vestry minutes of the 1660s included the pleas of churchwardens who were unable to enforce the collection of tithes needed to maintain a resident vicar.[13] The parish bordered on the countryside and was quite rural in character in places. Yeoman and husbandman were common among the few occupations stated by grooms from the parish. In the eyes of the sons and nubile daughters of hinterland farmers, St Philip and Jacob was doubtless a more attractive and accessible setting than one of the inner-city parishes. Nevertheless, migrants from the nearby villages never made up more than a tiny fraction of the spouses registered in St Philip and Jacob between the 1660s and the 1780s. That small percentage actually declined after 1760, when the vestiges of *rus in urbe* gave way to an emerging brickmaking industry,[14] a sudden concentration of people, and new, or newly subdivided, buildings in the parish.

The most startling feature of marriage patterns in St Philip and Jacob was the extreme affinity that Bristolians showed for one another. (Table 4.1.) Between 80 per cent and 97 per cent of all marriages registered in St Philip and Jacob during seven five-year periods involved the marriage of one Bristolian to another. During the first five years of the 1780s, nearly 92 per cent of all marriages registered in St Philip and Jacob united one parishioner to another even as the total number of marriages registered increased. Endogamy was most intense at the end of the early modern period, suggesting that urbanisation produced a more intensified inward-looking sociability, especially in those urban parishes most heavily inundated with migrants. Thus an immediate or exclusive association of xenophobia and parochialism with rural life deserves reconsideration.

Migrants wed in St Philip and Jacob showed similar topographical affinities. Their geographical mobility and relocation to the city did not result in a significant expansion of their immediate social sphere. From 1660 to 1664 in

*Cultural forms and affinities*

Table 4.1 Spouses' places of origin, St Philip and Jacob, Bristol
(% in parentheses)

|  | 1660 –1664 | 1673 –1677 | 1700 –1704 | 1720 –1724 | 1740 –1744 | 1760 –1764 | 1780 –1784 |
|---|---|---|---|---|---|---|---|
| Total marriages | 113 | 108 | 216 | 413 | 453 | 534 | 563 |
| Both spouses from Bristol | 91 (80·5) | 102 (94·4) | 197 (91·2) | 383 (92·7) | 399 (88·1) | 506 (94·8) | 546 (97.0) |
| Both spouses from St. P&J | 72 (63·7) | 86 (79·6) | 183 (84·7) | 339 (82·1) | 350 (77·3) | 423 (79·2) | 515 (91·5) |

*Source:* B.R.O. P/StP&J/R/1(c)(d)(e)(h) and P/StP&J/R/3(a)(b).

St Philip and Jacob, five of the six marriages in which no Bristol resident was involved united men and women who had in common with their chosen spouses exactly the same place of origin. In the period 1673–77 only seven people from outside the city of Bristol were married in St Philip and Jacob, and two of these extramural spouses, who were from the very same remote town, married each other. This trend continued during the first five years of the eighteenth century, when every one of the extramural spouses courted and wed someone from his or her very own village or town. Eventually the attachment that migrants felt for people from their own place of origin affected marriage patterns less. In the periods 1760–64 and 1780–84 there were no marriages registered in St Philip and Jacob in which both spouses were extramural. It appears that courtship across topographical lines very rarely took place in Bristol until a century or more after the Restoration. Even then, the percentage of native Bristolians married to fellow parishioners remained extremely high.

St Werburgh, Bristol, was an inner-city parish, densely settled and geographically compact. It serves as a useful contrast to St Philip and Jacob in this regard. St Werburgh was bordered on all sides by other urban parishes which were in turn enclosed on three sides by the rivers Avon and Frome. It was therefore insulated from the countryside surrounding Bristol, and the marriage patterns of its inhabitants were similarly confined, despite the relative wealth of the parishioners.[15] Except for the decades immediately following 1660 (and the middle decades of the eighteenth century, when the number of extramural spouses was negligible) the presence of local villagers among St Werburgh's spouses was at all times less pronounced than that of migrant spouses from

more remote places of origin. Naturally the collective population of settlements farther than ten miles from an English city was greater in absolute
terms than the collective population of villages within that city's immediate
hinterland. But from the point of view of Bristol's social composition, and the
local perception of the outside world, local villagers were relatively under-
represented in the married population of the city.

The degree of endogamy exhibited by St Werburgh's parishioners, although not always as high as that found in St Philip and Jacob, was still
remarkable. (Table 4.2.) Until the later eighteenth century, the percentages of
marriages composed exclusively of Bristolians rose steadily from one generation to the next in St Werburgh. Unlike the situation in St Philip and Jacob,
where endogamy peaked at the end of the early modern period, the trend was
dramatically reversed in St Werburgh in the last generation of the period;
social barriers between urban and rural spheres remained most intense at the
boundary between city and village. We may suppose that at all times wealthier
inner-city residents were more likely to court outside parish circles, perhaps
among the elite of other cities and towns, or even among members of the
gentry. The total number of marriages in St Philip and Jacob steadily increased
over the entire period while the number of marriages in St Werburgh generally declined. Almost certainly a growing portion of St Werburgh's residents
married outside the parish as the urban renaissance progressed.[16] The precipitous decline of marriages among fellow parishioners in St Werburgh after
1750 or so may even reflect the movement of wealthier Bristolians out of the
city altogether to establish homes in the new suburban development at the
end of the early modern period. Nevertheless, courtship between St Werburgh's
parishioners and local villagers was never very active. From 1694 to 1753, only
two (0·8 per cent) of the 249 marriages registered in St Werburgh represented a successful courtship between a person of local rural origin and a

Table 4.2 Spouses' places of origin, St Werburgh, Bristol (% in parentheses)

|  | 1664–93 | 1694–1723 | 1724–53 | 1754–83 |
| --- | --- | --- | --- | --- |
| Total marriages | 146 | 112 | 137 | 61 |
| Both spouses from Bristol | 124 (84·9) | 100 (89·3) | 135 (98·5) | 49 (80·3) |
| Both spouses from St. Werburgh | 82 (56·2) | 84 (75·0) | 128 (93·4) | 16 (26·2) |

*Source:* B.R.O. P/StW/R/1 and P/StW/R/2(a).

Bristol resident of any parish. St Werburgh's parishioners certainly met and married people from outside the city, but they displayed surprisingly little connection at all with migrants whose villages of origin were close to Bristol.

In St Werburgh, newcomers to the city courted one another, as they did in St Philip and Jacob, but not exclusively. Between 1664 and 1693, only twenty-two (7·5 per cent) of the spouses wed in St Werburgh were from nearby villages, but ten of them married people who were already recognised as Bristolians. At the same time, however, the other twelve migrants from the local villages all married one another, and eight of them were drawn to people whose villages of origin were the very same as their own. Two of the three spouses who migrated from urban areas beyond the local villages and married in St Werburgh between 1664 and 1693 came from the same coastal town of Poole, Dorset. They eventually married each other. During the following thirty years, nine migrants from other urban areas married in St Werburgh and four of them (44 per cent) took spouses who had come from their own city or town. In the second quarter of the eighteenth century four local villagers married in the parish and all of them took as spouses fellow migrants from their own villages.

Courtship hardly provided a connection between Bristol and its nearby villages, despite rural migration to the city. Between 1664 and 1693 only ten spouses registered in St Werburgh (or 3 per cent of the total) were local villagers who married native or settled Bristolians. The figure dropped below 1 per cent for the period 1694–1723. Between 1724 and 1753 there were no marriages at all between local villagers and Bristolians registered in St Werburgh, despite an absolute increase in registrations. After 1753 the percentage of local villagers marrying Bristolians in St Werburgh did increase, but the absolute number of local villagers among in-migrant spouses did not. Bristol's natives or established residents, who made up well over 90 per cent of the people wed in St Werburgh, were even more endogamous than rural migrants to the city during the first quarter of the eighteenth century; roughly 75 per cent of them courted people from their own parish during this period. In short, people of urban as well as of rural origin, even when living side by side, courted in separate circles and displayed strong personal affinities linked with the topographical settings with which they identified.

It is apparent that a high degree of endogamy obtained throughout Bristol. There were, for example, the cases of Bristolians who married in St Philip and Jacob rather than their own parishes.[17] In the five years from 1660 to 1664, nineteen marriages registered in St Philip and Jacob involved spouses who were all from Bristol parishes. Of those thirty-eight spouses, sixteen (over 42 per cent) married people from their own Bristol parishes even though they married in a Bristol parish other than their own. From 1720 to 1724 this figure rose to nearly 78 per cent. Most strikingly, for more than a century following

1660, only a very small portion of the marriages performed in St Philip and Jacob united a person from any city or town to a person from any village. The figures were highest early on (at 11·5 per cent between 1660 and 1664), when the parish was quite rural in character. They actually declined during the urban revival (sinking to 2·5 per cent during the period 1780–84) as the parish became thoroughly built-up.[18]

Bristol's inner-city quayside parish of St Stephen was heavily populated with mariners,[19] a widely travelled group. In over 95 per cent of the 223 marriages registered in St Stephen from 1754 to 1758 one Bristolian wed another. Between 1777 and 1786 this figure rose to nearly 98 per cent. The large totals involved surely accounted for the majority of the parish's married population, so only a few of St Stephen's parishioners, seafaring or otherwise, married outside the city altogether. In fact, between 1754 and 1758 inclusive of the 223 marriages registered in St Stephen 38 per cent of the couples were neighbours from the same street.[20] Even those Bristolians who ploughed the salt wave the wide world over returned to familiar soil, and their fellow urban dwellers, to form their closest bonds.

There is no evidence to suggest that this astonishingly high degree of urban endogamy was matched anywhere in Bristol's rural environs. Nevertheless, the relatively high percentage of extraparochial spouses registered in local villages did not reflect a steady expansion of the city's demographic sphere or any urban gravitational force channelling migrants through Bristol's rural environs *en route* to the city. Brislington, Somerset, for example, was clearly rural, but by no means off the beaten track. In the seventeenth and eighteenth centuries, Brislington was a large nucleated village. The centre of the village was somewhere between one and two miles down the Bath road from St Mary, Redcliffe, the nearest Bristol parish. There is reason to believe that roughly half Brislington's adult residents married elsewhere.[21] There were occasional references to Brislington villagers in Bristol marriage registers, but hardly enough to account for even a small portion of Brislington's mobile parishioners, whose names were conspicuously absent from their own village's marriage registers. That is to say, something approaching half the villagers courted and wed outside their parish, far more than could be expected to do so in Bristol. During the 1730s and 1740s, people from the surrounding countryside were more common than Bristol residents among Brislington's courtship circles. (Table 4.3.) Grooms and brides from Bristol appeared more often in Brislington's registers than vice versa. Rather than moving closer to some urban gravitational field, the villagers living in the city's immediate surroundings exerted a persistent force of attraction on each other. The shared affinity felt for a particular topographical setting by lovers, suitors and spouses was more influential than the size or proximity of a nearby city in shaping rural marriage patterns.

Table 4.3 Spouses' places of origin, Brislington, Somerset (% in parentheses)

|  | 1661–1707 | 1733–52 | 1754–80 |
| --- | --- | --- | --- |
| Total marriages | 45 | 71 | 111 |
| Both spouses from local villages | 35 (77·8) | 53 (74·6) | 85 (76·6) |
| Both spouses from Brislington | 32 (71·1) | 45 (63·4) | 69 (62·2) |
| Total spouses | 90 | 142 | 222 |
| Spouses from other villages | 5 (5·5) | 21 (14·8) | 20 (9·0) |
| Spouses from Bristol | 7 (7·8) | 13 (9·2) | 20 (9·0) |

*Source:* B.R.O. P/StLB/R/1(b)(c) and P/StLB/R/4(a), Parish
Registers of St. Luke, Brislington, Somerset

Despite the ready accessibility of Bristol's large population and the geographical mobility of local villagers, courting activity moved villagers about the countryside, or away from the region altogether, rather than into the city. It has been shown that women who lived away from home had more power to choose their husband than women living at home or with kin, and this may have provided the initial inducement for some village women to migrate to a city.[22] But villagers formed more extensive marital ties with other villagers – regardless of how far they had travelled – than with Bristol residents. The villagers of Olveston, Gloucestershire, lived only nine miles north-east of Bristol. In four sample decades spanning the period 1697 to 1784, over 93 per cent of the marriages registered in Olveston involved local villagers exclusively. Only three (0·8 per cent) of the spouses involved were from Bristol and not one of them was registered until the second half of the eighteenth century. People came to Olveston from outside the village to court and wed there, but they came from other villages within Bristol's rural environs. (Table 4.4.) Between 1775 and 1784, only one of the sixty-three marriages registered in Olveston involved someone other than a resident of Olveston or another local village. The earliest marriage between an Olveston parishioner and a Bristol resident on record in the Olveston registers after 1660 took place in 1756. In general, people of rural origin made up a declining portion of all spouses in the city until nearly a century after the Restoration, while in the villages the

Table 4.4 Spouses' places of origin, Olveston, Gloucestershire (% in parentheses)

|  | 1697–1707 | 1743–53 | 1754–63 | 1775–84 |
|---|---|---|---|---|
| Total marriages | 20 | 39 | 61 | 63 |
| Both spouses from local villages | 19 (95·0) | 36 (92·3) | 54 (88·5) | 62 (98·4) |
| Both spouses from Olveston | 13 (65·0) | 23 (59·0) | 42 (68·9) | 53 (84·1) |
| Total spouses | 40 | 78 | 122 | 126 |
| Spouses from other villages | 8 (20.0) | 20 (25.6) | 16 (13.1) | 9 (7.1) |
| Spouses from Bristol | 0 | 0 | 2 (1.6) | 1 (0.8) |

*Source:* B.R.O. P/OV/R/1(d)(f) and P/OV/R/3(a), Marriage
Registers of St Mary, Olveston, Gloucestershire.

opposite trend applied and continued right through the early modern period. That is to suggest that the convergence of urban and rural social spheres, once presumed to have been a product of late seventeenth and early eighteenth-century urbanisation, appears to have coincided more closely with the transplanting of urban dwellers to rural retreats, especially near the end of the early modern period.

Of course, parish registers do not provide a complete picture of marriage patterns because they tell us nothing about those marriages that people formed outside the Anglican church. The marriage patterns of religious nonconformists can be studied through the excellent records of the Society of Friends, or Quakers, a group closely associated with Bristol and the neighbouring counties.[23] The marriage patterns of Quakers present a picture not focused on the activity of a single parish but drawn from the entire region in which Bristol and the nearby villages were located. Nevertheless, the most thorough treatments of the social history of early Quakers do not consider the extent to which their sociability may have effected an urban–rural merger in the form of courtship and marriage patterns, despite the power of Quaker devotional practices and family formation to cultivate far-reaching, even transatlantic, ties.[24]

We might expect the widely but thinly dispersed Quaker population to be less geographically confined where the sociability surrounding courtship is concerned. Some geographical mobility was a practical requirement of communal worship for most early Quakers. The most celebrated meeting house in the Bristol region was located not in the city but in the nearby village of Frenchay, Gloucestershire. Other meeting houses in Bristol's rural environs were located in Chew Magna, Somerset, where Quaker weddings were held as early as 1680, and in Keynsham, Somerset, where they were held as early as 1724. By 1760 Quaker marriages were recorded as having taken place at no fewer than six other Somerset villages and towns.[25] In 1660 a Quaker couple from the Somerset town of Bridgwater travelled to Glastonbury, a smaller town over fifteen miles away, in order to have their wedding held at an organised Quaker meeting. Indeed, Quakers moved about a great deal in order to interact with one another. Quakers formed a national organisation that cultivated a geographically extensive social network for its members. For devotional reasons, however, Quakers were counselled to confine their sociability, and their courtship especially, to the Society of Friends, a relatively small group.[26]

A high degree of urban localism was reflected in the marriage patterns of Bristol Quakers. Quaker weddings were held in the city of Bristol as early as the 1660s, despite the Clarendon Code. In each of seven sample years taken at twenty-year intervals throughout the period 1660–1780, marriages in which two Bristol residents were united were more common than any other arrangement involving Bristol and Somerset Quakers. This is scarcely surprising in view of the fact that the largest portion of the region's married Quaker population resided in Bristol. The number of Quaker spouses registered in the whole region declined after 1680, a year in which forty-two new Quaker spouses were registered. But the portion of Quaker spouses coming from Bristol increased from 30 per cent in 1660 to over 61 per cent in 1720. The portion peaked in 1740, when nine of the ten spouses registered in that year were from Bristol. During the eighteenth century, Bristol's Quaker Meeting House, situated in the parish of Temple, eventually became somewhat of an urban landmark.[27]

Although not bound to the parish ties exhibited by conformists, Quakers were just as topographically divided in their courtship and marriage patterns as members of the conformist majority. Of the sixty-eight marriages registered in the seven sample years between 1660 and 1780 inclusive, only nine (13 per cent) involved the marriage of a Bristol Quaker to anyone from outside the city, and none of these took place in the years before 1700.[28] Of even greater interest is the fact that, in the five sample years spanning the century between 1660 and 1760, there was not a single marriage between a Bristolian and a local villager. At times, high levels of endogamy applied not only to Quaker couples from Bristol but to local village Quakers and to Quakers beyond Bristol's immediate environs as well. In 1660, not one of the twenty newly married Quakers identified by the Bristol and Somerset Meeting took a spouse from outside his or her own village or town. By contrast, of the twenty-one Quaker marriages recorded in 1680, seven united people from separate places of origin. Still, not one of these involved a Bristolian or local villager. Rarely, before the mid-eighteenth century, did the prospect of a Bristol match attract the more highly mobile rural Quakers. During the eighteenth century, however, Quakers from other cities and towns (as far away as London, Cork, and Dublin in some cases) travelled to Bristol, where they courted and wed. Levels of endogamy varied over time and from place to place, but the division of urban and rural courtship circles remained a constant until the last decades of the early modern period.

While Quakers who lived in or near the city continued to look no farther than their own back yards, Quakers living greater distances from the city courted more widely. In six of the seven cases involving nuptial mobility in 1680, the spouses originated from places more than twenty-two miles apart.[29] This trend continued in all the sample years in the eighteenth century, in which nine of thirty-seven marriages involved spouses originating from places more than twenty-two miles apart. In all but one of these marriages, the long-range courtship was experienced by Quakers who lived beyond Bristol's nearby villages. Thus most remotely situated Quakers, unlike those living in or near Bristol, courted over considerable distances. For a century following 1660 their romantic excursions and their closest personal ties took them away from the city of Bristol rather than towards it, despite the concentration of Friends there. As we have seen, the few Quakers who travelled to Bristol for marriage were of urban origin themselves. Religious nonconformists conformed with the courting tendencies of the general population. Patterns of courtship and marriage, whether they were endogamous or exogamous, conformist or nonconformist, reflected a fundamental divide between urban and rural social spheres.

In the cases of some rural religious dissenters, the home village of neither spouse served as the location of the wedding ceremony itself. Well into the eighteenth century it remained difficult for some nonconformists in rural areas to persuade their local pastor to perform the service. Dissenting villagers resorted to ceremonies involving a trip into a city or town, hasty procedures, and strange officiants. During the second quarter of the eighteenth century, more rural people seeking settlement in the Gloucestershire village of Bitton were married in Bath than in nearby Bristol. These villagers had no intention of settling in either city; they appeared in Bath for a day because a 'lawless minister' there, 'a man in a black coat', regularly agreed to perform marriages surreptitiously.[30] An abandoned wife (presumed to be a widow) who sought settlement in the village of Bitton in 1749 recalled for her examiner the hazy details of her wedding, which had taken place ten years earlier. In 1739 she married a fellow rural dweller, a horse driver from the nearby manor of Wick and Abson. The wedding was held in a public house or tavern on the outskirts of Bath, six or seven miles away. The ceremony was performed by a person unknown to her whom she believed to be the proprietor of the pub, the name of which escaped her. Her memory vastly improved concerning liturgical points bearing directly on the efficacy of her marriage and thus on her weak settlement claim. She assured her Anglican examiner that a 'reading over that part of the ceremony used in the Church of England ... and also the ceremony with the ring was performed'.[31]

Not all courtship resulted in permanently shared residence, much less marriage, formally approved or otherwise. Nevertheless, premarital and extra-marital sexual intimacy conformed to the same pattern of separate urban and rural social spheres for which there is strong evidence beyond marriage registers. Bastardy and paternity examinations often dealt quite explicitly with the location of social activity, or at least with the exact whereabouts of sexual encounters. An illegitimate father's place of residence was invariably of inter-est to parish officials. As unwed mothers knew, administerers of settlement examinations got right to the heart of the matter and left little doubt about the origins of unwed parents. Parish overseers could be cruelly hostile toward unwed pregnant strangers, even to the point of carting a woman in labour across rugged terrain in order to lay her newborn at the feet of some other parish. It is unlikely that many abandoned women would have risked forfeit-ing their claims for settlement and aid by traipsing after lovers from other parishes, although some especially brave ones probably did.

In dalliance, as in marriage, the proximity of Bristol did little to lure local villagers away from one another or diminish their rural affinities. The parents of illegitimate children in the villages did not travel far for their liaisons. In the records of six local villages between 1691 and 1781, seventy-five (over 86 per cent) of the eighty-seven bastards whose mothers were from villages near Bristol had fathers who were from villages in Bristol's rural environs.[32] In forty-eight out of these cases (over 55 per cent), the fathers of illegitimate children resided in the very same village where the pregnancy had developed or the child was born. Like marriages, the conception of illegitimate children rarely involved interaction between Bristolians and local villagers. In general, the few mothers who asked villages to aid their illegitimate children fathered by Bristol men had come from Bristol, where they had conceived those children. These women and their children were removed back to the city by village overseers. Only two women from villages in the Bristol environs identi-fied Bristol men as the fathers of their illegitimate children. Moreover, only one man from these villages was sued for paternity by the parish of a Bristol woman and that did not occur until 1750.[33]

That localism prevailed in these matters was expressed even further by the common strategy employed by men who, in groups of four or five, collectively signed bonds for specified unwed mothers and their children. Ostensibly, as the convention had it, this was to 'keep a bastard child from falling upon the parish rates'. But, for the purposes of a collection of men who subscribed such a bond, this strategy conveniently obscured the exact identity, and liability, of the father. Collusion of this type satisfied the overseers while it allowed unwed mothers no measure of exoneration beyond the right to settle in the parish of their male sponsors. The practice identified male social circles, which, once again, tended to be highly localised.

All this is not to say that village women were not without well travelled lovers. Eight men from remote villages and towns, and one man described as being 'at sea', were identified as fathers of illegitimate children born within the countryside near Bristol. Five of these long-distance lovers were rural in origin. Some had visited the local villages from as far off as Warwickshire and Berkshire. The fathers of local village bastards included a post-chaise driver, a 'travelling hatter', a churchwarden, and two attorneys. In short, the prenuptial and extramarital lovers of local village women were a socially diverse group with highly local, or remote, rather than Bristol, connections.

Women were almost certainly geographically adventurous lovers them-selves. The fact that there were fewer extraparochial brides than extraparochial grooms – this held true for rural, urban, conformist, and nonconformist groups – may give the false impression that women were somehow immobile or passive in courtship. The wedding ceremony and its location, it seems safe to say, remained a traditionally uxorial affair in most cases. Locations of available men and women, or the locations of brides and grooms on their wedding days, do not explain the persistence of the urban–rural gulf. It is a firmly established fact that the majority of urban residents in eighteenth-century England were female.[34] This was attributable in part to the superior longevity of women. Nevertheless, a substantial portion of urban women were single, migrant, job-seeking women. Given the mobility of women, and the availability in the city of eligible women of rural origin, it is all the more puzzling that some conspicuous merger of urban and rural spheres of court-ship did not take place in the century following the urban revival. Clearly the eligibility, mobility, and availability of women by no means assured they would develop an affinity for an unfamiliar setting and its established resi-dents, much less consent to marriage under those circumstances.

Parish registers and paternity examinations tell us nothing about the migra-tions involved in homosexual relations and other forms of intimacy resulting in neither marriage nor offspring. Early modern English representations of same-sex desire in literary texts are readily found,[35] but information about the lives of early modern homosexuals in general is fragmentary or pieced to-gether from isolated court cases.[36] An estimated 15 per cent of the male gentry and nobility living between 1650 and 1750 were homosexual.[37] There is no reason to suppose that a smaller percentage of the general population experienced same-sex desire. There is the argument that potentially reproductive heterosexual intercourse became more 'popular' during the eighteenth century but that this was more an expression of the divergence of sexual practices into categories increasingly associated either with same-sex desire or not. The portion of society made up of heterosexuals was not expanding; rather, the range of sexual activity accepted by heterosexuals was becoming more narrowly defined.[38]

In May 1743 Edward Knight, a Bristol cordwainer brought before the quarter sessions there, complained that two men had raped him on the third floor of a house in the Bristol parish of St James.[39] One of the accused, a thirty-year-old shoemaker from the city of Gloucester, admitted knowing Knight but denied having had sexual relations with him. He went on to inform the court that his alleged accomplice, a forty-three-year-old cordwainer from the town of Ludlow in Shropshire, had been a friend of Knight's and 'for some years had worked and lay with him'. The proceedings revealed that Knight had indeed known this accused assailant for ten years and had first met him in the city of Worcester. On the evening in question, Knight, the defendants, and a fourth man had shared three rounds of ale in a St James pub before retiring as a group to bed. The sharing of beds by members of the same sex or the same family without any sexual activity was common in this period. Another cordwainer, who had overheard their conversation in the pub, however, testified that a lovers' quarrel had taken place. This raised questions about Knight's testimony and his sexuality; it appeared that the whole trial itself had been used by Knight as a vindictive gesture designed to spurn a lover while exonerating himself from what was then the serious crime of wilful sodomy.[40]

At first glance this may seem like an isolated and unhappy incident with little to tell us about the separation of urban and rural personal ties. Let us not overlook the fact that the three principal actors in the episode had more in common than their gender and a crowded bed. Their private interaction was long-term, deliberate, intimate, and involved considerable geographical mobility. They were all members of a set of closely related skilled trades. Most significantly, their places of origin and work, their arenas of sociability, the locations of their first and last encounters were exclusively urban. It would be ridiculous to suggest that all male homosexuals confined their social activity to the urban setting. On the other hand, the notion that urban dwellers, regardless of their sex lives, tended to form intimate associations with residents of other cities and towns deserves serious consideration.

The possibility that sexual intimacy and marriage were related to localised expressions of occupational solidarity should not be ignored. In the case of Bristol and its rural environs, however, factors of topography seemed to have been more important than occupational gregariousness for the movements of spouses, at least. Certain villages were heavily populated with feltmakers and others with miners, but these concentrations were the result of local resources rather than some tendency of miners or feltmakers to court and settle along occupational lines. Some Bristol parishes were noted for particular occupational profiles. St Stephen, heavily dominated by mariners until their precipitous decline by the 1770s, provides the most extreme example of such a parish, but its history does not suggest that the influence of occupational solidarity discouraged extraparochial suitors. On the contrary, the percentage of marriages on which both spouses were from St Stephen was greater (over 90 per cent) in the period 1777–82 than it was in the earlier period 1754–58 (77 per cent), when the parish was far more occupationally homogeneous.[41]

The patterns of sexual relations and marriage formed by the actions of provincial urban dwellers and villagers, Anglicans, nonconformists, and extramarital lovers hardly conformed to those supposed by a model of an urban sphere of influence. The degree of localism and topographical affinity shown by lovers of many types was remarkably high, but no more so in the villages near Bristol than in the heart of the city itself. This situation persisted until 1760 or so, despite the urbanisation during the preceding century or more. Those men and women who did exhibit mobility in courtship failed, by and large, to forge a closer or more expansive connection between the city and its rural environs until the last decades of the early modern period. In their interactions with lovers and future spouses, geographically mobile villagers either circumvented the nearby city or looked beyond their immediate surroundings altogether.

## NOTES

1  S.R.O. Q/SR/127(2–3), Somerset Quarter Sessions (Midsummmer, 1675).

2  S.R.O. Q/SR/124(34), Somerset Quarter Sessions (Easter, 1674).

3  S.R.O. Q/SR/115(43), Somerset Quarter Sessions (Michaelmas, 1671).

4  S.R.O. D/D/Cd/108, Deposition for the Bishop of Bath and Wells (1700/1), p. 114.

5  P. Clark and D. Souden (eds), *Migration and Society in Early Modern England* (London, 1987); R. Finlay, *Population and Metropolis: The Demography of London 1580–1650* (Cambridge, 1981), especially pp. 51–69; P. Clark, 'Migration in England during the late seventeenth and early eighteenth centuries', *Past and Present* 83 (1979), pp. 57–90; R. A. Houston and C. W. J. Withers, 'Population mobility in Scotland and Europe 1600–1900: a comparative perspective', *Annales de démographie historique* (1990), pp. 285–308.

6  I. K. Ben-Amos, *Adolescence and Youth in Early Modern England* (New Haven, Conn., 1994), p. 69; G. Mayhew, 'Life-cycle, service and the family unit in early modern Rye', *Continuity and Change* 6 (1991), pp. 201–26; M. K. McIntosh, 'Servants in the house-

hold unit in an Elizabethan English community', *Journal of Family History* 9 (1984), pp. 15–16; A. Kussmaul, *Servants in Husbandry in Early Modern England* (Cambridge, 1981), pp. 51–7.

7   J. Horn, *Adapting to a New World: English Society in the Seventeenth-Century Chesapeake* (Chapel Hill, N.C., 1994), pp. 39–48. Between 1654 and 1686, of 701 free migrants bound from Bristol for the Chesapeake alone, 245 (35 per cent) came from within twenty miles of Bristol but did not settle there. I owe this reference to my colleague, Alex Bontemps.

8   L. W., *A Merry Dialogue between Andrew and his Sweetheart* (seventeenth century). This is included in R. Thompson (ed.), *Samuel Pepys' Penny Merriments: Being a Collection of Chapbooks* (New York, 1977), pp. 102–3.

9   *The History of Mother Bunch of the West, containing many Rarities out of her Golden Closet of Curiosities* (London, early eighteenth century). This is included in J. Ashton (ed.), *Chapbooks of the Eighteenth Century* (London, 1882), pp. 84–7.

10  S.R.O. DD/SF/1343, Poem in Somerset dialect about travel to London (manuscript, late seventeenth century).

11  J. Patten, *Rural–urban Migration in Pre-industrial England*, Oxford University School of Geography Research Papers 6 (Oxford, 1973); M. Drake and T. Barker (eds), *Population and Society in Britain 1850–1980* (New York, 1982); B. Maltby, 'Easingwold marriage horizons', *Local Population Studies* 2 (1969), pp. 36–9. Easingwold is a village roughly twelve miles north-west of York. M. Drake, *Population and Society in Norway 1735–1865* (London, 1969), a study of Norway, has shown that these tendencies were typical of rural societies outside England as well.

12  B.R.O. P/StP&J/R/1(c)(d)(e)(h) and P/StP&J/R/3(a)(b), Parish of St Philip and Jacob Registers of Christenings, Marriages, and Burials. Clerks in some Bristol parishes were in the habit of identifying spouses by their place of origin at least a century before parliamentary legislation required such thoroughness. They appear to have done so regardless of legal technicalities which awarded settlement to migrants after a residence period approaching two months, providing they had not petitioned for parish aid. Marriages in which both spouses were identified as extramural were common enough in Bristol to suggest a high level of anxiety and scrutiny concerning the nativity and pre-migration origins of people setting up new households in the city. In short, a person identified as a Bristolian by contemporaries was certainly a resident of the city during courtship and was, in all probability, regarded by neighbours and parish vestry as someone other than a migrant.

13  B.R.O. P/StP&J/V/1, St Philip and Jacob Resolution Book (1649–1722).

14  B.R.O. Diocese of Bristol Probate Inventories and Cause Papers. The earliest brickmaker's inventories extant from St Philip and Jacob are those of Peter Dalton in 1736 and John Hill in 1737.

15  B.R.O. P/StW/R/1 and P/StW/R/2(a), Marriage Registers of St Werburgh, City of Bristol.

16  It is unlikely that the decline of marriages in St Werburgh is an illusory effect of the source. On the contrary, we should expect registration to have been more, not less, complete after the Hardwicke Marriage Act of 1753.

17  Apart from St Philip and Jacob and St Werburgh, few Bristol parishes have left marriage registers identifying places of origin for large numbers of spouses before the Marriage Act of 1753.

18  B.R.O. P/StP&J/R/1(c) and P/StP&J/R/3(b) for the years 1660–64, 1680–84, 1700–04, 1720–24, 1740–44, 1760–64, and 1780–84.

19  E. and S. George (eds), *Guide to the Probate Inventories of the Bristol Deanery of the Diocese of Bristol 1542–1804* (Bristol, 1988), p. 283 and throughout.

20  B.R.O. P/StS/R/3(a)(b), Marriage Register Book of St Stephen, Bristol.

21  From 1647 to 1713 more than 960 people were christened, married, and buried in the village of Brislington. Births and deaths were each roughly ten times more common in the village than weddings were. That both deaths and births should exceed marriages by a factor more than double the average family size should arouse suspicion. No marriages were recorded in Brislington between 1639 and 1660, a period during which the practices of particular clerks may have combined with the disturbances of the civil war and interregnum to threaten the storage and survival of marriage records in the village. Nevertheless, between 1661 (when marriage records resumed in the parish) and 1713 (when the series volume ends) only forty-five marriages were registered in Brislington. If the average couple raised three children there should have been roughly five deaths per marriage, not ten, especially since infant mortality declined over time. Peter Laslett calculated the average household size, based on rural parish records in Kent, to be 4·45 individuals in 1676. He concluded that this figure was 'quite normal' for all of pre-industrial England. See P. Laslett, *The World We Have Lost: England before the Industrial Age* (New York, 2nd ed. 1973), p. 66. More recently the definitive work on early modern English population has shown some fluctuation in household size but points to the remarkable persistence of an overall figure somewhere between four and five. See E. A. Wrigley and R. S. Schofield, *The Population History of England: A Reconstruction 1541–1871* (Cambridge, Mass., 1981).

22  V. Brodsky Elliott, 'Single women in the London marriage market: age, status and mobility 1598–1619', in R. B. Outhwaite (ed.), *Marriage and Society: Studies in the History of Marriage* (London, 1981), pp. 81–100.

23  B.R.O. SF/R1/3 and SF/R1/4, Society of Friends Quarterly Meetings of Bristol and Somersetshire, Marriages (1659–1816). Quaker marriage registers exist for the entire early modern period following 1660 and, unlike most Church of England registers prior to the Marriage Act of 1753, they invariably report spouses' place of origin. They even provide information regarding parental place of residence on which an unusually complete and reliable understanding of individual settlement histories can be based.

24  R. T. Vann, *The Social Development of English Quakerism 1655–1755* (Cambridge, Mass., 1969); B. Reay, *The Quakers and the English Revolution* (New York, 1985); B. Levy, *Quakers and the American Family: British Settlement in the Delaware Valley* (New York, 1988). On the marriage of George Fox see H. L. Ingle, *First among Friends: George Fox and the Creation of Quakerism* (New York, 1994), pp. 207–28.

25  Street (1658), Glastonbury (1660), Barrington (1680), Taunton (1680), Milverton (1740), and Wellington (1760).

26  B.R.O. MS SF/C1/1(a), Letters and Papers of George Fox and other early Friends (1667–1719); B.C.L. MS #20097, Diary of Rachael Tucker; B.C.L. MS #20095, Diary of William Dyer (1745–1801); *Epistles of the Yearly Meeting of Friends held in London from 1681 to 1817* (London, 1817).

27  *Donne's Map of Bristol 1773*, of which Bristol City Museum, Braikenridge Collection, Reg. No. M745, is a copy.

28  B.R.O. SF/R1/3 and SF/R1/4.

29  The diameter of Bristol's local environs, as we have defined it, is twenty-two miles, the greatest distance local villagers would have had to travel to court one another.

30  B.R.O. P/B/OP/6/g(6, 13), Bitton, Gloucestershire, Overseers of the Poor Settlement Examinations (1723–49).

31  B.R.O. P/B/OP/6/g(29), Bitton, Gloucestershire, Overseers of the Poor Settlement Examinations (1723–49).

32  The bastardy and paternity examinations on which these figures are based were recorded between 1691 and 1781 by the vestrymen and overseers of six villages within Bristol's rural environs: B.R.O. P/B/OP/8(a)(c), Bitton, Gloucestershire, Overseers of the Poor; B.R.O. P/OV/OP/13(1–20), Olveston, Gloucestershire, Overseers of the Poor; B.R.O.P/W/OP/11 and 12, Westerleigh, Gloucesterhsire, Overseers of the Poor; B.R.O. P/Puc/OP/4, Pucklechurch, Gloucestershire, Overseers of the Poor; B.R.O. P/StLB/ OP/14(g), Brislington, Somerset, Overseers of the Poor; B.R.O. P/FC/OP/6, Frampton Cotterell, Gloucestershire, Overseers of the Poor.

33  B.R.O. P/StLB//OP/14(g), St Luke, Brislington, Somerset, Overseers of the Poor.

34  P. J. Corfield, *The Impact of English Towns 1700–1800* (Oxford, 1982), p. 99.

35  The scholarship on this subject for early modern England alone is so extensive that we could only touch the surface here. Two references serve to illustrate that literary representations of same-sex desire were well known, and have been closely studied, even for those members of society whose sexuality has been construed as least visible: J. Mueller, 'Troping Utopia: Donne's brief for lesbianism', in J. G. Turner (ed.), *Sexuality and Gender in Early Modern Europe: Institutions, Texts, Images* (Cambridge, 1993), pp. 182– 207; L. Faderman, *Surpassing the Love of Men: Romantic Friendship and Love between Women from the Renaissance to the Present* (New York, 1981).

36  A. Bray, *Homosexuality in Renaissance England* (London, 1982, and New York, 1995), and T. Hitchcock, *English Sexualities 1700–1800* (New York, 1997), pp. 58–75, provide general treatments of the subject. For the contruction of homosexual identity and laws concerning homosexuality in early modern England, see R. Trumbach, 'The birth of the queen: sodomy and the emergence of gender equality in modern culture 1660–1750', in M. B. Duberman, M. Vicinus, and G. Chauncey (eds), *Hidden from History: Reclaiming the Gay and Lesbian Past* (New York, 1989), pp. 129–40, which considers the association of homosexual sociability with the urban setting, and this warrants more extensive investigation; R. Trumbach, 'London's sodomites: homosexual behavior and Western culture in the eighteenth century', *Journal of Social History* 11 (1977), pp. 1–33. For narratives of early modern English sodomy trials see R. Trumbach (ed.), *Sodomy Trials* (New York, 1986); C. Bingham, 'Seventeenth-century attitiudes toward deviant sex', *Journal of Interdisciplinary History* 1 (1971), pp. 446–68. The use of sodomy trial records tends to stress the male experience, although the concept of female sodomy did exist.

37  L. Stone, *The Family, Sex and Marriage in England 1500–1800* (New York, abridged ed. 1979), pp. 39 and 337.

38  As far as I am aware, this argument is attributable entirely to H. Abelove, 'Some speculations on the history of sexual intercourse during the long eighteenth century in England', *Genders* 6 (1989), pp. 125–30. According to the argument, the deduced increase in the popularity of reproductive intercourse, resulting in a higher rate of

conception, is borne out, one might say, by the dramatic increase in population over the period in question.

39  B.R.O. Bristol Quarter Sessions: Papers, bundle 1742–98.

40  B.R.O. #13847(51), A List of Persons executed at Bristol since the Year 1741. Between 1753 and 1761 at least three men were executed publicly in Bristol for what were regarded as homosexual offences. In 1781 two men were executed publicly as a couple in Bristol.

41  B.R.O. P/StS/R/3(a)(b), St Stephen, Bristol: Marriage Registers. For occupational profiles of Bristol parishes, see George and George, *Guide to the Probate Inventories of the Bristol Deanery*.

# Chapter 5

## Personal culture: training and work

The performance of a job or the transmission of occupational skills were important bases of long-term personal associations in early modern England. The typical term of apprenticeship in seventeenth-century and eighteenth-century England was five to seven years. Adolescents who located apprenticeships in major cities were introduced to formal occupational instruction the successful completion of which conferred burgess status upon them. Apprentices could evolve into some of the most socially and politically conspicuous, if not always powerful, members of urban society.[1] But admission to the trained labour force was by no means assurance of widespread social interaction. As for apprenticeships, even service under highly skilled urban masters placed constant limitations on the geographical mobility of indentured adolescents and young adults. The indenturing of a child to an adult member of his or her own household was not the least bit rare. In 1699 a boy from rural Yorkshire, apprenticed to his own uncle in London, abandoned his apprenticeship after a brief period despite the kinship ties. The removal from his native setting was too much to bear.[2]

In most cases, migrants apprenticed in cities were apprenticed to complete strangers.[3] In the second half of the seventeenth century, children who went to Bristol apprenticeships were known to be 'spirited' away overseas before they had a chance to form any bonds at all in the city.[4] Ports were teeming with mariners, but the vast majority of them were identified as urban in origin or were so transient as to have established no roots outside the seafaring community.[5] By the 1650s, the Bristol boatbuilder Francis Bailey had more than eighty employees in his shipyard, but this was dramatically atypical.[6] In seventeenth-century Bristol, between half and a third of all apprentices were solitary.[7] More fortunate apprentices may have entered into a network of supporting relationships, but it is questionable how many urban and rural apprentices interacted long enough or closely enough to form such bonds with one another. Very few village girls were ever apprenticed to Bristol freemen[8] or, it seems safe to say, to skilled trades in any provincial city. Village girls in cities served solitary 'housewifery' apprenticeships, often under bachelors or widowers whose influence on their long-term development must have been of limited value at best.

The workshop of a busy urban artisan could be the gateway to broader social horizons for the luckiest of apprentices. There was nothing new about apprentices coming to Bristol from remote, even exotic places. In 1700 the son of a planter from the island of Antigua in the West Indies apprenticed himself to a Bristol merchant. In 1780 Sam Blinman, a successful Bristol ropemaker, apprenticed three boys.[9] One was the son of a London wigmaker and the other two were sons of Bristol labourers. These boys of different social stations shared access to an extensive urban occupational network. As a result, the son of the Bristol labourer associated, night and day for seven years, with the son of a London fashion tradesman. Blinman's fellow burgess, shipwright Paul Farr (whose shop must have been even more prosperous), apprenticed a grand total of eleven boys in 1780. Four were from Bristol itself, two were from other cities, one was from the little village of Bishop's Lydeard, about fifty miles away, near Taunton, and four were from villages near Bristol. Blinman's ropeworks and Farr's shipyard were exceptional, however, in the sense that they fostered the collaboration of urban and rural workers.

The widespread interaction of urban and rural apprentices under the same masters did not develop until a century or more after the urban revival. In early modern Bristol more than half the apprentices were solitary apprentices and in some trades (woodworking in particular) about two-thirds of the masters had only one apprentice at any given time. The minority of rural migrants who stayed on in Bristol long enough to become masters there tended to recruit their apprentices out of the very same villages from which they themselves had come.[10] So those apprentices who did form close associations under the same master tended to be drawn from the same setting. During the sixteenth and early seventeenth centuries, villagers had made up an increasing portion of all migrants apprenticed in cities, rising from less than half to more than two-thirds in Bristol and reaching four-fifths in London by the mid-seventeenth century. The trend was markedly reversed after the 1650s, when rural migrants made up a declining portion of urban apprentices.[11] In the case of Bristol, as in London, the early seventeenth century had marked a shrinking in the distances travelled by most migrants apprenticed in the city; in that sense one may speak of the counties of a particular region as forming a greater hinterland beyond the confines of a major city.[12] In the late seventeenth century urban masters organised hiring fairs aimed at recruiting apprentices from the countryside.[13]

Apart from occasional periods when very small concentrations of villagers appeared in the city's textile, leather working, and building trades, adolescents from Bristol and those from the rural environs did not converge in the same trades. It was even less common for urban and rural adults to co-operate in the workplace. It must be said that despite stark contrasts between urban and rural environments, some remarkably similar jobs were performed in both settings. In the early eighteenth century, 85 per cent of a sample group of apprentices in Sheffield came from the 'immediate vicinity', an area within a five-mile radius of the centre of that town.[14] But this figure includes apprentices from Sheffield itself, a calculation consistent with the general tendency to analyse an urban area and its rural environs as a single region or social unit. The apprentices in this Sheffield example are all taken from a single company, the cutlers, whose craft techniques were readily accessible in advance for many nearby villagers already engaged in making their own sheep-shearing tools and scythes.[15] Shared occupational heritage, the predisposition of skills, and geographical mobility were not enough to effect a wider merger of urban and rural social spheres.

In view of all this, there must have been some larger meaning in the fact that the portion of Bristol's apprentices coming from nearby villages – as opposed to apprentices from remote places or other urban areas – actually declined significantly for generations after 1660. Youthful migration to port cities in particular became an increasingly fearful prospect from the 1650s on. In the eighteenth century, migrant apprentices to cities and coastal towns still risked being sold into the hardship of maritime service.[16] One disillusioned seaman's apprentice observed that those who were tricked, forced or sold into martime and overseas service were usually 'country people'.[17] Even those urban apprenticeships under honourable masters involved terms of indenture that could be unattractive and fees that could be prohibitive while indentureship in general offered little protection from abusive treatment and all the other pitfalls strewn about an unfamiliar setting.[18] Apprentices of urban origin were granted recuperation allowances – one London apprentice was awarded a holiday in Bath during his illness – while ailing apprentices from the villages were more likely to lose their urban apprenticeship and retreat home to recover.[19] The representation of local villagers among Bristol apprentices did not recover its pre-Restoration levels until the end of the early modern period, when the power and size of the guilds had declined. (Table 5.1.) The urban renaissance, the influence of the exclusive urban network, robust civic institutions, and urban privileges may have hampered rather than promoted occupational interaction between Bristolians and local villagers.

Apprenticeship arrangements in Bristol almost always involved indenture premiums and masters' fees that were high by village standards, in some cases amounting to nothing short of a middle-class fortune. In 1740 128 new apprentices promised to pay masters' fees. These fees totalled £4,447 17s, or

Table 5.1 Places of origin of apprentices registered in Bristol (%)

| Place | 1660 | 1680 | 1700 | 1720 | 1740 | 1760 | 1780 |
|---|---|---|---|---|---|---|---|
| Total No. | 115 | 245 | 264 | 212 | 187 | 157 | 159 |
| Bristol | 42.6 | 45·7 | 49·7 | 46·7 | 51·9 | 56·1 | 59·7 |
| Local rural | 20·9 | 15·9 | 12·5 | 8·0 | 9·1 | 11·4 | 19·5 |
| Remote urban | 12·2 | 16·7 | 18·9 | 24·1 | 18·2 | 13·4 | 8·8 |
| Remote rural | 24.3 | 21·7 | 18·9 | 21·2 | 20·8 | 19·1 | 12·0 |

*Source:* B.R.O. #04357(2) (1660); #04353(1)b (1680); #04353(3) (1700); #04353(4) (1720); #04353(6) (1740); #04353(6) and #04357(7) (1760); and #04356(15) (1780), Corporation of Bristol Apprenticeship Registers. The complete registers survive, so yearly fluctuations in apprentice totals reflect historical trends and not accidents of record survival. There are examples of girls registered as apprentices in Bristol in some years, but these are rare. All 1,442 apprentices registered by the corportion in these seven sample years were boys. Of these, the exact places of origin are known for 1,339.

roughly £34 15s per apprentice, on average. Two apprentices that year promised to pay their masters the staggering fee of £315. Poorer apprentices in the nearby villages rarely paid fees unless their masters were skilled in some trade. Apprenticeship fees exceeding £2 paid by parish overseers on behalf of village children were very rare. The highest such payment received by a master in Bristol's rural environs was £6 6s paid to a Westerleigh cordwainer by the parish officials of nearby Frampton Cotterell,[20] and that arrangement was not made until 1779.

The principal, if not the only, aim of parish subsidies for apprenticeships was to train, and possibly remove, those children who might otherwise develop a lifetime dependence upon the parish.[21] Whenever possible, poor village children were simply taken from their own families and 'apprenticed' within the parish to other households more capable of supporting them or of teaching them to be self-sufficient. The families of some poorer apprentices were openly resentful of the embarrassment and hardship this caused, but those who resisted the official relocation of their children risked having their own poor relief revoked as a punitive measure.[22] Thus it was the poorer village children with little choice in the matter who were sent to Bristol. Of 326 poor apprentices under the control of the overseers in four villages near Bristol, forty-one (12·6 per cent) were sent to the city, where such children were not favourably placed.[23]

The degree of geographical mobility experienced by poor urban apprentices was lower than that shown by their rural counterparts. Of thirty-three apprenticeships arranged between 1660 and 1725 by the overseers of the poor in the Bristol parish of St Stephen, thirty-one (nearly 94 per cent) were served in the city. The two poor parishioners who left Bristol were apprenticed in the city of Worcester, over sixty miles away,[24] despite the fact that there were trades to be learned and a considerable amount of textile manufacturing in the local villages. This illustrates the operation of an urban network in yet another phase of direct personal interaction. Why were no poor Bristol apprentices sent to, or accepted by, more affordable masters in the nearby rural villages? Studied closely, the issue of fees raises a difficult question: how did virtually all the poorest apprentices of Bristol origin afford to remain confined to the city if the fees of Bristol masters were so dramatically beyond what most local villagers were willing or able to pay?

Perhaps poor children from Bristol were restricted by masters, parish overseers, and urban philanthropists to apprenticeships in unskilled occupations. This, however, does not appear to have been the case. Of the twenty-three poor boys from St Stephen who were apprenticed to Bristol masters between 1660 and 1725, at least nineteen (83 per cent) served in skilled trades. Their masters included four navigators, three weavers, three cordwainers, two blacksmiths, two horners, a tailor, a shipwright, a hooper, and a cooper. Both the poor boys from St Stephen who were apprenticed in another city during this period were placed in a skilled trade or profession. There were eight poor girls from St Stephen apprenticed in Bristol during this period. Only one, a pinmaker, was engaged in a skilled trade of any kind. The others were indentured to 'housewifery'. Skilled apprenticeships were made available to poor Bristol boys in their own city. Gender and place of origin, rather than wealth, shaped the agreements reached between Bristol masters and the sponsors of their poorer apprentices. It is important to remember that both parties knew full well that anyone admitted to apprenticeship might become a privileged member of the civic community. Even if the commercial and occupational rights of freemen gradually assumed a greater symbolic than legal meaning as the guild system waned, the right to settlement remained a popular concern throughout the early modern period, as an abundance of urban and rural removal orders testifies.

As for the rural point of view and the declining movement of job-seeking adolescents from local villages into Bristol, the identification of skills specific to the two settings does not yield a complete, or even satisfactory, explanation. There were twenty-one different trades in which a total of 169 boys from five villages near Bristol were apprenticed in either the city or its rural environs between 1680 and 1780.[25] There were eight trades in which none of these boys was apprenticed in Bristol and eight other trades in which none was apprenticed in a local village. The five remaining trades were common to Bristol and the local villages and were taught in both settings. Surely this constituted more than enough local specialisation among masters to motivate an urban–rural exchange of children seeking training unavailable in their native setting. Nevertheless, only fifteen (8·9 per cent) of these 169 children of rural origin took advantage of urban specialisation and entered the eight trades that were taught in Bristol but not in their own villages.

There is an alternative theory that the rural apprentices would have been more likely to move to Bristol into occupations for which some preliminary training was available at home. If this were so, the paucity of trades common to masters in both settings would explain the reluctance of local villagers to venture into the city. The evidence does not support this theory, however. We should expect the five common trades – those of the malster-mealman, carpenter, cordwainer, tiler-plasterer, and blacksmith – to be among the most popular with villagers bound for Bristol. The group of rural adolescents apprenticed in Bristol to these familiar trades was even tinier than that group of rural apprentices in Bristol whose chosen trades were not taught by village masters. This was not for lack of mealmen, carpenters, cordwainers, tilers, plasterers, or blacksmiths in Bristol.[26]

The apprenticeship patterns of local villagers must have been shaped by some other trend, or personal affinity, and not by the occupational profiles of the city and the countryside. There was no general pattern to the occupational differentiation of the urban and rural masters under whom these 169 apprentices served. The only clerk and the only papermaker, for example, were located in the countryside despite the strong association of the city with writing, printing, luxury trades, and professions. The only butchers, bakers, and tailors served were in the villages, but these trades were almost certainly ubiquitous. What took place, around Bristol at least, was not the pursuit or rejection of certain trades but the circumvention of the city by local villagers.

The popularity of feltmaking in the villages can be understood more fully as an occupational context for the expression of local and topographical affinity. The appeal of feltmaking from the point of view of rural adolescents may have been that it allowed them to stay and work in the local countryside. Of the 169 village boys for whom apprenticeships were arranged in twenty-one different trades in Bristol and its nearby villages between 1680 and 1780, ninety-one (54 per cent) served in the single occupation of feltmaking.[27] In all, fifty-five (71 per cent) of the seventy-eight rural boys in the other twenty occupations combined stayed in the local villages, and twenty-seven (35 per cent) of those seventy-eight boys stayed in their home villages. Every one of the ninety-one local village boys in feltmaking served his apprenticeship in one of the villages within Bristol's rural environs. Of the trades more readily available in the city or remoter places, those trades in which few if any local villagers indentured apprentices, weaving was clearly the one most commonly pursued by the other boys in this group, but the prospect of a weaving apprenticeship in Bristol attracted only seven of them, or 4 per cent of the total. To be sure, village weavers, who were connected with urban distributors, were an intergral force in early modern textile production.[28] But it appears that the training experiences of many rural weavers either involved an early retreat from urban apprenticeship or took place at the feet of fellow villagers in the rural setting, outside the administrative conventions and cultural context of the urban guild system.

Weaving and feltmaking were different in many important respects. Feltmaking was a craft at which rural folk could work without leaving their yards and hearths. A considerable amount of weaving was done in the cottages of Somerset and Gloucestershire, but boiling and pressing wool were a far cry from weaving, which involved complex and expensive machinery. Weavers, links in a chain of specialised textile workers, collected spun fleece from various sources beyond their own villages and towns. Feltmakers operated on a small scale and could get by with raw fleece from their own sheep.[29] Consequently the feltmaking operation and its labour force were highly localised. The fathers of rural feltmakers were feltmakers themselves, with the exception of a few labourers and miners. Feltmakers were neither geographically nor socially mobile and surely more than one boy lost his apprenticeship when his feltmaking father was 'reduced to poverty'.[30]

Feltmaking was the typical craft of the rural poor but no city as large as Bristol could be without practitioners of such a common trade. In fact, Bristol feltmakers took on apprentices throughout the century or so following 1660. During seven sample years taken at twenty-year intervals, nine boys apprenticed themselves to feltmaking in Bristol.[31] Five of these were of Bristol origin and their fathers included a mason and a pewterer. In 1720 the son of a brewer from Dublin, Ireland, and the son of a weaver from a remote English village apprenticed themselves to Bristol feltmakers. The indenture fees were minimal and in at least one case were paid by one of Bristol's charitable organisations. If there was an affordable craft in Bristol to which local village boys or girls were predisposed it was feltmaking. And yet, of roughly 180 local villagers apprenticed in the city in these sample years spanning more than a century, only two apprenticed themselves to Bristol feltmakers. The case of feltmaking illustrates that the geographical, financial, and technical accessibility of a popular apprenticeship was not enough to draw job-seeking local villagers into Bristol's urban workplace.

There is one set of related trades which no study of Bristol's work force can ignore: the building, repairing, stocking, rigging, and, above all, sailing of ships. Alexander Pope, a visitor to Bristol in the early eighteenth century, remarked that as one approached the city it appeared to be made up of a thousand vessels, 'their masts as thick as they can stand by one another'.[32] The visibility of mariners, combined with the dangerous and precarious nature of their employment, made fluctuations in their number and casualties conspicuous signs of more general trends in a port city's economy and society.[33] During wartime, men were actually pressed into naval service and died in droves. A dramatic rise in the numbers of Bristol mariners in the first half of the eighteenth century was a barometer of Bristol's changing status among English ports. The history of England's eighteenth-century maritime communities features the furious rivalry between Bristol and Liverpool. Bristol's import and export tonnage continued to increase after 1760 but by that time Bristol had been boldly eclipsed by Liverpool in virtually every department. Unlike Liverpool, Bristol had failed to channel the raw materials from its own rural environs into exports.[34] As we have seen, Bristol's command over the human resources of the nearby villages was also limited.

Bristol's vitality as an international port created a local demand for a host of support occupations far too diverse in character to form a single category. These occupations are conventionally referred to collectively as maritime trades, but the term mariner applies only to seafaring sailors, navigators, and officers. The skills and tools that urban shipwrights and anchorsmiths used were also at the disposal of carpenters and blacksmiths working in landlocked hinterland villages. On the other hand, mariners, more than Bristol's other workers, held jobs that were linked inextricably with the natural and artificial environments in which they were performed. Mariners were openly aware of the extent to which their work environment was a unique and defining characteristic of their occupational identity, reflected in their specialised language, garb, and code of conduct.[35] Only a small portion of Bristol's mariners bothered to apprentice themselves, because their chosen trade could be plied without freeman status. They were, as Marcus Rediker has argued, citizens of an Atlantic community.

Is it possible that the port of Bristol and the villages in the surrounding countryside were so economically specialised, in distinct ways, that the residents of the two settings found interaction difficult? Was the occupational profile of Bristol so alien to the neighbouring villagers that the city could neither attract job seekers from within the confines of its own rural environs nor train its own citizens to work in the rural setting? After all, Bristol was swarming with mariners whom contemporaries openly regarded as undisciplined, 'rowdy', and 'foul-mouthed'.[36] Let us not limit our discussion to farmers, feltmakers and mariners. Consider the relations among occupational heritage, occupational inclination and geographical origin for all types of Bristol apprentices.[37]

The occupation held by a child's father, either urban or rural, did not play a role, to any surprising degree, in determining whether that child would become an apprentice in Bristol. In the early seventeenth century, there was an apparent tendency for those children who were apprenticed in Bristol to follow in their fathers' footsteps[38] but this did not translate into any clear relationship between occupational heritage and apprentice migration to the city during the century after 1660. A few patterns did take shape. It is scarcely surprising, however, that those apprentices who came to Bristol from rural areas tended to be the sons of farmers, husbandmen and yeomen, members of the most common occupations in the villages. Professionals' and gentlemen's sons also arrived in significantly high numbers from more distant rural areas, but not from villages near Bristol. Mariners' sons from villages beyond Bristol's own rural environs were significantly rare among Bristol apprentices in the seventeenth century; either extramural mariners were rare or an affinity for rural life was stronger than one for an occupation at sea. The number of apprentices of Bristol origin who came from woodworkers' and builders' households was surprisingly high from one year to the next. Apart from this, the assortment of occupations held by the fathers of apprentices from Bristol itself did not conform to any strong patterns. Indeed, for the most part the occupational heritage of urban and rural children and adolescents apprenticed in Bristol after 1660 was not part of some ordered pattern linked to geographical mobility or place of origin.

Similarly, with only a few exceptions, the various occupations of the Bristol masters with whom both migrant apprentices and those of Bristol origin placed themselves were not readily distinguishable in terms of the geographical origins of the apprentices drawn to them. In the seventeenth century, the few local villagers who did apprentice themselves in Bristol did tend to associate themselves with leather and textile work, manual arts which made use of materials familiar to rural migrants. Apprentices from more remote villages also followed this trend, which persisted until the middle of the eighteenth century despite the tidal influx of mariners and the growing emphasis on maritime trades which could be learned in the city. There was a significant expansion of local villagers into Bristol's food and beverage industry by 1720. This was short-lived, however, and within two decades they were entirely displaced by food and beverage apprentices from areas beyond Bristol's rural environs. In the late seventeenth century, apprentices from more distant villages were associated with mariners, but within forty years they made a thorough transition to commerce and developed a significant and absolute aversion to seafaring apprenticeships. Apprentices who came to Bristol from other cities and towns exhibited no significant preferences for any occupation except for a brief inclination towards commerce in the mid-eighteenth century. Bristol adolescents who took up apprenticeships in their own city were even more randomly distributed among all occupational groups. In sum, the few correlations between apprentices' place of origin and their chosen occupation were temporary and fluctuated wildly, in contradictory fashions, over time. Thus the consistently poor showing of local villagers among Bristol's apprentices can hardly be explained by their occupational inclinations.

Perhaps the connections governing long-term, personal interaction in the workplace were formed among practitioners of similar trades, regardless of their places of origin. If this were true of urban and rural interaction, we should expect to find some meaningful correlations between the occupations of Bristol masters and the occupations of the village fathers whose sons were apprenticed in the city. There were a few interesting combinations of occupational heritage and inclination that suggest possible business connections between the fathers and masters of a handful of apprentices in Bristol. In 1680 a Clifton lighterman, or small boat pilot, apprenticed his son to a Bristol shipwright, as did a Clifton mariner in 1700. In 1780 a butcher from Stoke Gifford apprenticed his son to a Bristol currier of leather. Examples such as these are uncommon, but they invite further examination of the question.

Consider the 179 apprentices from local villages who were entered into apprenticeships in Bristol in seven sample years at twenty-year intervals from 1660 through 1780. The occupations of the local villagers whose sons were apprenticed in Bristol and the occupations of the Bristol masters themselves fell into nine widely recognised general categories: mariner, service, woodwork and construction, leather and textile work, metal and mineral work, food and drink preparation, professions, agriculture, and, of course, commerce.[39] Specific comparisons between the chosen trades of apprentices and those of their fathers suggest that neither occupational affinity nor the availability of urban masters discouraged or promoted the movement of local villagers into urban apprenticeships; very few of the relationships were significantly common or significantly rare.[40] (Table 5.2.) The four gentlemen's and professionals' sons apprenticed in Bristol's service sector were surprisingly numerous, given the very limited number gentlemen's and professionals' sons spread through a range of seven general occupational categories. That three of the six sons of village merchants attached themselves to metal or mineral work is worth noting, but no close practical link between commerce and forging is obvious (unless we imagine that Bristol metalworkers privately minted coins). At the same time, professionals, a group we may associate with merchants, were noteworthy for sending no sons at all into Bristol's metal trades. The fraction of the whole group involved in any meaningful correlatation was far too small to suggest that connections between rural fathers and urban masters explained the apprenticeship choices of young villagers living near Bristol.[41]

Village children were too rarely apprenticed in Bristol in their fathers' trades to indicate that occupational affinity was the principal influence behind the movement of rural apprentices to the city, or the lack of such movement. There was an abundance of woodworking and building masters in Bristol, enough to take fifty-three apprentices from the nearby villages alone. This made woodwork and construction the most popular group of trades among local village children and adolescents apprenticed in Bristol. The widespread

Table 5.2 Occupational heritage and inclination of local villagers apprenticed in Bristol in seven sample years, 1660–1780

| Fathers' occupation | Bristol masters' occupations | | | | | | | | | |
|---|---|---|---|---|---|---|---|---|---|---|
| | Agr. | Mar. | Com. | Ser. | B&W | T&L | M&M | F&D | Pro. | Totals |
| Agriculture | o | 3 | 11 | 4 | 27 | 19 | 7 | 4 | o | 75 |
| Maritime | o | o | 1 | 1 | 2 | o | 2 | o | o | 6 |
| Commerce | o | 1 | o | o | 1 | o | **3+** | 1 | o | 6 |
| Service | o | o | 1 | o | 1 | 1 | o | o | o | 3 |
| Building and woodwork | o | 1 | 2 | o | 9 | 4 | 2 | 1 | o | 19 |
| Textile and leatherwork | o | 3 | 1 | 1 | 2 | 8 | 4 | 2 | o | 21 |
| Mineral and metalwork | o | 1 | 1 | o | 7 | 7 | 5 | 3 | o | 24 |
| Food and drink preparation | o | o | 1 | o | 2 | 2 | 1 | 1 | o | 7 |
| Professional | o | **3+** | 3 | **4+** | **2−** | 4 | **0−** | 2 | o | 18 |
| Totals | o | 12 | 21 | 10 | 53 | 45 | 24 | 14 | o | 179 |

*Note:* Bold figures indicate contingencies that were significantly common (+) or rare (−).
*Source:* B.R.O. Corporation of Bristol Apprenticeship Registers.

activity of that trade in the rural setting as well was indicated by the nineteen sons of village builders and woodworkers. The other such occupational group was leather and textile work. With forty-five apprentices it was second only to woodworking and construction in popularity among local villagers apprenticed in Bristol. Twenty-one fathers of apprentices who went to Bristol practised leather work or textile work in the nearby villages. It was true that, in the case of the two most popular occupational groups among migrant apprentices, seventeen (43 per cent) of the forty rural children of men in these occupations went to Bristol into the same occupations, or ones quite similar. But this accounted for less than one tenth of all the Bristol apprentices drawn from the nearby villages. Moreover, woodwork, construction, leather work, and textile work accounted for most of the apprenticeships held in Bristol by local villagers in general. Of the seventy-five local farmers' children apprenticed in Bristol, forty-six (61 per cent) were in these two occupational groups, with no apparent heritable affinity for them. Among local villagers, the children of fathers who engaged in metal or mineral work were second only to farmers' children in Bristol apprenticeships, but they were drawn more often to construction and woodworking or leather and textile work than to metalwork, their fathers' own trade.

Adults at work also moved through separate urban and rural spheres. Of course not all of Bristol's freemen lived in the city. In 1720 a shipwright living in the neighbouring village of Clifton, Gloucestershire, took his own son as an apprentice and registered him with the Bristol corporation.[42] The activity of extramural merchants and artisans in the city diminished, rather than increased, during the urban renaissance until the enforcement of corporate statutes began to relax after the middle of the eighteenth century. Legal action taken against unprivileged businesses was common before the general decline of the guild system. In the late seventeenth century local trade laws barring non-freemen were even invoked strategically by Bristolians, in isolated instances, to harass political opponents and religious dissenters[43] or to exclude outsiders who tried to establish permanent retail shops in the city.[44] Bristol's lively seasonal fairs did encourage extramural people to conduct their business in the city on a temporary basis, but artisans and vendors who travelled to the city on these terms were mainly urban in origin.

The employment of specialised artisans from other cities was a common practice of urban parish vestries. As early as 1678 All Saints employed a full-time church maintenance staff, including a carpenter, a plumber, a mason, and a tiler. They were all from Bristol. But in the eighteenth century, when the All Saints vestry no longer confined its work force to fellow Bristol residents, they recruited artisans through the extended urban network. In 1738 the vestry of All Saints paid the healthy sum of £250 to an organ builder whom they brought in from the county town of Warwick. Eleven years earlier they had hired a bellfounder to undertake the recasting of the church bells. He came down from the city of Gloucester to do the job.[45]

By the same token, parishes in Bristol's rural environs were reluctant to tap the urban supply of professionals and specialised artisans. In 1737, when All Saints hired a lawyer to attend to the vestry's budget management, it selected one from among several readily available in the city. Only two years later, the parish officials in Brislington, Somerset, were forced to look outside their own village when they needed to engage the full-time services of an attorney. They hired a lawyer from the large village of Keynsham, Somerset, not from the city of Bristol, which was, in fact, closer.[46] There were periodic demands for bell repairs in the village churches near Bristol. But in 1765, when Brislington required the expertise of a bellfounder, the parish officials hired one from Chew Stoke, in Somerset, not from the nearby city. There is remarkably little evidence of Bristol artisans working for rural vestries until the end of the early modern period. In December 1771 the vestry of St Luke, Brislington, began an ambitious new parish housing project, a sign of suburban development in the villages. By that time they did advertise for masons and carpenters in a Bristol newspaper.[47] As for wealthy individuals in the surrounding countryside, the gentry exhibited an early preference for London professionals and artisans, or for members of their own family who occasionally took up residence in Bristol. By the last decades of the early modern period, gentry with residences in the nearby countryside did patronise Bristol's own fashionable specialists. In 1764 Sir John Hugh Smyth of Somerset's Ashton Court wrote in his accounts, 'paid Mr Paty for a chimney piece ... in my room at Ashton £23 19s 6d'. Few villagers would have paid that much for a fireplace.[48]

Even those rural adults who were highly mobile did not come to rest in the Bristol workplace and many skirted it. Of all extant settlement examinations administered in villages near Bristol, thirty-one (twenty-five men and six women) give details regarding the lifelong itineraries of working applicants for parish settlement. The evidence offers a look at skilled and mobile adults, with considerable experience and lengthy occupational histories, whose examinations were held throughout our period in various parts of Bristol's rural environs.[49] It is important to stress that these villagers were steadily employed, with only rare and brief lapses into jobless wanderings. All told, these rural workers made more than ninety moves to places of residence and occupations other than their own villages of origin. This amounts to an average of three moves per person.[50] One unmarried woman, identified as a servant in 1750, had moved more than seven times before her twentieth birthday. By the time she applied for settlement in the village of Bitton, five miles from Bristol, she had never lived or worked in the city. Barbers, perukemakers, masons and other skilled villagers reported having moved at least four times. Out of this entire sample of working villagers, only four had lived or worked in Bristol at any time. There is no record in these settlement examinations of any local villager living or working in Bristol between 1743 and 1767. There was an earlier lengthier period between 1695 and 1741 during which none of these mobile villagers was employed in the nearby city. An equal number of settlement applicants had moved through areas beyond Bristol's rural environs, but the vast majority of the local villagers simply moved about within ten miles of the city. There was no overlap between the two small groups who either ventured into Bristol or directly away from it. Around the time of the Restoration, one man who was steadily employed in Bristol for a period of four years chose to move about the countryside with his wife, living in the Somerset villages of Odcombe, Street, and Bruton, rather than reside in the city.[51] Apparently, as adults, most able-bodied villagers of all skill levels stayed put, left the vicinity of Bristol altogether, or engaged in a deliberate circumvention of the city throughout their adult working careers.

The patterns of movement in and around Bristol between 1660 and 1780 directly challenge, rather than support, the notion of an urban sphere of influence. They suggest that popular awareness and cultural forces, and not just the mechanics of economy, demography, and mobility, were behind the separation of urban and rural social spheres. As we have seen, an effort to explain this gulf through some analysis of the roles of wealth, occupation, gender, and age supplies neither sufficient nor consistent answers. On the other hand, the one constant was the tendency of urban and rural dwellers alike to associate closely with people whose setting of origin was similar to their own. That is to say, the patterns of deliberate, long-term, close personal interaction observed for Bristol and its rural environs may be explained in large part by the powerful influence of environmental affinities. Urbanisation, the process whereby rates of population growth in cities and towns exceed those of society as a whole, was taking place, without a doubt, in early modern England. It is widely accepted that migration, rather than natural growth or declining mortality, was the principal cause of early modern urbanisation.[52] These demographic facts are in no way inconsistent with the picture of personal interaction presented here. Migrants from remote areas contributed far more than local villagers did to Bristol's urbanisation. Neither proximity to a major city nor movement through it drew many villagers into close association with urban people. It is not clear that those villagers whose movements through cities were recorded stayed for long. Considering that a villager could put a brief stint of urban training happily to use, free of guild restrictions, back home in the rural setting, we should not assume that citizenship was the aim of every rural apprentice in a city.[53]

The unpleasant experiences of some villagers were linked in their minds with life and work in the city. Some time around 1692 Deborah Monck, a single woman from the Gloucestershire village of Oldland, made the short trip into Bristol, where she took a position as servant in the household of a shipwright in St Stephen. By 1694 she was petitioning Oldland's parish overseers to let her return to the village. They refused, on the grounds that she would need parish aid. She blamed her desperate condition on the fact that the Bristol shipwright's apprentice had got her pregnant and then abandoned her when the shipwright turned both of them out.[54] Fifty years later, an applicant for settlement in the village of Bitton in 1742 related that he had moved there from the village of Keynsham, Somerset, some years earlier, at the age of eleven, to live with his father for one year. He took an apprenticeship with a Bristol weaver in St Stephen, but after only six months the weaver persuaded a man in St Philip and Jacob to make use of the boy. The boy was so severely abused by his new master that he fled back to the country after having spent less than a year in the city. He 'lurked about' until the Bitton village blacksmith rescued him and taught him to cook.[55] Unpleasant experiences of this kind were not unique to the urban setting. Nevertheless, the observation that villagers migrated to cities and towns must be tempered by consideration of the fact that, for many rural migrants, their encounters with the city were alienating and brief.

The lack of long-term, deliberate personal interaction between members of the urban and rural populations and the surprisingly high levels of endogamy, localism, and segregation in both Bristol and its rural environs cannot be explained simply by reference to impersonal forces. The citizens of Bristol and the inhabitants of nearby villages interacted far less closely than we might expect, given the geographical mobility of the population and the size and economic importance of the city. The persistent urban–rural gulf was an expression of choices informed by attitudes and environmental affinities. Thus we must move from an understanding of the limited interaction between urban and rural social spheres to an exploration of the humanly determined physical surroundings, or material cultures, with which members of those urban and rural spheres identified.

## NOTES

1  S. R. Smith, 'London apprentices as seventeenth-century adolescents', *Past and Present* 61 (1973), pp. 149–61. In 'The social and geographical origins of London apprentices 1630–1660', *Guildhall Miscellany* 4 (1973), pp. 195–206, Smith argues that London's catchment area expanded but offers no detailed analysis of the interaction of urban and rural apprentices in the same workshops.

2  James Fretwell, *A Family History*, cited in I. K. Ben-Amos, *Adolescence and Youth in Early Modern England* (New Haven, Conn., 1994), p. 68.

3  Ben-Amos, *Adolescence and Youth in Early Modern England*, pp. 100–1.

4  D. H. Sacks, *The Widening Gate: Bristol and the Atlantic Economy 1450–1700* (Berkeley, Cal., 1991), pp. 252–3.

5  E. and S. George (eds), *Guide to the Probate Inventories of the Bristol Deanery of the Diocese of Bristol 1542–1804* (Bristol, 1988), pp. 270, 283, and throughout. In the eighteenth century half the probate inventories recorded by the Bristol diocese were for mariners who had no property apart from what they had aboard ship.

6  B. Little, *The City and County of Bristol: A Study in Atlantic Civilization* (London, 1954), p. 142.

7  Ben-Amos, *Adolescence and Youth in Early Modern England*, p. 102.

8  Examples are found in B.R.O. P/StLB/OP/15(h)ii (Nos 82, 88, 105, and 106); B.R.O. P/W/OP/15 (Nos 16, 26, and 73).

9  B.R.O. #04356(15), Corporation of Bristol Apprenticeship Registers (1770–87).

10  Ben-Amos, *Adolescence and Youth in Early Modern England*, pp. 102 and 177–82.

11  *Ibid.*, pp. 85–86, 99, and 282–3; S. Rappaport, *Worlds within Worlds: Structures of Life in Sixteenth-Century London* (Cambridge, 1989), p. 81; M. J. Kitch, 'Capital and kingdom: migration to later Stuart London', in A. L. Beier and R. Finlay (eds), *London 1500–1700: The Making of the Metropolis* (London, 1986), p. 234.

12  Sacks, *The Widening Gate*, p. 351, and *Trade, Society and Politics in Bristol 1500–1640*, 2 vols (Garland, 1985), pp. 502–5; J. R. Holman, 'Apprenticeship as a factor in migration:

Bristol, 1675–1726', *Transactions of the Bristol and Gloucestershire Archaeological Society* 97 (1979), pp. 85–92; J. Wareing, 'Changes in the geographical distribution of the recruitment of apprentices to the London companies 1486–1750', *Journal of Historical Geography* 7 (1981), pp. 241–50.

13 P. Clark, 'Migrants in the city: the process of social adaptation in English towns 1500–1800', in Clark and Souden, *Migration and Society in Early Modern England*, pp. 285–6.

14 P. Corfield, *The Impact of English Towns 1700–1800* (Oxford, 1982), p. 102.

15 For the pre-adaptation of rural shepherds and farmers to metalworking trades, see P. Large, 'Urban growth and agricultural change in the West Midlands during the seventeenth and eighteenth centuries', in P. Clark (ed.), *The Transformation of English Provincial Towns 1600–1800* (London, 1984), pp. 175–6.

16 Sacks, *The Widening Gate*, pp. 252–3; P. W. Coldham, 'The "spiriting" of London children to Virginia 1648–1685', *Virginia Magazine of History and Biography* 83 (1975), pp. 280–8. Sacks also presents a thorough analysis of P. W. Coldham (ed.), *The Bristol Registers of Servants sent to Foreign Plantations 1654–86* (Baltimore, Md, 1988).

17 M. Rediker, *Between the Devil and the Deep Blue Sea: Merchant Seamen, Pirates, and the Anglo-American Maritime World 1700–50* (Cambridge, 1987), pp. 13–14 and 81–2; E. Barlow, *Barlow's Journal of his Life at Sea 1659–1703*, ed. B. Lubbock (London, 1934), pp. 81–2.

18 Ben-Amos, *Adolescence and Youth in Early Modern England*, especially chs 2–6; R. Porter, *English Society in the Eighteenth Century* (Harmondsworth, 1982), pp. 100–4; P. Seaver, 'A social contract? Master against servant in the Court of Requests', *History Today* 39 (1989), pp. 50–6; anon., *Relief of Apprentices wronged by their Masters* (1687).

19 M. Pelling, 'Child health as a social value in early modern England', *Social History of Medicine* 1 (1988), pp. 135–64; L. M. Beier, *Sufferers and Healers: The Experience of Illness in Seventeenth-Century England* (London, 1987), pp. 56–7 and 170–1; A. Kussmaul, *Servants in Husbandry in Early Modern England* (Cambridge, 1981), p. 32. For the case of the apprentice at the Bath spa, see Chancery Court C3/304/68 (Claye v. Quashe, 1620), as cited in Ben-Amos, *Adolescence and Youth in Early Modern England*, p. 172.

20 B.R.O. P/FC/OP/5(48), Frampton Cotterell, Gloucestershire: Overseers of the Poor.

21 P. Sharpe, 'Poor children as apprentices in Colyton 1598–1830', *Continuity and Change* 6 (1991), pp. 253–69.

22 See, for example, B.R.O. P/StLB/V/1, St Luke, Brislington, Somerset: Vestry Book (1741–46).

23 B.R.O. P/OV/OP/14(1–42), Olveston, Gloucestershire: Overseers of the Poor; B.R.O. P/B/OP/7a(1–62), Bitton, Gloucestershire: Overseers of the Poor; B.R.O. P/StLB/OP/15(h)i, ii(1–33), St Luke, Brislington, Somerset: Overseers of the Poor; B.R.O. P/W/OP/15(1–249), Westerleigh, Gloucestershire: Overseers of the Poor.

24 B.R.O. P/StS/OP, St Stephen, Bristol: Overseers of the Poor.

25 B.R.O. P/OV/OP/14(1–42); B.R.O. P/FC/OP/5(1–86); B.R.O. P/B/OP/7a(1–62); B.R.O. P/StLB/OP/15(h)i(1–77), ii(78–123); B.R.O. P/W/OP/15(1–249). The villages are Olveston, Frampton Cotterell, Bitton, and Westerleigh in Gloucestershire, and Brislington in Somerset.

26 George and George, *Guide to the Probate Inventories of the Bristol Deanery*, pp. 276–8,

281–2, and 285. Practitioners of these trades were among the more abundant ones in Bristol over the entire early modern period. Of the five occupational groups, tilers and plasterers left the fewest extant inventories.

27  B.R.O. P/OV/OP/14(1–42); B.R.O. P/FC/OP/5(1–86); B.R.O. P/B/OP/7a(1–62); B.R.O. P/StLB/OP/15(h)i(1–77), ii(78–123); B.R.O. P/W/OP/15(1–249).

28  M. Spufford, *The Great Reclothing of Rural England: Petty Chapmen and their Wares in the Seventeenth Century* (London, 1984); J. de L. Mann, *The Cloth Industry in the West of England from 1640 to 1880* (Oxford, 1971).

29  De L. Mann, *The Cloth Industry in the West of England*, provides a thorough treatment of the rural textile industry and its connections with urban centres. For a brief explanation of the craft techniques, see D. Hartley, *Lost Country Life* (New York, 1979), p. 135.

30  B.R.O. P/FC/OP/5(1), Overseers of the Poor of Frampton Cotterell Apprenticeship Indentures (1737).

31  B.R.O. Corporation of Bristol Apprenticeship Registers. The sample years are 1660, 1680, 1700, 1720, 1740, 1760, and 1780.

32  W. Hunt, *Bristol* (London, 1895), p. 175, as cited in Rediker, *Between the Devil and the Deep Blue Sea*, p. 42.

33  B.R.O. Diocese of Bristol Probate Inventories and Cause Papers. Nearly 20 per cent of all Bristol inventories taken from 1701 to 1709 were for mariners and 34·5 per cent from 1710 through 1729. But in 1764 only 14 per cent of all Bristol inventories were for mariners.

34  K. Morgan, *Bristol and the Atlantic Trade in the Eighteenth Century* (Cambridge, 1993); F. E. Hyde (ed.), *Liverpool and the Mersey: An Economic History of a Port, 1700–1970* (Newton Abbot, 1971); W. E. Minchinton (ed.), *The Trade of Bristol in the Eighteenth Century* (Bristol, 1957). A good summary of the rivalry between the two ports is provided in P. Corfield, *The Impact of English Towns 1700–1800* (Oxford, 1982), pp. 41–2. For the additional point that Bristol's commitment to the slave trade contributed to its decline, see D. Eltis, *Economic Growth and the Ending of the Transatlantic Slave Trade* (Oxford, 1987), chs 1 and 2; and C. B. Estabrook, 'Bristol and the Atlantic Trade in the Eighteenth Century: a review', *Albion* 27 no. 2 (1995), pp. 312–13.

35  Rediker, *Between the Devil and the Deep Blue Sea*, ch. 4.

36  *Ibid.*, p. 153.

37  Several two-way contingency tables are needed to analyse the correlations involving the occupations of apprentices' fathers, the occupations of apprentices' masters, and the apprentices' places of origin for the 1,442 apprentices registered by the corporation of Bristol during the sample years 1660, 1680, 1700, 1720, 1740, 1760, and 1780. My remarks here are based on repeated analyses performed on such contingency tables with the use of a computerised technique as explained in C. B. Estabrook and G. F. Estabrook, 'ACTUS: a solution to the problem of small samples in the analysis of two-way contingency tables', *Historical Methods* 22 no. 1 (1989), pp. 5–8.

38  Ben-Amos, *Adolescence and Youth in Early Modern England*, pp. 159 and 282.

39  In addition to conforming to categories used in comparable studies, these analytical groupings have the advantage of emphasising the materials and skills involved in an occupation and not the locally variable levels of social status associated with those occupations. W. A. Armstrong, 'The use of information about occupation', in E. A. Wrigley (ed.), *Nineteenth-Century Society* (Cambridge, 1971), pp. 191–253. These categories

are adopted in studies of early modern occupational profiles as well. See, for example, J. Ellis, 'A dynamic society: social relations in Newcastle-upon-Tyne 1660–1760', in Clark, *The Transformation of English Provincial Towns*, p. 194; J. Boulton, *Neighbourhood and Society: A London Suburb in the Seventeenth Century* (Cambridge, 1987), pp. 66–73.

40 Estabrook and Estabrook, 'ACTUS', explains the method of quantitative analysis applied to the contingency tables in this book.

41 Out of the 179 Bristol apprentices of local rural origin only twelve (6·1 per cent ) were involved in statistically significant or noteworthy correlations between father's occupation and master's occupation. Out of the eighty-one occupational pairings (nine categories for fathers and masters), only five (6·2 per cent ) were statistically significant or noteworthy contingencies, and one of these (the pairing of professional father and metalworking master) was noteworthy for the lack of any apprentice with that combination of occupational choice and occupational heritage.

42 B.R.O. #04354, Corporation of Bristol Apprenticeship Registers (1711–24).

43 See, for example, B.R.O. #04452(1), Bristol Quarter Sessions (Easter term, 1682).

44 See, for example: B.R.O. #04452(1), Bristol Quarter Sessions (Michaelmas term, 1694).

45 B.R.O. P/AS/V/1(a), All Saints, Bristol: Order Book (1650–1750).

46 B.R.O. P/StLB/V/1, St Luke, Brislington, Somerset: Vestry Book (1739–53).

47 B.R.O. P/StLB/V/2, St Luke, Brislington, Somerset: Vestry Book (1753–1825).

48 A. Bantock (ed.), *The Later Smyths of Ashton Court from their Letters 1741–1802* (Bristol, 1984), p. 128.

49 B.R.O. P/B/OP/6/g(1–36), Bitton, Gloucestershire, Overseers of the Poor: Settlement Examinations (1723–49); B.R.O. P/StLB/OP/10/(1–15), St Luke, Brislington, Somerset, Overseers of the Poor: Settlement Examinations (1695–1780); B.R.O. P/FC/OP/4/(1–14), Frampton Cotterell, Gloucestershire, Overseers of the Poor: Settlement Examinations (1733–79). At least fifteen of these itinerant villagers had held jobs requiring a high level of skill. The ages of sixteen applicants are known and all but one applicant was over the age of twenty at the time of his or her examination. All but five were over the age of thirty and some of these were over forty. Of the nineteen whose marital status was recorded, fifteen were married.

50 Named destinations are counted here as one move. References to 'diverse places' are counted as 1·5 moves. Thus these calculations present a conservative picture of mobility.

51 S.R.O. Q/SR/102(46), Somerset Quarter Sessions (Midsummer term, 1662).

52 J. de Vries, *European Urbanization 1500–1800* (Cambridge, Mass., 1984); R. Finlay and A. Sharlin, 'Debate: natural decrease in early modern cities', *Past and Present* 92 (1981), pp. 169–80.

53 Rappaport, *Worlds within Worlds*, pp. 76–7 and 311–14; I. K. Ben-Amos, 'The failure to become freemen: urban apprentices in early modern England', *Social History* 16 no. 2 (1991), p. 157, and *Adolescence and Youth in Early Modern England*, pp. 120–1, 130, and 301.

54 B.R.O. P/StS/OP, Overseers of the Poor of St Stephen, Bristol: Settlement Papers (1695–1712).

55 B.R.O. P/B/OP/6/g(12), Bitton, Gloucestershire, Overseers of the Poor: Settlement Examinations (1742–43).

# Chapter 6

## Material culture: dwellings and possessions

J oseph Marks occupied a comfortable house in the city of Bristol during the urban renaissance.[1] Marks was not struggling, but neither was he wealthy. All his assets, credits, and possessions combined were valued at only £48 17s 7d prior to the payment of his debts and the settlement of his estate in April 1746. Despite his relatively humble means, Marks occupied eight rooms and had access to a cellar. His dwelling space was vertically arranged on three levels: four rooms on the ground level, two in the storey above the ground floor, and two more in the storey above that.[2] This type of multi-level dwelling, only one room in width but extending two or more rooms back from the street, conformed to an early modern standard of urban architectural design and was typical of houses occupied by rich and poor alike in English towns and cities from the fifteenth century through the eighteenth.[3] Two of the ground-floor rooms (the 'pantry' and the 'back parlour') were clearly subordinate spaces attached to the 'kitchen' and 'parlour'. All four of the upper rooms in the house contained beds. As Marks walked through the first storey toward the back of the house he came to the most expensively and most comfortably furnished of these bedrooms, the first-storey 'back room'. It was located in the warmth above the kitchen and was insulated, by the other first-storey room, from the noises, smells and commotion of the street below. Marks had plenty of speciality items in the rooms downstairs and thirteen pictures were on display there. One of the rooms at street level was well equipped to welcome guests with hospitality. Marks brewed coffee in his kitchen, at the back of the house, but served his guests in his 'parlour', where he kept a dozen china cups and saucers, eight 'chocolate cups', a teapot, a pier glass, a clock and case valued at £2 2s, a 'japanned' cupboard and five silver spoons. Wigs hung in his wardrobe. In the warmth of his kitchen, below his own bedroom, Marks may have dressed and performed morning ablutions before the mirror there.

John Jayne was nearly eight times wealthier than Joseph Marks, his urban contemporary whose home we just visited, but Jayne's house in a spacious village had six rooms, two fewer than Marks's dwelling.[4] Jayne was a yeoman farmer in Almondsbury, a Gloucestershire village only seven miles north of the centre of Bristol. In 1752 his total assets were valued at £381 18s 5d. His house included garrets, or spaces beneath the rafters, where Jayne stored ample supplies of cheese but little else. Jayne and his family did all their sleeping, eating, socialising, and living on the ground floor of the house. Jayne and his family had no parlour; the centre of household and private social gatherings in their home was the kitchen. While Marks used a portion of his income to buy a tea service, pictures, mirrors, and wigs Jayne was committed to a significant investment in livestock and arable land by virtue of his livelihood. It ought to be noted of farmers such as Jayne that their land, unlike Marks's chocolate pot, produced revenue. From one of his tenants farming in Somerset[5] Jayne collected £6 5s per annum, enough to buy, every year, a new matching set of all the most valuable finished goods in Joseph Marks's parlour. And yet Jayne chose not to do anything of the sort. He possessed only one such item, a clock and case valued at £2 12s 6d.

These two homes and their furnishings, as examples of the contrasting dwelling spaces and possessions of an urban dweller and a villager in provincial England, are representative rather than exceptional. Although people like Marks and Jayne had neither the resources nor the power of the gentry, the artificial surroundings that they maintained expressed active choices and meaningful preferences. A close examination of thousands of other dwellings, and the objects that their occupants used and cared for, provides some revealing glimpses into the divergent material cultures of early modern England. The extent to which urban manufactured goods and imported items made their way out of the urban market place and achieved some connection between the separate worlds of urban and rural dwellers was surprisingly limited for much of the early modern period. Dwellings and possessions, through which sociability was mediated, conveyed a constellation of signals about status, values, taste, and power. Material culture must be discussed with reference to wealth, occupations, and gender awareness, but the strongest factors guiding the ownership of possessions and the uses of dwelling space were the urbane and rustic attitudes associated with topographical settings.

Sadly, there are very few buildings still standing in Bristol that date from the seventeenth and eighteenth centuries. We can still visit the house in which Thomas Chatterton, the ill-fated poet, was born in 1752, but the Pineapple, his local tavern, is gone. The impressive Llandoger Trow, built in 1664 in King Street and named for the Welsh barges that docked near by, survives as an example of a multi-storey urban inn and tavern. It was certainly a colourful gathering spot, full of maritime characters, including, quite probably, Alexander Selkirk, the sailor whose life inspired Defoe's creation of Robinson

Crusoe.[6] What did visitors to the homes of real urban and rural dwellers encounter in the century or so after 1660? Did the material culture of the domestic scene represent a tie or another gulf between urban and rural social spheres? What evidence survives to move us into this private theatre of manners to bring the actors, with their props and costumes, to life? English probate inventories, even more than architectural remains and literary impressions, are an abundant and appropriate source on which to base a systematic analysis of domestic material culture and its place in social interaction.

It must now be said that English inventories of the early modern period are more useful to the cultural historian than to the economic historian. These documents record what ordinary people thought various possessions were worth, not the actual value of goods (the prices at which goods had been bought and sold).[7] By the same token, as we will see, these sources provide a wonderful sense of perspective; they tell us a great deal about the range of attitudes concerning domestic spaces, physical objects, and their use. It is the very idiosyncratic nature of early modern English inventories that helps to expose perceived hierarchies of possessions, to identify the perceived places of various objects in the home or in relation to each other, and to characterise the roles of various rooms in urban and rural dwellings. Assessors, who took the inventories, sometimes itemised household objects in groups according to perceived types rather than room locations. This was one way in which assessors expressed various attitudes towards possessions of special interest. For example, as objects books were either given special attention by assessors or inventoried in combination with a varied assortment of possessions ranging from leather goods and linens to medicines and spectacles. Far more than just tallying a deceased testator's gross assets, therefore, an English probate inventory captured a picture of a house and its contents as seen and interpreted by the occupant's neighbours, friends or relatives who drew up the account.[8] The vocabulary, detail, and emphasis of an English inventory are likely to convey something of the prevailing mentality of the home it describes.

An English probate inventory, although exhibited to a diocese for approval, was created by an ordinary person who was usually very familiar with the deceased and quite possibly of the same status or occupation. The inventory of one house in the village of Stapleton tells us that the assessor was the former occupant's illiterate sister, who dictated her survey of the house to a clerk.[9] The 1693 inventory of William Hayman, a Bristol cooper, was obviously drawn by his fellow artisan. The inventory drew very fine distinctions among 'racking cocks', 'bottling cocks', 'racking bores', and 'wimple bores', Hayman's specialised tools. The horses of a Bristol haulier's widow were all listed individually by the assessor, who treated the diocesan officials to some shrewd descriptions: 'an old black gelding with a great joint ... an old flea-bitten nag ... an old brown hollow-backed nag ... an old bay club-footed gelding

... a lame one-eyed mare'.[10] The assessor of a Bristol smith's goods gave special names – 'orlip', 'cafford', and 'scuppor' – to no fewer than three different types of nails located in the house and shop.[11] The complete separation of home and workplace was uncommon enough among merchants and artisans to warrant special mention in those exceptional cases.[12] Where work space and living space were under the same roof, separate valuation of goods explicitly identified as 'in the shop' was the standard practice of assessors. The commodities of public hospitality were found in conspicuously large quantities (thirty brass candlesticks, ten gallons of rum) and proprietors gave alluring names (Dolphin, Unicorn, Saracen, Angel) to the rooms of taverns and inns. Of course, some disappointing inventories consisted of broad references to utensils, apparel, and 'sundry items'. An assessor of one Bristol scrivener's goods and assets worth £71 3s 4d made separate references to his pictures, ink, books, and debtors but summed up all the remaining items as 'things out of sight and out of mind'.[13] A useful portion of all extant English inventories unveils the interiors of homes with organisational details and colourful terms at the level of individual rooms. These invite the reader to imagine the assessor as he or she went from room to room examining the contents just as the deceased relative or neighbour had last handled, shared, or displayed them.[14] Contemporaries observed conventions whereby many different rooms of a house were reserved for specific functions and activites.[15] These conventions varied significantly from city to village. The terms and organising principles employed by assessors as they surveyed the homes of their neighbours and friends suggest historically grounded analytical categories.

Some objections have been raised about juxtaposing the concepts 'luxury' and 'essential' in order to construe patterns of ownership and aspects of consumer behaviour.[16] Although contemporaries surely drew distinctions along these lines, it is also clear that one person's essential item was another person's luxury. Possessions that reflected the discretionary disposal of wealth might easily have been in the service of life's non-material essentials such as companionship, recreation, and spiritual fulfilment. Some early modern social commentators denounced luxury, when they associated it with envy and ambition, as morally suspect. An understanding of the gulf between urban and rural material cultures need not rest on moral judgements, although addressing a variety of objects in collective terms does require the observation of some convention. The term 'populuxe' applied to inferior copies of expensive luxury items has been introduced by the debate over the role of material culture in the emulation of social superiors.[17] Given our aim of locating possessions in particular settings, we can apply the term 'luxury' to finished goods likely to have been of urban origin or imported through urban markets.[18] That these so-called luxury items also tended to be prominently displayed in the home, as well as singled out and highly valued by assessors, need not make them signs of rectitude, turpitude, pretension, or status in the eye of every beholder. The levels at which villagers owned such items, measured in absolute terms and as portions of overall wealth, were significantly lower than urban levels of ownership. Urban and rural patterns of material culture, shaped in part by the ownership and place of items associated with urban sources, expressed conscious conformity to clearly distinct urban and rural conventions.

In this comparison of urban and rural material culture, all 5,095 extant inventories and cause papers drawn up in Bristol and the nearby villages between 1660 and 1780 have a place.[19] Of the entire extant collection, 1,455 cases also qualify for more complete comparative analysis.[20] These 1,455 cases, what we can call the comparison group, are documented by all extant inventories showing the testator to have been either: (1) a creditor as a lender, investor, or an owner of real estate;[21] (2) an owner of printed materials;[22] (3) an owner of luxury items, specified finished goods more likely to have been of urban or foreign origin than of local village origin; or (4) any combination of these. In short, these inventories describe the assets, dwellings, and vital information of people whose resources were coupled with a demonstrated decision to consume products from the urban network (however modestly), or invest (however cautiously), or both. Overall, distinctions between urban and rural patterns of ownership were largely the result of free choices, not of financial constraints. We will consider the entire pool of extant inventories to provide the basic social context for broader comparisons to the extent that the less detailed inventories allow. Along these lines, the comparison group, nearly a third of the entire extant collection, is representative of the range of wealth, occupational diversity and gender ratios expressed overall. With all this in view, we can use inventories to demonstrate how urban and rural people expressed their distinct preferences, not just their limitations, through material culture.

The singling out of possessions and wares in inventories brings the past to life in a way that makes the material culture of early modern England seem both distant and familiar. One can only wonder how successful the St Mary Redcliffe chapman John Austin was in finding buyers for his 'two dozen pocket sundials' in 1661. One Bristol innkeeper had an umbrella on hand during the early eighteenth century. John Davis, a Bristol surgeon, had an entire skeleton hanging in his house in 1741. Samuel and Mary Smith of Bristol, worth over £1,717 in 1776, had a wealth of unusual items, including a telescope, a useful symbol of their expanded horizons.[23] In the eighteenth century it became fashionable to display caged birds, especially exotic ones, in private homes. Caged birds were on display in the houses of all sorts of people: a linen draper worth over £1,611 in 1729, a poor farrier worth only £12 8s 9d in 1731, surgeons, fishmongers, mariners, grocers, and artisans. One victualler owned seven live caged birds in 1762. Nevertheless, all but one of the fifteen houses where assessors noted the presence of caged birds were in the city. The lone bird owner in a nearby village was the vicar of Bedminster, Somerset.[24]

The divergence of urban and rural material cultures also occurred at the most basic levels, but with larger implications. The central role played by food in the most widely observed of social rituals gave food and its origins added significance. It is even possible to speak of addictiveness, respectability, distinctiveness, or 'preciosity' as qualities increasingly associated with certain foods in all social circles by the late seventeenth century.[25] Knives and forks were rarely seen at the dining table, even in major provincial towns and cities, until the mid-eighteenth century,[26] but the implements of food preparation varied from town to country long before then. Katherine Burd, a Bristol widow worth only £39 6s 6d in 1678, owned and operated a 'dog wheel'. This was a type of fireplace rotisserie powered by a dog in a revolving cage, a device that was cruel but not unusual among Bristol residents. Sixteen years later in the rural village of Westbury-on-Trym, the assessors of Roger Grant's goods and assets (worth £76 7s 6d) found very few extraordinary items in his house (only a mirror), but made special reference to his 'apple roaster'. On the other hand, Samuel Smith of Bristol ate too few apples and required the use of a 'gouty cradle'. No list of items, however colourful or ordinary, will prove that cruelty, self-indulgence, extravagance, frugality, refinement, or any other value-laden quality was, in an absolute sense, a distinguishing aspect of urban or rural society. We need to consider the prominence of the categorical distinction between urbane and rustic because contemporaries openly expressed their experience of material culture in terms of setting.

When we look more closely at the ownership of musical instruments, to dwell for a bit on a pleasing set of objects, we see that although assessed values of instruments remained fairly constant from one setting to the other, the likelihood of finding a musical instrument was significantly greater in an urban home than a rural one. Moreover, the very small group of rural dwellers who owned instruments amounted to a collection of urbane villagers, exceptions who proved the rule. All but one of the villagers who owned musical instruments also owned some other so-called luxury item, a book, or both. Between 1660 and 1740, over 70 per cent of musical instrument owners in Bristol also owned books, and in the eighteenth century the figure was over 80 per cent. Only about 50 per cent of the villagers who owned musical instruments between 1660 and 1740 were book owners, but book ownership among rural owners of musical instruments was far above general levels of book ownership in the villages. Villagers who owned musical instruments tended to keep them in close proximity to their books in rooms sometimes identified as 'studies' or 'galleries' that were rarely found in ordinary rural homes. Among luxury owners in Bristol and the surrounding countryside, villagers were

Table 6.1 Ownership of musical instruments in all 915 households with luxury
items in Bristol and the nearby villages, 1660–1740

|  | All luxury owners | Instrument owners | As % of all luxury owners |
|---|---|---|---|
| Urban | 697 | 28 | 4·0 |
| Rural | 218 | 8 | 3·7 |

*Source:* B.R.O. Probate Inventories and Cause Papers.

nearly as likely as city dwellers to own a musical instrument. (Table 6.1.) As we
will see, rural dwellers in general had to reach a higher level of wealth than
urban dwellers before they would spend money on any luxury item; like urban
luxury owners, the rural instrument owners had less money than other villagers whose possessions and credit records represented discretionary expenditure or investment. On average, instrument owners in the villages were even
less wealthy than their fellow instrumentalists in the city, many of whom,
especially the professional musicians, had very little money indeed. (Table
6.2.) There were at least four professional musicians who kept several instruments in their Bristol homes: two violinists; Thomas Adeane, the late seventeenth-century cathedral organist; and one of his successors at Bristol cathedral, Joseph Gibson.[27] Although none of the instrument owners in the villages
near Bristol was a professional musician, of the four instrument owners in the
villages whose occupations were identified, two were farmers with other
luxury items and books, one kept a tavern in Clifton directly outside the city,
and one was the rector of Winterbourne.[28] Three times as many men as
unmarried women owned instruments in the villages; exactly the same ratio
applied to their fellow intrumentalists in the city. (Table 6.3.) In short, the

Table 6.2 Levels of wealth exhibited by owners of musical instruments in
Bristol and the nearby villages, 1660–1740

| Levels of wealth | Urban | Rural |
|---|---|---|
| Over £1,000 | 1 | 0 |
| £500–£1,000 | 2 | 0 |
| £200–£499 | 1 | 2 |
| £50–£199 | 10 | 1 |
| Under £50 | 14 | 5 |
| Average | £184 11s | £110 11s |
| Range | £3–£2,083 | £15–£378 |

*Source:* B.R.O. Probate Inventories and Cause Papers.

Table 6.3 Heads of households with musical instruments in Bristol and the nearby villages, 1660–1740, by gender

|       | Urban | Rural |
|-------|-------|-------|
| Women | 7     | 2     |
| Men   | 21    | 6     |

*Note:* Both unmarried women who owned instruments in the villages were widows, while the urban group included two 'spinsters'.
*Source:* B.R.O. Probate inventories and Cause Papers.

material culture and social profiles of rural instrument owners resembled those of urban instrumentalists more than they resembled the material culture and social profiles of their own neighbours in the villages.

Patterns of musical instrument ownership provide an example of how specific objects were associated with specific settings as well as the identities linked with those settings. Among instrument owners the rural dwellers did resemble the urban dwellers in their preference for virginals, but eight (29 per cent) of the city dwellers owned multiple instruments while no villager owned more than one instrument. (Table 6.4.) In the city one could see in private homes a much wider spectrum of instruments, including expensive keyboard instruments, such as harpsichords, as well as viols, dulcimers, and percussion instruments. In the city one could even hear organs being played in private homes, if not in those of the cathedral organists. Adeane had only viols and virginals at home and Gibson's private instrument was a harpsichord. But one organ valued at £20 was installed in 'the hall' of a Bristol arms painter shortly before his death in 1678 and another could be found in the 'parlour' of a clergyman's thirteen-room house near the cathedral.[29] In the villages the circle

Table 6.4 Owners of musical instruments in Bristol and the nearby villages, by the instruments they owned, 1660–1740 (% in parentheses)

|                 | Urban    | Rural   |
|-----------------|----------|---------|
| Only virginals  | 18 (64)  | 5 (62)  |
| Only viols      | 3 (11)   | 1 (13)  |
| Both            | 2 (7)    | 0       |
| Other           | 5 (18)   | 2 (25)  |

*Note:* All told, in the urban group twenty (71%) owned virginals and five (18%) owned viols.
*Source:* B.R.O. Probate Inventories and Cause Papers.

of people who played musical instruments in their homes formed a very tiny social sphere indeed. The wonderful image of Hugh Rumney accompanying, on his virginals, the violin playing of a young Richard White, a fellow farmer in Henbury, brings this sharply into focus and it would have strained the limits of comprehension for their urbane contemporary, Samuel Pepys, had he ever known them. On at least one revealing occasion, derisive terms used by Pepys, the quintessential man-about-town in Restoration London, pointed explicitly to his perceived connections among the possession of a musical instrument, its proper use, and urbane notions of rusticity: 'They have a kinswoman they call a daughter in the house, a short, ugly, red-haired slut that plays upon the virginals and sings, but after such a country manner, I was weary of it.'[30]

If we regard Bristol and the villages in the city's rural environs as the location of a single consumer population under the cultural influence of the urban renaissance, we should expect at least a third of all inventoried houses containing luxury items after 1660 to have been rural.[31] In fact, the portion was between a quarter and a fifth.[32] The portion increased slightly over time, but did not approach parity with urban figures at any time before 1740 or so. (Table 6.5.) Raw figures, as well as those adjusted for population estimates and locally variable rates of probate administration, point to the same basic trends. During most of the period associated with the urban renaissance, rural folk did not conform to the levels and patterns of ownership established by their urban counterparts.

Perhaps urban dwellers were wealthier than their rural counterparts. This does not appear to have been the case, however. Among urban workers below the status of artisans, sailors may have had the highest wages, but they were not steadily paid. Thomas Horne, a Bristol mariner, was paid £2 10s per month, but in 1720 his captain paid him for five months aboard ship. At his

Table 6.5 Urban and rural portions of all extant inventories of known origin for households containing luxury items over three forty-year periods

|  | 1660–99 | | 1700–39 | | 1740–80[a] | |
|---|---|---|---|---|---|---|
|  | Urban | Rural | Urban | Rural | Urban | Rural |
| Households | 376 | 104 | 321 | 114 | 90 | 15 |
| % of total | 78·3 | 21·7 | 73·8 | 26·2 | 85·7 | 14·3 |

*Note:* (a) Period in which probate was more closely limited to cause papers, inventories of disputed, more valuable, estates.
*Source:* B.R.O. Probate Inventories and Cause Papers.

death, Horne was worth only £19.[33] The work of rural labourers was so unsteady that they were paid by the day. At 12d per day[34] a male agricultural labourer working as an unskilled builder off-season could earn around £15 a year, although his wife and children, if he had a family, surely contributed less than that to the household income. The domestic servant in the city earned as little as one-third of this even though compensatory room and board were included as income.[35] It is true that twelve of the fourteen wealthiest estates recorded by the diocese in Bristol and the nearby villages between 1660 and 1780 were those of urban dwellers. But the portion of very wealthy citizens was higher for London than for provincial cities during the early phase of the urban renaissance. An estimated 38 per cent of all London freemen in the seventeenth century, including those with no credit and no highly valued or

Table 6.6 The distribution of wealth by setting over three forty-year periods for urban and rural households in the comparison group (% in parentheses)

| | 1660–99 | | 1700–39 | | 1740–80 | |
| --- | --- | --- | --- | --- | --- | --- |
| | Urban | Rural | Urban | Rural | Urban | Rural |
| Over £1,000 | 3 (0·5) | 1 (0·5) | 7 (1·8) | 1 (0·7) | 2 (2·0) | 0 |
| £501–£1,000 | 14 (2·5) | 10 (5·1) | 18 (4·6) | 8 (5·1) | 6 (6·0) | 0 |
| £201–£500 | 68 (12·2) | 40 (20·2) | 44 (11·2) | 47 (30·1) | 16 (16·3) | 7 (41·2) |
| £51–£200 | 182 (32·7) | 99 (50·0) | 115 (29·2) | 70 (44·9) | 34 (34·8) | 5 (29·4) |
| £11–£50 | 207 (37·3) | 43 (21·7) | 142 (36·0) | 25 (16·0) | 30 (30·7) | 4 (23·5) |
| Under £11 | 82 (14·8) | 5 (2·5) | 68 (17·2) | 5 (3·2) | 10 (10·2) | 1 (5·9) |
| Totals | 556 (100) | 198 (100) | 394 (100) | 156 (100) | 98 (100) | 17 (100) |
| Average wealth | £108 | £160 | £143 | £196 | £172 | £171 |
| £51–£1,000 | 264 (47·4) | 149 (75·3) | 177 (45·0) | 125 (80·1) | 56 (57·1) | 12 (70·6) |

*Note:* Of the 1,455 households in the comparison group, the settings for 1,419 are known.

*Source:* B.R.O. Probate Inventories and Cause Papers.

remarkable possessions, were worth over £500.[36] Only 3 per cent of Bristol citizens in our comparison group were worth over £500 between 1660 and 1699. In Bristol and the nearby villages a higher percentage of rural households than urban ones had estates valued between £51 and £1,000 throughout our entire period. (Table 6.6.) By urban standards a significant portion of villagers in southern Gloucestershire and northern Somerset controlled financial resources secure enough to permit the exercise of considerable choice over their expenditure or investment.

The level of wealth urban or rural dwellers would attain before choosing to buy a luxury item said something about the range of attitudes conveyed in material culture. In general, the level of financial security at which urban dwellers chose to buy such items was considerably lower than that observed by villagers. The average wealth of Bristolians who owned luxury items during the last forty years of the seventeenth century was £114, or £69 less than £183, the average wealth of the nearby villagers who owned such items during that period. The gap closed slightly during the first forty years of the eighteenth century, when the relevant figures were £166 for urban dwellers and £201 for villagers. It was not until the last forty years of the entire period that the average wealth of urban and rural owners of such items finally approached parity at £172 for urban dwellers and £174 for villagers. Over the entire period 1660–1780 there were only three households in the villages (0·8 per cent of the 371 rural households in the comparison group) in which more than one-fifth of the household's total wealth was in the form of luxury items. The portion of the urban comparison group achieving that level of ownership rose steadily over the entire period, reaching over 14 per cent after 1740.[37] During the century following 1660, most rural dwellers with any degree of financial cushion chose instead to improve their means outside the dwelling space in their stables, pastures, and fields. Horses, used by hauliers, were the animals most likely to be kept in the city. One Bristol baker was found to have a live pig locked in his cellar. In 1681 George Jocelin, a butcher in St Philip and Jacob, had sixteen sheep, but it is doubtful whether he kept so many in the city, even at that time. In 1758 William Tock, a farmer in Westbury-on-Trym, was worth £165 10s, slightly less than the average wealth of those villagers who owned luxury goods. Nevertheless, Tock's neighbours in Westbury could hardly have failed to notice some very visible signs of his success: thirty-six sheep and twelve lambs worth £11, thirteen cows and two yearlings worth £62, and three pigs worth £4 10s.[38]

Very few rural households with total assets of £30 or less owned any luxury goods, with the possible exception of a clock.[39] The assessed value of a clock was usually about £1 and those few poorer villagers who had clocks rarely owned any other luxury items.[40] There were three villagers of such modest means who owned virginals, keyboard instruments conventionally assessed at

£5 througout the period, but they owned no other items of high value.[41] By contrast, households in Bristol with total assets valued at £30 or less but in possession of luxury items were too numerous to describe beyond a few illustrative examples.[42] In 1734 Richard Holton of Bristol had assets amounting to only £21 5s 6d, and more than half that total was accounted for by luxury goods: six pictures, a silver tankard, a silver cup, silver spoons, a silver watch and chain, and mirrors. Elizabeth Mann, a Bristol widow worth only £19 12s 2d in 1725, owned gold and silver jewellery, a silver service and cutlery, twelve pictures, and mirrors, all of which accounted for nearly half her total wealth. Samuel Parrett, a tinplate maker in St James, Bristol, was worth only £11 10s 9d in 1713 but was £14 18s 6d in debt at his death. Nevertheless he owned a virginal, a decorative map and two pictures, eleven pieces of china coffee service, and a mirror. Mirrors, the most common luxury item owned by urban dwellers, were in the possession of many Bristolians whose total assets amounted to less than £5, and in a some cases only £1. From 1660 to 1740, around 16 per cent of all urban owners of the specified luxury goods had total assets of £10 or less, while only about 2 per cent of villagers with similar possessions were that poor. (Table 6.7.)

As for occupation, that too was less of a factor than setting in shaping levels of expenditure. Mariners did not usually take up residence in the countryside, but those who did live in the villages surrounding Bristol exhibited consumer behaviour unlike that of the mariners in the city. Only one mariner in our comparison group went without luxury items in the rural setting, but those mariners who did own such items in the villages were wealthier than rural

Table 6.7 Poorest owners of luxury items in Bristol and the nearby villages (% in parentheses)

| | 1660–99 | | 1700–39 | | 1740–80 | |
|---|---|---|---|---|---|---|
| | Urban | Rural | Urban | Rural | Urban | Rural |
| Total households with luxury items | 376 | 104 | 321 | 114 | 90 | 15 |
| Total assets of £30 or less | 154 (41·1) | 15 (14·4) | 134 (41·7) | 12 (10·5) | 24 (26·7) | 3 (20·0) |
| Total assets of £10 or less | 61 (16·2) | 2 (1·9) | 50 (15·6) | 3 (2·6) | 9 (10·0) | 1 (6·7) |

*Source:* B.R.O. Probate Inventories and Cause Papers.

mariners as a group; the villagers in this occupational group showed little expenditure on luxury possessions until they reached a higher level of wealth. Quite the opposite was true in the city, where there was an enormous community of urban mariners whose levels of luxury ownership were higher than those reached by their rural shipmates. At £57 total wealth, the average urban mariner in our comparison group who opted to possess any luxury item was £31 poorer than the average member of his occupation in the comparison group as a whole. Apart from members of occupational groups with relatively few rural practitioners (cordwainers, shoemakers, and leather crafters), gentlemen, professionals, and a few rural merchants were the only villagers who, as a group, devoted noteworthy portions of their wealth to luxury items. Rural gentlemen and professionals who possessed luxury items were poorer, on average, than other members of their social status in the rural setting. That is to say, the urban pattern of possessing higly valued finished goods at a lower level of total wealth, regardless of occupation, was displayed in the rural setting by a very small number of people whose occupations were most closely associated with the urban setting.

Villagers of every occupational group, with the exceptions just noted, were less likely than their urban counterparts to spend whatever surplus wealth they controlled on luxury possessions. One 'single woman' in the village of Henbury owned furnishings valued at £160 but dwelt in an austere house because she was in the rather odd business of hiring out furniture to other people.[43] Farmers, members of the largest and most representative rural occupation, were the most frugal members of the rural society in the second half of the seventeenth century, despite their wealth. Between 1660 and 1700 the average luxury-owning farmer, at £246, was £43 wealthier than farmers who limited their outlay of surplus wealth to lending, real estate investment, or the purchase of books. A farmer would have accumulated quite a bit more money than his neighbour before she or he would spend it on a luxury item. A villager might have been tempted to claim that consumer restraint led to a higher level of wealth. For urban dwellers, however, luxury items were not an expression of indulgence. As we will see, they were an expression of justifiable social conformity and conventions governing power and initiative in social spheres. In the urban setting, luxury items could be seen as an investment in social capital. At the very least we must see that two value systems, one urbane and one rustic, were in operation.

In general, those rural dwellers who did include luxury items among their possessions most often distinguished themselves from their urban counterparts by gravitating towards items holding some mechanical fascination or having some practical outdoor use. (Table 6.8.) In the early eighteenth century, timepieces became the most common luxury item in rural households, although they were still mentioned in only one-fifth of all extant inventories

Table 6.8 The relative popularity of some specified luxury items owned by rural dwellers in Bristol's nearby villages

| Specified items | 1660–99 | | | 1700–40 | | |
|---|---|---|---|---|---|---|
| | Total no. of owners | As % of luxury owners | As % of all extant | Total no. of owners | As % of luxury owners | As % of all extant |
| Firearms | 31 | 29·8 | 4·0 | 31 | 27·2 | 8·3 |
| Timepieces | 23 | 22·1 | 3·0 | 82 | 71·9 | 21·9 |
| Silver | 15 | 14·4 | 1·9 | 22 | 19·3 | 5·9 |
| Mirrors | 12 | 11·5 | 1·5 | 23 | 20·2 | 6·1 |
| Blades[a] | 11 | 10·6 | 1·4 | 7 | 6·1 | 1·9 |
| Jewelry | 7 | 6·7 | 0·9 | 4 | 3·5 | 1·1 |
| Gold | 7 | 6·7 | 0·9 | 4 | 3·5 | 1·1 |
| Instruments[b] | 7 | 6·7 | 0·9 | 2 | 1·8 | 0·5 |
| Pictures | 5 | 4·8 | 0·6 | 7 | 6·1 | 1·9 |
| China | 0 | 0 | 0 | 2 | 1·8 | 0·5 |

*Notes:* (a) Bladed weapons, including swords. (b) Musical instruments.
*Source:* B.R.O. Probate Inventories and Cause Papers

taken in villages near Bristol. It is surprising to discover that rural life, known more for its seasonal rhythms than for the discipline of punctuality, should have placed clocks in such a prominent position in rural material culture. Watches became as common as clocks in the city but remained relatively rare among possessions in the villages, where timepieces appeared in the home rather than about the body. As we have seen, firearms came into play on 'solemn occasions of rejoicing' and may have had recreational as well as practical uses in the rural setting.

Among the possessions of urban luxury owners, throughout the period between 1660 and 1740, mirrors, pictures of all sorts, and silver items (apart from silver watches) all remained more common than any sort of timepiece. Mirrors were nearly ubiquitous among the possessions of those urban mariners who owned luxury items. Perhaps sailors who travelled from port to port were dealers in mirrors and other small wares. It is tempting to speculate that mariners hung mirrors below deck to create an illusion of space in confined quarters, or that they carried mirrors as a grim precaution, used to beckon rescuers at sea. In general, it was the urban emphasis on appearances, images, and image projection that was revealed in the prominence of pictures and mirrors throughout the private homes of urban residents.

There is every reason to believe that gender awareness informed attitudes toward material objects in general, not just the decorative possessions seemingly favoured by single women.[44] It has been argued that married women, by virtue of the limited power they exercised over discretionary expenditure,[45] tended to express these attitudes more in the manipulation of items than in their acquisition, even – or perhaps especially – in the homes of wealthier couples, where household servants were involved.[46] A range of circumstances applied in households where women lived without men. Wealthier widows were the least likely to remarry but the most likely to liquidate possessions to become creditors. Single women tended to 'cluster' and this made for a communal rather than possessive material culture in their households.[47] Possessions found in homes with male heads of households almost certainly included items for which other members of those households, male or female, were responsible. Under rare circumstances possessions and assets in some households were recognised as jointly held by couples, by men and women together rather than by husbands alone.[48] As expressions of gender-specific patterns of ownership, however, inventories drawn up for individual women, especially so-called 'single women' or 'spinsters', are far more reliable than inventories indentified with men who may have been considered heads of mixed households. To be sure, some widows were heads of mixed households containing possessions inherited from their husbands, but even those widows whose husbands died intestate made legally independent decisions about which of those possessions to retain and which to liquidate.[49] Furthermore,

Table 6.9 Luxury owners, by gender, in Bristol and the nearby villages (% in parentheses)

|  | 1660–99 | | 1700–39 | | 1740–80 | | Totals | |
|---|---|---|---|---|---|---|---|---|
|  | Women | Men | Women | Men | Women | Men | Women | Men |
| Entire comparison group | 192 (25) | 585 (75) | 111 (20) | 452 (80) | 14 (12) | 101 (88) | 317 (22) | 1,138 (78) |
| All luxury owners | 112 (23) | 380 (77) | 84 (19) | 362 (81) | 11 (11) | 94 (89) | 207 (20) | 836 (80) |

*Note:* It should be made clear that luxury ownership, in general, was not particularly gender-specific. The relative numbers of men and women who owned luxury were directly proportional to the numbers of men and women in the overall comparison group of 1,455 cases.
*Source:* B.R.O. Probate Inventories and Cause Papers.

objects could inspire deep feelings and a high degree of 'sensibility' which, during the eighteenth century, was increasingly associated with a feminised psyche and bourgeois consumerism.[50]

Women's separate inventories made up about 22 per cent of our entire comparison group and their distribution between the city and the nearby countryside was directly proportional to the representation of urban dwellers and villagers in general.[51] Only five of the separate inventories for women failed to identify the place of residence, a true mark of obscurity in early modern society. All five of these accounts were drawn up before 1710, assessed estates valued at less than £30 each, and (with the exception of one grocer's inventory) attributed no occupation at all to the woman in question. Most women with separately inventoried possessions and assets were identified as 'widows', 'spinsters', or 'single women', but a good portion of the total (about 13 per cent in both settings) were identified as having specific occupations.[52] Of all inventories containing luxury items, the portion belonging specifically to women was remarkably consistent with the representation of women's separate inventories in the overall group, and was even consistent over time as women's inventories became a smaller portion of the group containing luxury. (Table 6.9.) That is to say, if the profiles of women who are known to have headed households or maintained homes and possessions separately from men were any indication, the ownership of luxury was not particularly gender-specific in provincial England between 1660 and 1780.

On the other hand, as in the case of occupational considerations, there were

Table 6.10 Influence of setting on luxury ownership, by gender and setting, for the 1,419 cases in the comparison group for whom place of residence was given (% in parentheses)

| | 1660–99 | | 1700–39 | | 1740–80 | | Totals | |
|---|---|---|---|---|---|---|---|---|
| | Women | Men | Women | Men | Women | Men | Women | Men |
| *Urban* | | | | | | | | |
| Cases | 140 | 416 | 81 | 313 | 10 | 88 | 231 | 817 |
| Owners of | 89 | 287 | 67 | 254 | 8 | 82 | 164 | 623 |
| luxury | (64) | (69) | (83) | (81) | (80) | (93) | (71) | (76) |
| *Rural* | | | | | | | | |
| Cases | 49 | 149 | 28 | 128 | 4 | 13 | 81 | 290 |
| Owners of | 21 | 83 | 16 | 98 | 3 | 12 | 40 | 193 |
| luxury | (43) | (56) | (57) | (77) | (75) | (92) | (49) | (67) |

*Source:* B.R.O. Probate Inventories and Cause Papers.

clear trends in ownership associated with the influence of setting. When we divide inventories into urban and rural groups and compare levels of luxury ownership exhibited by women as a group with those exhibited by men, we see marked contrasts in the two settings. (Table 6.10.) In the city, women and men were equally likely to have a portion of their own assets in the form of luxury possessions. For women and men in the urban setting, ownership of luxury became increasingly popular over time, and gender parity along these lines was not disrupted until after 1740. In fact, the portion of urban women owning luxury items independently was slightly higher than that of urban men in the early eighteenth century and slightly lower in the earlier period. By contrast, in the villages men were far more likely than women to have luxury possessions. As we have already seen, the extent to which women overall were less likely than men to own luxury items was nearly negligible. Thus it is particularly striking that until the end of the early modern period the separate possessions of city women were far more likely than those of village men, as well as of village women, to include luxury items; minor distinctions along gender lines were far outweighed by the principal distinction, which was between urban and rural. Not only were rural women with their own assets wealthier on average than similarly independent urban women, they were wealthier on average than urban men. (Table 6.11.) Nevertheless, urban women, the least wealthy group of all, were more likely than villagers of either sex to own luxury possessions during this long period.

Choices made by women who were widows at the time of their death resembled, in patterns of credit and selective ownership, those choices of women who had remained single their entire lives. (Table 6.12.) In both settings, a few of the women with separate inventories did conform to the literary stereotype of the wealthy widow: a woman whose assets were not controlled by a man. In real life, as in print, such a woman was faced with problematic, and revealing, choices. A widow of means was criticised as unruly if she resisted remarriage or was resented, by her new husband's cohorts, as a symbol of male aging, impotence, and mortality if she did remarry.[53] Widows who chose to remain luxury owners were unlikely to have liquidated a high portion of their assets to set themselves up as independent creditors. Women in both settings exercised revealing choices about what to acquire or keep if they were unmarried. The choice to remain independent from men correlated closely, among women who owned luxury items, with the ownership of what might have been construed, by that group, as women's possessions.

Despite the importance of gender awareness in the use of material culture, unmarried women's attitudes concerning possessions varied according to the settings in which they lived. Unlike creditors among unmarried women in the city, those village widows who did transform the major portion of their assets

Table 6.11 Average wealth and range of wealth, by gender and setting, for the 1,419 cases in the comparison group for whom place of residence was given

| | 1660–99 | | 1700–39 | | 1740–80 | |
|---|---|---|---|---|---|---|
| | Women | Men | Women | Men | Women | Men |
| *Urban* | | | | | | |
| Cases | 140 | 416 | 81 | 313 | 10 | 88 |
| Average | £92 | £113 | £107 | £154 | £180 | £172 |
| Range | £1–£498 | £1–£2,083 | £2–£856 | £1–£5,060 | £1–£746 | £5–£1,717 |
| *Rural* | | | | | | |
| Cases | 49 | 149 | 28 | 128 | 4 | 13 |
| Average | £116 | £174 | £200 | £196 | £149 | £179 |
| Range | £7–£409 | £7–£1,023 | £6–£1,345 | £4–£925 | £20–£289 | £7–£381 |

*Source:* B.R.O. Probate Inventories and Cause Papers.

into credit tended not to acquire or keep any luxury at all, and those few village single women whose assets were mainly in the form of credit conformed to the same rural practice.[54] Urban unmarried women were so much less likely than men to own pictures, escutcheons, weapons, timepieces, and large furnishings that luxury owners in the city appeared to draw sharper distinctions according to gender constructions of certain items. Unmarried village women were less likely than their urban counterparts to own even those specific items that might have distinguished women's own material culture from that of men. Rural widows were overwhelmingly represented by women who managed their own land and livestock and operated their own farms. Widow farmers acquired, or kept, firearms and clocks just as their husbands would have done. Throughout the early modern period urban widows chose to keep or acquire possessions that aided in hospitaity or adorned the body. They were more inclined to keep their wedding rings, or more likely to have been given them, even if they were poor.[55] Deborah James, a Bristol widow worth more than £420 at the time of her death in 1672, had over £361 in the form of credit, loans she had extended, amounting to 86 per cent of her total assets. But she also acquired, or kept from her marriage, a silver service worth £12, knives and forks with agate hafts, silk cushions and silk clothing, and a valuable jewellery collection, including a bracelet of 'bloodstones' worth £3 and a gold chain.[56] Elizabeth Lawrence, a Bristol widow worth over £420 in 1752, collected all the loans she had extended and had, at the time of her death,

Table 6.12 The relationship between luxury possessions and credit as controlled by unmarried women[a]

| | 1660–99 | | | | 1700–40 | | | |
| | Urban | | Rural | | Urban | | Rural | |
| % wealth in credit | luxury? | | luxury? | | luxury? | | luxury? | |
| | yes | no | yes | no | yes | no | yes | no |
|---|---|---|---|---|---|---|---|---|
| Over 50 | 7 | 10 | 3 | 10 | 10 | 6 | 1 | 6 |
| 31–50 | 5 | 6 | 1 | 0 | 2 | 2 | 1 | 3 |
| 11–30 | 14 | 7 | 2 | 3 | 4 | 4 | 1 | 0 |
| 1–10 | 7 | 4 | 2 | 5 | 1 | 1 | 1 | 0 |
| No credit | 41 | 14 | 9 | 7 | 41 | 1 | 7 | 2 |
| All creditors | 33 | 27 | 8 | 18 | 17 | 13 | 4 | 9 |
| Totals | 74 | 41 | 17 | 25 | 58 | 14 | 11 | 11 |

*Note:* (a) Widows, 'spinsters' and 'single women'. There are only ten inventories for unmarried women in the comparison group dating from after 1740, but the inverse relationship between luxury ownership and credit is even more pronounced in these: among the seven urban women, four of the five luxury owners had extended no credit, whereas the two women without luxury had over 50% of their assets in the form of credit; among the three villagers, the two women with luxury had extended no credit, whereas the woman without luxury had over 50) of her total assets in the form of credit.

*Source:* B.R.O. Probate Inventories and Cause Papers.

over £336 in cash (£70 of which was Spanish and German). Despite her apparent need for liquidity, she retained five jewelled rings (including a diamond) worth nearly £4, a very extensive collection of clothes valued at £24 11s, coffee, tea, and chocolate pots, china and a snuffbox. It must be noted also that Deborah James had 'twelve reading books' in her Bristol home at the time of her death in 1672. Elizabeth Lawrence, eighty years later, had thirty-two books in her 'parlour', including eight bound volumes of *The Spectator*. Books were possessions that many of their owners, women in particular, placed at the centre of gender-specific social spheres even to the extent of transcending the topographical divide.

The descriptive qualities of inventories capture the urban preoccupation with the real or perceived value imparted to an object by its geographical origins. The vast majority of inventory references in which an object was described in terms of its city or country of manufacture appeared in urban inventories. Joan Gray's assessor in Westbury-on-Trym did note that she had three carpets 'of Bristol making', and the assessor of Thomas Daunsey's goods remarked on a 'parcel of Dutch ware' in that gentleman's Stapleton home in 1710, but few rural inventories contained similar descriptions. Urban assessors were inclined to identify objects according to style names derived from foreign or exotic places. In the 1740s 'japanned' cupboards and clock cases began cropping up in urban 'parlours'. Most clocks with cases were valued between £1 and £3 whereas clocks identified as having cases lacquered in the 'japanned' style were assessed between £4 and £5.[57] Asian goods – especially textiles, beverages, and items associated with far-flung maritime travel – were identified with the fashionable urban classes in the seventeenth and eighteenth centuries.[58] It is scarcely surprising that the most common users and retainers of foreign coins were mariners. Some were paid routinely in West Indian coins. In Bristol members of other occupations and widows also had coins from the Caribbean, the Carolinas, Holland, Spain, Portugal, Ireland, Sweden, France, and German-speaking countries. In Bristol and the nearby villages every inventory offering explicit references to foreign coins was urban. Villagers appear not to have accepted or used foreign money which entered circulation through the urban network.

As the story goes in a popular seventeenth-century chapbook, the country mouse was amazed at the diet of his friend the city mouse.[59] One September in the 1760s, John Warner, a St James churchwarden, drew up that year's account of the annual Fair Dinner attended by the parishioners who had presided over the stall rentals in July and August. The dinner (which provided the vestry with enough ale, cider, and cheese for a breakfast the following day) cost the considerable sum of £5 3s 2d and captured the flavour of the fair itself, which was a mixture of exotic treats.[60] The diners treated themselves to imported wine, 1s 10d worth of tobacco, a quart of rum ('without the consent of the churchwarden') costing the parish still another 2s 6d, and fourteen lemons priced at 2s 4d. Sugar, which was still relatively rare in the rural diet of the early seventeenth century, became one of the most popular foreign imports in England. Between 1660 and 1750 the portion of imported sugar retained for domestic consumption (as opposed to re-export) rose by a factor of ten to reach a level of 90 per cent, while the level of annual sugar importation rose from about 2 lb of sugar *per capita* to 16 lb.[61] During that time, the price of 1 lb of sugar had dropped from about 1s, its early seventeenth-century level, to somewhere between 4d and 6d.[62] The importation of sugar was related primarily to the popularisation of stimulant beverages (tea, coffee, and chocolate), although the production of rum, molasses, and baked confections certainly contributed.

The transformation of stimulant beverages, sweetened with sugar, from 'edible luxuries' to 'everyday necessities'[63] took place in the urban setting. As early as 1681, there was a Bristol merchant earning a comfortable living specialising as a 'coffee seller'.[64] The first English coffee house was opened by a Turkish merchant in London in 1652.[65] Bristol's first public coffee house was established in 1666 and by the 1680s several more had appeared around the Tolzey market centre, along the river, and close to the cathedral up the hill.[66] Coffee houses were flourishing as hospitable and informative gathering places in nearly every provincial city and town by the early eighteenth century. By the 1730s, as a result of coastal smuggling,[67] tea that had circumvented regulated urban markets could be readily had by consumers in villages as well as towns. The private provision of coffee and chocolate, on the other hand, was clearly an expression of urbane hospitality.

The material culture of Bristol homes, far more than that of the homes in nearby villages, conformed to trends established by commercial gathering places found in the urban setting. The appearance in Bristol's private dwellings of paraphernalia used in preparing hospitable beverages, marking the increase in their private consumption in the city, was accompanied by an avalanche of china cups, saucers, and pots in which those drinks were served in style at all levels of urban society. Anne Garraway, a single woman in Bristol who was worth only £39 in 1712, owned a chocolate pot, thirty pieces of china, one stuffed parlour chair for herself and another for her guests. A Bristol tinplate maker by the name of Parrett was worth only £11 10s 9d in 1713, but he owned eleven 'coffee dishes'.[68] More than eight times as many homes in Bristol as in the nearby villages contained hospitality items specifically identified with coffee or chocolate as opposed to tea; Bristol homes contained almost fourteen times as many items specifically identified with coffee or chocolate. Before 1720 the only item specifically identified with coffee or chocolate in a rural home was a solitary chocolate pot in the possession of William Manning, the vicar of Bedminster, by 1702.[69] Samuel and Mary Smith of Bristol had a chocolate pot, a silver coffee pot and five teapots (two 'foreign China' and three 'English'), 188 pieces of china, two silver tankards, snuff, and twenty-six drinking glasses in their house in 1776. Between 1660 and 1720 Bristol homes had more than eight times as many punchbowls, tankards, pots, and china cups as village homes had, and this urban–rural distinction actually intensified over time; between 1720 and 1780 Bristol homes contained nearly forty times more items associated with hospitality beverages than were found in village homes. (Table 6.13.) Rural owners of china had three pieces at most and usually only one token china item. Bristol owners of china had more than fourteen pieces per household on average. One Bristol sailmaker had fifty-five pieces of china in his house, thirty-one of which were in his 'parlour'.[70] Bristol braziers and shopkeepers sold toy coffee pots, charming items with the power to inculcate an adult appreciation of urban luxury and private hospitality within the very domestic sphere of imitative child's play.[71]

Hospitality, and the manipulation of the material culture through which it

Table 6.13 Punchbowls, tankards, coffee pots, tea pots, chocolate pots, and china items found in 1,419 homes inventoried in Bristol and the nearby villages

|  | 1660–1719 | | 1720–1780 | | Totals | |
|---|---|---|---|---|---|---|
|  | Urban | Rural | Urban | Rural | Urban | Rural |
| Items | 75 | 9 | 519 | 13 | 594 | 22 |
| Owners | 27 | 5 | 73 | 10 | 100 | 15 |
| Owners as % of all luxury owners | 4·9 | 2·9 | 31·5 | 16·4 | 12·7 | 6·4 |

*Note:* These figures exclude such items found in public taverns, inns, and coffee houses. In view of the timing of tea's popularisation, the equal division of the chronology at 1720 (and not at forty-year intervals) is more relevant for this table.
*Source:* B.R.O. Probate Inventories and Cause Papers.

was conveyed, involved the subtle exercise of power within private spaces. A great deal of emphasis has been justifiably placed on the widespread importance of public taverns and inns as arenas of sociability, formal and informal political activity, and information exchange.[72] On the other hand, we should not overlook the persistent, or even growing, importance of private hospitality and the power of extrafamilial social activity to transform the home and define the boundaries of social spheres.[73] In the homes of the urban middle classes, as in those of the gentry, one source of power that women claimed in material affairs was their control over household objects, not always at the point of purchase but in the home, in some cases through special servants whose very presence was justified by the routine manipulation of possessions.[74] Salaried maids (as distinct from indentured servants in the household) were nearly eight times more common in Bristol than in the homes of nearby villagers, greater evidence still that the urban host's objective was to command – both the servant and the social opportunity – not to serve. Hospitality, as mediated through servants, also created a formal, albeit polite, distance between host and guest.

Urbane guests understood the importance of concealment, although this is often overlooked in modern discussions acknowledging the power of display. The use of rooms above stairs concealed intimate activites and possessions; linens (which were nearly eight times more common in the city than in the villages) concealed beds or rough-hewn tables; window curtains (which urban dwellers were five times more likely to own)[75] concealed interiors from passers by; and exotic spices concealed the lack of freshness in stored meats. Samuel Pepys, in recounting his progress through Restoration London's social and political circles, regarded admission to the upper regions of a house as a noteworthy detail because allegiances were formed, on the basis of confidentiality, 'upstairs'. At one particularly rollicking victory celebration, Pepys knew he had won the loyalty of his host as he recalled, 'upstairs we went ... dancing ... and dressing, him and I like women'. Pepys, who once said that 'painted' faces 'would make a man mad', was fond of pointing out that clothing suitable for receiving guests of the opposite sex should not be worn as costume, plumage, or decorative garb; to his urbane way of thinking, in which notions of female propriety and male aggression were both accommodated, fashionable attire should be worn as a form of concealment the control of which might be an arousing subject of negotiation.[76] In the urbane sensibility, proprietorial rights over dwellings and possessions empowered hosts to reveal or conceal aspects of their material culture as guided by their own public and private ambitions.

Rural folk were doubtless as convivial as city dwellers, but their domestic sociability involved less elaborate manipulation of luxury possessions and hospitality items of the kind found in taverns, inns, coffee houses, and homes in the urban setting. Most rural sociability involving luxury took place outside the home. In the case of Bristol and its nearby villages, all thirteen assessors' references to tobacco on offer in private homes appeared in urban inventories. Private homes offering liquor were more than four times more common in Bristol than in the surrounding villages, where not a single reference to liquor was made in any household inventories drawn up during the last forty years of the seventeenth century. In the city there was equipment for all sorts of games – including skittles, shuffleboard, and bowls – in private dwellings. Perhaps, in the villages, ordinary household items, not immediately indentifiable in an inventory as the stuff of games, led double lives as tools and toys inside rural homes. There were, however, rural examples of gaming equipment described in the inventories of public taverns such as the Hope and Anchor in Westbury-on-Trym where Joseph Floyd's patrons played shuffleboard in 1717. Much of the more public rural sociability could, in fact, affirm communal (as opposed to private) life or express, to a greater extent than the contents of their homes, the relative social positions and ambitions of the participants. The most luxuriously equipped dwellings in the rural setting, apart from those of the local squires, were the rectories and vicarages which acted on the occasions of church ales and social functions as public, rather than private, dispensaries of hospitality. William Manning, the hospitable vicar of Bedminster, whose chocolate pot was something of a rural novelty, also had liquor and thirteen casks of beer on hand.[77] The only house in Bristol's rural environs with an inventory showing more than eight rooms was the rectory of the parish of Winterbourne.[78]

The urban emphasis on the display of luxury goods, hospitality items and images led to the transformation of the urban house designed to contain public and private spaces under the control of the resident. An urban distinction between forms of comfort and sociability suitable on the ground level and those suitable above stairs was joined in eighteenth-century Bristol by the development of more specialised rooms throughout the house. The most fully equipped room in village homes, the kitchen, combined intimate life and group activity in one space, all on the ground floor, suggesting that urbane conventions distancing the privileged spaces of residents from the controlled spaces of their guests did not apply in the countryside outside gentry social spheres.

The few rural dwellers who had luxury items were likely to concentrate them in their kitchens, not in the rooms containing their beds. To the rustic turn of mind, beds belonged with other beds or with sacks of fruit and vegetables in rooms reserved for sleeping bodies and stored goods.[79] Rural dwellings rarely had furnished rooms above stairs. A rare rural example of a luxurious upstairs bedroom was the only room above stairs in the home of a Littleton-on-Severn 'gentleman' worth £186 13s in 1681. His bedchamber had additional furnishings valued at £30.[80] Near the end of the early modern period a mirror could be seen in the bedchamber of a farmer in the village of Elberton, Gloucestershire. Even then the three beds in that one room were joined by four sacks of potatoes.[81] Samuel Seager, a wealthy farmer with a seven-room house in the village of Almondsbury and assets valued at more than £1,023 in 1699, had no luxury items in his bedchambers apart from beds and sacks of stored food, although the value of his clothing (£12) makes one wonder where his wardrobe was kept. His only luxury possessions apart from a pair of gold rings were some silver items kept in a back room off his kitchen.[82] In the villages near Bristol, of the six homes with both parlours and pictures, five (83 per cent) had all the pictures on display in the parlour. Only three village homes near Bristol had hospitality items – none of them assessed before 1727 – but in all three of these homes all such items were in the parlour. With these rare exceptions, in the villages near Bristol all luxury items remained in the kitchen. In village homes, the few beds that appeared in rooms with other types of possessions were in kitchens.

Bedchambers retained much of their additional importance as separate centres of comfort and display for urban dwellers of all ranks. The 1681 inventory of Charles Blewett's house in the central Bristol parish of St Leonard shows that Blewett lived on two floors and that the most lavishly furnished room, with goods valued at £6 6s, was 'over the dining room'. Of the eighty-four Bristol homes we can entirely reconstitute room by room, fifty-eight (69 per cent) had pictures, paintings, or prints on display in them. In twenty-three (40 per cent) of these homes there were images hung in bedrooms, but in only nine (16 per cent) were all the pictures in the occupant's possession on display in a bedroom. Bedrooms were the centre of hospitality in more modest urban homes, while they were the intimate spaces of comfort among the increasingly differentiated interiors of homes occupied by more prosperous urban artisans and professionals. Humphrey Brent, minister of St Thomas in 1677, owned and occupied a house worth £100 near the Bristol Bridge. He had over £170 in other assets, including 'a study of books' worth £35. His 'parlour' had only £2 worth of goods in it. But his best bedroom, the 'middle chamber over the kitchen', contained £20 worth of furnishings. As late as 1767 William Toghill, a butcher worth over £180 in St Philip and Jacob, kept all his china and his best 'Virginia leather' chairs in his bedroom despite the existence of seven other rooms in the house. That the most intimate portion of the house was once the centre of urban sociability and display takes on larger significance when we consider the example set by seventeenth-century monarchs who directed affairs of state from the comfort and splendour of their baroque boudoirs.

During the eighteenth century urban dwellers increasingly identified an assortment of household rooms with a spectrum of activities – dining, intimate comforts, more public entertaining, reading and quiet reflection – some more fully exposed to guests than others. In the city even the guests of poorer bakers, masons, grocers, clerks, tailors, and leather workers, among others, also found themselves entertained in parlours.[83] As early as 1681 there was among the ten rooms inhabited by James Hayes, a Bristol merchant, a room specifically for 'dining'. The room contained three tables, a sideboard, chairs, a map, and a copy of the royal coat of arms. The assessors of only two of the village homes near Bristol mentioned dining rooms at all over the entire period from 1660 to 1780. The two rural exceptions in this regard were the home of a wealthy victualler in the village of Alveston, as assessed in 1768, and the nine-room rectory of Winterbourne.[84] The influence of urbanity on rural dwellings was significantly delayed and very limited.

On the other hand, urban dwellers may have got some of their notions from the country homes of the gentry and applied them to their own urban aims.[85] Beginning in the 1680s, the gentry directed their estate managers and architects to remove kitchens from manor houses and relegate them to separate pavilions, partly to control fire but mainly to elevate the formal house above the mundane activities of social inferiors.[86] After 1720 or so the location of domestic hospitality in the manor house had clearly shifted from the storeys to the ground floor.[87] The distinction drawn by the gentry between the privacy of the upstairs and the public nature of the ground floor was imitated by urban dwellers. Some of the clearest expressions of the segregation of intimate spaces from spaces on display were provided by the subjects of paintings and prints and the location of certain pictures in the home. Charles Foxell, a

Bristol joiner worth £580 3s 8d in 1739, owned twenty-three pictures. All his 'family pictures' were hung in bedrooms upstairs, while his portrait of George Whitefield, the famous Methodist who often preached in Bristol, was in the parlour with Foxell's coat of arms for all to see. Thus Foxell announced his religious affiliation and his lineage to his guests but kept more sentimental images from public view.[88]

To see that attitudes governing sociability and display varied from one topographical setting to the other and contributed to the conscious and visible maintenance of the urban–rural gulf, we need look no further than the bodies of urban and rural dwellers, as they appeared inside and outside the home, in life and in death. Proportionately more urban dwellers than villagers spent lavish amounts on clothing. Eighteen (78·3 per cent) of the twenty-three clothing collections assessed at £5 or more were worn by urban dwellers. The five most expensive wardrobes, all worth more than £20 and one more than £25, were urban. More significantly, even those very few villagers who did spend £5 or more on clothing tended to be wealthy enough to do so within their means. Only one of the five villagers who owned at least £5 worth of clothes had 20 per cent or more of his total assets in that form. On the other hand, nine of the eighteen urban dwellers whose inventories identified such expensive wardrobes devoted this same portion of their material wealth to garments. Although the gap narrowed in the eighteenth century, jewellery – as in the case of wigs, robes, and other ornamental garb – was clearly more popular among urban dwellers. (Table 6.14.)

The funeral expenses of ordinary urban dwellers often exceeded those of even the most substantial rural yeoman. Eleven of the twelve most costly funerals recorded in probate accounts of the 1760s and 1770s were for urban dwellers of various levels of wealth and status. Elaborate last rites were hardly

Table 6.14 The ownership of jewellery shown in all 3,787 extant inventories taken of 2,637 homes in Bristol and 1,150 homes in the nearby villages, 1660–1740

|  | 1660–99 | | | 1700–40 | | |
|---|---|---|---|---|---|---|
|  | Total no. of owners | As % of luxury owners | As % of all extant | Total no. of owners | As % of luxury owners | As % of all extant |
| Urban | 37 | 9·8 | 2·8 | 28 | 8·7 | 2·1 |
| Rural | 7 | 6·7 | 0·9 | 4 | 3·5 | 1·1 |

*Source:* Probate Inventories and Cause Papers.

new to the urban setting. In 1677 £6, or roughly 22 per cent of John Tyler's total estate, was spent on his funeral in St Peter. When John Thomas, a Bristol cooper worth only £31, died in 1707 his estate paid for seven hours of bell ringing in his parish according to his own wishes. In the city, not even poverty was grounds for exclusion from the urbane ritual of an elaborate funeral. Margaret Neady, a Bristol widow whose total assets at her death amounted to less than £2 (in fact, she was £24 8s 6d in debt), was laid to rest at a cost of £15 19s 4d in 1748. It is not clear who paid this lavish amount, although Neady's executor, a Bristol merchant named John Angier, may have provided what he regarded as a proper burial. In 1764 Edward Crane, a Bristol coach painter worth £692, was sent to his final resting place in grand style. The ceremony cost his estate £14 5s 8d, of which 15s was spent on cosmetic work for the corpse, a fitting expenditure for a man whose clothes were valued at £22. Crane's will stipulated that he wanted hours of bell ringing, a chaise hearse, twelve uniformed pallbearers, and ample liquor for all his mourners. The funeral was as much a celebration of Crane's powers of earthly accumulation as it was his ritual of passage into the afterlife.[89]

The view that urban material culture had a widespread influence outside cities and towns during most of the early modern period is misleading. It rests on the unsafe assumption that a commercial revolution in urban centres of advertising, marketing, and production was tantamount to imitative consumerism everywhere else.[90] To be sure, the mechanisms for the distribution of possessions associated with the urban network were firmly in place before the Restoration. Urban markets and fairs were attended by villagers. In fact, itinerant chapmen made it possible for rural consumers to buy an array of luxury goods without going to urban markets for them.[91] Nevertheless, villagers of all kinds conformed consistently to their own, lower, levels of consumption where finished items likely to be of urban or foreign origin were involved. There were many rural dwellers whose total assets exceeded £300 in value but included no luxury possessions at all.[92] Even though some of the most sophisticated analyses of English material culture in the latter half of the early modern period recognise the role of conscious aims in consumer behaviour, they still attribute patterns of acquisition primarily to wealth and disposable income.[93] Others have argued convincingly that consumer demand was not a function of real wages and, moreover, that there was no 'consumer revolution' in early modern England.[94] Although wealth did play some role in shaping patterns of consumption, the uneven distribution of wealth in early modern England explains neither the relative paucity of luxury items in the homes of prosperous yeomen in the countryside surrounding Bristol nor the consistently more common appearance of such items in the city, even in the possession of poorer people. The material culture of an English provincial city of substantial size and importance did not exert any particular regional influence. Rather, the material culture on display in urban homes and the forms of sociability that it served were imitative of trends established in the rural setting by the privileged landed classes. Over the extended period, in the urban setting some artisans and merchants even exceeded levels of luxury owner-ship established by the lesser gentry in the countryside,[95] while most villagers of both sexes and all levels of wealth exhibited a preference for material culture that asserted, in the face of urban resurgence, their own preserved detachment from the conventions of city life. During the urban renaissance villagers resisted urbane cultural hegemony.[96]

By the second half of the eighteenth century, villagers were more likely to see expressions of urbane sensibility in the homes and possessions of their neighbours. In the 1760s a traveller on the Gloucester road could stop ten miles from Bristol for a sip of French brandy, as well as a draught of West Country cider, at John Hewett's in the village of Alveston. A friend visiting the home of John Hewett, the victualler, could move about its seven rooms, gazing at eighteen different printed scenes on display throughout the house, both upstairs and down. From the 'new kitchen', where Hewett's best clock kept time, one might see, reflected in either of two mirrors, a painting in his 'dining room'. After dinner, there would be coffee in the 'parlour', served in china cups expressly for the purpose, or perhaps something stronger from the silver tankard. When John Hewett died in 1768, thirty-two people still owed him money amounting to more than £140. Hewett's widow decided to sell the pigs for £63 9s 9d, but she kept the luxury items in her home. As her husband's executrix she marked, but could not sign, the probate records and, in at least one sense, Widow Hewett still resembled most of her rural neigh-bours: she owned no books at all.[97]

## NOTES

1  B.R.O. Diocese of Bristol Probate Inventories and Cause Papers (Joseph Marks, 1746).

2  Throughout this study, the term 'storey' will be used, as it was in the inventories themselves, to refer to building levels above the ground floor. That is, first-storey rooms are directly above ground-floor rooms and just beneath second-storey rooms.

3  M. Laithwaite, 'Totnes houses 1500–1800', in P. Clark (ed.), *The Transformation of English Provincial Towns 1600–1800* (London, 1984), pp. 62–98. Bristol's domestic spaces resembled closely those of early modern Paris, suggesting that the cultural divide was along topographical and not national lines. See A. Paradailhe-Galabrun, *The Birth of Intimacy: Privacy and Domestic Life in Early Modern Paris* (Philadelphia, 1991), pp. 40–67.

4  B.R.O. Probate Inventories (John Jayne, 1752).

5  Jayne's inventory reports rents collected on fields in either Compton Dando or Compton Martin, both of which were rural Somerset parishes near Bristol.

6   L. J. Kaplan, *Thomas Chatterton: The Family Romance of the Impostor-Poet* (Berkeley, Cal., 1987), pp. 33–40; R. L. Megroz, *The Real Robinson Crusoe* (London, 1939).

7   J. de Vries, 'Between purchasing power and the world of goods: understanding the household economy in early modern Europe', in J. Brewer and R. Porter (eds), *Consumption and the World of Goods* (London, 1993), pp. 98–102; M. Spufford, 'The limitations of the probate inventory', in J. Chartres and D. Hey (eds), *English Rural Society 1500–1800* (Cambridge, 1990), pp. 139–74; J. and N. Cox, 'Valuations in probate inventories', *Local Historian* 16 no. 8 (1985), pp. 467–77.

8   The mentalities of English colonists and early Americans have also been explored by examining the language employed, as well as the items identified, in probate inventories. See A. E. Yentsch, *A Chesapeake Family and their Slaves: A Study in Historical Archaeology* (Cambridge, 1994); L. H. Foote and C. L. Haines, 'Household vernacular in Concord, Massachusetts, probate inventories 1655–1800', *Dublin Seminar for New England Folk Life Annual Proceedings* (Boston, Mass., 1983), pp. 55–69. By contrast, French inventories reflected a more standardised procedure conducted by notaries and official assessors. See C. Fairchilds, 'The production and marketing of *populuxe* goods in eighteenth-century Paris', in Brewer and Porter, *Consumption and the World of Goods*, p. 229; M. Baulant, A. Schuurman, and P. Servais (eds), *Inventaires après décès et ventes de meubles* (Louvain-la-Neuve, 1987); P. Benedict, 'Towards the comparative study of the popular market for art: the ownership of paintings in seventeenth-century Metz', *Past and Present* 109 (1985), pp. 100–17.

9   B.R.O. Probate Inventories (Anthony King, 1681).

10  B.R.O. Probate Inventories (Widow of John Brayne, 1687).

11  B.R.O. Probate Inventories (Lawrence Joyner, 1682).

12  The inventory of Francis Little, a Bristol saddler worth £489 17s 4d in 1681, shows that his shop was in Broad Street and his house was down on the quays. His probate account shows the payment of two separate rents for these.

13  B.R.O. Probate Inventories (Samuel Ware, 1712).

14  The importance of taking a household inventory promptly after the occupant's death, before items could be removed by self-interested creditors or heirs, was observed by executors in order to protect estates and prevent costly inheritance disputes. Cases in which a year or more elapsed between the taking of an inventory and its exhibition to the diocese were rare.

15  P. J. Corfield and U. Priestly, 'Rooms and room use in Norwich housing 1580–1730', *Post-medieval Archaeology* 16 (1982), pp. 93–123.

16  L. Weatherill, 'The meaning of consumer behaviour in late seventeenth- and early eighteenth-century England', in Brewer and Porter, *Consumption and the World of Goods*, pp. 206–27.

17  Fairchilds, 'The production and marketing of *populuxe* goods in eighteenth-century Paris', pp. 228–48; T. Hine, *Populuxe* (New York, 1986); L. Weatherill, 'Patterns of Consumption in Britain *c.* 1660–1760: Problems and Sources', unpublished paper, Clark Library Seminars (October 1988), asserts, 'There is no evidence that most people of middle rank wanted to be like the gentry, although they may have wanted the goods for their own purposes.'

18  The category 'luxury' includes: pewter, silver and gold items (other than coins); pictures,

paintings, and prints; watches and clocks; mirrors; firearms; swords and other bladed weapons; musical instruments; jewellery; china; glass; liquor or wine (not beer); tobacco; chocolate; special furniture (desks, scriptores, leather chairs, carpets, tapestries); and all items explicitly identified by assessors as urban or foreign in origin or style. ('Japanned' items, 'Manchester' cloth, 'Delft' plates, 'Barbados' shells, and 'Turkey' carpets are all examples.) Thus the category 'luxury' as used here includes all items, other than books, specified throughout Brewer and Porter, *Consumption and the World of Goods*, and L. Weatherill, *Consumer Behaviour and Material Culture in Britain 1660–1760* (London, 1988), with the exception of earthenware, saucepans, and eating utensils, all of which are regarded as noteworthy by Weatherill, who avoids the term 'luxury'. Weatherill, in 'The meaning of consumer behaviour', table 10.2, shows that pewter items were very common in rural and urban areas alike, 1675–1725. Items identified in an inventory as the deceased's occupational tools, stock-in-trade, wares, commodities for sale, or livestock have not been considered here as luxury possessions in the home.

19  Of the entire extant collection: 3,560 are from Bristol's own parishes, all of which are urban; 1,192 are from the twenty-four nearby villages in the city's rural environs; 343 are from unspecified parishes in either setting.

20  Of the 1,455 households represented in the comparison group the place of residence is known for 1,419. Of these 1,048 (74 per cent) are urban and 371 (26 per cent) are rural.

21  This includes loans extended, vessels, land, buildings, houses – other than the deceased's own residence – from which the deceased derived income in the form of rent, interest, or dividends on shares.

22  This includes printed books, pamphlets, broadsides, folios, ballads, and chapbooks. It also includes newspapers and other printed ephemera, although these were rarely itemised in probate.

23  B.R.O. Probate Inventories (John Austin, 1661; Thomas Hopper, 1717 (this may have been a very early example of an umbrella); John Davis, 1741; Samuel Smith, 1776).

24  B.R.O. Probate Inventories (William Manning, 1702).

25  S. W. Mintz, 'The changing roles of food in the study of consumption', in Brewer and Porter, *Consumption and the World of Goods*, pp. 261–73; W. Schivelbusch, *Tastes of Paradise: A Social History of Spices, Stimulants, and Intoxicants*, trans. D. Jacobson (New York, 1992).

26  Between 1675 and 1725 only 6 per cent of the extant inventories for the citizens of Berwick, Cambridge, Canterbury, Carlisle, Durham, Liverpool, Manchester, Newcastle, Shrewsbury, Southampton, and Winchester had knives and forks among their eating utensils, while only about 2 per cent of village households in the same diocese had knives and forks at that time. See Weatherill, *Consumer Behaviour and Material Culture in Britain* and 'The meaning of consumer behaviour', table 10.2.

27  B.R.O. Probate Inventories (Thomas Adeane, 1668; Joseph Gibson, 1700; George Browne, 1698; Nathaniel Tyndale, 1756). There is no assurance that the last of these resided in Bristol before 1740, but he does conform to the pattern of poor, but urbane, musicians established by his predecessors in Bristol, whose assets at death ranged between £10 and £91. Tyndale's total assets were only £19 at his death, but in addition to his violin and oboe he owned valuable 'parcels' of music and books, all in his upstairs bedroom, a clock, prints, pictures, mirrors, a tea service, and two wigs.

28  B.R.O. Probate Inventories (Hugh Rumney, yeoman farmer in Henbury, 1671; Richard

White, yeoman farmer in Henbury, 1695; George Wheeler, victualler in Clifton, 1736; John Griffyth, rector of Winterbourne, 1687/88). The occupations of musical instrument owners in Bristol were far more varied, but professionals and gentlemen made up the largest single group. Between 1660 and 1740, Bristol's musical instrument owners included two gentlemen, a clergyman, two cathedral organists, another professional musician, two surgeons, a corporation official, two merchants, a cooper, a horner, a button maker, an arms painter, a cordwainer, a tinplate maker, a mariner, five widows and two spinsters (with no specified occupations), and three other persons of unspecified occupation.

29 B.R.O. Probate Inventories (John Bevill, 1678); (John Massey, 1685).

30 Samuel Pepys, *Diary* (24 July 1663); R. Latham (ed.), *The Illustrated Pepys: Extracts from the Diary* (Berkeley, Cal., 1983), p. 55.

31 The population of Bristol at the end of the early modern was roughly 38,484. This excludes the populations of St George, St Paul, Clifton, Stapleton, Mangotsfield, and Bedminster, absorbed by the city between 1756 and the 1801 census. The population of the twenty-two relevant rural parishes and their hamlets was roughly 19,543. See W. Page (ed.), *The Victoria History of the County of Somerset* II (London, 1911) and *The Victoria History of the County of Gloucester* II (London, 1907).

32 Of all 4,752 inventories of known origin dating from the entire period 1660–1780, 1,020 were for households with owners of luxury items – those finished goods most often singled out by assessors for specific mention, most highly valued by assessors, and most likely to have been derived from the urban network. Of those 1,020 households, 787 (77·2 per cent) were urban and only 233 (22·8 per cent) were rural.

33 B.R.O. Probate Inventories (Thomas Horne, 1720).

34 This figure applies to the second half of the seventeenth century and is supplied by J. Thirsk (ed.), *The Agrarian History of England and Wales* IV (Cambridge, 1967), p. 864.

35 According to the 1714 inventory of a Bristol widow, Elizabeth Dexter, she paid her maid £2 per year. The maid's room, if Mrs Dexter supplied her with one, may have spared the maid £2 or £3 annual rent.

36 R. Grassby, 'Personal wealth of the business community in seventeenth-century England', *Economic History Review*, 2nd ser. 23 (1970), pp. 224–9.

37 Portion of urban households in the comparison group having more than 20 per cent of total assets in the form of the specified items: 1660–99, 3·7 per cent (14:376); 1700–39, 6·2 per cent (20:321); 1740–80, 14·4 per cent (13:90).

38 B.R.O. Probate Inventories (William Tock, 1758). Per animal, the value of livestock, as indicated by Tock's inventory, was as follows: 4s 6d per sheep/lamb; £4 2s per cow/yearling; £1 10s per pig. Tock also had a cart and harness worth £8. According to hauliers' inventories, a horse was valued between £1 and £2.

39 B.R.O. Probate Inventories. See, for example: William Ford, a coal miner in Mangotsfield, worth £10 15s 6d at his death in 1703; J. Llewellyn, a coal miner in Mangotsfield, worth £7 17s 6d at his death in 1711, and his son, J. Llewellyn, a coal miner in Mangotsfield, worth £4 17s 8d at his death in 1732; E. Davis, a yeoman in Stapleton, worth £15 at his death in 1731; J. Horne, a yeoman in Olveston, worth £19 16s 6d at his death in 1747; J. Stephens, a schoolmaster in Winterbourne, worth £7 6s at his death in 1748.

40 B.R.O. Probate Inventories (George Wheeler, 1736). George Wheeler, a victualler in Clifton worth only £15 3s 9d at his death, provides the exceptional case; in addition to his encased clock, assessed at £1, he owned ten pictures, a mirror, and three musical instruments.

41 B.R.O. Probate Inventories (William Longdon, of Stapleton, worth £30 10s at his death in 1674; Ann Culme, a widow in Mangotsfield, worth £22 1s 6d at her death in 1688; M. Branch, a widow in Clifton, worth £28 9s at her death in 1687).

42 B.R.O. Probate Inventories. For the period 1660–1780, 312 Bristol households with total assets of £30 or less owned luxury items. In the villages there were thirty such households, and only one of these had more than one of the specified items.

43 This valuable 'chattel lease' is described in the 1686 probate inventory of Elizabeth Credd. It constituted nearly 90 per cent of her total wealth.

44 L. Weatherill, 'A possession of one's own: women and consumer behaviour in England 1660–1740', *Journal of British Studies* 25 (1986), pp. 131–56. Weatherill herself acknowledges here that it is difficult to assign attitudes about particular possessions specifically to men or women.

45 S. Staves, *Married Women's Separate Property in England 1660–1833* (Cambridge, Mass., 1990), especially pp. 131–61. Throughout the period under consideration, the law held a husband liable for his wife's expenditure and answerable to her creditors, and so the law also undermined women's independent acquisition of possessions.

46 A. Vickery, 'Women and the world of goods: a Lancashire consumer and her possessions 1751–81', in Brewer and Porter, *Consumption and the World of Goods*, pp. 274–301. In attempting to address the question of gender-specific attitudes about certain possessions, Vickery argues primarily from the evidence generated by one subject, Elizabeth Shackleton, a literate member of London and gentry society whose diary is located at the Lancashire Record Office, L.R.O. DDB/81/1–39.

47 A. L. Erickson, *Women and Property in Early Modern England* (London, 1993), pp. 187–203.

48 B.R.O. Probate Inventories (Samuel and Mary Smith, 1776). Samuel and Mary Smith, whose total assets exceeded £1,717, resided in Bristol in a large house with a silver service, china, teapots, drinking glasses, pictures, mirrors, jewellery, comfortable furnishings, a dining room, a parlour, and a study full of books. Mary made out her own will in 1775 and joint possession of items assessed in the couple's inventory was undoubtedly made clear for the assessor in their wills.

49 Erickson, *Women and Property in Early Modern England*, pp. 156–86.

50 G. J. Barker-Benfield, *The Culture of Sensibility: Sex and Society in Eighteenth-Century Britain* (Chicago, 1996), pp. 154–214.

51 Of the 317 women with their own inventories, 231 (75 per cent) resided in the city and eighty-one (25 per cent) resided in the nearby villages.

52 The specified occupations of the urban women included: apothecary, blockmaker, boarding-house keeper, castor maker, cheese vendor, cobbler, cooper, cordwainer, grocer, haulier, innkeeper, locksmith, merchant, nurse-keeper, pinkmaker, shopkeeper, soap boiler, victualler, watch seller, weaver, whitawer, wool dealer, and writing mistress. The specified occupations of the village women included: farmer (especially sheep or dairy farmer), oatmeal maker, schoolmistress, and smallware mercer.

53  B. J. Todd, 'The remarrying widow: a stereotype reconsidered', in M. Prior (ed.), *Women in English Society 1500–1800* (London, 1985), pp. 54–92.

54  There were many unmarried women in the villages who conformed to this rural trend of high levels of assets in the form of credit but no luxury possessions at all. For examples, see B.R.O. Probate Inventories (Dorothy Orchard, a Henbury 'spinster' worth over £112, of which 89 per cent was in the form of credit, all on bond, in 1660; Joan Atkins, an Almondsbury widow worth over £309, of which 79 per cent was in the form of credit, all on bond, in 1661; Joan Witchell, a Mangotsfield widow worth £171, of which 94 per cent was in the form of cash and credit, in 1676; Frances Stephens, a Henbury 'spinster' worth over £88, of which 93 per cent was in the form of credit, in 1680; Elizabeth Mills, a Henbury widow worth £62, of which 58 per cent was in credit, all on bond, in 1684; Sarah Werrett, an Alveston 'spinster' worth over £128, of which 97 per cent was in the form of credit, in 1685; Jane Richards, a Henbury 'spinster' worth over £132, of which 84 per cent was in the form of bonded credit and collected interest, in 1705; Anne Cullum, a Mangotsfield widow worth over £82, of which 73 per cent was in the form of credit, all on bond, in 1714; Sarah Lloyd, a Mangotsfield widow worth over £289, of which 93 per cent was in the form of credit, all on bond, in 1748).

55  See, for example, B.R.O. Probate Inventories (Sarah Browning, 1715). Sarah Browning, a Bristol widow worth only £14 9s, owned only three items that were singled out by her assessor: a looking glass; a Bible with a silver clasp; and a gold band worth £1 10s, identified as her wedding ring.

56  B.R.O. Probate Inventories (Deborah James, 1672).

57  B.R.O. Probate Inventories (Stephen Rogers, mariner, 1764; Jacob Milsome, victualler, 1762).

58  J. E. Wills, junior, 'European consumption and Asian production in the seventeenth and eighteenth centuries', in Brewer and Porter, *Consumption and the World of Goods*, pp. 133–47.

59  *The Country Mouse and the City Mouse* (London, 12th ed. 1683). For a further discussion of urban–rural themes emerging from the chapbook collection of Samuel Pepys see M. Spufford, *Small Books and Pleasant Histories: Popular Fiction and its Readership in Seventeenth-Century England* (Cambridge, 1981), pp. 57–64.

60  B.R.O. P/StJ/F/21(1). Bristol merchants imported wines from Spain and France, tobacco from Maryland, Virginia, and the West Indies, rum and sugar from the West Indies, citrus fruits from southern Spain, Jamaica, and Nevis. See P. McGrath (ed.), *Merchants and Merchandise in Seventeenth-Century Bristol* (Bristol, 1955), pp. 288–93. There were unsuccessful attempts at growing tobacco in southern Gloucestershire as early as 1593, according to B. Little, *The City and County of Bristol: A Study in Atlantic Civilization* (London, 1954), p. 110. See also Joan Thirsk, 'New crops and their diffusion: tobacco-growing in seventeenth-century England', in C. W. Chalklin and M. A. Havinden (eds), *Rural Change and Urban Growth 1500–1800* (London, 1974).

61  K. Morgan, *Bristol and the Atlantic Trade in the Eighteenth Century* (Cambridge, 1993), pp. 184–218; D. C. Coleman, *The Economy of England 1450–1750* (Oxford, 1977), p. 118; C. Shammas, 'Changes in English and Anglo-American consumption from 1550 to 1800', in Brewer and Porter, *Consumption and the World of Goods*, p. 182.

62  C. Shammas, 'Changes in English and Anglo-American consumption from 1550 to 1800', p. 182.

63  S. W. Mintz, 'The changing role of food in the study of consumption', p. 261.

64  B.R.O. Probate Inventories (John Kimber, 1681). To Jonathan Barry I owe the information that John Kimber ran a radical coffee house that was continued, after Kimber's
death, by his widow.

65  S. W. Mintz, *Sweetness and Power: The Place of Sugar in Modern History* (Harmondsworth, 1985), p. 111.

66  J. Barry, 'Popular culture in seventeenth-century Bristol', in B. Reay (ed.), *Popular
Culture in Seventeenth-Century England* (London and New York, 1985), p. 68.

67  C. Winslow, 'Sussex smugglers', in D. Hay, P. Linebaugh, J. G. Rule, E. P. Thompson,
and C. Winslow (eds), *Albion's Fatal Tree: Crime and Society in Eighteenth-Century
England* (New York, 1975), pp. 124–5. By 1740 3 million lb of tea was smuggled annually;
that was three times the amount brought in legally through ports.

68  B.R.O. Probate Inventories (Anne Garraway, 1712 and 1714; Samuel Parrett, or Parrot,
1713).

69  B.R.O. Probate Inventories (William Manning, 1702). The complete absence of china
from the entire extant probate record for villages near Bristol in the late seventeenth
century is more likely a reflection of a highly significant paucity than a complete lack of
china in that setting. In a sampling of 2,075 rural inventories taken in eight English
dioceses between 1675 and 1725, only 1 per cent contained references to china. I suspect
that most of those references date from the eighteenth century. See Weatherill, 'The
meaning of consumer behaviour in late seventeenth- and early eighteenth-century
England', table 10.2.

70  B.R.O. Probate Inventories (George Fenton, 1749).

71  B.R.O. Probate Inventories (Thomas Westell, 1734).

72  P. Clark, *Sociability and Urbanity: Clubs and Societies in the Eighteenth-Century City*
(Leicester, 1986) and *The English Alehouse: A Social History 1200–1830* (London, 1983).

73  See especially F. Heal, *Hospitality in Early Modern England* (Oxford, 1990).

74  Vickery, 'Women and the world of goods', especially pp. 281–8.

75  Weatherill, 'The meaning of consumer behaviour in late seventeenth- and early eighteenth-century England', table 10.2. Here Weatherill, who does not emphasise concealment, shows that 43 per cent of 319 London inventories, 27 per cent of 217 inventories
in eleven major towns, and 15 per cent of 291 inventories of other towns contained
window curtains; from this I calculate that roughly 29 per cent of all urban inventories
in her sample contained window curtains. Of 2,075 rural inventories in her sample only
6 per cent contained window curtains. Bristol inventories were not included in her
sample.

76  Samuel Pepys, *Diary*. See, for example, 22 November 1660, 14 August 1666, and 5
October 1667. The openly flirtatious Pepys, who had a mistress, reprimanded his wife if
she violated even his notion of proper dress.

77  B.R.O. Probate Inventories (William Manning, 1702).

78  B.R.O. Probate Inventories (John Griffyth, 1697).

79  See, for example, the inventory of an Elberton yeoman, T. Collins, assessed at a healthy
£214 8s 5d in 1767, or the inventory of Henbury farmer, William Shepperd, worth £202

15s in 1746. Both households had rooms with at least three beds and little else other than apples or sacks of potatoes in them.

80  B.R.O. Probate Inventories (John Hopton, 1681).

81  B.R.O. Probate Inventories (Thomas Collins, 1767).

82  B.R.O. Probate Inventories (Samuel Seager, 1699).

83  See, for examples: B.R.O. Probate Inventories (Walter Carpenter, a Bristol baker with total assets of £33 2s 11d, in 1680; John Massey, a Bristol clerk with total assets of £59 1s, in 1685; John Robins, a Bristol mason with total assets of £18 1d, in 1734; Isaac Crump, a Bristol grocer with total assets of £72, in 1736; John Trotman, a Bristol saddle tree maker with total assets of £42 5s, in 1741; Daniel Badger, a Bristol tailor with assets of £41 12s 6d, in 1776).

84  B.R.O. Probate Inventories (John Hewett, a victualler with total assets of £358 12s 8d, in 1768; John Griffyth, rector of Winterbourne, with total assets of £378, in 1678).

85  This is a point of considerable debate. For the view that conscious choices shaping material culture are not a product of imitative behaviour see: Weatherill, 'The meaning of consumer behaviour in late seventeenth- and early eighteenth-century England', especially p. 208, where she states flatly: 'There is no evidence that most people of middle rank wanted to be like the gentry, although they may have wanted some of the new goods for their own purposes.'

86  M. Girouard, *Life in the English Country House: A Social and Achitectural History* (New Haven, Conn., 1978), p. 151. The country estate of Nether Lypiatt in Gloucestershire provides an early example of this.

87  Girouard, *Life in the English Country House*, p. 189.

88  B.R.O. Probate Inventories (George Foxell, 1739). George Whitefield was a native of Gloucester but made Bristol one of his preaching centres. Whitefield was identified by name as the subject of the protrait listed in this inventory.

89  B.R.O. Probate Inventories (John Tyler, 1677; John Thomas, 1707; Margaret Neady, 1748; Edward Crane, 1764).

90  N. McKendrick, 'Commercialization and the economy', in

N. McKendrick, J. Brewer, and J. H. Plumb, *The Birth of a Consumer Society: The Commercialization of Eighteenth-Century England* (Bloomington, Ind., 1982), pp. 1–194.

91  Spufford, *Small Books and Pleasant Histories*, ch. 5, and *The Great Reclothing of Rural England: Petty Chapmen and their Wares in the Seventeenth Century* (London, 1984).

92  Examples of very wealthy villagers with no luxury possessions date mainly from the first half of the urban renaissance. See, for example: B.R.O. Probate Inventories (William Stevens, worth £351, 1683; John Cox, worth £648 3s 8d, 1695; R. Bracy, worth £806 5s, 1701; John Baker, worth £841 17s 2d, 1701).

93  C. Shammas, *The Pre-industrial Consumer in England and America* (Oxford, 1990) and 'Changes in English and Anglo-American consumption from 1550 to 1800', in Brewer and Porter, *Consumption and the World of Goods*, pp. 177–295, especially pp. 194–9; Weatherill, *Consumer Behaviour and Material Culture in Britain*.

94  J. de Vries, 'Between purchasing power and the world of goods', especially p. 107, where Jan de Vries writes: 'The term "consumer revolution" should probably be suppressed

before frequent repetition secures for it a place in the used-car lot of explanatory vehicles reserved for historical concepts that break down directly after purchase by the passing scholar.'

95  Weatherill, *Consumer Behaviour and Material Culture in Britain*, pp. 25–42 and 168–89.

96  A detailed Dutch study of the material culture of farmers and townspeople in the seventeenth and eighteenth centuries concluded that rural dwellers, regardless of wealth or proximity to Amsterdam, preserved more traditional material culture as a self-conscious expression of distinctly rural taste. See H. van Koolbergen, 'De materiele cultuur van Weesp en Weesperkarspel in de zeventiende en achttiende eeuw', *Volkskundig Bulletin* 9, no. 1 (1983), pp. 3–52.

97  B.R.O. Probate Inventories (John Hewett, 1768).

# Chapter 7

Print culture:
books and printed matter

An understanding of print culture is essential to the study of early modern cultural ties and social networks. Print culture and oral culture are distinct in form, but in early modern England they had in common many purposes and social contexts.[1] Even if we cannot always know the titles and contents of cheap books, pamphlets, or even more valuable bound books, we can identify who the owners of printed materials were and where they lived. We can weigh the relative importance of gender, occupation, and wealth as determinants in the ownership of printed material. Patterns in the ownership of the printed word, like patterns in material culture and direct personal interaction, expressed an observable divide that was most pronounced along topographical lines. As we will see in the next chapter, the textual component of print culture explicitly corroborated and endorsed the separation of urban and rural spheres. The arrival of printers in provincial cities during the urban renaissance did not extend urban cultural influence over villagers, it intensified urban–rural distinctions. Until the middle of the eighteenth century, this urban–rural divide may have been more profound than that divide by which others typically distinguish so-called popular and elite cultures linked with wealth and literacy.

Some of the most detailed analyses of printed material as a feature of English life in the seventeenth and eighteenth centuries, the latter of which is often assigned special meaning as an age of commercialisation, focus almost entirely on the mechanisms of distribution and supply rather than on the identities and attitudes of actual book owners.[2] According to some, in the case of the most affordable and abundant books detailed profiles of the owners are least available.[3] The inclusiveness of early modern 'consumer culture', as opposed to the modern elitism of 'high art', is invoked convincingly as one means to explain the appeal of printed texts.[4] Other studies posing many of the essential questions regarding the social composition of book owners approach books as objects but confine themselves to the discussion of urban areas.[5] To understand the role of print as a cultural tie among people, without ignoring the influence of personal taste, we must first understand the distinct social and material contexts to which books were assigned.

During much of the earlier modern period before the eighteenth century, the origins of printed material in England were themselves severely circum-scribed. By extension of royal charter in 1557, printing in England became virtually monopolised by the Stationers' Company of London. There were, in periods of civil war or shifting religious policy, sporadic appearances of printing presses outside London and the university cities. A printing press was in operation in Bristol as early as 1546, a sign of the city's cultural and political significance. The press existed to produce religious pamphlets from within the protective confines of Bristol Castle. This provincial press was operating in the service of the Henrician reformation and was a short-lived venture. Nearly a century later, when royalists gained control of Bristol in July 1643, some talk of moving Charles's wartime court to Bristol resulted in the temporary establishment of a Royalist printing press there. A Laudian Prayer Book was printed in Bristol in 1644.[6] Normally, however, a combination of the Stationers' charter and the Licensing Act (more specifically the Printing Act) effectively restricted English printing to the cities of London, Oxford, and Cambridge.

In 1695 the Licensing Act was allowed to lapse and the emergence of legal and permanent provincial presses after that watershed was, in John Feather's view, 'to transform the trade and create whole new mechanisms of distribu-tion'. Printers of provincial newspapers, for example, became the most active agents for London book dealers in the first half of the eighteenth century.[7] In 1695 William Bonny wasted no time setting up his press in the city of Bristol when the corporation there granted him special dispensation to appease the local freemen at work in related book trades. The first Bristol newspaper, *The Bristol Post Boy*, began circulating some time in 1702, less than a year after the *Norwich Post*, England's first provincial newspaper, made its appearance.[8] In 1696 Bristol had 134 licensed chapmen (itinerant salesmen of petty items, cloth, and small books) and was second only to London, which had 501.[9] By 1775 at the latest, Bristol had thirty-three resident book dealers of its own.[10] The mechanisms of print production and distribution, strong signs of cultural and economic vitality, were present in a number of provincial cities by the early eighteenth century.

In a manner consistent with a widespread tendency to place revived urban areas at the centre of English life in general, historians have tended to lump provincial towns and their rural environs together into one collective market for books.[11] This is symptomatic of a familiar emphasis taken from the per-spective of supply, distribution, and marketing. Patterns of consumption, which varied from one setting to another, reflected the place of books in urban or rural social spheres. In the generations before the civil war, levels of book ownership varied from one type of town, or small urban area, to another. Moreover, these levels varied more from town to town than they did with the degrees of wealth exhibited by the consumer population.[12] Clearly, levels of book ownership varied from one urban location to another before the Licensing Act lapsed in 1695. The extent to which the establishment of printing presses in provincial cities promoted comparable levels of urban and rural consumption, revised attitudes toward printed materials, or drew rural dwellers into closer contact with urban culture remains to be shown. The eighty-year period following the Restoration is divided almost exactly in two by the arrival of permanent printing operations in Bristol and provides ample scope in which to assess the influence of a celebrated urban cultural development upon life in nearby villages.

Book ownership in the city of Bristol itself had declined in the seventeenth century before resident printers arrived there.[13] The recovery of book ownership in the city was sluggish during the first forty years of the eighteenth century. These trends may have been related to a general decline in the quality and availability of schooling in much of England during the period in question.[14] On the other hand, in the north of England the availability of teachers and schools may have improved after the Restoration.[15] It has been suggested that, with a decline in piety, the popularity of oral culture hampered the recovery of print culture of which religious tracts were once such a buoyant staple,[16] but this seems unlikely given the long history of a ubiquitous oral culture and the place of importance enjoyed by printed sermons in provincial publishing.

The contexts of print, more than the texts in print or the extent of their potential readership, help us assign meaning to patterns of consumption during the urban renaissance. The titles of books, and not just physical descriptions of them, were less commonly provided in inventories between 1700 and 1740 than they were before or after that period.[17] In the urban material culture of the early eighteenth century consumers differentiated more clearly between books and luxury items while the latter gained a higher profile in the urban hierarchy of possessions. In 1729 the vestry of St Philip and Jacob, one of the poorer Bristol parishes, actually sold two of the parish Bibles and seven of its Prayer Books, among other items, in order to purchase an engraved silver flagon, matching silver plate and a new surplice.[18] Urban bibliophilia would return after the Augustan age, but in the early eighteenth century printed material was marketed increasingly as a vehicle for disposable information.[19] The availability of newspapers and other locally printed ephemera at increasingly popular and numerous coffee houses created a temporary replacement for privately owned books in provincial cities and towns. These trends meant that, until the last decades of the early modern period, the power of privately owned printed material to expand social spheres was diminished, not enhanced. Some villagers may have read in urban coffee houses rather than in their own homes, but it is unlikely, given the form and context of print culture in the rural setting, that many villagers would have travelled into a city for such a purpose.

Despite new vitality in urban centres and the introduction of printing there, rural levels of book ownership were not elevated and print culture did not bring villagers into some expanding urban sphere of influence during the eighty years following the Restoration. Among members of our urban–rural comparison group, the percentage of rural dwellers who owned books declined from nearly 34 per cent in the forty years before 1700 to less than 15 per cent in the forty years after 1700. The decline in urban book ownership from about 44 per cent to under 33 per cent in the urban households was far less dramatic than that exhibited in the nearby villages.[20] Even studies that do not provide urban–rural comparisons have detected similar trends in urban book ownership.[21] An overall decline in book ownership from 18 per cent in 1675 to 13 per cent in 1725 has been observed for English rural households in general. It has been shown that over the same crucial period book ownership in provincial towns and cities overall actually increased from 20 per cent to 36 per cent, and from 18 per cent to an impressive 56 per cent in London.[22] Urban levels of book ownership were higher than rural ones in Cumbria, Cambridgeshire, and the north-west by a factor of roughly half, nearly twice as high as rural ones in Kent and the London area, and three times higher in the north-east and the Midlands.[23] The growth in the print-related trades in Bristol was not seen at all in the nearby villages.[24] The overall decline in rural book ownership in the late seventeenth and early eighteenth centuries may have reflected the polarisation of rural society, the contraction in the number of self-sufficient farmers, and the expansion in the ranks of dislocated agricultural wage labourers. These are sensible theories, but we should not assume that the distribution of wealth was the principal determinant of book ownership. As we will see, even patterns of literacy were not reliable indicators of the place of books among urban and rural dwellers in this period. The patterns of consumption and book ownership exhibited by villagers and urban residents were, to a significant degree, an expression of conscious choices. What is striking about relative trends in book distribution and ownership is that the period after the arrival of printing in Bristol saw the cultural gap between the city and the surrounding countryside accentuated rather than mediated. As in other respects, the topographical divide was bridged later in the eighteenth century, not during the earlier period associated with the urban renaissance.

The urban–rural gulf applied at the level of individual households as well as at the level of settings. Those villagers who did own books tended to own fewer than their counterparts in the nearby city. The distinction between intensive and extensive reading, observed for early modern France,[25] can be used to distinguish patterns of book ownership as well. In early modern England, rural patterns were characterised by the presence of fewer books of fewer types in fewer homes and fewer rooms. Urban book ownership was extensive. It is possible to combine explicitly reported figures and additional inventory details to identify any urban or rural dweller in one of four useful ways: as an owner of no books, of exactly one book, of 'some' books, or of 'many' books.[26] In the countryside around Bristol the number of villagers without books remained significantly large between 1700 and 1740, while villagers with 'many' and 'some' books became significantly rare. At the same time, the city's proportion of all book owners with more than one book, or even 'many' books, became significantly large while the city's proportion of the entire comparison group with no books at all became significantly small. (Table 7.1.)

Table 7.1 Comparison of urban and rural levels of book ownership in the city of Bristol and the nearby villages during two consecutive forty-year periods (% in parentheses)

| Levels of book ownership | 1660–99 | | 1700–40 | |
|---|---|---|---|---|
| | Urban | Rural | Urban | Rural |
| *Comparison group* | | | | |
| Many books | 68 (12) | 17 (9) | **50** (13)+ | **6** (4)– |
| Some books | 147 (26) | 40 (20) | **73** (19)+ | **12** (8)– |
| One book | 32 (6) | 8 (4) | 10 (3) | 5 (3) |
| No books | 309 (56) | **133** (67)+ | **261** (66)– | **133** (85)+ |
| Totals | 556 (100) | 198 (100) | 394 (100) | 156 (100) |
| | | | | |
| *All extant inventories* | | | | |
| With books | 247 (19) | 65 (8) | 133 (10) | 23 (6) |
| Without books | 1,053 (81) | 711 (92) | 1,204 (90) | 351 (94) |
| Totals | 1,300 (100) | 776 (100) | 1,337 (100) | 374 (100) |

*Note:* This table embodies four separately analysed contingency tables; the comparison group and the entire extant collection were analysed separately for each period. Bold figures indicate contingencies that were significantly common (+) or rare (–).
*Source:* B.R.O. Probate Inventories and Cause Papers.

A knowledge of book values acts as another means of assessing levels, and types, of book ownership. Single books valued at £1 or more were extremely rare and were usually identified separately by title. The average value of a book, calculated from actual holdings shown in the comparison group of inventories, was 1s 7d.[27] Thus the assessed values of parcels and bundles provide good evidence regarding the numbers, and types, of books they contained. The possibility that this estimate of average book value is high and that cheaper books were less likely to be given detailed assessment, or 'were not worth listing' in most probate inventories, should be considered.[28] Despite this, assessors in and around Bristol recorded no fewer than six collections of many books valued at a total of less than 1s before 1780. In fact, book collections with values between 2d and 6d per book were noted by assessors. Urban and rural assessors provided book totals with nearly the same frequency, so there is no reason to suspect that any large book collection, whatever its assessed value, was more likely to have been inventoried in a misleading fashion simply because its owner was rural.[29]

The act of collection, extensive ownership of a recognised class of possessions, can be understood as a systematic application of a cultural form (in this case printed material) to the collector's attempted mastery over that form.[30] In this way the collection is in the service of the collector's abstract claims about his or her place in the world. Collection is an active project involving not only the enjoyment of similar possessions but the continuing selection, preservation, and accumulation of them as a demonstration of collectors' control over the classification of objects and, by extension, themselves. Collectors of printed material are in the process of defining themselves as masters of that cultural form. By contrast, the ownership of a solitary prized object is not a process. It is a condition under which an isolated object assumes not a role subordinate to the owner but a detached role, perhaps even as a passive object of reverence. The possession of a solitary object may express its owner's identity, but the identity is not that of a collector. Understood in these terms, collectors of printed material were urbane rather than rustic.

Those villagers who did own books showed a strong preference for physically impressive, durable, and heritable books, but a rural household with books typically had a limited holding of only one or two volumes. Rural book owners had a few cherished books or perhaps a solitary volume. Such books had value beyond their amusing, edifying, or sacred texts; they had intrinsic worth, sentimental importance, aesthetic appeal, and ritual uses. Family Bibles were by far the most commonly owned type of book in rural homes. These large, decorative, and heritable volumes contained not only scripture but, according to conventional practice, hand-written entries of personal interest such as records of birth, marriage, and death. A great Bible was almost always assessed at £1 or £2. Such a volume, all by itself, could represent the limit of expenditure on books observed in the vast majority of rural homes. Henry Brereton of Westbury-on-Trym was exceptional among rural book owners in the extent to which his wealth was devoted to book ownership. He was worth over £109 in 1668 and had books worth £10, or 9·2 per cent of his total wealth.

Book owners in the city, regardless of their means, were generally more willing than villagers to commit a large portion of their wealth to the owner-ship of books, many of which were relatively cheap. Edward Ellis of the fashionable Bristol parish of St Augustine had books valued at £7 13s, or 5·3 per cent of his total wealth, in 1663. Anthony Browne of Bristol was worth £102 8s 2d in 1669, when he held £11, or nearly 11 per cent of his total wealth, in books. Samuel Harris, a brewer in St Mary-le-Port, was worth only £10 but he owned 'several' books which made up a tenth of his total wealth in 1664. Urban levels of personal investment in books were more conspicuous in the late seventeenth century than in the early eighteenth, after the printing of cheap ephemera had become an established success in the city. Newspapers and other printed ephemera so rarely appear in probate inventories that the pattern of their consumption is difficult to determine, although their contents clearly addressed an urban readership.[31] Urban dwellers assigned lasting value to books whose intrinsic or material worth may have been minimal. Collec-tions of chapbooks were to be found in the city far more than in the country-side.[32] By the mid-eighteenth century, bound collections of serial publications began to find their way into private homes and, like chapbooks, serial publica-tions were collected by city dwellers rather than by farmers and other villag-ers.[33] The arrival of local printing in Bristol, which did little to bring rural patterns into compliance with urban trends, may have shifted urban taste in favour of chapbooks and printed ephemera, rather than valuable or durable books, thus making the distinctions between urban and rural patterns of ownership even more pronounced.

It is generally accepted on the strength of publication and distribution records, that cheap books were widely owned, but where chapbooks wound up and what became of them after they were purchased are two of the more thorny issues regarding early modern book ownership. Chapbooks could be had for something between 2d and 4d, so it was possible to purchase several books and not spend a great deal of money. Urban dwellers had the largest book collections and, in general, clearly had larger book collections than rural dwellers. The distribution of book collections according to their total values, however, did not vary significantly from one setting to the other. (Table 7.2.) Thus, in the simplest terms, it was the urban book owners who had the cheaper books. Samuel Pepys's private library in London showed that chapbook collection was hardly an activity restricted to the poor and obscure. It was an activity more specific to setting; references to 'small books' and 'little

Table 7.2 Values of book collections in the city of Bristol and the nearby villages in two forty-year periods (% in parentheses)

| | 1660–99 | | 1700–40 | |
|---|---|---|---|---|
| | Urban | Rural | Urban | Rural |
| £10 or more | 5 (2·0) | 1 (1·5) | 0 | 1 (4·3) |
| £5–£9 19s 11d | 4 (1·6) | 2 (3·1) | 3 (2·3) | 0 |
| £2–£4 19s 11d | 16 (6·5) | 5 (7·7) | 7 (5·3) | 1 (4·3) |
| £1–£1 19s 11d | 24 (9·7) | 6 (9·2) | 9 (6·8) | 3 (13·0) |
| 10s–19s 11d | 41 (16·6) | 13 (20·0) | 16 (12·0) | 1 (4·3) |
| 1s–9s 11d | 96 (38·9) | 27 (41·6) | 53 (39·8) | 8 (43·9) |
| Less than 1s | 4 (1·6) | 0   0 | 0 | |
| Value unknown | 57 (23·1) | 11 (16·9) | 45 (33·8) | 9 (39·2) |
| Totals | 247 (100) | 65 (100) | 133 (100) | 23 (100) |

*Note:* Two contingency tables are shown here: one for 1660–99 and another for 1700-40. Note that although there were few collections worth less than 1s or more than £10, there were no contingencies common enough or rare enough to indicate a cause other than random distribution with respect to setting and the total values of individual book collections..

*Source:* B.R.O. Probate Inventories and Cause Papers.


books' were made by assessors of Bristol homes but not by assessors of homes in the nearby villages.[34] Some villagers must have owned chapbooks even though assessors in both settings gave fewer details about these. If chapbooks were likely to be lumped in with small items for collective evaluation, then chapbooks were clearly more common in the city than in the villages before the eighteenth century. Henry Cousten, a coal miner in the Gloucestershire village of Stapleton, did have books worth a total of 6d in his kitchen in 1713. The existence of this isolated case of cheap book ownership in the rural setting suggests that rural assessors would have identified chapbooks if villagers had collected them. Surely some villagers made the initial purchase of a chapbook but assessors very rarely found these among the lasting possessions in rural homes; villagers were not preservers, accumulators, and collectors of cheap books. With the exception of the chapbooks in Henry Cousten's modest Stapleton cottage, inventoried book collections which averaged 4d per book or less were exclusively urban in the case of Bristol and the nearby villages, further evidence that the urban setting was the dominant niche of chapbooks.[35]

The largest book collections of known size found in village homes near Bristol were small by urban standards. Between 1660 and 1700 the largest rural collection did not exceed four books. In that period, only three local villagers of distinct profiles had as many as four books: a farmer worth over £596, a haberdasher worth £67, and a man worth only £39 whose occupation was unspecified by his assessor. Thomas Adlam, a gentleman worth £103 in 1732, kept fourteen books worth roughly 5d apiece in his Henbury home six miles out of Bristol. In the city there were at least ten contemporaries of Adlam, including a poor mariner, who had collections larger than his. Nevertheless, with fourteen books, Adlam was a major book collector by rural standards among those below the rank of gentry. The second most active book collector among the villagers in the early decades of the eighteenth century was a yeoman farmer in Henbury, Adlam's own village. He had four books. Fewer inventories date from 1740 or later, but it is worth noting that eleven Bristol residents owning ten or more books, and five with more than thirty books, lived in this late period associated with the bourgeois bibliophile. The largest collection of known size inventoried after 1740 in the villages near Bristol contained two books, hardly conforming to the urban fashion of collection.

There is little doubt that the larger collections of books were in the city rather than in the surrounding countryside after the arrival of printing in Bristol as well as before that time. Between 1660 and 1700, all twenty-two of the very largest book collections of known size and location were in Bristol homes. Richard Blinman, an ejected minister residing in Bristol, had total assets worth only £40 in 1681, but he owned forty-nine books valued at £10 all told. This was a large collection of volumes which, at 4s per book on average, was by no means dominated by twopenny chapbooks. Blinman was clearly a collector of books who valued their preservation, evidenced by the fact that he singled out his books in his will and catalogued them there for his heirs. One owner of one of Bristol's ten largest collections in this period was a poor sievemaker worth only £14 who had fifteen books, while another was a jeweller worth over £838. The city remained the site of the largest book collections in the early decades of printing in Bristol. During the forty years following 1700, all ten of the very largest inventoried collections were in Bristol homes. Of the thirty-four largest collections assessed in or near Bristol during this period, thirty-three (97 per cent) were urban and in the hands of a diverse group. Henry Bryan, a Bristol mariner worth only £4, amassed a collection of twenty-four books in his St Philip and Jacob lodgings. The assessed value of these books fell between 2d and 3d apiece on average and almost certainly included a number of chapbooks. The owners of Bristol's largest book collections assessed in this period made up a highly varied assortment of types who appeared to have had little in common apart from their urban surroundings and their demonstrated attachment to books.

Women became slightly less well represented among the bigger collectors of books in Bristol in the eighteenth century. Only two women, widows who may have inherited books, were among the top ten private book collectors in the city after the arrival of printers there. One of the widows, Anne Teast, had eighty 'bound books' in 1729. At 6d per book on average her collection probably contained a mixture of chapbooks and more durable, elegant or scriptural volumes. Before the establishment of printing in Bristol, four of the ten largest book collections had been owned by women who lived in the city. One of these women had thirty-nine books in her home. At least one of Bristol's most extensive book collections in the late seventeenth century had been owned by a woman whose books were entirely her own and not her husband's, for she had never married.[36]

Clearly women could and did acquire their own books, but many widows surely became book owners directly from the estates of their deceased husbands. The 1684 inventory of Bristol widow Sarah Keene included books. In all likelihood they had belonged to her husband, Thomas Keene, sergeant of the Bristol sheriff who actually signed Sarah's will for her. Of the fifty widows known to have owned books in Bristol and the nearby villages between 1660 and 1740, exactly half could not sign their will. The proportion was only slightly lower in Bristol than in the countryside. Ecclesiastical court evidence taken from breach of promise cases shows that, as an act of courtship, suitors traditionally bought mirrors or bracelets rather than little books to present to girls.[37] It is not safe to assume that every book in a married couple's household belonged to the husband rather than the wife, but cases resembling Sarah Keene's reinforce the notion that, even after literate members of a household had passed away, heirs may have retained their books as sentimental tokens or valued artefacts. A woman with books, whether she inherited them or acquired her own, was far more likely to be found living in the urban setting.

Attitudes relating book ownership to gender varied significantly from city to village. Urban book owners identified a fair mixture of men and women as recipients of heritable books. Urban testators with several heirs singled out some books as willed items intended specifically for women and girls. In 1710 a carpenter in St Mary, Redcliffe, by the name of John Davies willed his 'large Bible' and silver goods to his grandson, a mirror and a Bible to one granddaughter, and a Bible and a Book of Common Prayer to another granddaughter. In 1666 Joan Griffith of Bristol gave her Bible to her son, Richard, but passed all her 'books' to another woman, possibly her daughter-in-law. Urban women made an effort to share books with one another. During the entire year following Easter 1663 Jane Parsons, a married woman living in the small Somerset city of Wells, kept in her house a Bible 'which was left with her in her custody' by her friend, Jane Daws, also of Wells. To the great dismay of the two Janes, this Bible, the cherished centrepiece of the firm friendship between the two women, was ultimately stolen by a transient lodger who claimed he was drunk at the time.[38] One Bristol widow, Sara Browning, was not able to sign her own will in 1715, but the only stipulation she made beyond a general reference to 'chattels, money and plate' was that her sister-in-law to whom she willed a 'biboll with the silver clasps' should share it with another woman.

By contrast, when the recipients of books were identified in rural wills they were nearly always men or boys. Rural testators, men and women alike, tended to pass over their own daughters in preference to men, occasionally of remoter connection, when bequeathing books. This was true even among the more highly educated members of rural society. John Hawkins, the son of the vicar of the village of Stoke Gifford, was left his father's entire collection of books in 1664. John's sister Margaret, on the other hand, inherited apparel rather than books.[39] The one rural exception was William Davis of Shire-hampton, who was worth only £78 in 1701. Two years earlier in his will he left 'apparel and books and other things' to his niece. Even in this case, however, a female heir was not identified as the recipient of books which had been singled out for her. Books were simply included among all the testator's movable possessions of which a woman happened to be the principal heir. The fact that rural testators preferred to bequeath books to male heirs may have been a logical consequence of male:female literacy rates, but even at three to one these were more equitable than the rural distribution of books to heirs. At a time when literacy rates among women were rising and books were increasingly identified as symbols of feminised 'sensibility' in cities and towns,[40] rural society apparently clung to the old image of a book as a masculine possession or, perhaps, an emblem of paternalism.

It is worth considering the possibility that the different occupational profiles of Bristol and the nearby villages accounted for the difference between urban and rural levels of book ownership. In Kentish towns during the late sixteenth and early seventeenth centuries the incidence of book ownership was relatively high among gentlemen, professionals, and members of the clothing and leather trades, but low among victuallers and builders.[41] If we combine the residents of Bristol and the nearby rural villages, in order to isolate the possible influence of occupation upon book ownership, some initial assumptions are encouraged: in both periods, before and after the introduction of printing in Bristol, professionals and gentlemen had large book collections, while few farmers, agricultural labourers, and gardeners had books. The figures produced in this way, without reference to setting, do indeed correspond to statistically significant relationships, as do the large number of farmers (of all degrees) and small number of professionals who did not own books. These are the only correlations between levels of book ownership and general occupation that are significant in the period 1660–99. (Table 7.3.) Figures for the forty-year period beginning in 1700 reveal the development of additional book ownership patterns along occupational lines. (Table 7.4.) The

Table 7.3 Levels of book ownership related to occupational categories of Bristol residents and nearby villagers combined, 1660–99 (% in parentheses)

| Occupational categories | No books | One book | Some books | Many books | Totals |
|---|---|---|---|---|---|
| Agriculture | **60+** | 3 | 18 | **2–** | 83 |
| | (72·3) | (3·6) | (21·7) | (2·4) | (100) |
| Maritime | 29 | 5 | 13 | 5 | 52 |
| | (55·8) | (9·6) | (25·0) | (9·6) | (100) |
| Commerce | 18 | 0 | 12 | 6 | 36 |
| | (50·0) | (0) | (33·3) | (16·7) | (100) |
| Service | 18 | 3 | 8 | 6 | 35 |
| | (51·4) | (8·6) | (22·9) | (17·1) | (100) |
| Building & woodwork | 41 | 3 | 17 | 4 | 65 |
| | (63·1) | (4·6) | (26·2) | (6·1) | (100) |
| Textiles & leatherwork | 36 | 6 | 16 | 9 | 67 |
| | (53·7) | (9·0) | (23·9) | (13·4) | (100) |
| Minerals & metalwork | 25 | 2 | 10 | 4 | 41 |
| | (61·0) | (4·9) | (24·4) | (9·7) | (100) |
| Food & drink preparation | 25 | 2 | 15 | 4 | 46 |
| | (54·4) | (4·3) | (32·6) | (8·7) | (100) |
| Professional | **10–** | 1 | 10 | **18+** | 39 |
| | (25·6) | (2·6) | (25·6) | (46·2) | (100) |
| Single woman[a] | 13 | 2 | 5 | 2 | 22 |
| | (59·1) | (9·1) | (22·7) | (9·1) | (100) |

*Notes:* (a) Widows and women whose occupations were stated are included in the appropriate occupational categories. Bold figures indicate contingencies that were significantly common (+) or rare (–).
*Source:* B.R.O. Probate Inventories and Cause Papers.

numbers of mariners and single women with exactly one book (probably a Bible) became significantly high. Members of the service sector who owned many books (possibly chapbooks) also became significantly common during the later of the two periods.[42]

A closer look at some specific occupations gives the impression that the ownership of books may have played a part in expressing redefined occupational identities. Barbers and surgeons were members of the service sector who, in the early eighteenth century, became significantly well represented among owners of more extensive book collections. In the seventeenth century, physicians in and around Bristol invariably owned books, while surgeons were

Table 7.4 Levels of book ownership related to occupational categories of Bristol residents and nearby villagers combined, 1700–40 (% in parentheses)

| Occupational categories | No books | One book | Some books | Many books | Totals |
|---|---|---|---|---|---|
| Agriculture | **67+** | 1 | **3–** | **2–** | 73 |
| | (91·8) | (1·4) | (4·1) | (2·7) | (100) |
| Maritime | 39 | 5+ | 13 | 3 | 60 |
| | (65·0) | (8·3) | (21·7) | (5·0) | (100) |
| Commerce | 47 | 0 | 9 | 5 | 61 |
| | (77·0) | (0) | (14·8) | (8·2) | (100) |
| Service | 23 | 0 | 5 | 9+ | 37 |
| | (62·2) | (0) | (13·5) | (24·3) | (100) |
| Building and woodwork | 32 | 1 | 12 | 5 | 50 |
| | (64·0) | (2·0) | (24·0) | (10·0) | (100) |
| Textiles and leatherwork | 32 | 0 | 10 | 6 | 48 |
| | (66·7) | (0) | (20·8) | (12·5) | (100) |
| Minerals and metalwork | 21 | 1– | 1 | 2 | 25 |
| | (84·0) | (4·0) | (4·0) | (8·0) | (100) |
| Food and drink preparation | 20 | 1 | 6 | 4 | 31 |
| | (64·5) | (3·2) | (19·4) | (12·9) | (100) |
| Professional | **7–** | 1 | **8+** | **8+** | 24 |
| | (29·2) | (4·2) | (33·3) | (33·3) | (100) |
| Single woman[a] | 13 | 3+ | 4 | 1 | 21 |
| | (61·9) | (14·3) | (19·0) | (4·8) | (100) |

*Notes:* (a) Widows and women whose occupations were stated are included in the appropriate occupational categories. Bold figures indicate contingencies that were significantly common (+) or rare (–).
*Source:* B.R.O. Probate Inventories and Cause Papers.

less likely to have them. During the first forty years of the eighteenth century, however, surgeons joined professionals such as musicians, clerks, clergy, and physicians to form a group of occupations whose members were almost universally in possession of books. The old distinction between physicians (professionals who held degrees and worked with their minds) and surgeons (who underwent apprenticeships and performed a service with their hands) was beginning to be challenged by the book-owning tendencies of eighteenth-century surgeons. When a Bristol surgeon named William Burgess drew up his will in 1721 his very first provision was that his instruments and his 'books treating of surgery' were bequeathed to his son, Joseph. Burgess stipulated that Joseph would not be entitled to the books and instruments until his twenty-first birthday, at the completion of his apprenticeship, a clear indication that the books were conferred as a symbol of maturity and occupational commitment. In some circles the ownership of books was associated with the acquisition of occupational skill and perceived as an emblem of occupational status.

At the same time, the masters of some crafts who valued the preservation of manual art forms jealously guarded traditional methods and doggedly clung, it seems, to oral culture, perhaps even resisting the influence of print culture in their workshops. Certain members of the building and woodworking trades, who were already noteworthy in the seventeenth century for their lack of book collections, were rarely book owners at all by the early eighteenth century. Among all members of the urban–rural comparison group between 1700 and 1740, eight (73 per cent) of eleven coopers and six (75 per cent) of eight carpenters had no books at all. Of the four carpenters in the comparison group who died between 1740 and 1780, not one had a book. Similarly, those artisans who worked with minerals and metals rarely owned books during the entire century following 1660. Five (83 per cent) of the six glassmakers and thirteen (81 per cent) of the sixteen blacksmiths, horse shoers, and nail forgers in the entire comparison group were without books. Not one of the four brick or soap makers had a book. The ownership of books may have contributed to the progressive differentiation among groups within broader occupational categories. Thirteen (87 per cent) of the fifteen tailors after 1700 had no books at all, but thirteen of the twenty weavers and clothworkers, more than half, owned books. The one Bristol bookseller whose private inventory survives possessed many books apart from the contents of his shop. By contrast, the one Bristol bookbinder whose private inventory survives owned no books at all. The two men were late seventeenth-century contemporaries, but the distinctions drawn between a retailer of books and a manual craftsman associated with the same product were central to identity formation on the part of these potential consumers of print culture. Distinctions along these lines may have been as important as literacy to patterns of book ownership in some occupational circles.

The importance of books for certain occupational identities reinforced, rather than mediated, the urban–rural divide. The differences between the occupational profiles of the city and the countryside accounted, in part, for the divergent patterns of book ownership specific to those settings. Those who worked in agriculture tended not to own books, and farming was far more prominent in the countryside than in the city. But the profound effect of setting itself becomes even more clear when urban and rural members of the same occupational groups are compared rather than combined. In general contrast to the urban setting, where several levels of book ownership, including

Table 7.5 Levels of book ownership related to occupational categories in the city of Bristol (% in parentheses)

| | 1660–99 | | | | | 1700–40 | | | | |
|---|---|---|---|---|---|---|---|---|---|---|
| | No books | One book | Some books | Many books | Total | No books | One book | Some books | Many books | Total |
| Agriculture | 3 (75.0) | 1 (25.0) | 0 | 0 | 4 (100) | 0 | 0 | 1 (100) | 0 | 1 (100) |
| Maritime | 26 (54.2) | 5 (10.4) | 13 (27.1) | 4 (8.3) | 48 (100) | 36 (66.6) | 4+ (7.4) | 11 (20.4) | 3– (5.6) | 54 (100) |
| Commerce | 16 (48.5) | 0 | 11 (33.3) | 6 (18.2) | 33 (100) | 44 (77.2) | 0 | 8 (14.0) | 5 (8.8) | 57 (100) |
| Service | 16 (51.6) | 3 (9.6) | 6 (19.4) | 6 (19.4) | 31 (100) | 19 (63.4) | 0 | 4 (13.3) | 7 (23.3) | 30 (100) |
| Building and woodwork | 41+ (66.1) | 2 (3.2) | 15 (24.2) | 4– (6.5) | 62 (100) | 29 (63.0) | 1 (2.2) | 11 (23.9) | 5 (10.9) | 46 (100) |
| Textiles and leatherwork | 29 (50.8) | 5 (8.8) | 14 (24.6) | 9 (15.8) | 57 (100) | 26 (63.4) | 0 | 9 (22.0) | 6 (14.6) | 41 (100) |
| Minerals and metal work | 23 (59.0) | 2 (5.1) | 10 (25.6) | 4 (10.3) | 39 (100) | 19+ (90.4) | 0 | 1– (4.8) | 1 (4.8) | 21 (100) |
| Food and drink | 23 (59.0) | 2 (5.1) | 11 (28.2) | 3 (7.7) | 39 (100) | 17 (63.0) | 1 (3.7) | 5 (18.5) | 4 (14.8) | 27 (100) |
| Professional | **3–** (13.6) | 0 | 8 (36.4) | **11+** (50.0) | 22 (100) | **5–** (27.8) | 1 (5.5) | 7+ (38.9) | 5+ (27.8) | 18 (100) |
| Single woman[a] | 6 (50.0) | 1 (8.3) | 3 (25.0) | 2 (16.7) | 12 (100) | 8 (53.3) | 2+ (13.3) | 4 (26.7) | 1 (6.7) | 15 (100) |

*Note:* Two contingency tables are shown here: one for 1660–99 and another for 1700–40. Bold figures indicate contingencies that were significantly common (+) or rare (–). Noteworthy contingencies are indicated as common (+) or rare (–). (a) Widows and women whose occupations were stated are included in the appropriate occupational categories.

| | 1660–99 | | | | | 1700–40 | | | | |
|---|---|---|---|---|---|---|---|---|---|---|
| | No books | One book | Some books | Many books | Total | No books | One book | Some books | Many books | Total |
| Agriculture | 57 (72·2) | 2 (2·5) | 18 (22·8) | 2– (2·5) | 79 (100) | 67 (93·0) | 1 (1·4) | 2– (2·8) | 2 (2·8) | 72 (100) |
| Maritime | 3 (75·0) | 0 | 0 | 1 (25·0) | 4 (100) | 3 (50·0) | 1 (16·7) | 2+ (33·3) | 0 | 6 (100) |
| Commerce | 2 (66·7) | 0 | 1 (33·3) | 0 | 3 (100) | 3 (75·0) | 0 | 1 (25·0) | 0 | 4 (100) |
| Service | 2 (66·7) | 0 | 1 (33·3) | 0 | 3 (100) | 4 (100) | 0 | 0 | 0 | 4 (100) |
| Building and woodwork | 0 | 1 (33·3) | 2 (66·7) | 0 | 3 (100) | 3 (75·0) | 0 | 1 (25·0) | 0 | 4 (100) |
| Textiles and leatherwork | 7 (87·5) | 1 (12·5) | 0 | 0 | 8 (100) | 4 (80·0) | 0 | 1 (20·0) | 0 | 5 (100) |
| Minerals and metalwork | 2 (100·0) | 0 | 0 | 0 | 2 (100) | 2 (66·7) | 1+ (33·3) | 0 | 0 | 3 (100) |
| Food and drink | 2 (50·0) | 0 | 2 (50·0) | 0 | 4 (100) | 3 (75·0) | 0 | 1 (25·0) | 0 | 4 (100) |
| Professional | 6 (40·0) | 1 (6·7) | 2 (13·3) | **6+** (40·0) | 15 (100) | 2 (33·3) | 0 | 1 (16·7) | **3+** (50·0) | 6 (100) |
| Single woman[a] | 7 (70·0) | 1 (10·0) | 2 (20·0) | 0 | 10 (100) | 5 (83·3) | 1 (16·7) | 0 | 0 | 6 (100) |

*Note*: Two contingency tables are shown here: one for 1660–99 and another for 1700–40. Bold figures indicate contingencies that were significantly common (+) or rare (–). Noteworthy contingencies are indicated as common (+) or rare (–). (a) Widows and women whose occupations were stated are included in the appropriate occupational categories.
*Source*: B.R.O. Probate Inventories and Cause Papers.

a notable lack of books, were linked with specific occupations (Table 7.5.), the distribution of books in the rural population was less attributable to occupation (Table 7.6.), after the arrival of printing in Bristol as well as before that time. Gentlemen and professionals, no matter where they lived, were more likely to own books, and in this sense they were outstanding exceptions to the rule of urban–rural contrasts. The few mariners who lived in the villages by the later period also exhibited book owning tendencies similar to those of their shipmates in Bristol. That book owning patterns in the case of mariners were tied more closely to occupation than to setting of residence constituted a revealing departure from the general trend; rural mariners, unlike their village neighbours, clearly took part in the social spheres and the cultural networks of the port city. The emphasis on book ownership as a subtle means of occupational differentiation was primarily an urbane one, as the professional pretensions of surgeons and the distinctions between the manufacturers and merchandisers of identical items, including books themselves, showed. That levels of book ownership correlated more widely with occupations in the city than with occupations in the countryside points to another contrast between urban and rural uses of print culture that intensified, rather than diminished, between 1660 and 1740.

The few rural dwellers whose levels of book ownership did appear to be linked with their occupation actually adhered to trends exactly opposite to those exhibited by urban members of similar or identical occupations. Agricultural workers, farmers, and gardeners made up a very large proportion of rural society, but it should be noted that the nature of their occupation *per se* cannot serve as an explanation for their lack of books; in the city, agricultural occupations bore no significant, or even noteworthy, relation to any level of book ownership. Mineral and metal work, one of the few occupations whose members developed noteworthy consumer tendencies in the countryside after 1700, correlated positively with book ownership in the rural cases, while blacksmiths, soapboilers, and other mineral and metal workers in the city developed exactly the opposite tendency, a noteworthy lack of books. The few artisans and merchants who lived in the rural setting tended to lack books. Thomas Smith, a clothier in Almondsbury, was worth over £655 at his death in 1683 but, like most of his neighbours in the village, owned no books. All five of the Bristol clerks represented by the sample for the period from 1660 to 1699 had books. Thomas Godwyn, a clerk in the village of Stapleton in 1675, the only rural clerk represented in the sample in this period, had no books at all. All three of Bristol's eighteenth-century schoolmasters represented in the sample had books, and one had many books. This seems hardly surprising at first. What is remarkable in view of the fact is that both rural dwellers identified as members of the teaching profession, a Henbury schoolmistress and a Winterbourne schoolmaster, had no books at all in their private possession,

Table 7.7 Book ownership related to levels of total wealth in the entire urban-rural comparison group (% in parentheses)

| | 1660–99 | | | 1700–40 | | |
|---|---|---|---|---|---|---|
| | No books | With books | Total | No books | With books | Total |
| Over £1,000 | 3 (75·0) | 1 (25·0) | 4 (100) | 4 (50·0) | 4 (50·0) | 8 (100) |
| £501–£1,000 | 13 (54·2) | 11 (45·8) | 24 (100) | 19 (73·1) | 7 (26·9) | 26 (100) |
| £201–£500 | 66 (61·1) | 42 (38·9) | 108 (100) | 72 (79·1) | 19 (20·9) | 91 (100) |
| £51–£200 | 165 (58·7) | 116 (41·3) | 281 (100) | 132 (71·4) | 53 (28·6) | 185 (100) |
| £11–£50 | 145 (58·0) | 105 (42·0) | 250 (100) | 114 (68·3) | 53 (31·7) | 167 (100) |
| Under £11 | 50 (57·5) | 37 (42·5) | 87 (100) | 53 (72·6) | 20 (27·4) | 73 (100) |

*Notes:* Two contingency tables are shown here: one for 1660–99 and another for 1700–40. Notice that although percentages vary with wealth there were no contingencies common enough or rare enough, in either period, to indicate a cause other than random distribution with respect to wealth and book ownership when rural and urban cases are analysed in combination.
*Source:* B.R.O. Probate Inventories and Cause Papers.

and both of them were alive in the mid-eighteenth century.[43] In short, the inconsistent – and in many cases directly opposed – effects of occupation upon book ownership should be regarded as another aspect of the comprehensive influence of setting.

The notion that patterns of book ownership were expressions of status raises the question of wealth. (Table 7.7.) It should be stressed that the association of book ownership with certain occupational identities in the city did not preclude ownership of books by the poor in either setting. The inventory of Samuel Read, a Bristol surgeon worth only £4 10s in 1716, makes special reference to only one group of items: his 'several books'. Moreover, not all the wealthiest members of society owned books. Nine (45 per cent) of the twenty wealthiest Bristolians who died between 1700 and 1740 left no books behind. The very wealthiest individual represented in the entire inventory collection, a Bristol merchant worth over £5,060, had no books at all.

Table 7.8 Book ownership related to levels of total wealth in the urban comparison group (% in parentheses)

| | 1660–99 | | | | | 1700–40 | | | | |
|---|---|---|---|---|---|---|---|---|---|---|
| | No books | One book | Some books | Many books | Total | No books | One book | Some books | Many books | Total |
| Over £1,000 | 2 (66.7) | 0 | 0 | 1 (33.3) | 3 (100) | 3 (42.9) | 0 | 4+ (57.1) | 0 | 7 (100) |
| £501–£1,000 | 6 (42.8) | 0 | 4 (28.6) | 4+ (28.6) | 14 (100) | 12 (66.7) | 0 | 4 (22.2) | 2 (11.1) | 18 (100) |
| £201–£500 | 37 (54.4) | 0– | 17 (25.0) | 14+ (20.6) | 68 (100) | 28 (63.6) | 1 (2.3) | 9 (20.5) | 6 (13.6) | 44 (100) |
| £51–£200 | 102 (56.0) | 10 (5.5) | 48 (26.4) | 22 (12.1) | 182 (100) | 76 (66.1) | 3 (2.6) | 15– (13.0) | 21+ (18.3) | 115 (100) |
| £11–£50 | 115 (55.6) | 11 (5.3) | 57 (27.5) | 24 (11.6) | 207 (100) | 92 (64.8) | 3 (2.1) | 31 (21.8) | 16 (11.3) | 142 (100) |
| Under £11 | 47 (57.3) | **11+** (13.4) | 21 (25.6) | **3–** (3.7) | 82 (100) | 50 (73.5) | 3 (4.4) | 10 (14.7) | 5 (7.4) | 68 (100) |

*Note:* Two contingency tables are shown here: one for 1660–99 and another for 1700–40. Bold figures indicate contingencies that were significantly common (+) or rare (–). Noteworthy contingencies are indicated as common (+) or rare (–).
*Source:* B.R.O. Probate Inventories and Cause Papers.

Table 7.9 Book ownership related to levels of total wealth in the rural comparison group (% in parentheses)

| | 1660–99 | | | | | 1700–40 | | | | |
|---|---|---|---|---|---|---|---|---|---|---|
| | No books | One book | Some books | Many books | Total | No books | One book | Some books | Many books | Total |
| Over £1,000 | 1 (100) | 0 | 0 | 0 | 1 (100) | 1 (100) | 0 | 0 | 0 | 1 (100) |
| £501–£1,000 | 7 (70.0) | 0 | 3 (30.0) | 0 | 10 (100) | 7 (87.5) | 0 | 0 | 1 (12.5) | 8 (100) |
| £201–£500 | 29 (72.5) | 1 (2.5) | 5 (12.5) | 5 (12.5) | 40 (100) | 44 (93.6) | 0 | 3 (6.4) | 0 | 47 (100) |
| £51–£200 | 63 (63.6) | 5 (5.1) | 22 (22.2) | 9 (9.1) | 99 (100) | 56 (80.0) | 4 (5.8) | 5 (7.1) | 5 (7.1) | 70 (100) |
| £11–£50 | 30 (69.8) | 1 (2.3) | 9 (20.9) | 3 (7.0) | 43 (100) | 22 (88.0) | 1 (4.0) | 2 (8.0) | 0 | 25 (100) |
| Under £11 | 3 (60.0) | 1 (20.0) | 1 (20.0) | 0 | 5 (100) | 3 (60.0) | 0 | 2 (40.0) | 0 | 5 (100) |

*Note*: Two contingency tables are shown here: one for 1660–99 and another for 1700–40. Notice that although percentages vary with wealth only one contingency was significant or even noteworthy in the rural setting; in the later period, the number of people with the least total wealth and 'some' books was larger than we should expect if the distribution of books was totally random with respect to wealth. For the most part, however, wealth was far more widely a factor in shaping patterns of book ownership in the urban setting, as indicated in the previous table.
*Source*: B.R.O. Probate Inventories and Cause Papers

There was, however, a far wider relationship between wealth and book ownership among urban residents (Table 7.8.) than there was among villagers (Table 7.9.) during the two forty-year periods on either side of the arrival of printing in provincial cities. In the city of Bristol from 1660 to 1699 the group of urban dwellers with large book collections was dominated by wealthy people. At the same time, the number of poorer Bristolians with many books was significantly small, as was the number of wealthy citizens without books. In the nearby villages there was no correlation whatsoever between levels of wealth and book ownership before the establishment of local printing. The only significant rural trend which emerged after 1700 indicates that the least wealthy group of villagers with 'some' books, although quite small, was larger than might be expected. It is possible that rural book owners of modest means were religious dissenters caught up in the enthusiasm of extraparochial worship in the generation or so following toleration. Regardless of its cause, even this solitary example of a rural book owning pattern with respect to wealth diverged from its counterparts in the urban setting, where poorer people were remarkably unlikely to have more than one book before the arrival of local printing and no longer exhibited any particular pattern at all with respect to book ownership during the early decades of the eighteenth century. It was clearly the case that book ownership was far more closely linked with the status of wealth in urban society than in the countryside, where it did not carry that significance. The arrival and expansion of local printing in the city during the urban renaissance did not cause villagers to adopt the urbane association of status and books before the middle of the eighteenth century.

Had factors of wealth exerted an influence on book owning tendencies beyond urban society we should expect the villagers to have been more, rather than less, likely than their urban counterparts to own books. Villagers in the comparison group were, on average, wealthier than their urban counterparts. The seven wealthiest Bristolians who died between 1700 and 1740 had some, but not many, books. The vast majority of the large collections in and around Bristol were in the possession of wealthy urban dwellers. By contrast, wealthy villagers were rarely collectors of books. Between 1700 and 1740 only two (7 per cent) of the thirty wealthiest rural dwellers had any books. Seven of the wealthiest villagers, including three worth over £800 apiece, had no books at all. As we have seen, the relevance of wealth to consumer behaviour, like the relevance of occupations, varied considerably from one setting to the other and underscores, rather than challenges, the basic observation: setting, more than wealth, occupation, gender, or even literacy, was at the root of the cultural divide.

It is possible that a startling portion of the book owners of common rank in early modern England did not read. Robert Browne, a gentleman from the village of Almondsbury, stipulated in his 1682 will that his 'great Bible with brass clasps' should go to his son, who was instructed 'to be constant in reading therein' and to 'endeavour to practice what he reads'. In 1731 William Alchurch of Bristol willed Bibles and a copy of Baxter's *Call to the Unconverted* to his brother and two nephews, 'hoping ... said brother and his children growing up may live a Godly, sober, life'. The wills of many known book owners survive for Bristol and its rural environs. However, the testimonies of Browne and Alchurch on behalf of reading and readers stand alone. To a large extent, literacy was a function of economic status in seventeenth-century England.[44] But there was no strong correlation between wealth and book ownership in provincial England, even after the urban renaissance there. Moreover, contrary to what we might suppose, the ownership of a book was not closely related to the factors governing a person's ability to read it. The argument that illness or feebleness may have prevented some testators from signing on the verge of death has been used to discredit wills as sources by which to calculate subscription rates.[45] The wills used in this analysis, however, were all studied in conjunction with inventories, so a comfortable interval (in some cases a matter of years) between the drafting of a will and the death of the testator is assured. Furthermore, the practice of labelling as 'nunciated'[46] those wills which the testator could only dictate from the deathbed was widely observed by executors, scriveners, and clerks of the diocese of Bristol, and all nunciated wills have been excluded from the calculations. Of the 190 known book owners from Bristol and the nearby villages whose wills survive from the period between 1660 and 1740, fifty-five (29 per cent) were unable to sign their own name.

Considerable debate surrounds the issue of the correlation between the ability to sign and the ability to read in early modern times. It is widely accepted that those children who attained a level of literacy in early modern England were taught to read before they were taught to write and that children who entered the work force instead of school may have learned to read but not to write.[47] In early modern France a number of people could read the catechism, but could not write.[48] In the 1740s a religious revival in a rural parish near Glasgow revolved around more than 100 villagers, three-quarters of whom were women; all the converts could read, according to examinations conducted by the minister himself, but it has been estimated that only a tenth of the women could write.[49] The notion of widespread literacy in early modern Scotland has been challenged on the grounds that about 70 per cent of Scottish women and 40 per cent of Scottish men in the mid-eighteenth century were unable to sign legal depositions.[50] Signatures of rural dwellers in early modern England were more likely to resemble childlike scrawl indicative of the ability to write little more than one's name.[51] The ability to sign one's name might be expected of any reader, even one for whom writing in a more extensive way was impossible. At least one established authority on this subject accepts the basic ability to sign one's name (hardly as impressive as composing complex sentences) as a functional indicator of literacy.[52]

Of particular interest is the fact that book owners in villages near Bristol were far more likely to be illiterate on these grounds than were book owners in the city. In the period between 1660 and 1740, of fifty rural book owners whose wills were examined, twenty-one (42 per cent) could only place an 'X' or a mark of some sort on their will, compared with thirty-four (roughly 24 per cent) of the urban book owners who were unable to write their name. At the very least, one might expect book owners, regardless of the setting in which they lived, to exhibit a more widespread ability to sign than members of the general population, but such may not always have been the case. Between 1660 and 1700 in villages near the city of Bristol, a literate region by the standards of the time,[53] there were more book owners who were unable to sign their will (eighteen) than there were book owners who could sign (fourteen). Roughly 56 per cent of the book owners in Bristol's rural environs at the end of the seventeenth century were unable to sign their own name. As little as 53 per cent of the general adult male population in the rural areas surrounding Bristol may have been unable to sign their names, a figure slightly better than the one calculated for book owners who lived in that same area a generation later.[54]

In view of all this, it is difficult to accept the notion that the appearance of print technology in an English provincial city in the late seventeenth century necessarily placed the hearts and minds of nearby villagers in the hands of urban printers or permitted cities to exert a greater cultural influence over their rural environs as an immediate consequence of the urban renaissance. It is clear that a book could be regarded as far more, or far less, than a collection of words. The historian's understanding of 'the book' must take into account the social, material, and cultural significance assigned to books in former times by non-readers as well as readers. The audience for the printed word was surprisingly diverse in its social composition, including children and adults, women and men, rich and poor in representative numbers. It excluded no occupational group. The relationship between gender and book ownership varied from city to village, as did the relationship of book ownership to wealth and occupation. The conspicuous differences in levels of book ownership and patterns of book use pointed to the primary influence of a topographical divide which amplified divisions along lines of occupation, wealth, status, or even degree of learning.

It is possible to study the role of the printed word, and the peculiar reverence for its power, as one basis of shared belief or community formation. As we will see, explicit messages conveyed in printed words that some villagers and urban residents actually read spoke to the very question of social, topographical, and cultural boundaries. Books, newspapers, and printed ephemera inscribed images of readers' familiar surroundings and offered glimpses beyond the horizon of personal experience. The evolution of affinities leading to a significant convergence of urban and rural social spheres, however, required an array of cultural forms, of which print was only a part, to be applied in new ways.

## NOTES

1  T. Watt, *Cheap Print and Popular Piety 1550–1640* (Cambridge, 1991); J. Barry, 'Literacy and literature in popular culture: reading and writing in historical perspective', in T. Harris (ed.), *Popular Culture in England* c. *1500–1850* (New York, 1995), pp. 69–94.

2  M. Spufford, *Small Books and Pleasant Histories: Popular Fiction and its Readership in Seventeenth-Century England* (Cambridge, 1981) and *The Great Reclothing of Rural England: Petty Chapmen and their Wares in the Seventeenth Century* (London, 1984); I. Rivers (ed.), *Books and their Readers in Eighteenth-Century England* (Leicester, 1982); J. Feather, *The Provincial Book Trade in Eighteenth-Century England* (Cambridge, 1985); R. Myers and M. Harris (eds), *Spreading the Word: The Distribution Networks of Print 1550–1850* (Winchester, 1990); J. Raven, *Judging New Wealth: Popular Publishing and Responses to Commerce in England 1750–1800* (Oxford, 1992).

3  A notable exception was the very large catalogued collection of chapbooks in the possession of Samuel Pepys in the late seventeenth century. See Spufford, *Small Books and Pleasant Histories*, and R. Thompson (ed.), Samuel Pepys' *Penny Merriments: Being a Collection of Chapbooks* (New York, 1977), for excerpts with commentary.

4  A. Bermingham and J. Brewer (eds), *The Consumption of Culture 1600–1800: Image, Object, Text* (London, 1995).

5  P. Clark, 'The ownership of books in England 1560–1640: the example of some Kentish townsfolk', in L. Stone (ed.), *Schooling and Society* (Baltimore, Md, 1976), pp. 95–111. Clark's principal sources here are probate inventories.

6  B. Little, *The City and County of Bristol: A Study in Atlantic Civilization* (London, 1954), pp. 105 and 130.

7  Feather, *The Provincial Book Trade*, pp. 1–2, 29, 64–5.

8  R. M. Wiles, *Freshest Advices: Early Provincial Newspapers in England* (Columbus, Oh., 1965), pp. 14–16.

9  Spufford, *Small Books and Pleasant Histories*, p. 119.

10  *Sketchley's Bristol Directory* (Bristol, 1775).

11  The tendency of production records to obscure differences between urban and rural patterns of consumption and ownership can be seen in Feather, *The Provincial Book Trade*, p. 32.

12  Clark, 'The ownership of books in England', pp. 97–100.

13  J. Barry, 'Popular culture in seventeenth-century Bristol', in B. Reay (ed.), *Popular Culture in Seventeenth-Century England* (London and New York, 1985), p. 67, suggests that the decline in inventory references to books may be dated from the Restoration and observes that 34·6 per cent of Bristol inventories contained references to books between 1620 and 1660, whereas only 21·8 per cent did between 1660 and 1710.

14  D. Cressy, 'Education and Literacy in London and East Anglia 1580–1700' (Ph.D. thesis, Cambridge University, 1972), pp. 99–100, 111–13, 129–35.

15  A. Smith, 'Endowed schools in the diocese of Lichfield and Coventry 1660–99', *History of Education* 4 no. 2 (1975), pp. 5–8; and 'Private schools and schoolmasters in the diocese of Lichfield and Coventry 1660–1999', *History of Education* 5 no. 2 (1976), pp. 117–26.

16  Barry, 'Popular culture in seventeenth-century Bristol', pp. 67–8.

17  Of the 247 Bristol inventories containing books in the period 1660–99, eighty-eight (35·6 per cent) provided titles; in 1700–39, thirty-five of 133 (only 26·3 per cent); in 1740–80, twenty-one or thirty-five (60·0 per cent). Rural percentages were slightly higher.

18  B.R.O. P/StP&J/V/2 St Philip and Jacob Minute Book (1723–1832).

19  J. Money, 'Teaching in the market-place, or "*Caesar adsum jam forte: Pompey aderat*": the retailing of knowledge in provincial England during the eighteenth century', and C. Y. Ferdinand, 'Selling it to the provinces: news and commerce round eighteenth-century Salisbury', in J. Brewer and R. Porter (eds), *Consumption and the World of Goods* (London, 1992), pp. 335–77 and 393–411.

20  Unless otherwise stated, for the remainder of this chapter the tabulated figures and the discussion of them will be based on the group of inventories from the comparison group. In the period 1660–1739, 777 of these inventories are from the period before the arrival of local printing, roughly speaking, and 563 date from the period immediately following it.

21  J. Barry, 'The Cultural Life of Bristol 1640–1775' (D.Phil. thesis, Oxford University, 1985), pp. 346–420, produces a slightly different set of inventory figures. Dr Barry includes ninety-one more inventories for the period 1660–99. These may include evaluations from wills, which I excluded, or from the parish of Barton Regis, which I treated as extramural. Dr Barry's study identifies 748 fewer inventories for the period 1700–39. Mariners' inventories in this period, which make up a large portion of my sample, included many with partial valuations, a category of inventory that Dr Barry excluded. Dr Barry's percentages for all extant inventories are quite close to mine, however, and this affords confidence given the large numbers of extant inventories located in both studies.

22  L. Weatherill, *Consumer Behaviour and Material Culture in Britain 1660–1760* (London, 1988), pp. 29, 80, and 88. The few localities not studied in some depth by Weatherill include Bristol and the neighbouring counties.

23  Weatherill, *Consumer Behaviour and Material Culture*, p. 80. Weatherill herself tabulates the percentages of urban and rural inventories containing books between 1675 and 1725 (urban percentage: rural percentage) as follows: London area 31:17; north-east 14:5; east Kent 40:32; Cambridgeshire 16:11; the north-west 27:19; north-west Midlands 26:12; Cumbria 21:16. In Hampshire a higher percentage of rural inventories (26 per cent) than of urban ones (19 per cent) had books, a fascinating local aberration that deserves further explanation.

24  Every extant inventory of a printer, stationer, bookseller or bookbinder proved between 1660 and 1780 in Bristol and the surrounding villages was for a resident of the city. For the rise in the print-related trades in Bristol in the eighteenth century, see Barry, 'Popular culture in seventeenth-century Bristol', pp. 65–6.

25  R. Darnton, *The Great Cat Massacre and other Episodes in French Cultural History* (New York, 1984), p. 249.

26  Between 1660 and 1780, of all surviving inventories from Bristol and the nearby villages, 533 were drawn up by assessors who made references to books. In 209 (39 per cent) cases, assessors recorded the exact number of books found in an urban or rural home. In the period from 1660 to 1740 assessors of 497 inventories made references to books and 187 (38 per cent) noted exact book totals. Many assessors reported 'parcels', 'bundles', or 'chests' of books, and others referred to 'some' or 'many' books. A book owner is said to have had 'some' books if the assessor used that very term or if there were from two to five books in the inventory (either exactly reported or estimated). Totals categorised here as 'many' were either described as such by the assessor or are known or estimated to have included six or more books. A 'parcel' of books is taken to have had three or more books. A few parcels of six or more books may have crept into the 'some' category.

27  Between 1660 and 1740, 138 inventories provided both exact numbers of books (totaling 828 books) and values attached exclusively to those books (totaling £65 1s 2d).

28  Spufford, *Small Books and Pleasant Histories*, p. 48.

29  Of the inventories showing book ownership from 1660 to 1740, 468 were for homes of known setting; 38 per cent of the urban ones and 32 per cent of the rural ones give exact book totals, so the impact of estimates upon our calculations varies only slightly with setting.

30  J. Baudrillard, 'The system of collecting', in J. Elsner and R. Cardinal (eds), *The Cultures of Collecting* (Cambridge, Mass., 1994), pp. 7–24.

31  G. A. Cranfield, *The Development of the Provincial Newspaper 1700–60* (Oxford, 1962), and Ferdinand, 'Selling it to the provinces', supply indirect evidence that early provincial newspapers were primarily the instruments of manufacturers, merchants, and entrepreneurs operating in the towns where the papers sprang up. See the following chapter for further analyses of newspapers and textual clues regarding the geographical distribution of the newspaper readership.

32  See, for example, the mariner in St Philip and Jacob who was worth only £4 18s 7d and had twenty-four books valued at 5s all told, or $2^1/2$d per book. B.R.O. Probate Inventories (H. Bryan, 1712). Spufford argues, however, that the readership of chapbooks was neither especially urban nor especially rural, a tentative conclusion that invites further investigation. See her *Small Books and Pleasant Histories*, pp. 45–61.

33  The probate evidence for the private collection of serial publications in and around Bristol appears exlusively in urban inventories. Elizabeth Lawrence (1752), a Bristol widow, had eight volumes of *Spectator* issues worth 9s all told; Thomas Bolt (1766), a Bristol sexton, had thirteen volumes of magazines worth £1 all told and eight volumes of *Spectator* issues worth 9s 6d all told; Samuel and Mary Smith (1776), a wealthy Bristol couple, had eight volumes of *Turkish Spy* issues worth 6s all told. Thomas Bolt's magazines may have been printed in Bristol but, it should be mentioned, neither the *Spectator* nor the *Turkish Spy* was a provincial publication.

34  B.R.O. Probate Inventories include four urban examples (E. Haggett, 1669; M. Spurgin, 1680; G. Williams, 1710; J. Richards, 1733) dating from before and after the arrival of local printers in Bristol.

35  B.R.O. Probate Inventories and Cause Papers include, for example, the inventories of

the following Bristolians: Mary Meredith (1681), a 'spinster' with twenty-four books worth 8s (4d apiece); John Griffin (1688), a sievemaker with twelve 'small books' worth 3s (3d apiece); Gibbion Williams (1710), a maltster with eight 'small books' worth 2s 6d (less than 4d apiece); Henry Bryan (1712), a mariner with a collection of twenty-four books worth 5s (less than 3d apiece); William Stirling (1713), a mariner with six books worth 1s (2d apiece); William Dutton (1718; 1728 bundle), possibly a West Indies trader with twenty-three 'bound books' worth 5s 6d (less than 3d apiece); Elizabeth Mann (1725), a widow with twelve books worth 1s 6d (less than 2d apiece); John Richards (1733), a baker with twenty-five 'small books' worth 6s (less than 3d apiece); Mary Williams (1735), a widow, with eleven books worth 1s (slightly more than 1d apiece); John Davis (1741), a surgeon with a collection of thirty-five books worth 10s (between 3d and 4d apiece).

36  The gender-specificity of book collection and use is a problematic and fascinating issue. It is difficult to separate a widow's possessions from those of her former husband. The only way to identify those books exclusively in the possession of women is to isolate the inventories of 'spinsters'. There is no way, in fact, to be certain that the books in a man's inventory were not acquired, in actuality, by his wife, daughter, or some other woman in the household.

37  Spufford, *Small Books and Pleasant Histories*, p. 169 cites A. Macfarlane, 'The Regulation of Marital and Sexual Relationships in Seventeenth-Century England, with Special Reference to the County of Essex' (M.Phil. thesis, University of London, 1968), p. 71.

38  S.R.O. Q/SR/105 Somerset Quarter Sessions (March 1664).

39  B.R.O. Probate Inventories (John Hawkins, 1664) and B.R.O. Wills (John Hawkins, 1614).

40  G. J. Barker-Benfield, *The Culture of Sensibility: Sex and Society in Eighteenth-Century Britain* (Chicago, 1996), pp. 154–214.

41  Clark, 'The ownership of books in England', p. 101.

42  The category 'single woman', a description commonly supplied in the inventories themselves, surely included domestic servants.

43  B.R.O. Probate Inventories (James Stephens, 1748, and Grace Leg, 1752).

44  D. Cressy, 'Educational opportunity in Tudor and Stuart England', *History of Education Quarterly* (1976), p. 314; and 'Literacy in seventeenth-century England: more evidence', *Journal of Interdisciplinary History* 8 no. 1 (1977), pp. 146–8.

45  R. O'Day, *Education and Society 1500–1800: The Social Foundations of Education in Early Modern Britain* (London, 1982), p. 14. The words of testators also provide qualitative evidence concerning systems of belief, social relations and general frame of mind, although some stock phrases were supplied by clerks, especially in nunciated wills. See M. Spufford, *Contrasting Communities: English Villagers in the Sixteenth and Seventeenth Centuries* (Cambridge, 1974), ch. 13.

46  In some cases the term 'nuncupative' was used.

47  R. S. Schofield, 'The measurement of literacy in pre-industrial England', in J. R. Goody (ed.), *Literacy in Traditional Societies* (Cambridge, 1968), pp. 318–25; M. Spufford, 'First steps in literacy: the reading and writing experiences of the humblest seventeenth-century spiritual autobiographers', *Social History* 4 no. 3 (1979), pp. 407–35 and in H. J. Graff (ed.), *Literacy and Social Development in the West* (Cambridge, 1981).

48 R. Chartier, M. M. Compere, and D. Julia, *L'Education en France du XVIe au XVIIIe siècle* (Paris, 1976), pp. 106–7.

49 T. C. Smout, 'Born again at Cambuslang: new evidence on popular religion and literacy in eighteenth-century Scotland', *Past and Present* 97 (1982), pp. 114–27.

50 R. Houston, 'The literacy myth? Illiteracy in Scotland 1630–1760', *Past and Present* 96 (1982), pp. 81–102.

51 L. Stone, 'Literacy and education in England 1640–1900', *Past and Present* 42 (1969), pp. 99–101.

52 Cressy, 'Educational opportunity in Tudor and Stuart England' and *Literacy and the Social Order* (Cambridge, 1980).

53 Recent estimates of overall illiteracy rates for women and men in both settings in the seventeenth century are presented in D. Cressy, 'Literacy in context: meaning and measurement in early modern England', in Brewer and Porter, *Consumption and the World of Goods*, p. 315, as: urban men, 45 per cent; urban women, 60 per cent; rural men, 68 per cent; rural women, 90 per cent.

54 An average illiteracy rate for adult males in rural England in the earlier half of the seventeenth century was something approaching 70 per cent, according to Stone, 'Literacy and education in England'. A re-examination of Stone's source, the Protestation Returns of 1642, sheds light on the highly localised variability of illiteracy rates, which were significantly lower in some rural areas than in others. See Cressy, *Literacy and the Social Order*, pp. 62–103.

# Chapter 8

---

# Print culture:
## community and strangeness

It is widely accepted that a printed text can cultivate in its readers a collective sense of social, political, or religious affiliation. By virtue of its replication and dissemination, the printed word even has the potential to serve as a cultural tie that transcends localism. In view of this, we may well wonder what impact printed texts had on the development of identities informed by a sense of place itself in early modern times. How did printed texts shape geographical awareness, construct popular images of remote places and alien types, and thereby prescribe the limits by which the very concepts of 'stranger' and 'community' were defined? It is clear that printed texts known to have been read in and around Bristol, an early centre of provincial printing, invoked the concepts of topography, boundaries, strangeness and familiarity to address the very issue of community.

An association of books and literacy with urbanity and broadened horizons makes a good deal of intuitive sense, but printing hardly served to create an increasing sense of regional identity or communal awareness extending beyond the confines of city or village until the middle of the eighteenth century. The expansion of horizons, heightened awareness of news and information concerning England and beyond, occurred quite some time before the bridging of the topographical divide closer to home.[1] From the very beginning, with Caxton's *The Description of Britain* (1480) and other English incunabula, the English representation of community in print tended to emphasise the close association of community with place and the intense localism of English communities separated by pronounced topographical boundaries and highly localised cultural ties. After the Restoration, these notions still constituted the conventional wisdom upheld by the likes of Evelyn and Aubrey and their antiquarian successors well into the eighteenth century.[2] Almanacs, newspapers, broadsides, books, and printed sermons circulating in and around Bristol during the century after 1660 replicated and disseminated information, ideas, and images that actually reinforced the real and perceived separation of urban and rural worlds. In fact, the xenophobia and parochialism which influenced relations between urban and rural dwellers, natives and foreigners, and members of different religious groups were caused in part by representations of the world, and of the community, in print. Collective identities rooted in status, occupation, religion, gender, and degrees of learning were all formed and expressed within the context of setting.

The problematic significance of widely read texts for shared belief, collective identity and community formation in the early modern period has hardly been lost on historians. For some readers religious or political ideology, rather than occupation or residence, was the basis of their social spheres.[3] According to one view, because subjects of interest varied from one reader to the next, what one read was a matter of personal taste rather than collective social awareness.[4] At least one theory of narrative compares that discursive form, of which newspaper reporting is but one example, to material culture and the purposeful collection of objects. Paradoxically, the personal possession of material signifiers and the subjective reporting of 'situations and events, characters and objects, places and atmospheres' both express the conscious perspective and construed environment of the commentator, or collector, as reliably as they represent the objective elements of experience. As utterances, therefore, texts are rooted in the surroundings of their source; the printed word, in this view, is as much a representation of locus as it is of nexus.[5] Others have argued persuasively for the sixteenth and seventeenth centuries that print culture was, by virtue of the standardising and 'corrective' influence of publishers, necessarily the expression of an elite, urbane mentality alone. The very process of publication altered beyond recognition the form and content of any oral and proverbial tradition, with all its regional variations, which peasant society might have accepted as its own.[6] This engaging argument comes provocatively close to denying the existence, or possibility, of a so-called popular press in the early modern period.

An active popular demand for reading material was at the very least perceived by members of the book trades, who, judging from their success, did indeed identify a socially broad market in early modern England. During the urban renaissance there was in circulation a growing number of pamphlets, newspapers, and books treating a widening spectrum of subjects and themes.[7] The increasing number and widening circulation of newspapers, for which there was a large popular audience in coffee houses and taverns alone, was a well known feature of English life, established in the provinces as well as London by the end of the seventeenth century and responsible for diminishing the gap between learned and uninformed readers.[8] Despite the flourishing of the newspaper and chapbook trades, which dealt partly in the recycling of popular lore or sordid, ribald, violent, and brief stories, it is entirely unsafe to

assume that these so-called popular reading materials were reserved for servants, unskilled workers, and other people of modest means. On the contrary,
Samuel Pepys, a high-ranking royal official, owned nearly 250 chapbooks,
making his collection one of the largest in late seventeenth-century England.
Pepys owned eighty-one chapbooks devoted to jests, burlesques, crime stories,
and sexual satire. In fact, these were the most common types of books in his
collection.[9]

The increased popularity of lending libraries also reflected the growth of a
reading audience across all ranks of society.[10] Some lending club members
could easily afford their own collections of books but were drawn to lending
circles as focal points for social entertainments of a refined and fashionable
nature such as musical recitals. Some people who set themselves up as lenders
were booksellers interested in promoting sales.[11] A considerable amount of
private book lending was a central aspect of gender-specific sociability and
extraparochial devotional life. The expansion of both the readership and the
range of subject matter did not necessarily polarise readers on an axis of
wealth and status. The complicated role of printed texts in the formation and
expression of collective identities cannot be understood without reference to
setting.

In the city of Bristol the connections between the subject matter of books
and the occupations of people who tended to own those books were not always
what we might suppose. (Table 8.1.) Artisans did not show an affinity for
books concerning crafts and trades until rather late in the early modern
period. This was almost surely a product of guild influence. Until the waning
of the guild system in the eighteenth century, occupational skills were highly
proprietorial and transmitted orally, to the brethren or indentured novices,
rather than indiscriminately divulged in print. Builders and woodworkers
showed a penchant for historical works. Throughout the first decades of the
urban renaissance there appears to have been a limited demand, in general,
for books on manual arts and techniques, but these subjects were eventually
given considerable attention in print by eighteenth-century encyclopaedists.
At the time of his death in 1772, James Waters, a millwright in the newly
annexed Bristol parish of St George, owned a copy of *Croker's Dictionary of Arts
and Sciences*.[12] During the eighteenth century, craft manuals began to appear
in households of all kinds. Bristol's lawyers, clergy, and gentlemen also acquired works on manual arts. In 1776 the wealthy Bristol couple Samuel and
Mary Smith had, in their parlour, a copy of 'Bradley on Gardening' and two
books on distilling.[13] An eighteenth-century trend of practical autodidacticism
revealed itself in the more general popularity of instructional books owned by
people other than artisans and full-time practitioners of manual crafts.

Individual cases did suggest how the reading tastes of book owners could
strongly reflect occupational identities in the urban setting. The few book

Table 8.1 Books of known titles arranged by theme and by the occupational categories of their owners in the city of Bristol, 1660–1780 (% in parentheses)

| | Pro. | Ser. | Art. | Mar. | Com. | Lab. | Wid.[a] | Totals |
|---|---|---|---|---|---|---|---|---|
| Piety and prayer[b] | 71 (53·8) | 12 (13·6) | 9 (45·0) | 3 (27·3) | 2 (100) | 0 | 5 (71·4) | 102 (38·9) |
| Nature and science | 6 (4·6) | 63 (70·8) | 0 | 0 | 0 | 0 | 0 | 69 (26·3) |
| Law and history | 28 (21·2) | 4 (4·5) | 7 (35·0) | 0 | 0 | 0 | 2 (28·6) | 41 (15·7) |
| Travel and geography | 8 (6·1) | 4 (4·5) | 0 | 6 (54·5) | 0 | 1 (100) | 0 | 19 (7·3) |
| Technical and manual arts | 4 (3·0) | 2 (2·2) | 3 (15·0) | 1 (9·1) | 0 | 0 | 0 | 10 (3·8) |
| *Belles-lettres* | 7 (5·3) | 1 (1·1) | 0 | 0 | 0 | 0 | 0 | 8 (3·1) |
| Lexicons and dictionaries | 2 (1·5) | 2 (2·2) | 1 (5·0) | 0 | 0 | 0 | 0 | 5 (1·9) |
| Classics and philosophy | 4 (3·0) | 1 (1·1) | 0 | 0 | 0 | 0 | 0 | 5 (1·9 |
| Stories and diversions | 2 (1·5) | 0 | 0 | 1 (9·1) | 0 | 0 | 0 | 3 (1·1) |
| Total books | 132 | 89 | 20 | 11 | 2 | 1 | 7 | 262 |

*Notes:* (a) Widows with stated occupations are included in the appropriate occupational categories. The occupational categories are: professional; service sector; artisan; martime; commerce; labour; widow.

(b) Other than Bibles, which were very commonly in the possession of book owners in general

owners of this kind had unusually large and thematically narrow book collections. By the eighteenth century, there were surgeons in Bristol who collected large numbers of books nearly all of which dealt with the subjects of anatomy, surgery, and medicine. Edward Turner, the surgeon aboard the ship *Leavant* in 1777, owned twenty-six books of which all but a Bible, Prayer Book, and one 'miscellany' dealt with medical arts and sciences.[14] As early as 1705, a surgeon in the Castle Precincts owned forty volumes on 'physic and surgery' and had no books of any other kind.[15] To be sure, the strong association of books on science and nature with members of the service sector was a result, in large part, of the interest surgeons took in the subject matter, but this was at a time when the popular demand for books on health and medicine was growing in general.[16]

Mariners, regardless of where they lived, showed an attachment to printed works concerning geography and travel, but in the city mariners were joined in this interest by a variety of people. Nearly all the bound navigational atlases and marine charts belonged to sailors, navigators, and merchant seamen. At the same time, printed maps and atlases of other kinds appeared in Bristol homes belonging to members of no fewer than twenty-seven different occupations.[17] One Bristol mariner did indeed own forty-eight maps in the early eighteenth century and many other mariners in Bristol owned several printed maps, charts, and atlases. But the maps in Bristol homes charted more than the vast regions of the briny deep. In fact, the significant majority of Bristol's map owners were not mariners at all. One Bristol cooper named John Evans owned ten maps in 1726. By contrast, the few owners of printed maps who did live in the rural setting all had maritime occupations or were members of the clergy. Like map owners in the city, the few villagers who owned printed maps tended to own books as well. Between 1660 and 1740, a time when only 7·7 per cent of local villagers owned books, five (over 71 per cent) of the seven rural map owners also had books; map ownership and book ownership were both highly exceptional and related in the rural setting. In absolute terms, the ownership of maps in conjunction with books was more frequently an urban phenomenon. For the same period, from 1660 to 1740, 14·4 per cent of all surviving Bristol inventories contained books. Twenty-seven (67·5 per cent) of the forty map owners of Bristol in this period also owned books. The conjunction of maps and books showed that map ownership, with its implications for extended horizons, was more closely connected with print culture itself than with any one occupation in the city, while in the villages map ownership was closely connected with occupations associated with port cities in particular or urbanity in general.

Ministers were another occupationally oriented group of readers. The private library of Richard Blinman, an ejected minister residing in Bristol in the 1670s, contained forty-nine books, all but three of which dealt with theology, scripture, or ecclesiastical history.[18] But books of theology and scripture were ubiquitous and the ownership of them hardly served as an identifying trait of any one occupation or social group. In Bristol those widows with no stated occupation tended in their book ownership to concentrate on pious works, with law and history placing a distant second. In general, however, an urban book owner, regardless of occupation, was much more likely than a villager to own books touching on a wide variety of subjects, including theology.

Rural readers of all occupations clearly identifed the Bible as the dominant text in print.[19] For a significant portion of rural book owners, a copy or copies of the Bible was the full extent of book ownership. Between 1660 and 1740 forty-five different book titles were noted in the inventories of homes in the villages near Bristol. All the books other than Bibles found in these homes delved into sacred themes. A copy of Perkins's works and a copy of Dr Mayer's writings were in the possession of a poor Mangotsfield woman who died in the spring of 1688. An Almondsbury widow had but one recognised book at the time of her death in 1694: a copy of Foxe's *Book of Martyrs.*[20] The villagers whose books were identified by title were a fairly representative sample of the rural population; no particular occupation was over-represented.[21] Rural readers surely came in contact with secular texts, including ones intended as much for diversion as for instruction, moral or otherwise. Affordable chapbooks covering a variety of subjects, both secular and sacred, were certainly available in the countryside. In the villages, however, books other than pious and sacred works were not noted, preserved, collected, and bequeathed. Contrary to the representation of rural people in print, the fact that villagers did not replicate patterns of print culture found in the city did not mean that they were myopic or that the full range of printed materials was beyond their grasp. The dominance of scripture among textual influences recognised by villagers persisted well into the eighteenth century, despite the proximity of a teeming centre of cosmopolitan culture and commerce, because villagers wanted it that way.

In a social fabric closely woven by conformity, the normative influence of scripture reinforced communal life that was resistant to alternative behaviour and outside influences. The reading of the Bible in its early modern Anglican context hardly encouraged extraparochial affiliations. On the contrary, it fostered a tribal mentality, provided some of the earliest tenets of the cult of domesticity, justified highly localised regulation of settlement rights and poor relief, and presented a pastoral and paternal, rather than cosmopolitan, ideal. To be sure, xenophobic parochialism was neither specifically rustic nor specifically urbane, but early modern readers of the Bible surely noted that cities were depicted as centres of corruption and suffering even in the Holy Land. Without straying from scripture itself Protestant dissenters, especially after these circles widened and became more socially prominent, eventually presented religious views and devotional practices that promoted an effective challenge to the established, parochial, notion of community. For much of the early modern period the traditional power and influence of scripture in England surely contributed to the xenophobic tendencies of communities of all kinds in urban, as well as rural, settings.[22]

It was only on the surface that ancient Judaeo-Christian scripture appeared to be the product of ideological and social forces drastically removed, culturally and temporally, from the lives of early modern English villagers and townspeople. The English reformation and its lengthy aftermath effected the nationalisation of an orthodoxy and in the process appropriated the imagery of Jerusalem as an image of England, the chosen land. Other metaphors were readily propagated. The Pope was Antichrist. All strangers beyond the communal boundary were the suspect aliens of Egypt, Babylon, and Sodom.[23]

That the perdition of such remote and unfamiliar peoples was didactically juxtaposed against the omnipresence of a personal saviour and a close band of humble disciples, whose movements were largely confined to a small area, reinforced some English secular attitudes concerning community as well as religious beliefs concerning the nature of the divine. The homily became an instrument of secular authority, making obedience to superiors and harmonious relations with one's fellow parishioners the principal Anglican virtues.[24]

Printed sermons addressed the theme of community with astonishing regularity. Printed copies of more than 100 sermons heard and read in and around Bristol from the 1670s to the 1770s are extant. An obsession with religious conformity was an established ingredient in the normative view of membership of the community as policed by the civic polity in the late seventeenth century, so the control of the printed medium itself took on new importance as an issue open to contention in the context of localism.[25] Anglican sermons printed throughout our period took localism as a theme and stressed that conformity to the established religion was a requirement not only of membership in a community but of the very order on which community itself depended.[26] In 1685, when Bristol's municipal leaders continued to wage official attacks on local dissenters and recusants in order to enforce civic purity,[27] corporate authoritarianism was reinforced by a printed sermon delivered at the bishop's visitation.[28] There was a healthy Anglican tradition, observed by Bristol's parish preachers, of justifying the power and authority of judges, magistrates and secular officials, especially in the local execution of their duties.[29] In 1683 a sermon of local authorship presented in the Bristol parish of St James preached on loyalties extending beyond the confines of the city, but this may have been a rare and timely concession to the thousands of visitors attending the annual St James fair held in the parish that very week in the midst of the city's anti-recusant furor.[30] Eighty years later a sermon delivered at another visitation, and printed shortly thereafter, still asserted the perceived need for a national religion and equated the community of orthodox faith with a community bound by shared space.[31] The issue had not been resolved with official toleration in the 1690s. Civic officials and their sympathisers in the pulpits were still determined, even in the middle of the eighteenth century, to prevent the idealised union of localism and conformity from losing its grip on popular sentiment. The connection between civic and religious loyalty persisted as a familiar theme in the Mayor's Chapel right up to the end of the early modern period.[32]

Charity was widely preached as a principal Christian virtue, but Bristol's published sermons of Anglican origin conspicuously emphasised the local application of generosity. If some sermons addressed themselves to the honourable nature and fraternal traditions of certain occupations,[33] many more of Bristol's printed sermons invoked the earthly and spiritual benefits of charity towards one's immediate neighbours, a notion consistent with the parochial organisation of the Anglican church itself. A community based on the sharing of material resources within a locally confined group was an attractive notion to its wealthy and powerful members.[34] It permitted them to exert didactic influence, in the guise of generosity, to display the 'perfection of Christian morality' quite visibly, and in material terms, among the people in their midst.[35] Until the late eighteenth century eulogies printed in Bristol, without exception, honoured local citizens whose contribution to the welfare of the city – as opposed to the surrounding villages, region, or nation – provided the principal theme of such sermons.[36] Eulogies for rural residents were not printed in Bristol until the 1770s. By the middle decades of the eighteenth century specially commissioned sermons honoured charitable ties within Bristol's county societies, organisations of migrants and their descendants whose common origin beyond the confines of the city formed the very basis of their close formal relationship.[37]

The conformist positions on difficult moral issues and abstract concepts were very much bound up with a more tangible sense of familiar spaces. In Anglican sermons, just as localism was presented as a sign of virtue, so the pain of expulsion or physical separation was equated with the essence of sin. Virtue, morality, sin, salvation, and grace were explained in terms of distance.[38] The so-called 'practical religion' and ethical instruction of conformist sermons dealt almost exclusively with recurring face-to-face relations and used neighbourliness as the principal measure of correct behaviour.[39] It was the law-abiding audience moving freely within the parish or city who heard chilling sermons equating hell with remoteness and sin with separation, expulsion, or isolation. Final sermons preached to imprisoned criminals on the eve of their execution offered solace in the notion that death constituted a return to the fold, a journey back to one's origins. Heaven, in this sense, could be understood as home.[40]

Writings attributable to dissenting preachers or dissenting congregations differed significantly from the local conformist publications in their presentation of abstractions, including the concept of community itself. The social spheres of dissenters contained occupational, sexual, and familial connections, but these were the products of 'spiritual tribalism' more than local tribalism.[41] Dissenting publications circulating in Bristol in the later decades of the seventeenth century promoted the view that spiritual communion, the basis of community, is achieved in a vast universe and that the time spent within spatial confinements, in corporeal form, is fleeting. The medieval image of the soul moving through the earthly edifice of life as a bird darting in one window and out another, back into the infinite darkness, was a favourite of Thomas Hardcastle, who preached before the Bristol Broadmead congregation in the 1670s.[42] Among dissenters, neither the community of like-minded believers on earth nor the community of souls in afterlife was bound by the confines of space by which conformists recognised their own communities. These competing visions of community expressed in print were also reflected in long-standing notions about the disposition of the body and the soul, as careful readings of the dissenting and conformist language used in seventeenth-century wills have shown.[43] In his will, composed in 1637, Thomas Adeane, a conformist parishioner in St Thomas, stressed his desire to be laid to rest within the city of Bristol. Adeane's exact contemporary in the city, a Baptist named Lawrence Joyner, requested instead to be buried among fellow believers, a subtle distinction pointing to the divergence of a community based on shared space and a community based on shared belief.[44] The sermons which Joyner's dissenting successors heard and read well into the next century still emphasised personal knowledge of the divine – spiritual intimacy rather than spatial closeness – as the basis of community as well as salvation.[45]

Some issues commonly believed to have separated dissenters and Anglicans, such as the role and authority of the clergy, were actually areas of convergence by the eighteenth century. Unitarians, for example, moved away from the strongly anti-Catholic depiction of the minister as a mere servant of the congregation while clergy of the Anglican establishment, preaching in Bristol cathedral itself, began to concede the possible 'frailty of its ministers'.[46] Dissenters did not neglect the issues of daily conduct and social interaction. On the contrary, they accepted accountability and respectability as means of advancing the cause of religious toleration in a divided society while glorifying their creator and saviour in heaven.[47]

Eighteenth-century evangelical revivalists did not see parochial worship, the sharing of sacred space with one's immediate neighbours, as a requirement of proper devotion. Indeed the assemblies of dissenters and the sermons of their preachers, Wesley's included, were hardly confined to the indoors, much less to one place of worship.[48] Wesley's sermon on grace preached in Bristol in 1740, and printed there shortly afterward, stated plainly that divine laws of salvation and repentance apply to 'all men, everywhere, every man in every place, without exception, either of place or person'.[49] His language may have been restrictive with respect to gender, but not with regard to place. In the 1750s William Dyer was an avid churchgoer and sampler of sermons. He attended several religious services and meetings every week at Anglican, Methodist, Quaker, and (eventually) Unitarian places of worship. He was present in November 1753 when George Whitefield preached at Bristol's Old Orchard in the 'new built Tabernacle', a place of worship so new that oiled paper covered the windows where the stained glass had not yet been inserted. Dyer attributed the new religious revival not to published theological works but to the power of inspired preaching and to the interaction of communicants drawn by spiritual, rather than parochial, ties.[50]

That Anglican communal worship rested on personal interaction and familiar ritual, rather than on more abstract spiritual ties, was obvious from parochial attitudes to print culture itself. In the 1750s William Dyer remarked that the parish clerk of St Nicholas, despite his permanent loss of vision in both eyes, 'continued his office ... he was able to repeat the Psalms and all the responses to the Church service'.[51] In 1729 the vestry of St Philip and Jacob sold both of the parish's additional 'great' Bibles and all seven Prayer Books from the congregation's pews and retained only those few volumes needed by the clergy for their observation of the liturgy. In 1735 the vestry of St Philip and Jacob contemplated buying two Common Prayer Books for the parish library but rejected them in favour of 'A Book of Articles, Canons, Injunctions, and Acts of Parliament' which it bought a year later.[52]

Urban readers, regardless of their wealth, gender or occupation, were far more likely than rural ones to own books that had significance for entirely non-spiritual aspects of life. This was true before and after the arrival of printers in provincial cities. (Table 8.2.) George Stearte, a Bristol surgeon worth only £40 in 1671, owned works of Bede and Ambrose Parey in additon to a copy of Riverin's *Practice of Phisicke* and a treatise entitled *The Five Senses*. Urban dwellers, rather than villagers, were the avid collectors of chapbooks. Godly and pious works made up the single smallest category of chapbooks from the point of view of supply, as well as demand, in late seventeenth-century England.[53] The heyday of religious chapbooks had been before the civil war. The career of John Andrewes, the 'market-place theologian' and best known of the 'penny godly' authors, had coincided with the decline of pious chapbooks and godly ballads in the early seventeenth century.[54] In the early decades of the eighteenth century, books in all formats on history, science, nature, geography, and travel combined to challenge the numerical supremacy of pious and religious texts in urban households. The collections of cheaper printed materials in urban homes after 1740 appeared in the form of bound periodicals, filled with social and political commentary of a secular nature. Even Bristol's trained theologians read well beyond the bounds of divinity. One Bristol theologian named Alexander Catcott was a member of a growing circle of avid amateur geologists that included deluvian theorists interested in reconciling scriptural and natural explanations of topographical variation. In January 1750 Alexander Catcott recorded in his diary the titles of 130 books and collected manuscripts which he had read on the subjects of natural history, science, and regional antiquity.[55] In 1762 a Bristol gentleman named William Whitton owned a biography of Oliver Cromwell, a multi-volume *Travels into India*, an alluring *Account of Time*, and numerous other books on history, travel, law, and crime, including a history of piracy which surely touched on all these themes.

In 1742 Benjamin Hickey's shop in the centre of Bristol advertised the

Table 8.2 Books of known titles, arranged according to thematic categories, for three forty-year periods during which their owners lived in the city of Bristol (% in parentheses)

| | 1660–99 | | 1700–39 | | 1740–80 | |
|---|---|---|---|---|---|---|
| | Books | Owners | Books | Owners | Books | Owners |
| Piety and prayer[a] | 41 (68.3) | 6 (60.0) | 13 (21.0) | 8 (66.7) | 48 (34.3) | 8 (80.0) |
| Nature and science | 5 (8.3) | 2 (20.0) | 41 (66.1) | 2 (16.7) | 23 (16.4) | 3 (30.0) |
| Law and history | 4 (6.7) | 2 (20.0) | 6 (9.7) | 5 (41.7) | 31 (22.1) | 5 (50.0) |
| Travel and geography | 6 (10.0) | 4 (40.0) | 0 | 0 | 12 (8.6) | 3 (30.0) |
| Technical and manual arts | 1 (1.7) | 1 (10.0) | 1 (1.6) | 1 (8.3) | 7 (5.0) | 4 (40.0) |
| *Belles-lettres* | 0 | 0 | 0 | 0 | 8 (5.7) | 2 (20.0) |
| Lexicons and dictionaries | 1 (1.7) | 1 (10.0) | 0 | 0 | 4 (2.8) | 4 (40.0) |
| Classics and philosophy | 0 | 0 | 0 | 0 | 5 (3.6) | 3 (30.0) |
| Stories and diversions | 2 (3.3) | 1 (10.0) | 1 (1.6) | 1 (8.3) | 2 (1.4) | 1 (10.0) |
| Totals | 60 | 10 | 62 | 12 | 140 | 10 |

*Note:* (a) Bibles, which were very commonly in the possession of book owners in general, are listed separately as follows:

| | | | | | | |
|---|---|---|---|---|---|---|
| Bibles | 123 | 86 | 36 | 29 | 22 | 16 |

*Source:* B.R.O. Probate Inventories and Cause Papers.

impending sale of 'many thousand' volumes, some formerly in the libraries of two Bristol gentlemen, one of them a clergyman.[56] Hickey's notice specified the titles of the most enticing editions. Of the forty-seven titles so noted, twelve were those of historical works, but only ten were those of theological works. Neither Bibles, despite their intrinsic value, nor Prayer Books were specifically promoted in the notice. The historical works, which included those of Rapin, Raleigh, and Camden, tended to feature England's past or that of some particular English county or city, as in the case of Drake's *Antiquity of York*. One of the seven legal works on offer, *The Trial of Captain Goodere*, dealt with a sensational Bristol murder case of great local interest. Five books dealing with geography and travel were included among those mentioned: Madox's works on the cities, boroughs, and land of England; Martland's surveys of London; and Le Bruyin on travels to Persia, Muscovy, and the East Indies. The advertisement also featured a Spanish dictionary and a copy of Telemachus in French. From a thematic point of view, the books in Bristol homes resembled those in foreign cities more closely than they resembled those found in the villages of southern Gloucestershire and northern Somerset.[57]

Almanacs ranged far and wide across the terrain of political commentary, historical memory, scientific inquiry, religious polemics, and astrological predictions[58] as they inscribed in print an awareness of geography and community. We know that a copy of Thomas Gallen's *New Almanac* was in the possession of a Bristol resident sometime between its date of publication in 1671 and 1674, when the owner, Francis Creswicke, wrote his name and several journal entries on its pages.[59] Creswicke read during the 'golden age of English almanacs'.[60] Of the thirty-two items in the almanac's 'compendious chronology of things memorable', most dealt with the conquests and wars of the English crown, astronomical events, and the chronicles of Christianity. All almanacs discussed celestial bodies in some way and turned the reader's attention to very remote places indeed. The scale of perception in these popular publications was grand and presumed a readership of similarly broad horizons. Gallen simply listed the points from which eclipses could be viewed in the year 1671: 'our antipodes and perioecis, as also in Nova Guinea, Insulis Solomnis, de los Turbarones, in Mare del Zur, the Kingdom of Quivira, straight of Anian, California, as also in Cathay, China, Borneo, Japan, India, intra and extra Gangem, the Philippine and Molucque Islands, and the adjacent places'. For whom would this list have been meaningful? There were a few items in Gallen's chronology – the invention of coaches, the paving of roads, the extension of navigable rivers, and the early importation of tobacco – that presumed the reader's preoccupation with travel and remote places. Gallen's almanac informed its readers that the very invention of print ranked with the creation of the world and the 'passion of Our Lord' among historical events most worthy of mention. Only the least perceptive reader would have failed to see an association among print technology, extended horizons, and urbanity.

The construed ideal of distinctly urban and rural worlds, discernible in the contents of all types of printed texts, including books, newspapers, pamphlets, and maps, was clearly presented in almanacs. Gallen stated plainly on his title page that the almanac was intended for 'such as use markets or fairs, also to travellers that coast the Kingdom', and twelve pages later he described the almanac as 'a true and plain description of the highways in England and Wales'. The almanac contained no information about agricultural practices and no references to rural areas or pastimes. All the information concerned London, other urban centres, or travel among them. Nearly a third of the items in the 'compendious chronology of things memorable' dealt specifically with London, its mayors, fires, buildings, and plagues. The almanac also reported the schedule of judicial sessions at Westminster and the opening of the Exchequer. The almanac's tide table listed cities including Hamburg, Lisbon, and Cadiz, but calculated the times of high water in all places relative to its occurrence in London. Bristol's high tide, the reader was informed, could be expected some three hours after high tide in the metropolis.

Almanacs cultivated a sense of an urban network superimposed over a murky rural landscape which was treated separately if at all. The mileage chart in Gallen's almanac listed cities ranging from forty-four miles (London and Cambridge) to 202 miles (London and St David's) apart.[61] The descriptions of routes connecting one city with another made references neither to villages nor to the expanses of rural areas either side of the roads. Instead, the almanac referred only to the towns appearing every eight to twelve miles *en route*, with the largest interval between noteworthy sites, by the almanac's reckoning, placed at twenty-five miles. The first landmark recognised along the highway from Bristol to Oxford was the town of 'Sadbury',[62] which was ten miles outside Bristol. This matches the conventional figure of ten miles as the radius encompassing an urban centre's rural environs. In the geography of social spheres presented by this very popular printed source, rural environs were assigned standard dimensions and were treated as spaces between the settlements of the construed readership rather than as settlements themselves. In this urbane view, rural environs were like the celestial void in which the cities, like heavenly bodies, were suspended.

In fact, foreign lands received more attention in print than English villages for much of the early modern period. The citizens of a bustling port, where mariners made up the single largest occupational group, surely developed some awareness of foreigners, strangers, exotic travellers, and their origins. One of the best-known examples of the eighteenth-century English literature of exotica, Defoe's *Robinson Crusoe* (1718), was conceived in Bristol, where the author encountered Alexander Selkirk, the seafarer whose adventures provided the inspiration for the book.[63] The themes of texts recognised in urban households embraced broadened horizons as an aspect of the urbane sensibility. In view of this, the condescending and xenophobic treatment that remote places and alien types received in printed texts circulating, or even published, in a cosmopolitan English city demands further explanation.

It is important to draw a distinction between the reception of images conveyed through print culture and the treatment of actual people. A popular fascination with exotica was readily apparent in the material and print cultures of the city and its residents well before the Restoration. Bristol was at the very forefront of English exploration and colonisation. The sixteenth-century voyager Martin Frobisher and his crew referred to the unfamiliar people they encountered abroad not only as 'savages' but as 'the countrey people'. These wretched strangers performed for the amusement and profit of their English captors and then died horribly of deficient immunity or pathetic isolation in English cities.[64] One of the fashionable periodicals collected by urban dwellers in the second half of the eighteenth century, *Turkish Spy*, featured exotic imagery but it is doubtful that readers of such a periodical would have welcomed a Turkish neighbour, suitor, employer, or apprentice.[65] The attitude of smug superiority with which so-called exotic people were regarded was gradually and subtly eclipsed by fear and suspicion regarding the 'strangers' within English communities themselves. The theological works included in Hickey's advertisement of 1742, *The History of Popery*, and *Tradition of the Jews*, or the *Doctrines and Expositions contained in the Talmud and other Rabbinical Writings*,[66] may have reflected an urbane shift away from a polemical distaste for recusancy and dissent and toward a more widespread curiosity in the scholarly aspects of all religions. But those Catholics, Jews, and all people associated with remoteness who encountered local personal culture, face-to-face interaction, were widely treated in English parochial life as intruders and proper targets of oppression and hatred. The importance of proximity was reflected in the heightened xenophobia displayed in the printed representation of those religious, ethnic, and transient groups who encroached on established communities during the urban renaissance.

Along with 'countrey people' and women of all ranks, immigrants were the favourite targets of abuse in seventeenth-century chapbook literature. In print the intensity of mockery increased as levels of immigration rose, with the cruellest barbs aimed mainly at ethnic groups whose influx was perceived to be the highest at the time. The most commonly burlesqued immigrants in Bristol were the Welsh, a group whose place of origin was visible from the mouth of the river Avon on a clear day. Anti-Welsh sentiment persisted thoughout the early modern period as anti-Irish and antisemitic xenophobia became even more intense with the steady influx of Irish labour and the official readmission of Jews to England during the 1650s. Innocent references to leeks and potatoes were no longer possible in the eighteenth-century provincial press, in which the Welsh and the Irish had been reduced to the status of edible plant life.[67]

The latter part of the seventeenth century saw the rise of a particularly vilified sect, the Society of Friends. William Prynne, in his pamphlet entitled *The Quakers unmasked* and clearly detected to be but the *Spawn of Romish Frogs, Jesuits and Franciscan Fryers*,[68] misrepresented Quaker theology in order to identify that dissenting group with Catholics. Prynne, who drew upon the Quakers' own publications,[69] was surely aware of the Quaker disdain for the tradition of beatification. Quakers refused, in all their writings, records, and speech to attach the preface 'saint' to the name of any parish, building or person. Nevertheless, Prynne wrongly cited the veneration of saints as a Quaker practice, an outrageous piece of sophistry intended to associate Quakers with Catholics. He claimed that the presence of Quakers in Italy, the geographical locus of popish power, was proof of their Catholicism, itself a popularly held symbol of foreignness. He pointed out that Bristol Quakers took refuge in the abandoned Dominican friary in Bristol's Broadmead and therefore must be, as occupants of a popish gathering space, Catholics and outsiders. Quakers had situated themselves in the heart of an English city, and by 'this their new stratagem' did more harm than 'ever they did by saying Mass, or preaching, printing any points of Popery in eighty years' time before'. One widely circulated broadside alleged that Quakers defecated in churches.[70] Prynne, a leading polemicist of his day, invoked the symbolic significance of space and its violation while he grossly misrepresented the philosophical implications of Quaker religious ideas.

The improved social status of nonconformists who won over their neighbours in mundane, rather than spiritual, ways as successful and philanthropic members of the working community[71] reduced hostility toward Protestant dissenters by the middle of the eighteenth century. Catholics and Jews, on the other hand, remained subject to vicious abuse in print and in person. Unlike Protestant dissenters, Jews and Catholics never escaped their association with social separation and remote places.[72] A late seventeenth-century book in the possession of a Bristol resident described the simple clothing, diet, customs, economy, and gender relations of Laplanders, but asserted the alien backwardness of their society on the strength of two revealing observations: the Laplanders were not Christians and they did not live in cities.[73] In view of the xenophobic tendency to merge representations of all socially marginalised types, it is scarcely surprising that villagers living on the verge of towns were commonly subjected to the sort of mockery and abuse that cheap books, broadsides, and local newspapers aimed at ethnic groups, foreigners, and religious dissenters.[74]

Early provincial newspapers hardly addressed a rural audience at all. The assumption based on at least one study of London newspaper mastheads, that English newspapers of the late seventeenth and early eighteenth centuries were 'intended primarily for circulation among readers in the rural areas or ... country readers as well as city readers',[75] is not a safe one. Until the mid-eighteenth century, Bristol's newspapers provided a link with London and focused on news from the urban network and areas abroad.[76] The early Bristol newspapers were mainly digest compilations of news printed first in London. The advertisements in Bristol papers were supplied by urban merchants, artisans, and professionals many of whom were Bristolians themselves. The

Bristol newspapers of the first half of the eighteenth century did not provide any sort of regional forum wherein news and opinion derived from the nearby villages could be found. The argument that provincial newspapers did not develop localist editorial tendencies until the end of the eighteenth century may overstate the case, but only slightly.[77] In any event, if the printed word did serve to promote urban–rural ties based on regionalism, we should expect provincial newspapers, the most explicitly localist application of print, to supply evidence of it.

As late as the 1720s, Bristol newspapers still presented a vague or uncertain picture of rural and regional geography. A Bristol report of the apprehension of a highwayman by his intended victim admitted: 'but whether this happened in Somerset or Devon we are at a loss because both counties meet thereabouts'.[78] Bristol newspapers reported incidents occurring in other cities and towns with their exact locations known but Bristol's reporters were mystified by the rural geography of the neighbouring counties. On 23 October 1725, *Farley's Bristol Newspaper* reported: 'Last week, a farmer going home from Warminster market in Somerset was met on the road by some rogues who first robbed and then murdered him.' Warminster is in Wiltshire. More revealing, perhaps, was the lack of attention to detail – the particular road, the name of the farmer or his village – beyond those needed to present the rural world in a generic sense as a self-evidently treacherous place removed from the urban experience.

On the other hand, the publishers of Bristol newspapers assumed a familiarity, on the part of the readership, with specific details of the English urban landscape. In 1725 the same *Farley's Bristol Newspaper* supplied an example: 'They write from Dover on Sunday last, a boy with some others on the cliffs there fell down off one of them, reckoned as high as the Monument in London, into the water.' The boy got up and ran away unharmed. The urban reader surely marvelled less, if at all, at the fact that a man-made civic structure in another city, rather than a natural formation such as the Avon gorge cliffs on the edge of Bristol, was used without additional explanation to convey to a readership in Bristol the approximate height of cliffs in Dover. In general terms, the readers of provincial newspapers were supplied with an urban, even metropolitan, frame of reference for their understanding of events everywhere.

Early provincial newspapers drew a distinction between direct personal interaction – the stuff of personal culture – and news. News was images and information derived from remote sources through print culture. The oldest surviving issue of *The Bristol Post Boy* appeared in the second week of August 1704 and contained no news of Bristol itself. It consisted of three London items, two Plymouth items, and one each from Falmouth and Yarmouth. These were all port towns, convenient receptors of news which, in that period, seemed to have been associated exclusively with remote or foreign cities, the origins of printed information itself.[79] The only reference to Bristol in this early *Post Boy* was an advertisement for a surgeon in King Street specialising in the treatment of venereal diseases. Early references to Bristol in its own papers were not news items but advertisements for goods and services. The only routine references to Bristol in its own newspapers during their first decades reinforced the image of the city as a junction in the extended urban and foreign network. The arrivals of ships, either coasters from other English cities or maritime vessels from across the Atlantic, were routinely reported in all the Bristol papers. The announcement of bankruptcies was another weekly item of interest aimed at members of the urban trade community. The bankruptcy notice of James Graham, a chapman 'late of Bristol', was the only reference to Bristol in Farley's entire issue of 23 October 1725.[80] These notices of business failures concerned themselves with members of the extended urban network and not with local farmers and the prospects of good or bad harvests. Early Bristol newspapers included no items at all concerning local rural villages.

Reports in Bristol papers of events in the local countryside began to appear in the mid-1720s, but these presented the rural experience as dangerous and gruesome, a disturbing image in stark contrast to that created for Bristol itself. The readership was presented with a picture of rural life shaped entirely by the imagery of danger, barbarity, and deviance. In the three-month period alone from late October 1725 to late January 1726, the items concerning nearby villages reported in *Farley's Bristol Newspaper* were enough to convey this impression. In this typical selection of the period, the Bristol paper's readers were told of gangs robbing and murdering along the rural roads in Somerset near Pensford, and Wells, and in the neighbouring county of Wiltshire; of the collapse of a glassmaking house in Pensford 'six miles off' and the gruesome details of the bodies discovered in the rubble; of two Bristol boat pilots who drowned in the murky waters off the shore at Kingsroad, the rural area at the mouth of the Avon; of an unfortunate somnambulist in a rural Gloucestershire inn who in the middle of the night, dreaming he was safely at home, plummeted from an upper storey window and writhed on the ground in pain unnoticed until the next day; of a particularly brutal murder 'instigated by the devil' in the Somerset village of Street; and of a Horfield farmer who was found in his cottage with his brains dashed out when his seven-year pact with the devil expired. It is also of no small significance that the newspaper had to identify for the readership the whereabouts of these nearby villages. Not only was the local rural landscape portrayed in print culture as something of a mystery, but the very dangers which typified the reported picture of rural life were linked, in two carefully detailed instances, with an irrational evil beyond human control.[81]

The relative isolation of villages and rural homes was presented by newspapers as a liability in times of trouble and a cause of trouble itself, stemming from behaviour unchecked by social contact. A servant in Street who murdered the mistress of the farm while her husband was away was said to have 'followed her out where she was milking the cows and with a hay knife almost cut off her head ... dragged her to the hay mow ... and made off before the neighbourhood was apprised of it'. The only mildly unsavoury story about Bristol reported in the entire year of 1725 was an anecdote, clearly intended to be humorous, about a drunken customs official who was caught urinating in plain view on Wine Street in the heart of the city.[82] Bristol's own criminals and deviants were conspicuously absent from the pages of Bristol newspapers until the second half of the eighteenth century, a delayed development consistent with urban reporting elsewhere in England.[83] Despite the constant danger of fire in cities and towns, and routine complaints about unsafe hearths or ovens in urban homes and workshops,[84] Bristol fires simply were not reported in Bristol newspapers. By contrast, *Farley's Bristol Newspaper* reported on 5 February 1726 that a farmer's wife in the village of Shirley Holmes, Hampshire, needing to make an excursion to 'a neighbouring farmhouse to get some milk', had locked her three children inside (for safety's sake) and returned some time later to find her house burned to the ground with the children inside because no one had been near to help. Defoe warned that old country roads were 'dangerous to travel through, especially for strangers'.[85] Readers learned from the 21 August 1731 issue of Farley's Bristol paper that a man was robbed of £25 right on the common in the village of Brislington, Somerset. Farley reported on 23 October 1725 of the ship *Samuel and Jane*, which strayed into treacherous coastal waters away from port and was tossed aground, where its wreck and salvage were 'carried away by country people'. It was a popular observation in London, Portsmouth, and Bristol papers that smugglers operating in these places were local farmers.[86] The rural setting was represented in print as an endemically dangerous space haunted by highwaymen, deviants, and harpies removed from the corrective vigilance and omnipresent supervision provided in civic society.

All the direct evidence concerning the extent to which newspapers from provincial cities actually reached a readership in the countryside begins with estimates of the printed supply and ends with the identification of the places through which the more successful provincial papers circulated. In addition to the newspapers spread about by dispatchers, Bristol's printers surely ran off enough copies to fill the city's coffee houses and taverns. The Hope and Anchor, the village gathering place in Westbury-on-Trym, might be expected to have had some newspapers on the premises. In 1727 Samuel Farley announced the dispatch of his newspaper 'by two or three running footmen ... for the convenience of people in the country', but their distribution points, with the exception of Westbury, were the towns of Somerset and Gloucester-shire, not the villages.[87] It would have been difficult for any courier to transport more than a handful of papers to a few regular subscribers. Felix Farley printed the following on the front page of his *Bristol Journal*:

> For the benefit of those who shall please to advertise in this journal, the proprietors hereof, at a considerable expense, extended its circulation every week to the following places, viz. London, Reading, Chippenham, Marshfield, Bath, Bradford, Trowbridge, Shepton, Devizes, Sodbury, Wells, Axbridge, Bridgwater, Taunton, Exeter, Tiverton, Barnstaple, Honiton, Plymouth, Launceston, Penzance, Hereford, Monmouth, Worcester, Evesham, Shrewsbury, Birmingham, Haverfordwest, Swansea, Abergavenny, Brecknock, Neath, Caermarthen, Chepstow, Cardiff, Oxford. We apprehend that by extending our paper in this manner it must undoubtedly give satisfaction to those who advertise therein.

This new circulation, the most extensive of a Bristol paper, was not announced until 1755 and it gives no indication of a rural readership. Furthermore, of all the places mentioned in this impressive list, only one, Chipping Sodbury, was within eleven miles of Bristol.

The advertisements in Bristol papers were also of urban origin from the very start. The advertisers, we may suppose, had an audience in mind when they invested in the printer's services. The advertisers in William Bonny's *Bristol Post Boy*, the city's first newspaper, were merchants, surgeons, and artisans of Bristol. Bonny advertised his own printing and bookselling business and in at least one instance offered 'Welch Common Prayer Books' which appealed to a remote or immigrant readership rather than a local rural one. Bonny's papers also advertised his 'shop books' and 'pocket books', and a 'new map of South Britain, or England and Wales, containing all the cities and market towns, with the roads from town to town'. There were no rural advertisers and no advertisements for items known to have been in rural households: livestock, farming tools, clocks, and firearms.[88] Even the early advertisements for parcels of land were placed by urban agents in Bristol or Bath.

The earliest explicit signs of a rural readership for Bristol newspapers appeared in the second quarter of the eighteenth century when a few rural readers communicated directly with the newspapers. In January 1733 someone advertised a reward for the recovery of a horse stolen or strayed from a paddock in 'Westbury in the county of Gloucester', as its owner or the newspaper saw fit to inform the readership.[89] James Pidding, the owner of a stray horse near Lawford's Gate, Bristol, may have imagined that his horse could have been found by a reader in the nearby countryside when he placed a notice in the newspaper.[90] In 1730 there appeared, for what may have been the first time in a Bristol paper, correspondence from a rural reader himself. As usual it was concerned with the recovery of lost goods, and it contributed to the urban picture of rurals as strife-torn and suspicious outsiders in the bargain:

Whereas Mary, the Wife of John Wall of Cleur in the parish of Wedman in the county of Somerset has [run away] from her husband, and has carried off some of his effects, this is therefore to caution all persons not to trust the said Mary Wall for he will pay you no debts contracted by her from the date hereof: 21 November 1730.[91]

Such notices, disclaiming liability for the debts of alienated wives, were fairly common, but it is important to note that Farley, the publisher, was still not familiar enough with the neighbouring countryside to identify properly the whereabouts of Clewer, which was only fifteen miles south-west of Bristol, near Wedmore (not 'Wedman') and Wells.

Andrew Hooke remained the publisher and writer of the Bristol *Oracle* after 1743 with a new printer, a new masthead, and a new title accommodating the startling inclusion of the countryside in the paper's new image: *The Oracle; or, Bristol Weekly Miscellany* became the *Bristol Oracle and Country Intelligencer.* Hooke was certainly aware of the implications of his paper's new name. He was a contentious sort who openly challenged the reports compiled by the Farleys, his local publishing rivals. He aimed barbed jests at the poor geographical sense of Felix Farley, whose paper, Hooke observed, occasionally placed the Russian fleet afloat in the hills of Transylvania.[92] Hooke once quipped that Farley should go shopping where geographical primers are sold if he should ever manage to locate such a place. Hooke advertised his personal accessibility at his Bristol haunts. Readers were routinely reminded by the Oracle that Hooke was 'at St Michael's Coffee House in Magdalen's Lane, and at the London Coffee House in Corn Street, where he may be spoke with every day'. Felix Farley did say of his own paper that it was printed in his house in Wine Street, but Farley's paper was merely assembled in Bristol. Many of the remarks in Hooke's paper were conceived in Bristol by the publisher himself. By offering Bristol a paper that was an extension of his own personality, Hooke provided a local identity in print and not simply a link with the urban network.

A Bristol auctioneer and appraiser by the name of Sketchley published his very first issue of *The Bee and Sketchley's Weekly Advertiser* on 27 October 1777. His aims were to provide a philosophical alternative to news and to depart from the xenophobic polemics of the age. 'I hope for the correspondence and kind assistance of the *ingenious* ... to recommend peace and *universal charity.*' Sketchley regarded the use of print as a means of soliciting and expressing the self-conscious identity of a community affiliated by shared values and a common readership. He ran a serial column in *The Bee* devoted to the history of the city of Bristol that served as a meaningful contrast to the historical vision of almanacs and earlier papers focused on London and abroad. Sketchley made references to local villages in this context. He informed his readers that John Locke 'the philosopher and one of the greatest men England has produced, was born at Wrington, in the county of Somerset, near Bristol'.[93] According to one of Sketchley's reports, when asked why he refused to tip his cap to the bishop a cantankerous elderly farmer explained that if the bishop's benediction were real it would have the strength to pass through a hat.[94] The printing of this anecdote was a transparent bid, by an urbane newpaper, to identify a more appealing rustic stereotype, but Sketchley's own philosophy consistently implied a divisive distinction between urbane civility and rustic eccentricity.

Sketchley purposely named *The Bee* after the natural creatures whose admirable lives served as his ideal model for the spatial and material bases of community formation. Front-page columns in the first three issues of the paper were devoted to the metaphorical use of the bee, 'an insect famous for its industry', an anatomical wonder and, by no coincidence, a communal being. The bee collects 'sweet juices extracted from flowers which the bee discharges into the cell of the magazine for the support of the community in the winter'. Sketchley went on to identify the community as a hive, a fully enclosed space distinguished by its self-sufficiency, isolation from its surroundings, and the adequate division of labour accomplished by its inhabitants, who live harmoniously at close quarters, despite their various ranks and social stations. Sketchley asked, in a pointedly rhetorical fashion, 'Considering the advantages arising from the labours of bees, is it not strange that our country people are not more solicitous about the preservation and increase of these animals?' He went on to remark that young bees who become separated from the swarm establish themselves in another hive, thus supplying more imagery of an urban network, centres of social and economic activity communicating across expanses of rural landscape. Between the 1740s and 1770s Bristol's newspapers and serial publications did finally become instruments of local sentiment and informers of a local identity. It is not clear, however, that the identity prescribed in print for Bristol readers ever fully overcame the representation of the rural world as detached and slightly alien. The development of local journalism in provincial England may have given new expression to a long-established mentality of civic isolationism.

It is possible to trace the thematic shifts in manuscript diaries as responses to the changes in locally printed newspapers, thereby gaining some fascinating clues about the purpose and scope of printed information as perceived by readers themselves. Early newspapers, the posts, were presented to the reader in epistolary form and diarists treated printed publications and scribbled personal accounts as supplements to one another. Alexander Catcott actually pasted newspaper clippings into the pages of his private journal next to his own handwritten entries.[95] At times William Dyer, who was another close reader of newspapers, used his diary to record his remarks about newspaper reports.[96] In one instance Dyer's careful reading of a newspaper gave him news of his uncle's death before members of his own family had contacted him about it.[97] Beginning in the 1740s Dyer wrote his diary, a highly detailed personal narrative ranging greatly in theme and scope, during the last decades of the early modern period as Bristol newspapers were beginning to print information and opinion with a local viewpoint. The relationship between text and reader in former times is difficult to ascertain, but in the person of William Dyer we have a devoted and astute commentator who responded to all types of printed information, ephemeral and durable. He was a thoughtful critic of sermons and a collector of books, to which he made numerous references. He compiled an index to his two-volume diary. He cited, by page numbers, cross-references to other entries in the diary and added editorial gloss upon later review. That is, Dyer organised and documented the private record of his life as if it were a publication but in keeping with the conventions of subjectivity common to devotional, occupational, political, pastoral and social diaries.[98]

As if in response to the changes in Bristol's printed texts, Dyer's diary exhibited subtle movements toward or away from dominant foci and themes. (Table 8.3.) William Dyer sought to place the record of his own personal

Table 8.3 Thematic and focal breakdown of William Dyer's diary entries for three five-year periods (% in parentheses)

|  | 1750–54 | 1760–64 | 1770–74 | Total |
|---|---|---|---|---|
| Local and personal | 120 | 132 | 159 | 411 |
|  | (52·6) | (50·2) | (58·0) | (53·7) |
| Local and impersonal | 60 | 56 | 28 | 144 |
|  | (26·3) | (21·3) | (10·2) | (18·8) |
| Remote and personal | 27 | 26 | 29 | 82 |
|  | (11·8) | (9·9) | (10·6) | (10·7) |
| Remote and impersonal | 9 | 12 | 20 | 41 |
|  | (4·0) | (4·6) | (7·3) | (5·4) |
| Sermons and philosophy | 9 | 20 | 7 | 36 |
|  | (4·0) | (7·6) | (2·6) | (4·7) |
| Dreams and imaginings | 1 | 8 | 20 | 29 |
|  | (0·4) | (3·0) | (7·3) | (3·8) |
| Printed books, | 2 | 9 | 11 | 22 |
| newspapers, etc. | (0·9) | (3·4) | (4·0) | (2·9) |
| Total entries | 228 | 263 | 274 | 765 |
|  | (100·0) | (100·0) | (100·0) | (100·0) |

*Source*: B.C.L. MS #20095, Diary of William Dyer (1745–1801).

development in the context of his perception of what was socially and histori-cally relevant, and his diary compensated for the deficiencies or changing emphases and themes of the printed record that was available to him. As we should expect, the diary maintained an emphasis on local subject matter of a personal nature. Nevertheless, from the very beginning, the portion of the diary devoted to local news outside Dyer's own personal experience declined. The rate fell off even more sharply in Dyer's accounts as the provision of local information became a routine and meaningful function of Bristol's newspa-pers by the 1760s or so; the advent of local news in print eventually relieved Dyer, somewhat, of his compulsion to record, in private, the public life of his city. What has been characterised as a bourgeois impulse to capture in writing the details of life in one's city was, at this very time, becoming more widely satisfied in print elsewhere in Europe as well.[99] Dyer and his own friends and relations do not seem to have travelled any more often in the later periods, but Dyer's attention to remote affairs of public interest became noticeably greater when the coverage of such events in local papers began to trail off and were replaced by ethnographic travel serials and philosophical commentary. His references to printed material steadily increased, reflecting its influence on his awareness, but these ran more and more towards the practical and secular, as did the reading tastes of his urban neighbours. At the same time, he became positively obsessed, in relative terms, with his own nightly dreams and imaginings, which he came to regard as sources of religious instruction. By the 1760s Dyer displayed a surging interest in his own philosophical musings attributable to his having cast about in search of inspired preaching outside the confines of his own parish. This was partly behind his contempla-tion of the rural existence and his move to the countryside near Bristol.

The printed word did contribute to the expression of communal identities based on a sense of place which was such an important aspect of early modern mentality. The introduction of local printing in the city of Bristol in the late seventeenth century, and the flourishing of printing, publishing, and newspa-per enterprises there, can be taken as a sign of the city's participation in an English urban renaissance itself. Nevertheless, printed texts hardly promoted the formation of a regional identity embracing urban and rural communities much before the middle of the eighteenth century. Books, almanacs, broad-sides, newspapers and other printed materials reified an urban network from which villages were virtually excluded. The widening of urban reading tastes reflected a smug fascination with exotica which extended Bristol's cultural horizons beyond its immediate hinterland. Xenophobia and its expression intensified, rather than diminished, as strangers and local commentators moved in closer physical proximity to one another. This effect produced, in print culture, a stereotyping of rural life and rural folk that resembled in its harsh detachment that medium's dismissive and abusive treatment of immigrants and religious dissenters. The Bible and its interpretation in the hands of Anglican preachers and conformists stressed the communal aspects of religious practice and sustained the traditional regard for direct personal interaction within the confines of shared spaces, in the interest of shared resources, as the bases of community. To the extent that this notion – parochialism in the purest sense – obtained in both city and village, it operated as a wedge, rather than as a tie, between urban and rural social spheres.

## NOTES

1  Caxton, England's first printer, published *Recuyell of the Historyes of Troye* as early as 1475 but in Bruges. Two years later he printed *The Dictes or Sayengs of the Philosophres*, probably the first book printed in England, at his shop at the Sign of the Red Pale near Westminster Abbey. For more on the incunabula printers, see W. Chappell, *A Short History of the Printed Word* (New York, 1970), pp. 59–83, and L. Hellinga, 'Importation of books printed on the continent into England and Scotland before *c.* 1520', in S. L. Hindman (ed.), *Printing the Written Word: The Social History of Books circa 1450–1520* (Ithaca, N.Y., 1991), pp. 205–24.

2  Peter Heylyn, *Microcosmos, or, A Little Description of the Whole World* (1621); *Cosmographie* (1652); John Norden, *England: An Intended Guyde for English Travailers* (1625), and Robert Fage, *A Description of the Whole World* (1658), were reprinted after 1660. The continuation of this tradition is readily detectable in John Evelyn, *Silva, or, A Discourse of Forest-Trees* (1664); Evelyn, *Tyrannus* (1661); John Ray, *Observations Topographical, Moral and Physiological, Made on a Journey* (1673); Moses Pitt, *The English Atlas* (1680–83); John Aubrey, *Remaines of Gentilisme and Judaisme* (1687); Edmund Bohun, *A Geographical Dictionary* (1688); William Stukeley, *Itinerarium Curiosum* (1724). Aubrey's manuscript *Monumenta Britannica: or, A Miscellany of British Antiquaries* conforms to this pattern, but only the portions included in Edmund Gibson's 1695 edition of Camden's *Britannia* appeared in print. In his own day, Aubrey was better known in print as the antiquarian of Wiltshire. Although not antiquarian in its approach, we should add Defoe's *A Tour through the Whole Island of Great Britain* (1724–26) to this partial list on the grounds that Defoe still viewed cities and villages as distinct communities divided by clear topographical boundaries and highly localised culture. For further discussion of the links between topography, natural surroundings, and collective identity as perceived by early modern commentators see B. J. Shapiro, *Probability and Certainty in the Seventeenth Century: A Study of the Relationships between Natural Science, Religion, History, Law, and Literature* (Princeton, N.J., 1983), pp. 119–62; K. Thomas, *Man and the Natural World: Changing Attitudes in England 1500–1800* (Harmondsworth, 1984), pp. 242–87; S. Schama, *Landscape and Memory* (New York, 1995).

3  See, for example, R. Darnton, 'La lecture rousseauiste et un lecteur "ordinaire" au XVIIIe siècle', in R. Chartier (ed.), *Pratiques de la lecture* (Paris, 1978), pp. 125–55; P. Benedict, 'Bibliothèques protestantes et catholiques à Metz au XVIIe siècle', *Annales E.S.C.* no. 2 (1985), pp. 343–70.

4  D. Mornet, 'Les enseignements de bibliothèques privées 1750–1780', *Revue d'histoire littéraire de la France* 17 (1910), pp. 449–92.

5   M. Bal, 'Telling objects: a narrative perspective on collecting', in J. Elsner and R. Cardinal (eds), *The Cultures of Collecting* (Cambridge, Mass., 1994), pp. 97–115.

6   N. Z. Davis, 'Proverbial wisdom and popular errors', in her *Society and Culture in Early Modern France* (Stanford, Cal., 1975), pp. 227–67.

7   B. Capp, *English Almanacs 1500–1800: Astrology and the Popular Press* (London and Ithaca, N.Y., 1979); M. Spufford, *Small Books and Pleasant Histories: Popular Fiction and its Readership in Seventeenth-Century England* (Cambridge, 1981), chs 3, 4, and 5; I. Rivers (ed.), *Books and their Readers in Eighteenth-Century England* (Leicester, 1982); J. Feather, *The Provincial Book Trade in Eighteenth-Century England* (Cambridge, 1985); J. Black, *The English Press in the Eighteenth Century* (Philadelphia, 1987); J. Barry, 'The Cultural Life of Bristol 1640–1775' (D.Phil. thesis, Oxford University, 1985), pp. 347–59.

8   R. M. Wiles, *Freshest Advices: Early Provincial Newspapers in England* (Columbus, Oh., 1965); H. R. F. Bourne, *English Newspapers: Chapters in the History of Journalism, 1621–1820* (New York, 1966); L. Cranfield, *The Development of the Provincial Newspaper 1700–60* (1962); H. L. Snyder, 'The circulation of newspapers in the reign of Queen Anne', *Library*, 5th ser. 23 (1968); R. B. Walker, 'Advertising in London newspapers 1650–1750', *Business History* 15 (1973), pp. 112–30; M. Harris, 'London printers and newspaper production during the first half of the eighteenth century', *Printing Historical Society Journal* 12 (1977–78); C. Y. Ferdinand, 'Selling it to the provinces: news and commerce round eighteenth-century Salisbury', in J. Brewer and R. Porter (eds), *Consumption and the World of Goods* (London, 1992), pp. 393–411.

9   R. Thompson (ed.), *Samuel Pepys' Penny Merriments: being a Collection of Chapbooks* (Columbia, 1977); Spufford, *Small Books and Pleasant Histories*, pp. 129–55.

10  A. D. McKillop, 'English circulating libraries, 1725–1750', *Library*, 5th ser. 14 (1934); H. Hamlyn, 'Eighteenth-century circulating libraries in England', *Library*, 5th ser. 1 (1946).

11  I owe these observations to Keith Manley, who presented his critique of Kaufman's findings in a paper on 6 November 1985 at the University of London Institute of Historical Research.

12  B.R.O. Probate Inventories (James Waters, 1772).

13  B.R.O. Probate Inventories (Samuel and Mary Smith, 1776).

14  B.R.O. Wills (Edward Turner, 1777).

15  B.R.O. Probate Inventories (William Nicklaus, 1705; 1708 bundle).

16  G. Smith, 'Prescribing the rules of health: self-help and advice in late eighteenth-century England', in R. Porter (ed.), *Patients and Practitioners: Lay Perceptions of Medicine in Pre-industrial Society* (Cambridge, 1985), pp. 249–82; M. Fissell, 'Readers, texts and contexts: vernacular medical works in early modern England', in R. Porter (ed.), *The Popularization of Medicine 1650–1850* (London, 1992), pp. 72–96; R. Porter, 'The people's health in Georgian England', in T. Harris (ed.), *Popular Culture in England c. 1500–1850* (New York, 1995), pp. 124–42.

17  B.R.O. Probate Inventories. The 1660–99 sample of map owners in Bristol included a surgeon, a blockmaker, a carpenter, a goldsmith, a soapmaker, a merchant, a butcher, two coopers, nine mariners, and one person of unknown occupation. The 1700–39 sample of map owners in Bristol included a baker, a tiler, a grocer, a surgeon, an innkeeper, a stuffmaker, a saddler, a hatter, a schoolmaster, a maritime merchant, a soapmaker, a hosier, a mealman, a haulier, a blockmaker, a tinplate maker, a barber,

three victuallers, two coopers, six mariners, two widows, and one other person of unknown occupation. The six different occupations of the seven known map owners in Bristol whose inventories appear in the markedly reduced sample from the period 1740–80 were: saddletree maker, surgeon, sexton, mariner, victualler, and fan maker.

18 B.R.O. Wills (Richard Blinman, 1681).

19 Assessors in the villages were at least as conscientious as urban assessors in reporting the titles of the books they mentioned. Of the 390 surviving Bristol inventories showing books in the possession of urban dwellers in the eighty years between 1660 and 1740, 123 (32·4 per cent) provide the title of at least one book. Of the eighty-eight rural inventories showing book ownership between 1660 and 1740, thirty-one (35·2 per cent) provide titles. M. Marion in *Les Bibliothèques privées à Paris au milieu du XVIIIe siècle 1750–59* (Paris, 1978), pp. 95 and 135–70, could assign titles to only 4 per cent of all the books identified in his sample of inventories.

20 B.R.O. Probate Inventories (Ann Culme, 1688; Elizabeth Bartlet, 1694).

21 The sample is made up of eleven yeoman, two husbandmen, eight widows, three spinsters, a gentleman, a wheelwright, a baker, a cordwainer, a blacksmith, a haulier, and a person of unknown occupation.

22 Numerous biblical references to people originating from beyond the spatial confines of the local community associate unfamilar people with evil, hostility, danger, sadness, poverty, burden, strife, or punishment. People of remote or unknown origin are thereby placed under the suspicion of the righteous. Prominent examples include Proverbs 18:1, Colossians 1:21, Job 19:15, Genesis 23:4, Psalms 69:8, Jonah 10:5, and Jeremiah 14:8 and 5:19. A slight variation on this theme may be seen in the Epistle to the Hebrews (13:2), in which Paul advises treating strangers with hospitality out of fear that they may be angels roaming the earth in judgement of mankind. So, at the very best, strangers are presented as wielders of intimidating powers. In the Gospel according to Matthew 25:35, Jesus does explain that in taking the form of a stranger he put the generosity of ordinary people to the test. So Jesus, understandably, serves as the exception.

23 H. Fisch, *Jerusalem and Albion: The Hebraic Factor in Seventeenth-Century Literature* (New York, 1964). C. Hill, *The World Turned Upside Down: Radical Ideas during the English Revolution* (Harmondsworth, 1975), pp. 321–2; *Milton and the English Revolution* (Harmondsworth, 1979), pp. 205–12; *The English Bible and the Seventeenth-Century Revolution* (Harmondsworth, 1994), pp. 109–25 and 264–97.

24 E. M. W. Tillyard, *The Elizabethan World Picture* (New York, 1944), pp. 9 and 88.

25 J. Barry, 'The press and the politics of culture in Bristol 1660–1775', in J. Black and J. Gregory (eds), *Culture, Politics and Society in Britain 1660–1800* (Manchester, 1991), pp. 49–81, and 'The politics of religion in Restoration Bristol', in T. Harris, P. Seaward, and M. Goldie (eds), *The Politics of Religion in Restoration England* (Oxford, 1990), pp. 163–90.

26 Sermons devoted to the subject of conformity as the remedy for chaos and the breakdown of community were often delivered and published within a day or two of the anniversary of Charles I's execution, regarded by Restoration conformists as an atrocity of religious divisiveness. See, for example, Thomas Jekyll, *Peace and Unity Recommended and Persuaded: Preached at Bristol, 31 January 1675* (London, Bristol, 1675), B.C.L. pamphlet #6594.

27 See grand jury presentments for the year 1680–86 in B.R.O. #04452(1), Bristol Quarter Sessions: Presentments and Convictions (1676–1700). The relevant presentment prior

to the visitation was recorded in the Easter Session of 1685 and complained of the absenteeism of Bristol parishioners.

28 John Gaskarth, *Sermon Preached before John, Lord Bishsop of Bristol, at his Primary Visitation, 30 October 1685* (London, 1685). B.C.L. #8004 is a copy of this.

29 It should be noted that many printed sermons in this vein, prior to their publication, had been delivered at the local session of the assizes or in the Mayor's Chapel on civic occasions. See, for example, Richard Standfast, *Sermon Preached at Christ Church, Bristol, before Sir Francis North at the Assizes held there 7 August 1675* (London, 1676), B.C.L. Braikenridge Collection #9707; Richard Thompson, Dean of Bristol, *Sermon preached at Cathedral Church, Bristol, 21 June 1685, before Henry, Duke of Beaufort, Lord Lieutenant of the City and County* (London, 1685), B.C.L. Braikenridge Collection #9914; John Gibb, *Mutual Duties of Magistrates and People: Preached at St Mary Redcliffe, Bristol, 29 May 1721, before the magistrates of Bristol* (Bristol, 1721), B.C.L. pamphlet #6218; A. S. Catcott, *Superior and Inferior Elahim: Preached before the Corporation of Bristol at the Mayor's Chapel, 16 August 1725, the Day before the Assizes* (Bristol, 2nd ed. 1742), B.C.L. pamphlet #1716 or #10496.

30 Richard Kingston, *Vivat Rex: preached at St James's Church, 25 July 1683, before the Mayor, Alderman, Council and Citizens of Bristol upon the Discovery of the late Treasonable, Phanatic Plot* (1683), B.C.L. pamphlet #1602.

31 William Taswell, *Expedience and Necessity of National Establishments in Religion, with Observations on that of the Church of England in particular* (1763). This was preached at the visitation of Thomas, Lord Bishop of Bristol, at St Stephen's Church, 14 July 1763. B.C.L. Braikenridge Collection #9583.

32 Coeruleus Archididascolos, *Union and Loyalty Recommended: Preached at the Mayor's Chapel, Bristol, 2 September 1754, by William Batt* (Bristol, 1754), B.C.L. #1563, or #1562 for Batt's original version; John Berejew, *Religion Essential to Civil Government: Assize Sermon Preached at the Mayor's Chapel, 2 August 1774* (Bristol, 1774), B.C.L. Braikenridge Collection #9924.

33 Samuel Crossman, Dean of Bristol, *Sermon Preached 23 April 1680 at the Cathedral Church of Bristol before the Gentlemen of the Artillery Company Newly Raised* (1680), B.C.L. Braikenridge Collection #9629; Charles Brent, *Honour the Lord with thy Substance: Preached before the Society of Merchants, Bristol, St Stephen's Church, 10 November 1708* (Bristol, 1708), B.C.L. Braikenridge Collection #9951; A. S. Catcott, *Antiquity and Honourableness of the Practice of Merchandise: Preached before the Worshipful Society of Merchants, Bristol, in the Parish Church of St Stephen, 10 November 1744* (Bristol, 1744), B.C.L. Braikenridge Collection #9552; John Price, *Advantages of Unity Considered: Preached before the Ancient and Honourable Society of Free and Accepted Masons, in the Parish Church of St John Baptist, Bristol, 28 December 1747* (Bristol, 1748), B.C.L. pamphlet #5860.

34 See, for example: Charles Brent, *Persuasions to a Publick Spirit: Preached before the Court of Guardians of the Poor, Bristol, St Peter's Church, 13 April 1704* (Bristol, 1704), B.C.L. pamphlet #5616; Charles Brent, *Money Essay'd; or, the True Value of it Tryed: Preached before the Society of Merchants, Bristol, 10 November 1727* (Bristol, 1728), B.C.L. pamphlet #2158; Carew Reynell, *Sermon Preached before the Contributors to the Bristol Infirmary*, at St James, Bristol, 12 December 1738 (Bristol, 1738), B.C.L. Braikenridge Collection #9956–7; John Castleman, *Sermon Preached before the Subscribers to the Bristol Infirmary, in the Parish Church of St James, 13 March 1743* (Bristol, 1744), B.C.L. pamphlet #5090.

35  Joshua Tucker, *Hospitals and Infirmaries Considered as Schools of Christian Education for the Adult Poor: Preached at St James, Bristol, 18 March 1745* (Bristol, 1746), B.C.L. pamphlet #1659; Thomas Broughton, senior, *The Perfection of Christian Morality Asserted: Preached at the Parish Church of St James, Bristol, 19 March 1752, before the Subscribers of the Infirmary of the City* (Bristol, 1752), B.C.L. pamphlet #9535 and #7363; Hugh Waterman, *Sermon Preached before the Court of Guardians of the Poor, Bristol, at St Peter's Church, 13 April 1699* (Bristol, 1699), B.C.L. pamphlet #5093 or Braikenridge Collection #9567.

36  The sermons for Edward Colston, Bristol's most famous philanthropist of the late seventeenth and early eighteenth centuries, were the most numerous. See for example, James Harcourt, *Sermon ... at the Death of Edward Colston, All Saints Bristol* (Bristol, 1721), B.C.L. pamphlet #508; Charles Brent, *Good Man's Surpassing Worth and Glory: Preached at Christ Church, Bristol, after the Death of Edward Colston* (Bristol, 1721), B.C.L. pamphlet #1592.

37  Joseph Horler, *Works of Charity Recommended from the Common Relation we bear to Christ: Preached at All Saints Church, Bristol, before the Wiltshire Society at their Annual Feast held in Merchants' Hall, 21 August 1729* (Bristol, 1729), B.C.L. Braikenridge Collection #10799; Joseph Horler, *Blessedness of Giving Superior to that of Receiving: Preached at Temple Church, Bristol, before the Annual Feast of the Wiltshire Society, 30 August 1750* (Bristol, 1750), B.C.L. Braikenridge Collection #9632; Joseph Horler, *Of Clothing the Naked: Preached at St Thomas Church, Bristol, before the Wiltshire Society Annual Feast, 30 August 1739* (Bristol, 1739), B.C.L. pamphlet #1440; Arthur Bedford, *Unity, Love and Peace: Preached before the Gloucestershire Society, 2 September 1714, their Anniversary Feast Day, at St Nicholas Parish Church, Bristol* (Bristol, 1714), B.C.L. pamphlet #6248; John Price, *Antiquity of the Festival of St David Asserted: Preached before the Society of Ancient Britons, 1 March 1754, in the Parish Church of St James, Bristol* (Bristol, 1754), B.C.L. Braikenridge Collection #9628. St David, of course, is the patron saint of the Welsh, or ancient Britons. It is worth noting that many of the sermons presented to national, county, or incomer societies were delivered in the city's outer parishes such as St James and Temple.

38  John Moore, *Banner of Corah, Dathan, and Abairam Display'd, and their Sin Discover'd: Several Sermons Preached at Bristol* (William Bonny, Bristol, 1696), B.C.L. Braikenridge Collection #10231 and #10232. William Goldwin, *God's Judgements on a Sinful People: Preached at St Nicholas, Bristol, 8 December* (Bristol, c. 1730), B.C.L. pamphlet #1593.

39  Edward Hancock, *Pastor's Last Legacy and Counsel: A Farewell Sermon Preached at St Philip's, Bristol, 24 August 1662* (1662), B.C.L. Braikenridge Collection #10615; Strickland Gough, *Sermons on Effectual Calling and ... Practical Religion: Preached in Bristol* (Bristol, 1709), B.C.L. Braikenridge Collection #10553; Matthew Hole, *True Liberty Described and the False Pretences of Liberty Discovered, Shewing the Nature, Use and Abuse of Christian Liberty: Preached at St Peter's Church, Bristol, 29 July 1711* (Bristol, 1711), B.C.L. Braikenridge Collection #9568; William Goldwin, *Light of an Exemplary Life: Preached at St Nicholas, Bristol, 1734, before a Society of Young Gentlemen Educated at the Grammar School* (Bristol, 1734), B.C.L. Braikenridge Collection #9624; Kirby Reyner, *Select Sermons upon Practical Subjects: Preached in Bristol* (Bristol, 1745), B.C.L. Braikenridge Collection #10492.

40  James Buller, *Sermon Preached before the Prisoners under Sentence of Death, in Newgate, Bristol, 24 September 1754* (Bristol, 1754), B.C.L. pamphlet #1316. In commenting on R. Coppin's *Truth's Testimony* (1655), Keith Thomas notes that congregations received with

scepticism the idea that heaven was farther away than could be imagined. See K. Thomas, *Religion and the Decline of Magic* (New York, 1971), p. 161.

41 B. Levy, *Quakers and the American Family: British Settlement in the Delaware Valley* (Oxford, 1988), pp. 53–85.

42 Thomas Hardcastle, *Christian Geography and Arithmetic; or, a True Survey of the World: Being the Substance of some Sermons Preached at Bristol* (London, 1674), p. B3. It is not clear from Hardcastle's sermon whether or not he expected his audience to be familiar with the works of Bede.

43 M. Spufford, *Contrasting Communities: English Villagers in the Sixteenth and Seventeenth Centuries* (Cambridge, 1974), ch. 13.

44 B.R.O. Wills (Thomas Adeane, 1637; Lawrence Joyner, 1637).

45 Kirby Reyner, *Knowledge of Christ and Him crucified: Five Sermons Preached at Tucker Street, Bristol* (Bristol, 1748), B.C.L. Braikenridge Collection #10504; Jonah Thompson, *Joshua's Resolution to Serve the Lord: Preached at the Conclusion of the Yearly Meeting of the People Called Quakers, at Bristol, 15 May 1745* (Bristol, 1745), B.C.L. pamphlet #6013, printed in Bristol by Samuel Farley.

46 Thomas Amory, *Ministers not Lords over the Faith of Christians, but Helpers of their Joy: Preached at Lewin's Mead, Bristol, 22 May 1751* (Bristol, 1751), B.C.L. pamphlet #1244, and Samuel Chandler, *Sermon Preached at the Ordination of Thomas Wright, at Lewin's Mead, Bristol, 31 May 1759* (Bristol, 1759), B.C.L. Braikenridge Collection, #10499. And see John Camplin, *Evidence of Christianity not Weakened by the Frailty of its Ministers: Preached at Bristol Cathedral, 29 June 1777, Occasioned by the Execution of William Dodd* (Bristol, 1777), B.C.L. pamphlet #1245.

47 R. T. Vann, *The Social Development of English Quakerism 1655–1755* (Cambridge, Mass., 1969), and B. Reay, 'The social origins of early Quakerism', *Journal of Interdisciplinary History* 11 no. 1 (1980), pp. 55–72, demonstrate the overtly respectable middling origins of early Quakers. For Methodist guidelines of social conduct see H. Abelove, *The Evangelist of Desire* (Stanford, Cal., 1990), pp. 96–109. That religious dissenters played an active role in the Bristol Society for the Reformation of Manners in the early eighteenth century is shown in J. Barry and K. Morgan (eds), *Reformation and Revival in Eighteenth-Century Bristol* (Bristol, 1994), pp. 3–62.

48 Sam Farley, Kirby Reyner's publisher, is known to have had Quaker connections and sympathies, but Reyner's religious affiliation seems to have been subject to change. He preached before a variety of congregations including one at Tucker Street in Bristol. The extensive nature of John Wesley's preaching itinerary is well known, but for further discussion see Abelove, *The Evangelist of Desire*.

49 John Wesley, *Free Grace: A Sermon Preached at Bristol* (Bristol, 1740–41), p. 28. I owe Dr Thomas Hamm and the Friends Collection of Earlham College my thanks for access to these and other related materials.

50 B.C.L. MS #20095, Diary of William Dyer I (June 1752). We know that Dyer collected books because he describes his attendance at book auctions (14 February 1752). Dyer refers to the efficacy of dreams and disembodied or inner voices in several diary entries, including those for 11 and 12 May, 5 December 1751, and 28 May 1762. In his entry of 25 November 1753 Dyer also marvels at the powers of a Mr Grimshaw, a celebrated preacher in Yorkshire whose 'church had been four times filled at administering the sacrament when thirty-five bottles of wine were expended only at one sacrament'.

Whitefield may have stressed the social, as opposed to the spiritual, aspects of religion more than Dyer thought necessary. See George Whitefield, *Nature and Necessity of Society: Preached at St Nicholas, Bristol* (Bristol, 1737), B.C.L. Braikenridge Collection #9625.

51  B.C.L. MS #20095, Diary of William Dyer I (17 March 1753).

52  B.R.O. P/StP&J/V/2, St Philip and Jacob Minute Book, (1723–1832).

53  Spufford, *Small Books and Pleasant Histories*, pp. 134–7. Spufford calculated, based on the advertisement lists of seven seventeenth-century chapbook publishers, that 71·6 per cent of those books were devoted to 'non-godly' subjects. Indeed, the subset of 'small merry books' accounted for over 42 per cent of the advertised stock, compared with only 28.4 per cent for 'godly' chapbooks. Samuel Pepys had nearly half (49 per cent) the chapbook trade list in his collection. He had 62 per cent of all 'merry' books on the list and 42 per cent of all 'histories', compared with only 34 per cent of the available 'godly' chapbooks.

54  T. Watt, *Cheap Print and Popular Piety 1550–1640* (Cambridge, 1991), pp. 55–73 and 296–320.

55  B.C.L. MS #6495(SR4B), Alexander Catcott's diaries of tours made in England and Wales (1748–74). Catcott had read antiquities and regional descriptions of Leicestershire, Middlesex, Cornwall, Dorset, Warwickshire, Yorkshire, Staffordshire, Nottinghamshire, Berkshire, Rutland, Scotland, Wales, Sicily, Jamaica, Chile, Peru, and the South Seas.

56  *Oracle; or, Bristol Weekly Miscellany* (31 December 1742), p.4.

57  P. Benedict, 'Bibliothèques protestantes et catholiques à Metz au XVIIe siècle', *Annales E.S.C.* no. 2 (1985), pp. 343–70; M.-H. Froeschle-Chopard, La Religion populaire en Provence orientale au XVIIIe siècle (Paris, 1980), pp. 268–70; J. Queniart, *Culture et société urbaines dans la France de l'ouest au XVIIIe siècle* (Paris, 1978); H.-J. Martin, *Livre, pouvoirs et société à Paris au XVIIe siècle* (Geneva, 1969); Marion, *Les Bibliothèques privées à Paris*, pp. 135–70.

58  Thomas, *Religion and the Decline of Magic*, pp. 283–385; Capp, *English Almanacs*, especially pp. 59–66; P. Curry, *Prophecy and Power: Astrology in Early Modern England* (Cambridge, 1989).

59  B.R.O. Creswicke MSS #9728(1).

60  Capp, *English Almanacs*, p. 23. Here Capp refers to the period 1640–1700.

61  Of course, St David's in Wales was regarded as a city, despite its smallness and remoteness, by virtue of its cathedral.

62  Chipping Sodbury, Gloucestershire.

63  The best original accounts of this and other South Seas adventures are provided in papers and early publications preserved in Bristol archives. See Woodes Rogers, *Cruising Voyage round the World … 1708–1711 … an Account of Alexander Selkirk's Living Alone for Four Years Four Months on an Island* (1712), B.C.L. #4400, Braikenridge Collection #10651–2; and Edward Cooke, *Voyage to the South Sea and round the World, Performed in the Years 1708–11 by the Ships 'Duke' and 'Duchess' of Bristol … wherein an Account is given of Alexander Selkirk*, 2 vols (1712), B.C.L. Braikenridge Collection #10649–50.

64  S. Greenblatt, *Marvelous Possessions: The Wonder of the New World* (Chicago, 1991), pp.

109–18. For an example of the capture and display of foreign natives see Hakluyt's account of Martin Frobisher's voyage to *Meta Incognita* from early August to October 1576.

65 B.R.O. Probate Inventories (Samuel and Mary Smith, 1776) show that eight volumes of this periodical were found in their parlour.

66 The latter was hailed by Hickey as a recent publication. The demonisation of Jews in early modern England is addressed in F. Felsenstein, *Anti-Semitic Stereotypes: A Paradigm of Otherness in English Popular Culture* (Baltimore, Md, 1995), especially pp. 27–39 and 266–70. The notion that Jews belonged in Jerusalem and not England is addressed in N. I. Matar, 'The idea of the restoration of the Jews in English Protestant thought 1661–1701', *Harvard Theological Review* 78 (1985), pp. 115–48.

67 See, for example, the 1754 pamphlet *Leek Justified and Potatoes Downfall* printed in Bristol at the time of a bitterly contested election in which naturalisation was a central issue. B.C.L. broadside, Braikenridge Collection #10964.

68 B.C.L. #SR122 is a copy of the second edition of this 1664 pamphlet published in London.

69 *Ibid.*, p. 5.

70 Anon., *Strange and Terrible Newes from Cambridge; the True Relation of the Quakers Bewitching Mary Phillips*, etc. (London, 1659).

71 B.C.L. Bristol Collection #10162, Minutes of the Society for the Reformation of Manners (1700–05); Williams Library, London MS34.4, John Evans List of Dissenting Congregations and Ministers (1715–29), fos. 99, 102, and 147. Both these appear in Barry and Morgan, *Reformation and Revival in Eighteenth-Century Bristol*. For further discussion of the improving social status of eighteenth-century nonconformists see W. C. Braithwaite, *The Second Period of Quakerism* (Cambridge, 1961); M. Watts, *The Dissenters* (Oxford, 1978), pp. 382–482; G. S. De Krey, *A Fractured Society: The Politics of London in the First Age of Party 1688–1715* (Oxford, 1985), pp. 74–120; M. Fissell, 'Charity Universal? Institutions and Moral Reform in Eighteenth-Century Bristol', in L. Davison, T. Hitchcock, T. Keirn, and R. B. Shoemaker (eds), *Stilling the Grumbling Hive: The Response to Social and Economic Problems in England 1689–1750* (New York, 1992), pp. 121–44, which does distinguish between the 'primitive Christianity' of earlier philanthropic movements and the social prominence of dissenting leadership essential to eighteenth-century charity movements. For the argument that the rising status of these groups had earlier origins, see B. Stevenson, 'The social and economic status of post-Restoration dissenters 1660–1725' and 'The social integration of post-Restoration dissenters', in M. Spufford (ed.), *The World of Rural Dissenters 1520–1725* (Cambridge, 1995), pp. 332–87.

72 *Felix Farley's Bristol Journal*, 27 December 1755, reported that a horribly destructive earthquake, perhaps blessed with divine intelligence, destroyed all of Lisbon's Roman Catholic churches and monuments and all the Jesuit schools and Dominican hospitals, while 'the corn houses' (where Bristol merchants did business in Lisbon) 'were happily saved'. For agitation against the naturalisation of Jews, see the broadsides *Liberty! No Placemen! No Naturalization!* (Bristol, 1754), B.C.L. Braikenridge Collection broadside #10952; *To the Worthy Freemen of Bristol: No Jews!* (Bristol, 1754), B.C.L. Braikenridge Collection broadside #10965; *News! News! Very Sad News! for Jews and a Certain Clergyman* (Bristol, 1754), B.C.L. Braikenridge Collection #10970. Josiah Tucker was the Bristol clergyman in question, who advocated, in Parliament, a Jewish naturalisation bill.

73 John Sheffer, *The History of Lapland* (Oxford, 1674). A copy of this belonging to a member of Bristol's Prideaux family is B.C.L. #20535 (286), Rudhall Notebooks, Diaries and Books.

74 Spufford, *Small Books and Pleasant Histories*, pp. 51–9 and 182–3. For an example of typical anti-rural chapbooks see the *The Sackfull of News* (1685) or *The Madmen of Gotham* (c. 1680), both included in Samuel Pepys's collection. Parts of these are reprinted in Thompson, *Samuel Pepys' Penny Merriments*, pp. 162–4 and 244–6.

75 Wiles, *Freshest Advices*, pp. 4–5. Wiles bases this conclusion on the titles of some London papers: John Houghton's *Collection for Letters for the Improvement of Husbandry and Trade* (1681–84) and his *Collection for Improvement of Husbandry and Trade* (1692–1704); *City and Country* Mercury (1667); *Country Gentleman's Courant* (1685); J. Morphew's *Country Gentleman's Courant: or, Universal Intelligence* (1706–07); *Country Gentleman* (1726); Dormer's *Country Tatler* (1736); *Country Magazine: or, Weekly Pacquet* (1739); and T. Cooper's *Country Oracle: A Weekly Newspaper containing answers to all Questions in All Sciences* (1741).

76 The oldest surviving issue of an English provincial newspaper is no. 91 of *The Bristol Post Boy* of 12 August 1704, printed by William Bonny, B.C.L. #B21561 BL7 Portfolio 7, B19887. The other Bristol newspapers circulating before 1750 included: *Sam Farley's Bristol Post Man* (1713–c. 1723); *Bristol Weekly Mercury* (1715–28); *Farley's Bristol Newspaper* (1725–c. 1742); *Oracle: or, Bristol Weekly Miscellany* (1742–43); *Bristol, Bath and Somerset Journal* (1742–44); *Bristol Oracle, and Country Intelligencer* (1743–46); *Bristol Oracle, and Country Advertiser* (1743–46); *Felix Farley's Bristol Journal* (1743–61); *Farley's Bristol Advertiser* (1743–49); *Bristol Oracle* (1745–50); *Bristol Mercury* (1746–50); and the *Bristol Weekly Intelligencer* (1749–60).

77 D. Read, *Press and People 1790–1850: Opinion in Three English Cities* (London, 1961).

78 *Farley's Bristol Newspaper* no. 22 (2 October 1725).

79 This trend continued for the life of *The Bristol Post Boy*. The issue for the week of 13–20 March 1709 (no. 281), for example, consisted of five London items, three from Edinburgh, two from Dundee, and one each from Portsmouth, Ostend, and Vienna. Nearly all the focal locations were urban ports.

80 In a sample period of one month from 25 September to 23 October 1725 the bankruptcies reported in *Farley's Bristol Newspaper* consisted of the following: a linen draper and a chapman from Boston (Lincolnshire), a baker from Bury St Edmunds, a dyer from Liverpool, a haberdasher from Leicester, a peruke-maker from St Mary Alechurch, a dyer from Wakefield, a vintner from Halifax, a peruke-maker from Cirencester, an innholder from Andover, a mercer from Fareham, and a chapman 'late of Bristol'.

81 *Farley's Bristol Newspaper* (18 December 1725) tells of the decapitation of a Somerset farming woman by a servant observed to be under the influence of the devil. The issue of 29 January 1726 tells of the Horfield farmer's fateful pact with the devil.

82 See Farley's issue of 11 December 1725.

83 P. King, 'Newspaper reporting, prosecution practice, and perceptions of urban crime: the Colchester crime wave of 1765', *Continuity and Change* 2 no. 3 (1987), pp. 423–54.

84 B.R.O. #04452(1) and #04452(2), Bristol Quarter Sessions: Presentments and Convictions (1676–1700 and 1728–95).

85 D. Defoe, *A Tour through the Whole Island of Great Britain*, ed. P. Rogers (Harmondsworth, 1971), p. 255.

86  See, for example, the report concerning smuggling in Portsmouth submitted by a London correspondent to the 30 October 1725 issue of *Farley's Bristol Newspaper*.

87  Wiles, *Freshest Advices*, p. 122.

88  *Bristol Post Boy* (1704–10), nos. 91, 281, 287, and 340.

89  *Farley's Bristol Newspaper* (27 January 1733).

90  *Ibid.* (4 December 1725).

91  *Ibid.* (28 November 1730).

92  Andrew Hooke in *Bristol Oracle; or, Bristol Weekly Miscellany* 21 (31 August 1742), p. 3.

93  *The Bee and Sketchley's Weekly Advertiser* (2 December 1777).

94  *The Bee and Sketchley's Weekly Advertiser* (3 and 24 November 1777).

95  B.C.L. MS #6495 (SR4B), Alexander Catcott's Diaries of Tours made in England and Wales (1748–74). See his entry of 6 May 1754.

96  B.C.L. MS #20095, Diary of William Dyer (1745–1801), 22 August 1756 or 6 January 1758, for example.

97  B.C.L. MS #20095, Diary of William Dyer (1745–1801), 3 June 1772.

98  P. Seaver, *Wallington's World: A Puritan Artisan in Seventeenth-Century London* (Stanford, Cal., 1985); A. Macfarlane, *The Family Life of Ralph Josselin* (Cambridge, 1970); R. Latham (ed.), *Diary of Samuel Pepys* (Cambridge, 1978); D. Vaisey (ed.), *The Diary of Thomas Turner 1754–65* (Oxford, 1984); J. Beresford (ed.), *James Woodforde: The Diary of a Country Parson 1758–1802*, 5 vols (London, 1924–31).

99  R. Darnton, 'A bourgeois puts his world in order: the city as a text', in *The Great Cat Massacre and other Episodes in French Cultural History* (New York, 1984), pp. 107–43.

# Part III

---

# Urban–rural convergence

# Chapter 9

## Communication across
## the topographical divide

Like many of the people for whom he wrote, Daniel Defoe was an admirer of those enterprises that transported across the land copious amounts of people, goods and correspondence more frequently and more swiftly than before. When Ralph Allen, the famous literary patron, adopted the project of linking post roads after 1720, avid travellers and correspondents became increasingly excited about the prospect of improved services and expanded connections. Defoe sang the praises of the new post roads connecting Plymouth, Exeter, Bristol, Gloucester, Worcester, Shrewsbury, Liverpool, Manchester, and running 'through all the western part of England ... to maintain the correspondence of merchants and men of business, of which all this side of the island is so full'.[1] What we might call the logistics of belief, the technology surrounding the distribution and acquisition of information and ideas, should not be overlooked nor its influence on the formation of expanded social spheres underestimated. The progressive technologies of literacy, print, and infrastructural development aided mobility and communication, but these alone were not enough to bridge the cultural and social divisions that existed between city and countryside through the middle of the eighteenth century. Urban and rural convergence on a significant scale required the wider acceptance of nonconformist extraparochialism and the acceptance of a transformation in topographical setting itself. The first of these, in connection with the logistics of belief, is the subject of this chapter.

It is reasonable to believe that shared access to printed texts, the exchange of private correspondence, and an ability to read and write allowed literate people to form social spheres beyond their immediate geographical confines. Social spheres based on shared ideas did have the greatest potential to transcend geographical limitations and strong local affinities, provided that members of those spheres were literate, mobile, or both. We should call into question, however, the notion that a separation of literate and illiterate spheres was more pronounced than the separation of urban and rural spheres for most of the period associated with the urban renaissance. In village and city alike literate people were drawn together in marriage, for example, but rarely across the topographical divide. Those social spheres that were formed and maintained through written correspondence operated in the urban network. The uneven distribution of literate skills and written materials did play a role in shaping patterns of social interaction prior to the second half of the eighteenth century. The affinity of literate people for one another and the importance of literacy to their identity as a group can be shown both quantitatively and qualitatively. But shared literacy emerged relatively late as a commonly experienced cultural tie among those people who, because of geographical or material divisions, might otherwise have remained separate. Outside the circles of a tiny elite, the localising tendencies of personal culture and material culture had a strong, persistent, and ubiquitous influence on the formation of early modern social spheres.

The formation of social spheres based on shared beliefs alone remained problematic for most of the early modern period despite improvements in communication. Literacy initiated and exacerbated bitter religious divisions as much as it bridged them. Well into the eighteenth century, printed words and images inscribed and sustained a dominant notion of strangeness that defined communities topographically according to highly localised boundaries and exclusive networks. Like the separatism of the urban network, the introspection of manorial bodies frustrated the tendencies of any literate or ideologically motivated villagers to make contacts beyond their immediate horizons. Shared ideas did little to overcome localism despite the ostensible functions of adjudicators and authorities in both settings: the regulation of communal values; the promulgation of codes; the interpretation of ideas; and the articulation of binding abstract principles. Shared spaces and resources were the enduring and widespread cultural ties on which most social spheres were based because recreational life, residential life, and confessional life were all highly localised by the influence of the parish in the Anglican tradition. Literate conformists, as much as illiterate ones, were subject to the dominance of localism perpetuated by the parish system of the Anglican church.

Dissenters rather than the conformist majority or indifferent bystanders provided the most extensive and influential cultural ties between the city of Bristol and the nearby villages during the urban renaissance. In 1673 alone the Quakers printed and distributed twenty-two copies of 'Friends Books' in Bristol, fifty-four in London, and 524 to county dwellers outside those cities.[2] Hardcastle, who preached before the Baptists at Bristol's Broadmead, recognised the importance of the printed word in the unity of a scattered fellowship of believers. He dedicated the printing of his *Christian Geography and Arithmetic* of 1674 to his congregation. Published copies of these sermons found their way into the homes of villagers well outside the confines of the city.[3] The few sermons printed in Bristol in which villagers were eulogised were the work of dissenting preachers and their congregations. These publications stressed the humility of the deceased in the face of eternity rather than the prestige of the deceased within a spatially confined social sphere.[4] The contribution of dissent to the formation of extraparochial and extramural communal ties around Bristol resulted in a sweeping cultural movement born out of religious divisiveness itself. Dissenters had been forced by the punitive measures of the authorities to reach beyond the enforcement of spatial boundaries which divided parishes from one another and cities from their surrounding villages. By the middle of the eighteenth century, Methodists preached in the open air in the countryside surrounding the city while hostility toward Protestant dissent began to dwindle into a few isolated episodes.

The overtly and gregariously extraparochial activites of religious nonconformists were essential, therefore, to the greater measure of urban–rural convergence experienced near the end of the early modern period. Social spheres that transcended localism as well as the topographical divide were few, but the importance of shared ideas as the cultural tie for rural dissenters had been clear since the days of sixteenth-century Lollards.[5] By the 1720s Defoe, an outspoken critic of localism and 'corporation-tyranny', observed that private academies established for the children of religious dissenters in provincial towns allowed more interaction and communication to take place across all kinds of existing barriers, expanses, and divides.[6] Defoe himself had been educated in the school of an ejected Independent minister and at a prominent dissenters' academy in the village of Newington Green, just outside London. In the 1750s Willam Dyer said of his friend Hester Phelps, 'She never learned to read but was truly taught of GOD and experienced a *birth* of the divine life brought forth in her soul.'[7] Dyer and Phelps were members of the growing number of Bristol's informally ecumenical citizens whose cultural ties and social spheres transcended the old divide between conformists and dissenters. They also transcended civic, village, and parochial localism. By the middle of the eighteenth century the social integration of dissenters who moved out of oppression into prominence, and the eventual acquiescence toward nonconformist practices outside the confines of established parishes as well as within them, contributed to the general expansion of social spheres across the topographical divide, even among the illiterate.

The vast majority of literate book owners did identify immediate social spheres that were entirely literate. Richard Blinman of Bristol drew up his will in 1681.[8] Books featured prominently in his final wishes and he bequeathed all forty-nine of his volumes by title. Blinman and all three of the witnesses to his will (Sam Lloyd, John Drew, and Christopher Roberts) were able to sign their names. They formed an entirely literate circle. The witnesses of a will were often the testator's three or four most trusted friends and relations. The ability to sign one's name, or provide any other evidence of literacy, was by no means required of witnesses many of whom simply made their marks near their names as inscribed by the clerk. In the city of Bristol, among the 140 wills whose testators are known to have owned books at some time between 1660 and 1740, 101 (72 per cent) of those wills are remarkable by virtue of the fact that every one of the witnesses involved, regardless of gender or occupation, could sign his or her name.[9] Moreover, in eighty-three (82 per cent) of those 101 cases, the testators themselves were able to sign. In the rural setting, where the level of literacy was relatively low and there were far fewer cases of book ownership, the affinity of literate book owners for one another was as strong as it was in the city. Fourteen wills drawn up by book owners living in villages near Bristol between 1660 and 1740 bear the signatures of all the witnesses involved. In every case but one the testator was also literate, despite the fact that roughly half the book owners in Bristol's rural environs were unable to sign their name. The remarkably high degree of shared literacy within these social circles was very meaningful.

Literate women were a minority in this period and the connections among them, in either setting, were conspicuous.[10] We have already seen that women tended to share their books with other women. Mary Meredith of Bristol owned books and, because she was a single woman rather than the widow of a literate husband, we can be reasonably sure that they were for her own use. The three witnesses of her will in 1681 were the clerk who drew it up and two women, one of whom could sign. When Frances Hodge, a literate book owner in St Mary Redcliffe, drew up her will in 1692 she called upon two witnesses both of whom were literate women. Anne Garraway, a Bristol single woman with books in her possession, drew up her will in her own hand in 1712, signed it and asked her friends, two literate women, to witness her testament. A year later, in the village of Winterbourne, where literate women were even more unusual, two of their signatures were placed on the will of Mary Pilourn. As a literate, rural, book-owning woman, Mary Pilourn, who was also a merchant, presented a rare combination of qualities indeed. Her close association with two of the few other literate women in her village can hardly be seen as an accident.[11] Literate women appear to have had closer ties with other women who were literate than with men who were not.

Literate women were very unlikely to marry illiterate men. In the three decades after 1750 or so, only about 3 per cent of marriages in Bristol brought together a literate bride and an illiterate groom.[12] In only about 4 per cent of the marriages registered in villages near Bristol did a literate woman take an illiterate man as her husband.[13] In all such cases the bride and groom were from the same village.[14] In December 1762 a literate woman married a labourer in Brislington, Somerset. Despite his humble social status, this labourer shared with his educated wife the skill of literacy. Not one of the thirteen illiterate labourers identified in Brislington registers from 1754 to 1784 married a literate woman. In the rare instances in which literate women married illiterate men of rural origin, in addition to whatever personal charms he may have possessed, the husband in these situations usually enjoyed high status associated with yeomanry and land ownership. It is a possibility that some of the few literate women who married illiterate men placed simple marks in the marriage registers rather than embarrass their husbands in a public record. Quite understandably, Mr Schimmelpenning's bride had some difficulty spelling her new name in the St Stephen parish register in 1756. There are two puzzling cases from Bristol, both dating from 1760, in which the bride, seeing that her husband had signed upon the lower of two lines provided, signed in a narrow blank space beneath his name rather than place her signature above his on the line remaining.[15]

Hardwicke's Marriage Act of 1753 required all spouses to place their own signatures or marks, depending on their ability, in an official church register. In Bristol during the three decades following the passage of the Hardwicke Act two-thirds of the literate spouses married other literate people. In the interior urban parish of St Werburgh, out of the 100 spouses who could sign, eighty-six married another literate person. We must bear in mind that there were fewer literate women than literate men, even in cities. Barring the existence of some virtually undetected population of literate single women, it was impossible for many literate men to marry literate women and, therefore, the number of marriages in which literate people had paired themselves was nearly as high as it could be.[16] Despite the limitations imposed by the shortage of literate women, about two-thirds of the literate spouses registered in villages outside Bristol during the thirty-year period following the passage of Hardwicke's Act married a man or woman who was also literate.[17] In this period, of those spouses who came from outside the village where they were married, about 78 per cent were literate, and of those about 81 per cent were drawn into the village by a literate mate.[18]

Marriage registers for the three decades after the mid-eighteenth century, when intimate bonds between urban and rural dwellers began to form more extensively, help us assess the role of literacy in the patterns of interaction across the topographical boundary. In 1688 Sarah Edwards, a Shirehampton widow who owned and read books, drew up her will and signed it, but not before expressing her 'love and respect' for her 'very good friends Nicholas Barnard of Bristol, brazier [and] Hugh Williams of Bristol, cooper'.[19] Although a few of the earlier social spheres in which ordinary Bristolians and local villagers associated had been those of readers and writers like Sarah Edwards and her 'very good friends' in the city, urban and rural convergence remained unusual until the middle of the eighteenth century. In the last three decades of our period, nineteen (17 per cent) of the 109 spouses wed in the village of Brislington were from the city of Bristol, with which that village shared a boundary. All but two of these geographically mobile spouses were literate and all but three of the literate Bristolians married villagers who were also literate. In the Gloucestershire village of Olveston during this period, all three spouses of Bristol origin were literate and all three of them married literate villagers. In October 1762 Mr William Jones of Bristol married Elizabeth Bayley, an Olveston villager. In this tidy example, both spouses were literate and the groom was a bookseller. At a June wedding in 1780 one self-consciously literate couple in Brislington registered neither the groom's occupation nor his place of settlement but recorded his affiliation with 'St John's College in the University of Cambridge' expressing volumes about the couple's view of themselves.[20]

An awareness of the conventions and cultural ties employed by others in the parish influenced the priority a couple assigned either to shared spaces or to shared literacy in the formal affirmation of their union. The proclamation of banns, the public declaration of the intent to marry, entitled a couple to be wed in the church where the banns were announced, barring any objection from the congregation. Banns were part of personal, as opposed to print, culture; they were spoken in person by the couple before their neighbours assembled in church on three consecutive Sundays. From the sixteenth century on, the early modern Church of England had required that a wedding should be performed under the roof of a parish church familiar to at least one of the betrothed as a requirement of the marriage's solemnisation.[21] It was possible, however, to affirm marriage through the more private means of obtaining a written licence. This option was available even to couples who were unable to sign their name or read a document.[22] In the thirty-year period after 1754, about 62 per cent of those Bristol couples in which both spouses were literate obtained marriage licences. In the interior parish of St Werburgh, where the highest percentage of literate spouses was to be found,[23] 81 per cent of literate couples acknowledged their union with a licence. Literate couples, especially those who lived and moved among more literate people, placed less emphasis on a communal and spatial context as a means of formalising personal ties.

By contrast, about 86 per cent of Bristol marriages in which neither spouse could sign were affirmed through the proclamation of banns. This correlation was especially strong in the peripheral urban parish of St Philip and Jacob. There 94 per cent of the illiterate couples chose to affirm their marriages, and their social sphere, through a cultural practice featuring the spoken word within the confines of communal space. In St Philip and Jacob, where the levels of literacy exhibited by spouses were the lowest,[24] even literate couples were likely to observe the proclamation of banns in church, and seventy-four

(54 per cent) of the parish's 138 literate couples did just that. Despite increasing levels of literacy and the local availability of printed documents, the general popularity of banns persisted well into the late eighteenth century, in urban parishes as well as in the villages.[25] All this points to the strong normative influence of direct personal interaction and shared spaces in the maintenance of conformist social spheres throughout the early modern period.

By the second half of the eighteenth century, some literate villagers began to transcend the localism imposed by traditional communal institutions. There were connections among the shifting functions of village manor courts, the level of manor court activity prompted by the villagers, and the extent to which manor court jurors constituted a literate group. The literacy rate of Abson and Wick manor court jurors at the beginning of our period was high, even compared with urban standards; in the years immediately preceding the acquisition of the manor by the Haynes family in 1665, roughly 85 per cent of the jurors had been able to sign the records.[26] In October 1660 the Abson and Wick manor court asserted that its presentments were those of a 'jury of the King of England, Scotland, France and Ireland'. More than a purely rhetorical concession to the spirit of the Restoration, this was a declaration of perceived associations formed by shared ideas transcending the confines of the village. In that year, when the manor court represented itself as an instrument of the King's law, the jurors also cited statutes. This practice was not repeated in later years.

Between 1675 and the 1750s the number of presentments entertained in Abson and Wick stayed consistently between twenty and thirty per year, but there was a steady decline in the number of literate jurors participating in the manor court there. The court remained an active focus of village attention despite the fact that in 1697 every single one of the jurors could sign, whereas in 1750 only half the jurors could sign.[27] The manor court evolved as an institution in which the culture of personal contact, rather than that of abstract codes, provided the principal ties among the participants. This is not to say that the manor court was unsuited to its role of providing the fair adjudication of disputes. On the contrary, the institution was still working nearly a century after the Restoration, but mainly with the participation and approval of those illiterate villagers whose cultural ties had not transcended their local sphere.

After the mid-eighteenth century, it finally became the sense of the increasingly litigious literate villagers that the manor court served a social, not a judicial, function. In 1756 litigators in the village of Abson and Wick insisted that serious offenders presented in the manor court there should be prosecuted elsewhere, to ensure legal satisfaction, and that the parish tithing revenues would cover the expense. By the 1770s the number of presentments in the Abson and Wick manor court had plummeted to an average of six per year and these dealt almost exclusively with the *pro forma* assignment of parish offices. By this last decade of the period, 78 per cent of the jurors could sign presentments and other manor records. This revival of literacy in the manor court at the end of the early modern period accompanied the eventual transformation of the institution from an introspective and closed social sphere into an advocate of village interests across the region, especially in opposition to turnpikes.[28]

The network of improved roads connecting cities and towns provided for the swifter transport not only of more people but of their correspondence as well. For most of the early modern period, however, it is doubtful that a majority of the general population in provincial England actually exchanged letters. Some historians include the development of a postal system in the same list of later eighteenth-century English accomplishments in which they mention the invention of toast.[29] Of course illiterate people could, and did, dictate letters. Most women were, at best, marginally literate for generations after the Restoration, as 'scrawled' letters – even those by female members of the gentry – beautifully illustrate.[30] Moreover, prior to the late eighteenth century, the post was so unreliable that even those people who could write were reluctant to entrust their correspondence to it.[31] In addition to highway robbery, poor transport made the post a risky proposition. There were no regular scheduled coaches between Bristol and Liverpool until the 1750s, for example. In 1746 the postal service came to a complete halt for months at a time because of Jacobite rebels.[32] The practical complications of maintaining social spheres that transcended localism were considerable.

As a result of such complications, virtually all of the Bristolians and villagers who relied heavily upon the exchange of the written word for the maintenance of their social spheres (a relatively small group) used familiar associates and friends as carriers, a fact that serves to emphasise the personal and intimate nature of written interaction and print culture in this period. William Dyer made use of his Quaker connections.

> Sent John the travelling Quaker with a letter to Messers Arthur and Benjamin Heywood ... agreeing to pay the said John three guineas provided he delivered said letter by noon on Monday the 13th instant. He was accustomed to walking or rather a walk and kind of trot and thereby conveying a letter with greater expedition than by Post ... If he kept sober, he generally (though on foot) performed a journey in less time than a single horse could do.[33]

As late as 1755 George Scullard sent letters to his correspondents in Bristol in the hands of a mutual friend and apologised on those rare occasions when the person who delivered his letters was unknown to the recipient. In one such case, Scullart pointed to the inadequacies of the postal system and explained, 'I did not know when I should have a convenient method of conveyance.' Scullard, it should be mentioned, sent his letters from London, and not from some rural corner of provincial England.[34] To the extent that the postal system succeeded at all it reflected the detachment of the urban network, and its cultural resources, from the rural world until well into the eighteenth century.

If the communications of Anglican conformists effected a local merger of urban and rural social spheres prior to the mid-eighteenth century, the development was less than widespread. This was even true of widely connected intellectuals. The correspondence of the Reverend A. Stopford Catcott, his son, Alexander Catcott, their associates and friends expressed the convergence of a group of intellectuals whose members were, in geographical terms, widely dispersed. The correspondents were closely and consciously bound together by shared ideas expressed in their own writings as well as those of others, in and out of print. There was an abundance of letters produced by that group, between the 1730s and 1770s, and these crossed two generations and thousands of miles. Communications sent to Alexander Catcott between 1736 and the 1770s had far-flung origins, including Edinburgh, Amsterdam, and Hungary. A. Stopford Catcott, a fellow of St John's, Oxford, was headmaster of the Bristol Grammar School from 1722 to 1743, after which he became rector of St Stephen's, Bristol. In 1729 he was appointed preacher of St Mark's, the mayor's chapel. Thus, unlike some other groups whose ideas and access to the written word were the primary bases of their social spheres, the Catcotts and their friends were situated comfortably in the Anglican establishment, despite the provocative nature of their ideas. The members of this group deserve attention on the strength of their creative thought alone and the possibility that they represented a kind of quasi-scientific resistance to Newtonian cosmology, long after its formulation, in the early stages of its popularisation. Of overarching relevance was their use of the written and printed word for the maintenance of close ties and the delayed inclusion of rural members in a conformist social sphere based on cultural ties transcending shared spaces and shared material resources.

The circle of correspondents to which the Catcotts belonged was held together by a shared interest in the promotion of what might be called diluvian theories of nature and the application of John Hutchinson's theological and etymological arguments to an interpretation of their observed surroundings. John Hutchinson was a correspondent of Charles Wesley by the 1750s.[35] Hutchinson was among the elder Catcott's regular correspondents. The title of Hutchinson's major work, *Moses' Principia* (1724–27), juxtaposes references to Newton's work and the word of God in tablature. In Hutchinson's cosmology, the word of God generated fire, light, and air, which operated directly on the material universe. Like many others after Newton, the Catcotts and their group were deeply interested in the reconciliation of natural science and scripture. They placed priority and causal significance squarely on the latter, with special emphasis on the power of the spirit to control matter and therefore govern all natural phenomena, including planetary motion and optics. For this group the deluge was a divine act from which all subsequent geological and biological forms were derived.[36]

They were hardly alone in this view, but the arguments put forth by the Catcotts, Hutchinson, and members of that circle were radically linguistic and etymological to the extent that they assigned a kinetic force to words themselves, a notion consistent with scriptural assertions that divine words have the power of creation. Catcott once argued, by asserting that the noises of animals themselves were Hebrew syllables, that the spirit acted directly on nature through language.[37] Members of this group referred to words, and their appearance in scripture or print, as 'proof' or as 'discoveries'.[38] Hutchinson devised formulae to measure the position of the earth relative to beams of sunlight. These formulae generated measurements the precision of which was incongruous considering that among the variables in Hutchinson's calculations were certain Hebrew participles.[39] Hutchinson published a tract asserting a connection between 'glory' and 'gravity' in which the former was the verbal equivalent of the latter, a physical phenomenon that remained mysterious for those who had yet to accept Newton unreservedly.[40] Even if Hutchinson's arguments and methods were not empirically compelling, their acceptance by the Catcott circle made them socially binding.[41]

Widely dispersed members of literate circles used written correspondence and books read in common as means of social interaction. A Bristol merchant by the name of Henley complained in a letter to the powerful landowner Edward Southwell, at his country estate in Kingsweston, that nowhere in Bristol was he able to find a copy of 'Hutchinson's Book', a publication of mutual interest. He asked if Southwell might locate a copy for him, presumedly in London.[42] The scarcity of current theological publications in a major provincial city decades after the arrival of local printing is, of course, worth noting. Arrangements concerning the sharing of printed books and pamphlets of special interest, usually in short supply or difficult to locate, were often the subject of letters produced by the Catcott circle.[43] Despite the fact that all the members of this social sphere lived in Bristol, London, or Oxford, or visited one of these cities regularly, they complained, well into the 1760s, about the difficulty of acquiring copies of important publications and professed the deepest indebtedness to one another for the collective use of their books. Hutchinson helped supervise the printing of Catcott's treatises in London. About 600 copies of any one of them would be produced at a time, and Catcott's friends would see personally to their distribution through connections in Oxford, London, and Bristol, but there were no rural points of dispersal.[44]

Some face-to-face interaction concerning the activites of the Catcott circle featured those co-operative persons who kindly delivered books and letters for their friends. One correspondent in London, who sent a letter containing sophisticated applications of Hebrew grammar, arranged to have the letter delivered in person by a Hebrew scholar who could aid its Bristol recipient with the letter's contents.[45] Alexander Catcott expressed open dissatisfaction with booksellers, book dealers, and their negligent carriers and agents, who confused authors or titles and often obtained the wrong books.[46] He made a point of carrying his father's letters to London and Winchester himself.[47] These books and letters, and the ways in which they circulated, expressed the personal nature of ties formed on the strength of shared access to written ideas.

A dispersed social sphere based on shared access to printed or scribbled words, and the ability to derive personally compelling ideas from them, could be as exclusive socially as it was expansive intellectually. Because of the limited appeal of Hutchinson's and Catcott's works, Bristol booksellers refused to carry them, even for the few customers who expressed genuine interest.[48] The Catcott circle, which consisted of literate men with Oxford and London connections, was restricted to polyglots. Members of the Catcott circle wrote to one another in English, French, Latin, Greek, and Hebrew and insisted that 'the great mystery of the Christian religion must depend entirely upon revelation and the true knowledge of that revelation upon the language wherein it was first taught'.[49] In 1738 Nicholas Trott sent a letter across the Atlantic to tell Alexander he had received one of the elder Catcott's published sermons in North Carolina. Upon reading the sermon, Trott became 'confirmed in the opinion that in order to [have] an exact knowledge of the Holy Scriptures it was absolutely necessary that a person be able to read the original text'.[50] Even among skilled printers Catcott had difficulty locating a collaborator in Bristol who was qualified in the necessary languages. He eventually came to an arrangement with a printer in London who hired 'a poor Jew' who could correct and prepare Catcott's proofs.[51] In 1737 Julius Bate in Bath wrote tactfully, yet pointedly, that he could 'dispose' of only fifty copies of Catcott's books but went on to suggest that if Catcott would publish in English, rather than Latin, 'Mr H[utchinson] has many female admirers who have sense enough though not Latin enough to read' such work.[52] Of the entire collection of letters, produced by no fewer than forty-six identifiable correspondents in the circle, only two letters were written by women. One of these letters Alexander Catcott received from his own sister some time between July and October in 1761, and the other was sent seven years later from Whitehall by the Duchess of Portland.[53]

The ability of these correspondents to communicate as well as they did was attributable to the location of their circle within the urban network. The Catcott correspondents wrote from London, Oxford, Bristol, Bath, Wells, Winchester, Northampton, Manchester, Newport, Gloucester, and Coventry. All the letters written by the elder Catcott to John Hutchinson from 1733 to 1736 were composed in Bristol and sent to London. All but two of Hutchinson's letters to Catcott were composed in London and sent to Bristol. The two exceptions originated in Oxford and in Walton-upon-Thames, the location of Hutchinson's village retreat in the shadow of the metropolis. The travel destinations mentioned in these letters were urban, and Oxford was predominant among them.[54] There were a few individuals who wrote from rural locations, but they were exceptional. The Bates brothers and a Mr Gardner wrote occasionally from Walton-upon-Thames in the 1730s while Hutchinson was alive, but they wrote from London or from Sutton, Sussex, within a very short ride from the city. Alexander did receive letters from a correspondent in Wadenhoe, Northamptonshire. In short, the geographical origins and destinations of these letters, clearly recorded by the correspondents, reflect the gradual, but surprisingly late, convergence of urban and rural social spheres despite the transcendent qualities of literacy and the printed word.

Most rural members of the circle were Oxford-trained Anglican clergy who had village posts but maintained their urban connections. Such was the case with Vicar Stevens, who wrote from Coalbrookdale in Shropshire.[55] A Thomas Gwillam wrote to Catcott from the village of Whitchurch, Herefordshire, to request books on behalf of his five colleagues, all of whom held graduate degrees. One was a justice of the peace. One was a physician in the town of Monmouth. Two were clergy at the cathedral in the city of Hereford and one was the rector of Stonehouse, Gloucestershire. Gwillam, who was a customer of 'Mr Croft's bookstore' in the city of Monmouth, was part of a literate circle whose members 'constantly go down every fortnight to Bristol', as he explained to Alexander Catcott.[56] There is little evidence that Anglican clergy in Bristol ventured into the social spheres of rural parishioners. Hutchinson urged Catcott to make the journey from Bristol to Hutchinson's London house near Charing Cross, where other correspondents interested in the spread of 'new doctrines' could gather. Hutchinson, who identified himself warmly as a 'brother quack', observed that these doctrines could make 'such bodies of clergy act in concert which they never did before'.[57] Members of the Catcott circle sensed the parochialism of Anglican clergy, even in major cities. As for his own city's elite, Catcott observed, 'the clergy here are almost all on the opposite side, or do not think these things worth minding, and our merchants have their affairs to think of'.[58] Nevertheless, the social spheres of Anglican clergy were, more than those of their parishioners, likely points of urban–rural convergence.

Surely there were readers in Bristol's nearby rural villages who were aware of Hutchinson's theories and knew that the Catcotts, who were associated with these exciting and provocative ideas, lived and preached near by in Bristol. In their field studies members of the Catcott circle moved through the countryside near Bristol and used what they observed in the natural landscape there as bases of their written arguments. The only letter the Catcotts received from a local villager before the second half of the eighteenth century was from a Stoke Gifford man who wrote only once. He asked to see one of the Catcotts in person at St Nicholas's church.[59] In January 1770 Thomas Jeffrey, an excavator from the Somerset village of Wrington, wrote to inform Alexander Catcott that the discovery of certain bones in Sandford Hill would, in his view, support diluvian theories of natural history.[60] This is the earliest evidence that a local rural villager acted as a corresponding member of the Catcott circle. Unlike nonconformists, who transcended Anglican parish spheres, even the most literate and urbane conformists, like the Catcotts who made intellectual excursions through the cosmos, were largely fixed in their social spheres and cultural ties to a particular setting until the last decades of the early modern period.

The process of community formation beyond parochial, village, or civic confines was, for most of the early modern period, undermined by hostility to religious nonconformity. This hostility was hardly diminished by the urban renaissance and it persisted well beyond the formal granting of toleration to Protestant dissenters in 1689. The resulting tension between those who advocated comprehensive diversity within an established church and those who accepted the private separatism of nonconformists outside that church actually widened the gulf between Anglicans and dissenters after official toleration became law.[61] Some have even argued that this division intensified urban–rural distinctions in the late seventeenth and early eighteenth centuries; when 'dissenters turned their back once and for all on Anglicanism ... popular Anglicanism was enmeshed more closely than ever within the social fabric of the English countryside'.[62] Despite declining attendance, increased lay–clerical tensions, and some neglect of strict observance in rural parishes, the devotional practices of villagers during the generations following the Restoration suggest that Anglicans in the countryside at least considered themselves as avidly conformist as their urban counterparts.[63] In any case, after the 1689 Act of Toleration, which did not repeal the penal laws against dissenters who worshipped in unlicensed congregations, Anglicans who neglected to kneel at prayer and communion, stand at the Creed and Gospel, or bow at the name of Jesus risked far less recrimination than dissenters who congregated for private worship behind closed doors or beyond the confines of the parish. The history of religious persecution in and during the generations after the Restoration shows that nonconformists, connected through the written word and extraparochial expression of their shared beliefs, were abused as much for the nature of their cultural ties and social spheres as for any of the abstract beliefs in question.

In the late seventeenth century, civic authorities launched an assault on all dissenters, but found that parishioners were accustomed to acting on their own notions of what constituted offensive nonconformity.[64] It is difficult to claim that parishioners justified disciplinary actions against nonconformists in purely spiritual terms. Private worship, an intellectual or spiritual activity, was unobjectionable in the view of parishioners, whereas failure to attend one's parish church at the appointed time and place was an offensive rejection of communal activity. During the turbulent 1680s Bristol constables openly refused to disrupt unlawful conventicles at the same time as they were routinely reporting parishioners for failure to attend church.[65] It is certain that some shopkeepers and artisans worked on Sundays rather than attend church, and this explains, in part, why people who simply absented themselves from church tended to be of a higher status than people who spent Sundays withdrawn from the parish for the sake of collective worship rather than personal profit. Those Bristol conventiclers who were apprehended were of low status; their association and arrest may have been a product as much of social alienation as of religious enthusiasm.[66] Attacks against the possessions and meeting houses of Quakers were readily mobilised by constables themselves. Acutely aware of this operative distinction between legal codes and communal ties, George Fox wrote in 1674 of the 'cruel spoiling of goods and violent taking away contrary to all law and justice, then coming with clubs and breaking down your stables and carrying away your goods'.[67] The material culture and personal culture of Quakers – their odd forms of speech and dress, their separate resources, their separate marriages, and especially their separate meeting places – were the targets most meaningful to ordinary parishioners.

The ability of ideologically sustained social spheres to transcend the geographical limitations of traditional parish or civic communities was demonstrated no more dramatically than in the experience of early Quakers, the most harshly treated group of religious dissenters in the late seventeenth century. From the very start, Quakers were organised regionally, rather than by city, village, or parish. The Society of Friends was more than a religious sect; it was an international organisation, a social network committed to the material, as well as spiritual, welfare of its members.[68] Bristol was a provincial centre of Quaker activity, beginning with the arrival of George Fox in the 1650s. During the 1670s the connections among widely dispersed Quaker homes and meeting houses permitted Fox to be conducted safely on his tours through Ireland and the Americas, in areas hostile to Friends, although he travelled great distances from one friendly contact to the next.[69] Like members of early modern English society in general, until the mid-eighteenth century or so, Quakers tended to marry people from within their own familiar setting. Quaker devotional practices, however, brought them into closely tied social spheres that combined urban and rural dwellers. Quakers maintained such close ties, despite official scrutiny and popular oppression, through routine mobility and the publication and dissemination of extensive correspondence, an extraordinary amount of which survives as a result of the special place it was deliberately accorded by the Society itself.

Quaker identity was self-consciously bound up with the printed word, which was, for Quakers, a means of salvation in many respects. Quaker belief in revelation did not rest entirely on the scriptures. At the same time, the belief in an illuminating inner voice, the moral and spiritual guide of every Quaker, found its outward expression and its defence in print to such an extent that personal testimony evolved into the Society of Friends' own corpus of devotional texts. The Society of Friends printed the papers and biographies of its members immediately upon their death. On one occasion, Fox related the news of a woman's death in Jamaica and instructed her son to 'gather up all her papers and her sufferings and send them to London that her life and death may be printed'.[70] Faced with the more mundane concerns of arrest and the confiscation of their property, Quakers also made a point of presenting published accounts, rather than verbal testimony, before the assize judges. Entire volumes of these narratives of 'tedious sufferings' were created and distributed because Quakers believed in the power of replicated documents to present a unified and consistent front and prove the merit of their case in the eyes of the law.[71]

George Fox asserted that his writings, like those of other Quakers, were a sign of his own inner light, God's guiding inspiration shining within him. Fox invoked 'election' not to refer in the Calvinist sense to exclusive predestination, but to identify his writings as the product of a personal vision. This vision was of a kind given to all believers who would heed their inner light granted 'by the grace of God'.[72]

> What I am I am by the grace of God in the election and can say it is God that justifies ... Hast you kept in the simplicity and the love of God, out of prejudice, you would never have judged as you hast done concerning my quotations; for hadst you and the rest stood in the true liberty and conscience, in the grace, truth, light, faith, and power of Jesus, you would not have taken my quotations ...[73]

Among Quakers false or surreptitious quotation was the equivalent of encroachment. Quakers were so proprietorial about words that to publish the words of a Quaker without consent was, in their view, to stray from the ways of God. At the same time, texts whose authors gave their consent and which met with the collective approval of Friends as determined at their regional meetings in Bristol and London were printed, bound, and personally distributed among fellow members of the Society. Between 1672 and 1674 Fox arranged to have travelling Quakers deliver Edward Burroughs's printed works in person to twenty friendly contacts across the Atlantic in Rhode Island, New York, Maryland, and Virginia.[74] True believers, the enlightened, and members of the social sphere were all one and the same to Quakers; all were identified through the shared publication, dissemination, and accession of replicated texts.

As we have seen, Quaker theology was thrust together, in the consciousness of the offended conformist community, with that of Catholics (Jesuits especially), who were condemned on similar grounds as alien. Far from accepting Catholic dogma, George Fox toured Ireland for the very purpose of identifying Quakers there and disputing Catholic theology in the midst of its genuine proponents.[75] The day after the Quaker party landed in Dublin, where 'the papists were angry and raged very much' at him, Fox challenged 'friars, monks, priests and Jesuits, and the Pope himself to come forth and try their God and their Christ that they had made of bread and wine'. In a continuing attack on Catholic tenets, Fox went from town to town in Ireland, inviting priests to say a mass for horses, arguing that 'the candles had a mass, and the lambs had a mass, why might not his horse have a mass as well as they – he is a good creature'. All Anglican positions concerning the eucharist and other liturgical concepts more closely resembled Catholicism than the Quaker position, which utterly rejected consubstantiation and transubstantiation alike. Quakers accepted the required renunciation of Catholic doctrine in good conscience, but the official affirmation of this involved swearing an oath, a practice abhorrent to Quakers.[76] So they found themselves in the situation of refusing to serve as jurors, a civic offence for which they repeatedly paid the find of 40s. The Quaker's modifying notion that inspiration and grace were not preordained by election was in sympathy with conformist anxiety about the possible residue of Calvinist zeal after the Restoration.[77] Perhaps differences between Anglican and Puritan theology were too subtle for most parishioners to argue about,[78] but even at the height of animosity towards Quakers, who distanced themselves from both doctrines, divisions along social, rather than doctrinal, lines persisted no matter how many tracts the Society of Friends printed.

Quakers were actually sympathetic in principle with civic authorities who waged a simultaneous war against swearers, gamers, ale vendors, and untimely revellers. In a printed circular, Fox appealed to the Bristol magistrates as fellow 'zealous Christians' against 'drunkards, swearers, cursers, fighters, cheaters, cuzeners, bawdy houses, whorehouses, wickedness, adulterers, liers, fornicators, thieves and such as followeth pleasures and live wantonly upon the Earth'.[79] Indeed, Fox argued that the magistrates did not deal harshly enough with 'pleasures, games, and sports which you keep on your idle days to dishonour God'. By 1705 a few Quakers eventually joined the new Bristol chapter of the Society for the Reformation of Manners, but despite the urgings of the Reverend Arthur Bedford, the Society for the Promotion of Christian Knowledge leader in Bristol at the time, the Anglican clergy there failed to convert Quakers to the Church of England.[80] Quakers could accept the rectitude of Anglican reformers without compromising their own separatist beliefs; it was the life style of their unsympathetic neighbours that the Quakers could not abide.

The principal objection of civic and ecclesiastical authorities echoed that of the pamphlet polemicists: Quakers sequestered themselves and convened in extraparochial space. In its own Easter letter of 1682 the grand jury of Bristol took umbrage at Quaker publications without citing a single passage, much less attacking any theological positions.

> The Quakers have presumed to publish another libel entitled *The Distressed Case of the People called Quakers in the City of Bristol and their Inhuman Usages for their Religious Peaceable Assemblies.* We present Charles Harford for being the author and dispenser of that libel. We present the Castle [Precincts] being extraparochial to be a receptacle of papists and fanatics and desire this court to find expedients whereby the inhabitants thereof to be liable to the law as well as other parts of the city.[81]

The title of the denounced pamphlet suggests that the Quakers themselves knew full well that it was 'extraparochial' assemblies, rather than beliefs, that rendered their Society offensive to civic conformists. Quakers dressed and spoke unlike their conformist neighbours. They sometimes refused to speak at all. Some were seen to walk about naked as a sign of faith but they refused to doff so much as a cap to make a gesture of social obeisance. They gathered in their own meeting houses and mockingly called parish churches 'steeple houses'. The socially conspicuous nonconformity and extraparochialism of Quakers left them accused of offences ranging from witchcraft to sexual abominations, to sedition. The Quaker view of themselves and Quaker conventions of social interaction were, from the point of view of their detractors, crimes of arrogance and of social, rather than religious, nonconformity which made them targets of absurd accusations. The activities of Quakers in the countryside alienated conformist villagers for the same reasons.[82]

In the diocese of Bristol more Quaker meetings gathered in the rural environs than in the city itself in the late seventeenth century, a situation which may have continued because of the emergence of Frenchay, near the village of Winterbourne, as the site of an important meeting house.[83] Before 1689, while the Restoration code of penalties for nonconformity was still in force, urban as well as rural dissenters were required to congregate at least five miles away from incorporated cities.[84] After restrictions against nonconformist gatherings in urban areas had been relaxed, the proportion of local Quakers residing or worshipping in Bristol, rather than the surrounding countryside, steadily increased. But, as their early history of oppression suggests, Quakers exerted little influence on patterns of social interaction outside their own social sphere during the first half of the urban renaissance.

If the cultural ties of dissenters had the potential to promote a local merger of certain urban and rural social spheres, this was largely unrealised until the mid-eighteenth century.

After the first divisive decades of toleration, Quakers were among the dissenters who, despite lingering poverty among them, achieved enough social prominence as a group to affect urban–rural interaction more broadly.[85] As early as 1716 John Evans, the London Presbyterian minister who conducted a survey of England's dissenting congregations and ministers, noted in Bristol 'a great body of Quakers' who were 'generally well affected to the present government, and large traders and very rich'. The Quakers of the five Bristol meetings were reported at the time to exceed 2,000 in number, with their collective wealth estimated at £500,000.[86] It is likely that the members of Bristol's Quaker congregations, the largest in England at that time, reached over 4,000 in number, with a combined wealth closer to £800,000.[87] At the turn of the century, the wealthiest congregation in all England outside London was quite possibly the dissenting congregation in Lewin's Mead meeting house in St James.[88] Arthur Bedford, as an Anglican clergyman, found he needed to defend himself against the complaints of his conformist SPCK correspondents concerned about the positions held by Baptists, Independents, Presbyterians and Quakers in the Bristol Society for the Reformation of Manners, which failed to survive early eighteenth-century sectarian animosity.[89] Acceptance was a slow process, even after official toleration. In November 1753, when Dyer visited a 'newbuilt tabernacle' for a dissenting congregation in Bristol, he remarked that it was so new that oiled paper glowed with sunlight in all the windows where stained glass had yet to be inserted.

By 1769 Donne's *Map of the Country Eleven Miles round the City of Bristol*, a large map which labelled the area's prominent houses and other buildings, identified Quaker meeting houses in the nearby villages of Brockley and Lawrence Weston as well as Methodist and Moravian meeting houses in Kingswood.[90] Quaker migrants drawn from the surrounding counties to the successes of Bristol Friends in the middle and late eighteenth century maintained connections with their origins in the countryside. In the later stages of this process, some came to Bristol, where they prospered, and then moved to more gracious homes in the nearby villages. Zephania Fry, a clothier from Sutton, Wiltshire, married Abigail Hiscox of Bristol in 1741 and resided there in Castle Street. By the time of Abigail's death in 1781 they had been living in the village of Stapleton, near Bristol, from which their son, Robert, maintained his role in a circle of affluent Quakers in the nearby city from the 1760s on.[91]

Rural as well as urban Quakers, when left to their own devices unmolested, formed lasting connections with the urban network. By 1740, close to 80 per cent of Quaker marriages in the region took place in the Bristol meeting. Quakers from Bristol and the nearby villages increasingly married across topographical lines after 1740 or so. Only one out of every eight Quaker marriages joined a Bristol resident to a villager over the entire period from 1660 to 1780, with little evidence at all of such marriages before the eighteenth century. By contrast, after 1740, during the last forty years of the period, nearly one out of every four Quaker marriages in the region brought Bristolians and villagers together.[92] Because a parochial construction of community did not apply to these nonconformists, many of the Quaker couples who transcended the topographical divide worshipped together before marriage, with villagers attending meetings in Bristol and Bristolians attending meetings in the countryside. It is not entirely surprising that some of the Bristol Quakers who married local villagers after the mid-eighteenth century had connections with printers.[93] The transformation of nonconformists from oppressed to tolerated, and then from socially vigorous to influential, promoted a convergence of urban and rural social spheres in a way that the norms and practices of parochial conformity had not.

A new and informal ecumenicalism featured people who worshipped more widely but still moved comfortably through Anglican social spheres. By the 1750s William Dyer, who had both Methodist and Quaker connections, wandered from one parish church to another, but made a point of attending Wednesday prayers in his own parish in Bristol. He wrote of his parish church in St James, 'I seem to have declined this church on Sundays and repaired to St Mary Port church where Mr Seyer frequently preached and made good discourses.'[94] Dyer, who believed in epiphany through dreams, was clearly theologically unorthodox as well as logistically unrestrained. So he actively sought like-minded people for spiritual kinship. On some Sundays Dyer attended four services in four separate places of worship, including 'Mr Wesley's room', where, like the Methodists around him, he felt guided by 'the small still voice ... the shepherd of his soul'. On the very same day he might have been found at the separatist gathering in Lewin's Mead,[95] associated later in Dyer's life with Bristol's Unitarian circle. But Anglican churches remained a social resource for Dyer, who even selected his barber over others on the grounds that he and Dyer regularly attended the same early morning prayer services in St Werburgh.[96] He mingled with the vicar and other clergy, including Mr Thomas Jones, vicar of Temple Church, whom Dyer privately regarded as a 'loose liver'.[97] He was married in his own parish of St James, as were other members of his family. Despite his intellectual and devotional eccentricities, which led him afield, Dyer remained connected socially with the parish in which he lived through personal ties affirmed in St James church.

Dyer's devotional and social meanderings led him into the villages near Bristol where Methodists had been especially active for a decade.

Sunday morning with my dear wife and Mrs Edwards at Kingswood School or Chapel, which we reached on foot, about eight o'clock and heard Mr Charles Westley [*sic*] preach who afterwards administered the sacrament. But, as strangers were not admitted, Mrs Edwards, who was of Mr Westley's Society, applied and we were permitted to partake and communicate with those of that community.[98]

The Methodist movement was a religious awakening which grew out of a circle of Oxford Anglicans, but the Methodist notion of strangeness was not guided by parochial concerns. In eighteenth-century nonconformist circles the invocation of 'stranger' was not derived from anxiety about places of origin. Those who presented themselves for inclusion in the social sphere of the spiritual community were not strangers.

Methodist sermons near Bristol drew urban dwellers to the countryside, where they joined, in massive crowds, the rustic Kingswood colliers and other villagers whose terrain the newspapers had once warned urbane travellers not to cross. What impressed Dyer most about Yorkshire Methodists was the great numbers in which they convened. On one occasion, he remarked, a single congregation in a small place filled a church four times over and consumed thirty-five bottles of communion wine.[99] The use of open-air sermons by the Methodists spoke not only to the importance of the rural – one should even say, pastoral – setting for this evangelical movement; such gatherings also amounted to the bursting of parochial confines by the burgeoning social spheres of eighteenth-century Protestant nonconformists. Despite the urban renaissance, the arena in which urban and rural social spheres converged through confessional ties was as much part of the rural setting as the urban setting.

The promotion of urban–rural convergence, long after the urban renaissance had got under way, was the result of shifting topographical affinities as well as changing attitudes concerning the nature of community. For most of the early modern period the immiscibility of urban and rural worlds was itself a persistent normative idea that sustained the cultural and social divide between those people who identified with the urbane and those who identified with the rustic. Defoe observed that if it were not for localist ideology and 'the chain of their own liberties', cities like Bristol, by the 1720s, could 'have swelled and increased in buildings and inhabitants, perhaps to double the magnitude'.[100] As we are about to see, transformations in attitudes about the land itself and how people should live upon it produced a topographical, as well as social, convergence of city and country in the late eighteenth century. But it was the lure of the country for urban dwellers, more than any gravitational pull of urban centres, that gave rise to suburbia in its modern form, the ultimate synthesis of antithetical city and village. The material and discursive reconstruction of the rural landscape under the early influence of bourgeois romanticism gave rise to modern suburbia, a conspicuous expression of urban–rural convergence that brought the early modern period to a close.

# NOTES

1 Daniel Defoe, *A Tour through the whole Island of Great Britain (1724–26)*, ed. P. Rogers (Harmondsworth, 1971), pp. 486 and 712n.

2 B.R.O. SF/C1/2, A Collection of Yearly Meeting Epistles from the Year 1666 to the Year 1840 inclusive (1673), item 5.

3 B.C.L. #B10191. One such home was that of J. Harris, who lived in the village of Stokes Croft, Gloucestershire.

4 As far as I am aware, there is only one surviving example of a eulogy printed in Bristol in which the honoured deceased was connected with a rural parish: Caleb Evans, *Hope of the Righteous Death: Preached at the New Chapel in Stapleton at the Internment of Joseph Mason* (Bristol, 1780), of which B.C.L. pamphlet #1169 is one copy. We know that Evans, who wrote no fewer than five eulogies printed between 1775 and 1790, preached for the Baptist congregation at Broadmead. See B.C.L. pamphlet #1625.

5 M. Spufford (ed.), *The World of Rural Dissenters 1520–1725* (Cambridge, 1995).

6 Defoe, *A Tour through the whole Island of Great Britain*, pp. 251–5 and 362.

7 B.C.L. MS #20095, Diary of William Dyer (1745–1801), entry of 6 June 1756. These are Dyer's own emphases.

8 B.R.O. Wills, Richard Blinman (6/1681).

9 In fact, on occasions on which women served as witnesses for book-owning men, both parties were literate. See, for example, B.R.O. Wills: James Hayes (1681); Francis Little (1681); George Londen (1723); Rees Lewis (1774).

10 The importance of books, reading, and educational experiences for the formation of friendships and shared identity among women has received more attention for post-colonial America than for early modern England. See N. F. Cott, *The Bonds of Womanhood: 'Woman's Sphere' in New England 1780–1835* (New Haven, Conn., 1977), and M. Kelley, *Private Woman, Public Stage: Literary Domesticity in Nineteenth-Century America* (Oxford, 1984). I am grateful to my colleague Mary Kelley for sharing her views on this subject with me.

11 More evidence of connections among literate book-owning women is provided in B.R.O. Wills: Elizabeth Milner (1690); Elizabeth Arundel (1691); Joan Perkins (1715); Sarah Webb (1733); Elizabeth Lawrens (1752); Nancy Bastable (1768).

12 B.R.O. P/StP&J/R/3(a), St Philip and Jacob Marriages (1760–64); P/StW/R/2(a), Marriage Registers of St Werburgh, City of Bristol (1754–1812); P/StS/R/3(a), Marriage Registers of St Stephen, Bristol (1754–61).

13 B.R.O. P/OV/R/3(a), Registers of the Parish of St Mary, Olveston, Gloucestershire (1754–63 and 1775–84); P/StLB/R/4(a), Marriage Registers of St Luke, Brislington, Somerset (1754–1808).

14 An illiterate miller from Olveston who married a literate woman from his own village in September 1759 and an illiterate butcher from Brislington who married a literate woman from his own village in August of 1764 are examples.

15 B.R.O. P/StP&J/R/3(a), St Philip and Jacob Marriages (1760–64).

16 B.R.O. P/StP&J/R/3(a), St Philip and Jacob Marriages (1760–64); P/StW/R/2(a), Marriage Registers for St Werburgh, City of Bristol (1754–1812); P/StS/R/3(a), Marriage

Registers for St Stephen, Bristol (1754–61). In the 819 marriages registered here, 556 of 868 literate spouses married other literate people. Of the 819 women who married in these Bristol parishes from 1754 to 1784, only 307 (38 per cent) could sign their name, as opposed to the 561 (69 per cent) of the 819 grooms who could sign.

17  B.R.O. P/OV/R/3(a), Registers of the Parish of St Mary, Olveston, Gloucestershire (1754–63 and 1775–84); P/StLB/R/4(a), Marriage Registers of St Luke, Brislington, Somerset (1754–1808). Of the 233 grooms registered in the villages of Olveston, Gloucestershire, and Brislington, Somerset, from 1754 to 1784, 123 (52·8 per cent) could sign their name. Only seventy-seven (33·0 per cent) of the 233 brides could sign. Nevertheless, of 203 literate spouses registered in those villages, 130 (64 per cent) formed a union with another literate person.

18  In the last three decades of our period, in the villages of Olveston and Brislington, forty-one spouses came from outside the villages where they married. Thirty-two were literate, and, of those, twenty-six married another literate person. Women married outside their own place of origin less often than men did, but after 1753 such women were found in Olveston in 1758, 1761, and 1775, and in Brislington in 1761, 1763, 1766, 1772–74, and 1777–78. Examples were more common in the city, where parishes were not insulated from one another by open space and where women were more likely to be literate.

19  B.R.O. Wills (Sarah Edwards, 1688).

20  B.R.O. P/OV/R/3(a), Registers of the Parish of St Mary, Olveston, Gloucestershire (1754–63 and 1775–84); P/StLB/R/4(a), Marriage Registers of St Luke, Brislington, Somerset (1754–1808).

21  L. Stone, *The Family, Sex, and Marriage in England, 1500–1800* (abridged ed., New York, 1979), pp. 30–1; J. R. Gillis, *For Better, for Worse: British Marriages, 1600 to the Present* (Oxford, 1985), pp. 56–70 and 151–2; A. Macfarlane, *Marriage and Love in England 1300–1840* (Oxford, 1986), pp. 225–6 and 304–6; M. Ingram, *Church Courts, Sex and Marriage in England 1570–1640* (Cambridge, 1987), pp. 132–4.

22  Between 1754 and 1784 thirty-two such couples opted for marriage licences in the three urban parishes of St Werburgh, St Stephen, and St Philip and Jacob, as indicated in the parish registers.

23  Of St Werburgh's sixty-nine grooms, fifty-three (76·8 per cent) could sign the register. Of the sixty-nine brides, forty-seven (68·1 per cent), a very high percentage indeed, could sign.

24  Of St Philip and Jacob's 534 grooms, 343 (64·2 per cent) could sign. Of the 534 brides, 158 (29·6 per cent), a remarkably low portion, could sign.

25  The popularity of banns was nearly identical in the two topographical settings. In the villages of Olveston and Brislington, 157 (67·4 per cent) of 233 couples observed the proclamation of banns, and in the three Bristol parishes in question 543 (66·3 per cent) of 819 couples observed banns.

26  B.R.O. #14581 HA/M.4, Haynes Manor Court Records (1657–1677). In 1680 only nineteen (79 per cent) of twenty-four grand jurors in the city of Bristol could sign a presentment against a widely perceived Jesuit plot. B.R.O. #04452(1), Bristol Quarter Sessions: Presentments and Convictions (Trinity, 1680).

27  B.R.O. #14581 HA/M.4, Haynes Manor Court Records (1657–77); HA/M.5, Haynes Manor Court Records (1697–1726); HA/M.6 Haynes Manor Court Records (1746–68).

28  B.R.O. #14581 HA/M.7, Haynes Manor Court: Presentments (1770–71).

29  R. Porter, *English Society in the Eighteenth Century* (Harmondsworth, 1982), pp. 291–2.

30  B.R.O. AC/C, AC/D, AC/F, AC/JS, AC/WO, AC/WH, and #36074. Anton Bantock, a transcriber of this collection, refers even to the early eighteenth century women's letters as 'Betty's Horrid Scrawls' in *The Earlier Smyths of Ashton Court from their Letters 1545–1741* (Bristol, 1982), pp. 214–40.

31  B.R.O. #09701, Letter of Thomas Trotman, in Siston, to Richard Haynes, Esq., of Bristol (18 April 1722).

32  R. M. Wiles, *Freshest Advices: Early Provincial Newspapers in England* (Columbus, Oh., 1965), p. 61.

33  B.C.L. #20095, Diary of William Dyer (entry of 11 June 1757).

34  B.C.L. #B26063 (SR43), Correspondence of Rev. A. S. Catcott and Rev. Alexander Catcott (1733–74), Letter of Scullard to Catcott (4 January 1755).

35  H. Abelove, *The Evangelist of Desire: John Wesley and the Methodists* (Stanford, Cal., 1990), p. 69.

36  B.C.L. MS #6495(SR4B), Alexander Catcott's Diaries of Tours made in England and Wales (1748–74).

37  B.C.L. #B26063 (SR43), Letter of Catcott to Hutchinson, (23 June 1734).

38  See, for example, B.C.L. #B26063 (SR43), Letter of Hutchinson to Catcott (29 October 1733).

39  B.C.L. #B26063 (SR43), Hutchinson to Catcott (21 September 1734); Hutchinson to Catcott (1 January 1734).

40  B.C.L. #B26062 (SR43), Hutchinson to Catcott (2 July 1734).

41  M. Neve and R. Porter, 'Alexander Catcott: glory and geology', *British Journal for the History of Science* 10 (1977), pp. 37–60, provides another treatment of this group and identifies scientific and empirical aspects of Catcott's thinking.

42  B.R.O. #12964(76), Somersetshire MSS, 1672–1741: Letter of Henley to Southwell (5 November 1720).

43  A few examples include: B.C.L. #B26063 (SR43), Catcott to Hutchinson (27 July 1733); Catcott to Hutchinson (29 October 1733); Hutchinson to Catcott (30 January 1734); Hutchinson to Catcott (11 May 1734); Hutchinson to Catcott (5 December 1734); Trott to Catcott (12 May 1738); Robertson to Catcott (17 April 1738); Gwillam to Catcott (10 May 1738); Robertson to Catcott (1 February 1747); Shaw to Catcott (20 September 1750); Stevens to Catcott (27 April 1752); Robertson to Catcott (10 October 1754); Frankcombe to Catcott (5 February 1761); and Brown to Catcott (15 January 1765).

44  B.C.L. #B26063 (SR43), Hutchinson to Catcott (1 June 1736).

45  B.C.L. #B26063 (SR43), Hutchinson to Catcott (20 August 1735).

46  B.C.L. #B26062 (SR43), Catcott to Hutchinson (27 July and 29 October 1733).

47  B.C.L. #B26063 (SR43), Catcott to a Winchester correspondent (20 December 1739).

48  B.C.L. #B26063 (SR43), Hutchinson to Catcott (5 August 1736).

49  B.C.L. #B26063 (SR43), Gwillam to Catcott (10 May 1738).

50  B.C.L. #B26063 (SR43), Trott to Catcott (12 May 1738).

51  B.C.L. #B26063 (SR43), The printer, W. Romaine, to Catcott (7 April 1745).

52  B.C.L. #B26063 (SR43), Julius Bate to Catcott (18 April 1737).

53  B.C.L. #B26063 (SR43), Mary Delany to Alexander Catcott (7 December 1768).

54  See, for example, B.C.L. #B26063 (SR43), Hutchinson to Catcott (26 July and 4 September 1734).

55  B.C.L. #B26063 (SR43), Stevens to Catcott (3 August 1751) and (28 March 1752).

56  B.C.L. #B26063 (SR43), Gwillam to Catcott (10 May 1738).

57  B.C.L. #B26063 (SR43), Hutchinson to Catcott (1 January 1735).

58  B.C.L. #B26063 (SR43), Catcott in a letter possibly intended for a relative (26 March 1737).

59  B.C.L. #B26063 (SR43), J. Hart to Catcott (29 November 1737).

60  B.C.L. #B26063 (SR43), Jeffrey to Catcott (30 January 1770).

61  G. V. Bennett, 'Conflict in the church', in G. Holmes (ed.), *Britain after the Glorious Revolution 1689–1714* (London, 1969); T. Harris, *Politics under the Later Stuarts: Party Conflict in a Divided Society 1660–1715* (London, 1993), pp. 139–40 and 178.

62  S. Doran and C. Durston, *Princes, Pastors and People: The Church and Religion in England 1529–1689* (London, 1991), pp. 91–2.

63  D. A. Spaeth, 'Parsons and parishioners: Lay–Clerical Conflict and Popular Piety in Wiltshire Villages 1660–1740' (Ph.D. thesis, Brown University, 1985); 'Common prayer? Popular observance of the Anglican liturgy in Restoration Wiltshire', in S. J. Wright (ed.), *Parish, Church and People: Local Studies in Lay Religion 1350–1750* (London, 1989), pp. 125–51; M. Ingram, 'From Reformation to toleration: popular religious cultures in England 1540–1690', in T. Harris (ed.), *Popular Culture in England, c. 1500–1850* (New York, 1995), pp. 120–3.

64  T. Harris, *London Crowds in the Reign of Charles II: Propaganda and Politics from the Restoration to the Exclusion Crisis* (Cambridge, 1987); J. Barry, 'The politics of religion in Restoration Bristol', in T. Harris, P. Seaward, and M. Goldie (eds), *The Politics of Religion in Restoration England* (Oxford, 1990), pp. 163–90.

65  B.R.O. #04452(1), Bristol Quarter Sessions: Presentments and Convictions (1676–1700). See, especially, Trinity, 1681.

66  B.R.O. #04452(1), Bristol Quarter Sessions: Presentments and Convictions (Michaelmas, 1681, and Epiphany, 1681/82). In Epiphany term 1682, 167 people in sixteen groups were presented at Bristol quarter sessions for 'illicit assembly' on Sundays. Of those, eighty-five were identified as labourers, fifty-four as unemployed or of no particular occupation, and four were spinsters. Only one gentleman was apprehended. The previous Michaelmas, 135 people were presented instead for absence from church. There were only two labourers among them. By contrast, that group did include two gentlemen, a physician, a schoolmaster, four apothecaries, fourteen members of a company of grocers, several other merchants, artisans, thirteen widows, and wives of other offenders.

67  B.R.O. SF/C1/1(a), Letter of George Fox to the Men's Meeting [in Bristol] (1674).

68  The most extensive social history of early Quakers is R. T. Vann, *The Social Development*

*of English Quakerism 1655–1755* (Cambridge, Mass., 1969). For the development of Quaker social institutions in America and the maintenance of transatlantic cultural ties see B. Levy, *Quakers and the American Family: British Settlement in the Delaware Valley* (Oxford, 1988). For the life and thought of George Fox see H. L. Ingle, *First among Friends: George Fox and the Creation of Quakerism* (Oxford, 1994).

69 B.R.O. SF/C1/1(a), Letters and Papers of George Fox and other early Friends (1667–1719). See, especially, letters of George Fox in Rhode Island to the Men's Meeting in Bristol, 19 April 1672, or Fox's letter from Dublin later in that decade.

70 B.R.O. SF/C1/1(a), Letters of George Fox to the Men's Meeting in Bristol (9 April 1672).

71 B.R.O. SF/C1/1(a), Letters of George Fox from London to Bristol Friends regarding the Imprisonment of Quakers there (24 April 1671); Letter of George Fox to the Bristol Men's Meeting (1 November 1699); Letter of George Fox to Men's Meeting (1674). For a more detailed analysis of Quaker legal strategies and the legal battles of early Quakers see C. W. Horle, *The Quakers and the English Legal System 1660–88* (Philadelphia, 1988).

72 M. Watts, *The Dissenters: From the Reformation to the French Revolution* (Oxford, 1978), pp. 186–8 and 203.

73 B.R.O. SF/C1/1(a), Letter of George Fox to W[illiam] R[ogers] (November 1678).

74 B.R.O. SF/C1/1(a).

75 B.R.O. SF/C1/1(a), G[eorge] F[ox]: his travels into Ireland and in and out of Ireland.

76 B.R.O. #0449(1), Bristol Quarter Sessions: Docket (1695–1703). See especially 1696.

77 R. J. Acheson, *Radical Puritans in England 1550–1660* (London, 1990), pp. 69–74; B. Reay, 'Quakerism and society' in J. McGregor and B. Reay (eds), *Radical Religion in the English Revolution* (Oxford, 1984). At the time of the Restoration, Calvinism was tainted by its association with Puritan zeal, civil war, and revolutionary violence. The restored Bishop of Winchester, George Morley, was a Calvinist. The attack on Calvinism launched by the Cambridge Platonists 'was directed more against the spirit which it encouraged than against the convictions which it held'. G. R. Cragg, *The Church in the Age of Reason 1648–1789* (Harmondsworth, 1960), pp. 65 and 68. For the observation that Quakers of the Restoration period also proudly invoked their separatism as 'dissenters' to distance themselves from Puritans, see J. Spurr, 'From Puritanism to dissent 1660–1700', in C. Durston and J. Eales (eds), *The Culture of English Puritanism 1560–1700* (New York, 1996), especially pp. 235–53.

78 D. D. Wallace, *Puritans and Predestination: Grace in English Theology, 1525–1695* (Chapel Hill, N.C., 1982); J. Barry, 'The parish in civic life: Bristol and its churches 1640–1750', in Wright, *Parish, Church and People*, pp. 160–1; J. E. Bradley, *Religion, Revolution and English Radicalism: Nonconformity in Eighteenth-Century Politics and Society* (Cambridge, 1990), pp. 1–2.

79 B.R.O. SF/C1/1(a), Letters and Papers of George Fox and other early Friends (1667–1719).

80 J. Barry and K. Morgan (eds), *Reformation and Revival in Eighteenth-Century Bristol* (Bristol, 1994), pp. 45–6.

81 B.R.O. #04452(1), Bristol Quarter Sessions: Presentments and Convictions (Easter, 1682).

82 R. Bauman, *Let your Words be Few: Symbolism of Speaking and Silence among the Seventeenth-Century Quakers* (Cambridge, 1983); B. Reay, 'Quakerism and society', in J.

McGregor and B. Reay (eds), *Radical Religion in the English Revolution* (Oxford, 1984); M. Ingram, 'From Reformation to toleration', p. 119.

83  *Notes on Bristol History* 5 (University of Bristol Department of Extramural Studies, 1962), p. 12. Churchwardens' diocesan presentments against Quakers also included those for Abbots Leigh, Bedminster, Shirehampton, Winterbourne, sixteen other Gloucestershire parishes, and the city of Bristol itself.

84  The Five Mile Act of 1665 was part of this code, which also included the Corporation Act (1661), the Act of Uniformity (1662), the Quaker Act (1662), the Conventicle Acts (1664 and 1670), which together required sworn acceptance of the Anglican Book of Common Prayer, removed nonconformists from municipal government, heavily fined nonconformists who assembled to worship, and removed all nonconformist and ejected ministers to a distance five miles from any incorporated cities or their former parishes. The sacramental tests imposed on all officials by the Test and Corporation Acts remained in place even after 1689.

85  B. Stevenson, 'The social and economic status of post-Restoration dissenters 1660–1725' and 'The social integration of post-Restoration dissenters 1660–1725' in Spufford, *The World of Rural Dissenters*, pp. 332–87.

86  Williams's Library, London, MS.34.4. The Evans list for Bristol (MS.34.4, fos. 99, 102, and 147) is included in Barry and Morgan, *Reformation and Revival in Eighteenth-Century Bristol*; see especially p. 71. The compilers of the county-by-county Evans lists surely identified Bristol as a prominent place for Quakers; only five of the Evans lists, compiled between 1716 and 1729, included information on Quakers whereas Baptists, Independents and Presbyterians appeared throughout the Evans lists.

87  N. Rogers, *Whigs and Cities: Popular Politics in the Age of Walpole and Pitt* (Oxford, 1989), pp. 268–9; R. S. Mortimer, 'Notes and queries', *Journal of the Friends' Historical Society* 57 no. 3 (1996), p. 312.

88  G. Holmes, *Augustan England: Professions, State, and Society 1680–1730* (London, 1982), p. 113. Holmes does not identify Lewin's Mead by name, but he uses the 1715 Evans list here, which refers to this Bristol congregation.

89  Mortimer, 'Notes and queries'. Documents concerning the involvement of a Bristol SPCK correspondent, Arthur Bedford, in Society for the Reformation of Manners activity are included in Barry and Morgan, *Reformation and Revival in Eighteenth-Century Bristol*; see pp. 6–13 for commentary concerning the tension surrounding dissenting involvement in the society.

90  B.R.O. #247 BP210, *Donne's Map of the Country Eleven Miles round the City of Bristol* (1769), 'sold by the author, B. Donn[e], at the Mathematical Academy in King Street, Bristol'.

91  London Society of Friends Library, Bristol and Somerset Quarterly Meeting Digest Register of Marriages (1657–1837), Book 116, p. 249, Fry and Hiscox (11 March 1741). J. W. Frost (ed.), *The Records and Recollections of James Jenkins 1753–1831* (Lewiston, N.Y., 1984), discusses Robert Fry. Evidence of the nonconformist conflation of urban and rural spheres in the Bristol environs appears in the 1766 diary of Andrew Parminter, a Moravian whose testimonies are included in Barry and Morgan, *Reformation and Revival in Eighteenth-Century Bristol*, see especially p. 142.

92  B.R.O. SF/R1/3 and SF/R1/4, Society of Friends Quarterly Meetings of Bristol and Somerset: Marriages (1659–1816). In seven sample years at twenty-year intervals from

1660 to 1780 inclusive, of sixty-eight Quaker marriages in the region, nine (13·2 per cent) united Bristolians and villagers with no such cases (0 per cent) before the sample year 1700. For contrast, see London Society of Friends Library, Bristol and Somerset Quarterly Meetings Digest Register of Marriages (1657–1837). Between 1740 and 1780 inclusive, of 275 marriages in the region, sixty-five (23·6 per cent) united Bristolians and villagers.

93   B.R.O. SF/R1/3–4, Society of Friends Quarterly Meetings of Bristol and Somersetshire: Marriages (1658–1816). The meeting in Frenchay, Gloucestershire, was especially popular among Bristol Quakers, who formed lasting social spheres there. See, for example, the Quaker marriages involving the Ash, Beck, and Champion families in 1769 and 1770. On 14 April 1761 Samuel Bonner, printer, of Keynsham, Somerset married Sarah Buckingham of Bristol.

94   B.C.L. #20095, Diary of William Dyer (1745–1801), 2 vols, MS. See the entry for 5 December 1753.

95   B.C.L. #20095, Diary of William Dyer (5 December 1751).

96   B.C.L. #20095, Diary of William Dyer (24 February 1752).

97   B.C.L. #20095, Diary of William Dyer (23 December 1751 and 26 February 1752). Members of the Dyer family obtained marriage licences.

98   B.C.L. #20095, Diary of William Dyer (28 October 1753).

99   B.C.L. #20095, Diary of William Dyer (25 November 1753).

100  Defoe, *A Tour through the Whole Island of Great Britain*, p. 362.

# Chapter 10

The origins of
modern suburbia

Come, come let us leave the town,
And in some lonely place,
Where crowds and noise were never known,
Resolve to spend our days.
          Henry Purcell's *The Fairy Queen* (1692)

The seeds of suburbia, in its modern sense, were planted in extramural villages where settlement patterns were altered by the transplanting of urban dwellers to rural environs outside their cities. During the last few decades of the early modern period villages were transformed by urban professionals and merchants who wanted to reside on insulated plots suitable for private residence conveniently close to a city. Before the mid-eighteenth century, people who commuted to an English provincial city from its rural environs to conduct their routine lives were members of a very small minority. In the early 1670s Sir Robert Yeamans, a Bristol councillor, actually lived in rural Redland, just outside the city, but his attachment to both settings can be explained in part by his having moved in gentry circles.[1] In Yeamans's lifetime, and for generations after, when people spoke of provincial suburbs they still referred to the peripheral parishes within a city's chartered confines. These were often the last urban parishes to be heavily developed. In view of the dramatic growth and revitalisation of urban centres beginning at the Restoration, the fact that extramural suburbia did not develop until almost a century later is remarkable. That provincial suburbia appeared so much later than the economic revivals and demographic pressures experienced by nearby cities cannot be explained without reference to the persistent and conscious resistance of rural dwellers to urban encroachment. Despite the importance of wealth for suburban development, urban–rural convergence on the landscape took place in the context of considerable controversy in which affinities, values, cultural practices, and resulting allegiances were more closely linked with urbane and rustic consciousness than with patrician and plebeian consciousness.

In April 1778 James Jenkins, a London merchant born in Bristol, toured the West Country in a private chaise. Upon visiting Bristol he was less favourably impressed with the city than with the transformation of the nearby settlements and their new inhabitants:

> I found this, my native city (but which I had not then seen since the days of my infancy) very different from either London or Dublin – most of the streets narrow, crooked and dirty, sledges drawn along them ... and the inhabitants talking much bad English – indeed a phraseology almost exclusively their own ... We left Bristol and passed several neat country houses, three of which (our driver informed us) belonged to a tin-man, a gardener and a tallow chandler, all occupations ... deemed mean, and followed by persons of small property ... Our young barrister expressed his astonishment and laughed.[2]

Since Jenkins's childhood many prosperous tradesmen and merchants, not just gentlemen, had appeared in the developing settlements just outside the city. As Jenkins approached Bristol from the south, he was struck by the mixture of urban and rural people on the Somerset landscape in close proximity to the city. The pleasing setting featured 'land of rich verdure and the country ornamented with several gentlemen's seats and, upon our nearer approach to Bristol, the country houses of its wealthy citizens were interspersed in a pleasing variety, and (if I may say so) rendered it rurally populous'. Before the development of extramural suburbia, James Jenkins's apologetic description of Bristol's environs as 'rurally populous' would have been understood as disturbingly oxymoronic.

If urbane and rustic people shared any attitudes about the distinct urban and rural settings it was that the boundary between them should be maintained with vigilance. During a transitional period in the middle of the eighteenth century the normative belief that urban and rural worlds should be kept separate lost much of its former influence. This marked a significant ideological transformation, or paradigmatic shift, from the descriptive and normative stance reflected in policy, commentary, and activity in provincial England for most of the early modern period despite the urban renaissance after 1660. In 1580 an Elizabethan proclamation forbade the expansion of cities beyond their chartered confines. A law of 1656 forbade the construction of new houses upon holdings of fewer than four acres within ten miles of cities. The Tudor statutes still prohibited any house within an enclosed parcel of less than 0·25 acre, regardless of whether the entire holding consisted of 4 acres or more. These laws were also invoked in the eighteenth century by urban officials themselves who wished to discourage immigration and to preserve the natural barrier between city and countryside. Extramural congestion was associated with vagrancy, disease, and disorder, in their view.[3] Even Daniel Defoe, the great advocate of an extended commercial network, regarded as thriving those towns that built and improved within their gates.[4] This value was reflected in the actual subdivision and intensification of Bristol's existing outer parishes as opposed to the possible sprawling development beyond the city's established confines.

At the same time, rural dwellers of all social stations actively preserved the rural quality of their chosen surroundings. Rural land holdings, even those of smaller tenants, were often made up of two or more parcels, pieces of land clearly delineated by an enclosing fence, hedge, road, stream, or other barrier. In the villages near Bristol, for more than an entire century following 1660, the parcels on which houses and cottages were set were nearly all an acre in size, at least four times larger than was needed to comply with all the surviving statutes. This was as true of tenants whose total holdings were confined to an acre as it was of those tenants who occupied several parcels and several acres. In 1727 the house plot occupied by a clerk in the village of Stapleton was only 0·5 acre in size, so once again village clergy, with university connections and other urbane affinities, provided exceptions to rustic mentality in the rural setting.[5] As a rule, regardless of the sizes of any accompanying pastures, orchards, forests, and arable fields, the delineated parcels on which rural dwellings stood reflected an immutable rustic notion of what constituted sufficient insular space for a place of residence. This aspect of rural life was not violated even in the consolidated estates or the most nucleated villages in the Bristol countryside.[6] As we will see, rural dwellers who resisted the encroachment of suburbia on their villages exhibited communal solidarity based on a shared affinity for setting that transcended the class divisions with which larger enclosures are associated.

The enclosure of large tracts of land by the privileged elite dislocated less successful tenants who had good reason to view engrossment as hostile,[7] but the long-term consolidation of estates by the gentry did not disturb the rural quality of village settlement patterns in close proximity to cities, nor did it create suburban plots to be conveyed, free and clear, to commuting urbanites. The largest parcels on manors and estates, such as the private parks, contained the great houses where the local gentry actually created larger tracts of less densely settled land between themselves and urban centres. The estate management maps and records on deeds show the deliberate acquisition of contiguous plots over more than a century by the Southwell family in rural Gloucestershire parishes just north of the city of Bristol. The result, and clearly the objective, by the second half of the eighteenth century was the rural isolation of their estate and tenants. In 1772 the family's private enclosure, Southwell Park, contained the largest parcel (92 acres) and the largest average parcel size (more than 12 acres) on the entire estate. Kingroad Farm, the location of tenants farthest from the park, had an average parcel size under 4 acres and its largest parcel covered fewer than 8 acres, but the farm was separated from Bristol by the spacious park itself. The size of the parcels diminished as they radiated from the great parks, but the consolidation of the large private estate nearer Bristol further insulated the tenants on one side of the park from the city on the other side.[8]

Eighteenth-century commentators noted the dilemma of urban dwellers for whom the estate management strategies of the established gentry were not an option. Citizens with urbane affinities were torn between two extremes: the intensifying urban environment of contained cities and the unfamiliar challenges of country life. The gendered language of urbane commentators in the sixteenth and seventeenth centuries represented cities as nurturing females, mediators between raw nature and refined culture. By the end of the eighteenth century there was a rising discourse of the masculine city with its beastly disposition and gluttonous predations.[9] Whereas cartographers and writers had used positive language to describe London in the seventeenth century, after the 1720s it had become the sprawling metropolis of which Defoe asked rhetorically, 'Whither will this monstrous city then extend?' Referring to London's newer portions, Defoe spoke contemptuously of 'little offices for clerks' and the 'private prisons and houses of confinement'. Defoe concluded in *The Complete English Tradesman* that 'trade is almost universally founded upon crime', an observation indicative of an urban dweller's shifting attitude toward the setting in which he lived.[10] Urban planners of the second half of the eighteenth century advocated a naturalist programme designed to introduce open and verdant space as a reaction to urban interior growth and density. Even then, urbane commentators like John Stewart fumed that *rus in urbe* was 'tinctured with absurdity' and a 'preposterous idea at best'. Of sheep brought in to graze in city squares for picturesque effect, Stewart scoffed: 'To see the poor things starting at every coach, and hurrying around their narrow bounds, requires a warm imagination indeed, to concert the scene into that of flocks ranging in fields, with all the concomitant ideas of innocence and a pastoral life.'[11] In the second half of the eighteenth century, urbane and affluent members of urban society were moved, therefore, to create for themselves a new environment, suburbia, between the confinements of the city and the feared deprivations of village life.

Behind this project were new urbane visions of the rural setting altered with the aid of artifice. The early invocations of rustic life as a corrective for urban ills represented the rural setting as a fantastic place, a mythical other world. After seeing a London production of Shakespeare's *A Midsummer Night's Dream* at the King's Theatre in 1662, Samuel Pepys denounced the bucolic fantasy as 'the most insipid ridiculous play that ever I saw in my life'.[12] The seventeenth-century notion of the 'poetic arcadia' of the rural 'landskip' was an idealised moral metaphor, not a place of habitation. By the eighteenth century, technical devices, tinted mirrors, foil-encrusted scopes and frames, were used by tourists and amateur painters to transform, in their vision, 'mere geology and vegetation' into 'picturesque' landscape.[13] Whereas earlier urbane representations of the rural setting had been invitations to the imagination, the product of urbane rusticators of the mid-eighteenth century, who actually took up residence outside cities, was an altered landscape made suitable for their habitation. Ornaments and furnishings in the 'japanned' style, for example, were common in Bristol homes throughout the urban renaissance but were not seen in the farmhouses and cottages of villagers.[14] Follies and architectural ornaments in an Asian style became so fashionable among the new bourgeois suburbanites that William Chambers published a guide to the subject in 1757. The rising popularity of Asian forms in the developing suburbs distressed William Gilpin, a more traditional defender of the rustic aesthetic, who remarked that 'above all ornaments we are disgusted with the Chinese'.[15] Suburbia, in general, introduced bourgeois taste and values to the rural environs of cities to such an extent that it gave rise to an entirely new setting.

The development of extramural suburbia was not the first concerted alteration of the English rural landscape by any means. Medieval and early modern forest management by the crown and its aristocratic clients left ancient woodlands so appallingly decimated that John Evelyn, with the blessing of the Royal Navy, pleaded in *Silva* for the careful stewardship of trees under the Restoration.[16] But the sweeping harvest of timber, for houses and ships, was the extraction of resources from the countryside, not the merger of urban and rural dwellers in a new setting. During the eighteenth century, few members of the aristocracy and gentry developed suburban parcels for transplanted members of the urban middle classes. The traditional rural elite, identifying with the noble qualities of the great English oak, engaged in patriotic reforestation on a grand scale befitting their station.[17] Agriculture, of course, had altered the countryside thousands of years before the growth of extramural suburbia.[18] The rural setting was not nature without culture; on the contrary, the lives of villagers had always been guided by rustic values, aesthetics and affinities as expressed through a range of cultural forms.

The use of land for agricultural purposes clearly conformed to rustic values, affinities, and, arguably, aesthetics. In a rural settlement parcels used in agriculture, whether they were farmed by freeholders or copyholders, were interspersed so that no one person's holdings were consolidated in one location.[19] These customary patterns of land tenure, resembling patchwork quilts, raised some awkward issues concerning trespass and access but obviated greater concern that flood, fire, wandering livestock or soil exhaustion in one cluster of parcels would wipe out any one farmer's entire crop. This practice was observed even by those gentlemen whose holdings exceeded hundreds of acres, provided these were preserved as active farms.[20] By contrast, in 1766 the Smyths of Ashton Court hired Benjamin Donne, the published cartographer of Bristol, to survey sixteen parcels amounting to only fifty acres in the neighbouring village of Bedminster, Somerset, bordering directly on the city of Bristol. These parcels ranged in size from only one to four acres and were let to eight different tenants, all of whom held contiguous, as opposed to interspersed, plots.[21] The holdings acquired by transplanted urbanites tended to be consolidations of contiguous plots. According to one value system, land was to be managed for agricultural productivity, while in another value system it was to be domesticated as a retreat.

When the rural environs of cities became subject to suburban development, the cultural product was contested ground on which urbane horticulturalists encountered rustic agriculturalists. Although the former were closely associated with learned institutions and the formal discipline of natural history, a working farmer, even in a year of high crop yields, would have been hard pressed to take seriously Batty Langley's anguished query of 1728: 'Is there anything more shocking than a stiff regular garden?'[22] To comply with the romantic notion that humans could be inserted comfortably into wilderness after all, the 'rude wildernesses' extolled by suburban gardeners had to be artistic creations providing the satisfying appearance of natural confusion, a 'polite kind of rudeness'.[23] It was not the villagers themselves who transformed villages into modern suburbia, it was bourgeois escapists tied to nearby cities.[24]

In view of the late eighteenth-century movement to romanticise the rural landscape, not on its own terms but as the inviting object of urbane creativity, we need to recognise that rustication – a flight from urbanisation – played an essential role in urban–rural convergence. In the study of early modern England an emphasis normally placed on dramatic urban development sustains an old view: urban growth was that society's measure of progress and the urban setting was the locus of urban–rural convergence.[25] Villages should not be seen as communities that failed to urbanise. The dynamic influence of the rural setting, and the changing place of countryside in the English imagination, were profoundly experienced by urban and well as rural people. An entire thatched village, Blaise Hamlet, was created in Henbury, Gloucestershire, by a wealthy landowner who intended it as a retirement community for his servants in the early nineteenth century. This cult of the picturesque, a programmatic reversion to a more rustic aesthetic in the design and management of country homes and estates, was visible in the reconstruction of villages near Chippenham, Cambridgeshire, as early as 1696.[26] By the 1750s new country homes of the elite had moved away from Palladian symmetry and the earlier emphasis on gentility upstairs. Rather, old great houses and new suburban retreats incorporated more natural and organic forms which blended into the scenery as cottages had always done; 'nature was refreshing but no longer frightening'.[27] One English tourist and man of leisure, enthralled with his discovery of the rustic mentality, commented in the 1770s that 'a hog is a much more valuable piece of goods than a set of tea things'.[28] In June 1774 the vestry of St Philip and Jacob had its annual banquet not in a Bristol tavern but at the village inn of Almondsbury.[29] It is worth considering that this conversion to the rustic was every bit as significant as any rural imitation of urban taste, if not more so. After all, ambitious Bristolians, in their urban homes, aspired to achieve the effect of a manor house far more than even the most prosperous villagers imitated urban trends in sociability and material culture.

Attempts at conversion to genuine rusticity on the part of urbane individuals could be woefully unsuccessful. Migration out of the city, like migration into it, did not necessarily transform attitudes and affinities rooted in a place of origin. In the 1730s A. S. Catcott built himself a small country retreat and wrote in cheerful anticipation that he had 'enclosed a moderate plot of ground with walls, not more than ten minutes walk from my [Bristol] house, but completely situated in the country air, quite out of the smoke of the city, but in full view of it'.[30] Less than a year later, he discovered that life outside the city did not suit his mentality.

> As I promised to you, and proposed to myself, I got my country house, as soon as the holy days began; but it proved very unhappy for me that I did so. Instead of pursuing the affair in hand, I rose every morning so exceedingly disordered as renders one quite incapable or reading, writing or thinking.[31]

Among his urbane friends Catcott was not alone in these sentiments. William Stevens, who had become vicar of Coalbrookdale in Shropshire complained of his rural isolation: 'This is a miserable place ... I should be glad to have a letter from you, and collect all the news you can in your way, for it is a desolate place I live in now.'[32]

Some villagers consciously alienated urbane types who ventured into the countryside. Urbane people were out of place in the rural setting and, as such, were a nuisance to villagers. In 1695 Amos Trevelyan, a member of a respected old family in the village of Nettlecombe, Somerset, had a running battle with the new parson, a fellow whose training made him more fit for the pulpit than for the farm. 'The parson's mare in my wheat all night,' Trevelyan complained in June. But there was more to come over the following weeks: the parson's heifers were in and out of Trevelyan's clover; his horses were in the wheat three days in a row; the parson's seven 'butter cows' joined his other cattle after that; and in one day Trevelyan found in his crops twenty-six of the parson's stray ewes and lambs. Surely some members of the clergy had rural origins, but this urbane clergyman could tend a flock in the metaphorical sense only. By July, Trevelyan was fed up with his incompetent neighbour, but instead of dealing directly with the parson, Trevelyan herded the clergyman's cattle off to the hundred pound in Wellington.[33] The keeper of the George inn in the large village of Bruton, Somerset, became so annoyed with soldiers and sailors from Bristol that by early 1716 he refused to serve them, calling them 'a pack of rogues all'.[34] Rustic villagers became newly disenchanted with some activities once these became associated with the encroachment of urbane taste. In 1727 the aptly named village of Banwell, Somerset, prohibited horse racing, a crowded form of sociability attracting urban dwellers that has been identified as an expression of the urban renaissance.[35]

Urbane travellers were as unimpressed as they were unwelcome in the countryside, where they could scarcely imagine settling. In the late seventeenth century John Walker, a member of a wealthy Bristol and London family, suffered through a series of tours in the countryside of England, Scotland, and Wales.[36] Why Walker took these tours is somewhat of a mystery; rustic charm was entirely lost on him, as is evidenced by his reaction to typical village dwellings and hospitality.

> A lamentable poor village. Houses all covered with turf instead of thatch. It is noted for a medicinal well a mile distant. The whole town would afford no provender for our horses. We were constrained to buy a little coarse malt and boil it. We were a little diverted by a prattling landlady.

He referred to country folk as 'poor creatures' and 'ill-favoured jades', and he avoided staying in their villages, preferring the hospitality of gentry friends. (He did, however, keep his horse in villages along the way.) On at least one occasion he had no choice and wound up trapped in a village, 'a miserable place [where] we lodged in a sow room upon straw beds [with] no window for any light'. Such solitary excursions by urban dwellers moving warily through the rural setting were accompanied by a new trend by the mid-eighteenth century. Enterprising developers transformed alien rural environs to accommodate the affinities, and imaginings, of rusticating citizens. These developments affected the movement of urbanites to suburbia in ways tourism had not.

Caleb Dickinson was typical of the urbane developers of the suburban landscape, although he was almost certainly more unsavoury than others. Dickinson, who started out as a soapmaker in Bristol, made his fortune, like so many other Bristol merchants in his day, at an alarming rate in the Atlantic rum and slave trade. In the 1740s, at a time when almost fifty slave ships sailed out of Bristol every year, slave traders made £8,000 profit for each shipment of African slaves.[37] In 1746 Dickinson moved his Bristol residence from Castle Green, in the old part of the city above the quays, to the fashionable St James's Square, a more recently developed neighbourhood noted for its park-like quality. Naturally, he owned a coach. He conducted most of his business in Bristol, where all his clothes were tailor-made and where he kept a substantial running tab with his apothecary.[38] His business correspondence – from London, Amsterdam, Lisbon, St Petersburg, Virginia, and Jamaica – arrived exclusively at his Bristol address. By 1746 Dickinson was also living in his newly acquired stately home in Kingsweston, Somerset. This was twenty-five miles from Bristol, an inconvenient distance, and altogether too rural. Even some of the wealthiest people once found it difficult to get about in the countryside. In 1666 Henry Walrond had written apologetically to John Pyne, another gentleman in rural Somerset, 'my sister ... will not adventure on horseback she being a very heavy woman and ye ways very dangerous'.[39] Dickinson did not plan to live stranded in the coutryside as others before him had.

Beginning in 1740, Dickinson toured the West of England taking note of the best roads and the most promising places to develop, not only for his own habitation but for profit.[40] His keen awareness of what would draw enchanted urbanites to suburban developments more than compensated for his lack of natural affinity for the rural setting. Of the village of Newport he snorted, 'nothing remarkable but an old castle belonging to the Berkeleys ... the manor ... subsists on the passage of strangers from Bristol to Gloucester ... has three publick houses of tolerable entertainment'. The entertainment was tolerable enough for Dickinson to spend 13s 9d in one afternoon there, close to what a servant would have taken three weeks to earn. He was generally unimpressed with the rural landscape and all the villages sprinkled in his path. 'Hardwicke, a little inconsiderable village ... gives little to the chancellor.' He described his trip through Shropshire as 'forty miles of unpleasant country abounding with heather'. Of Derbyshire he wrote, 'very wild ... here are no hedges for fence but the fields are divided by stone walls built holey for the wind to pass through or else they would never stand in this bleak country'. The Lancashire coutryside was no good because it was 'extreme sandy and troublesome for wheeled carriages'. Indeed, Dickinson's assessment of countryside was based, in part, on how easily one could fence off bits of it or pass through it.

Dickinson was interested in spaces with development potential in or near cities. In his view, villages were not places to enjoy for their closeness to nature; they were potential sources of revenue to be drawn into an urban sphere of influence. He made lengthy entries in his account about potential tourist traps near cities and towns. Sites associated with animism and pagan religions, which had captured the imagination of the fashionable public, looked promising. Dickinson paid for a tour through 'The Devil's Arse', a series of caves about fifteen miles from Manchester. This very same spot, which he compared to Wookey Hole near Bristol, also caught the attention of more learned surveyors John Walker and Alexander Catcott on completely separate occasions. He was certainly right about trends in attractions. The haunted Ostrich Inn and 'Druidical stones' appeared as landmarks in the

1769 edition of Benjamin Donne's printed guide map to Bristol and its environs.[41] Dickinson was also interested in spa development. He was generally unimpressed with Buxton, near Manchester, but thought it had potential.

> Buxton, situated between some hills, though not enough to screen it from the cold air – very bad. And no house that looks tolerable ... Then those of less figure – the sauciness of the servants, the extortion of the housekeepers and others one has to do withall – is cause of much wonder that anyone stays unto [this place] for pleasure. But I think the curiosity of the water is well worth seeing.

Upon investigation of the 'blood warm' baths there, Dickinson pronounced the waters to be 'very pleasant'. Near Leeds, Dickinson looked into Harrogate, where he noted 'there are springs famed for their mineral and medicinal qualities', but he dismissed the place because the sulphur waters smelled 'like rotten eggs' for miles around.

While investigating Matlock Wells near Chesterfield, another potential site for spa development, Dickinson visited Chatsworth, the great house of the Duke of Devonshire. The duke's sociability centred on Chesterfield and he became a celebrated host of urban elites in the assembly rooms there in the 1750s.[42] Dickinson's reaction to Chatsworth and its grounds was unlike his reaction to the countryside in which it was set.

> A good house pleasantly in a vale and makes a splendid figure with the wilderness ... It could be called a new building – it's only a new case to the old palace that stood here formerly ... nor is there anything uncommon attractive in the whole but the fine cascade of waterworks.

His emphasis was on the newness of the improvements, on the engineering involved, and on the system of fountains, a mechanical contrivance. While gazing across the groomed estate at Chatsworth he formed the odd impression that 'the place itself is very romantic and rural', with 'delightful views' and 'shady walks for company'. After his departure, however, while passing through the twenty miles of the rural territory leading to Sheffield, he complained of the journey 'from Chatsworth through very unpleasant counrty'. The very same land that Dickinson viewed with pleasure as a 'romantic' landscape became 'unpleasant' countryside as soon as Dickinson experienced it outside the context of the convivial duke's renovated estate. Although Dickinson described Stockport, Birmingham, and Preston as 'pretty' towns, he never used the word 'pretty' to describe a rural scene; instead, he applied the term 'romantic' to places where buildings and landscaping had civilised nature. As if to summarise the formula, an urbane tourist of the 1770s said tersely of a Somerset stately home he admired, 'art, nature, taste ... elegant'.[43]

By 1774 Dickinson had a finger in every pie offering a slice of suburban development near Bristol, in turnpike development, spa development, and enclosures. In 1774 he was poised to execute a plan that would revive a spa in

Clifton, a developing suburb between the city of Bristol and the spectacular Avon gorge. In the middle decades of the eighteenth century, leafy Clifton had become a desirable residential area for Bristol's commercial and professional classes. Over this period of time, Dickinson shrewdly acquired seemingly unattractive parcels – mainly grazing land – in the former manor between the city and the river. At a single stroke, through strategic awareness of the Hotwells spa, an attraction to urban tourists, Dickinson ensured the importance of the urban–rural artery passing directly in front of four rapidly appreciating roadside acres already in his possession.[44]

The acquisition of suburbia was an urbane initiative. In 1778, with the manor vacant in the village of Brislington bordering directly on the city, a group of affluent Bristolians seeking investment property formed an agreement to enclose and subdivide Brislington common. The development reconfigured the land into consolidated, as opposed to interspersed, lots of sizes appropriate neither to farming nor to parkland of interest to the gentry.[45] The new proprietors of Brislington common subdivided it into suburban parcels for their own residential purposes or for rent. The commissioners of the enclosure (Thomas Symes, Robert Wright, and William Blackborrow) were not residents of the village at all. Although they were not among the proposed proprietors of the Brislington enclosure, the commissioners had already acquired holdings individually in the nearby villages of Chewton Mendip, East Harptree and Downend. No resident squire was among the proposed proprietors. Instead, this group consisted of strange bedfellows: the Duke of Chandos; James Colston of the famously wealthy Bristol Colstons; John Dolman, the incumbent rector of St Luke's, Brislington; two Bristol clergymen (John Hughes and Sydenham Teast); and the overseers of the poor of Keynsham, whose large village had already been engulfed topographically by the Bristol conurbation. One of the tenants on the subdivisions came to 'occupy a certain close of ground called Hawkins Grove belonging to Mr Sydenham Teast as lessee under the mayor, burgesses and commonality of the City of Bristol'. At the time the deal was closed, the Bristol corporation acquired Hawkins Grove from John Pullen, who was handsomely compensated in the arrangement, with proprietorial rights over an access road through the new subdivisions connecting them with 'the turnpike road which leads from Bath to Bristol'.

In 1740, after a Mr S. T. Wylde of Bristol had acquired a house and land in 'Busselton' (by which he meant Brislington), he engaged as his surveyor a Mr Halfpenny, the Bristol architect who would go on to publish the plans of the Bristol Exchange.[46] Halfpenny did identify the sizes of parcels, but unlike farmers and rural estate managers, whose surveys labelled parcels according to what grew or grazed upon them, Halfpenny was interested in showing the location of Wylde's holding in relation to the urban network. Whereas farmers labelled their fields by name, Halfpenny indicated roads by name. Moreover, he named roads as a resident of Bristol, not Brislington, would view them: 'the Wells road' to the Somerset cathedral city and, revealingly, 'the Busselton road' from Bristol. Halfpenny amply illustrated the survey, unlike any farmer's survey, with vehicles, including a post coach, or perhaps a private coach, with its team of horses at full pace on a road conveniently running by the property.

The ownership of small farms, disturbed by other forms of development, was changing in this period through urban channels by which suburbanisers could acquire moderate rural holdings for recreational and residential purposes in close proximity to their urban centres of employment. One sign that Bristol newspapers had become promoters of urban–rural convergence was their eventual use to advertise the sale of land in the possession of rural dwellers. On 31 December 1742 John Elton, Esq., a rural gentleman in 'the county of Gloucester', advertised the availability of 'Ashley Farm consisting of 140 acres of meadow, arable and pasture land, well watered, wooded, having a good farmhouse and other conveniences within one mile of Bristol'. He presented the proximity of country and city as an attractive feature. The advertisement appeared in the *Oracle; or, Bristol Weekly Miscellany* just as it changed its name to the *Bristol Oracle and Country Intelligencer*. The revised representation of the rural setting as a financially and logistically accessible retreat appealed to a broader cross-section of urban dwellers dissatisfied with growing cities but unwilling to sustain their quality of life away from them.

There were distinctions between the customary role of a local squire and the aims of an urban middle-class developer in his newly acquired rural retreat. At his new Kingsweston home, Dickinson hardly exhibited aspirations of paternalism. He was not a pacifying figure earnestly adjudicating disputes or visibly co-operating with parish officials. He was not engaged in the management of a rural community, the cultivation of its land, or the supervision of local villagers, apart from using them as casual labour to mow his hay.[47] All the renovation of his newly acquired house and grounds in Kingweston was done by Bristol workers, as his accounts also show. Dickinson's occupation was the conduct of West Indies trade, which financed his speculative development of suburban land. He acquired land in the Somerset villages of Lydford, Babcary, and Congresbury as well as Kingsweston. When urban developers acquired land in more than one village, as they often did, tenants fell under the power of absentee landlords who had no social grounding in these village communities. Dickinson was on very poor terms with his rural neighbours and tenants. In January 1747 Dickinson ordered the tythingman to apprehend two women who gathered wood on his land; he demanded 10s from each of them and insisted that they should be 'publickly whipped' in Kingsweston.[48]

The first order of business for Dickinson as a suburban developer was to pressure working farmers into eviction. Early in Dickinson's programme of suburban expansion he began to accelerate the collection of debts from his new tenants. In the case of at least one debtor, Dickinson left him without any means of operating a farm. On 22 September 1746 Dickinson's agent, John Norton, drew up a list of 'goods taken in distress for rent due at Lady Day 1746 to Caleb Dickinson, Esquire, for an estate in East Lydford'. On two occasions that summer, Norton sold confiscated goods, including tools, livestock, and personal items, at auction, thus humiliating as well as ruining tenants. In December 1746, the same month that Dickinson laid out £2 to a Bristol wig maker, he welched on a debt owed to William Reeves, whose goods he had just confiscated a few months earlier. At the end of the year Reeves wrote to Dickinson, begging to be paid for wood he had cut and delivered. 'Pray be so good as to send that little som [sic], for every shilling to me is very precious ... sir, you no [sic] very well the goods ... and I hope you will be so good as to see me justice done.'[49]

The contentious aspects of suburban development may have had less to do with nascent class antagonism than with collective identities and social divisions based on setting. There is much to be said for the argument that patricians, by privatising land that had once been treated as a communal resource, abdicated their paternalistic role and the right to exact orderly deference along with it.[50] To be sure, local gentry families, such as the Smyths and Southwells, participated in the eighteenth-century enclosure trend near Bristol. The Southwells created a deer park bounded by enclosed orchards, pastures, and fields that were all productively, but privately, managed.[51] The Smyths of Ashton Court even acquired and consolidated smaller parcels suitable for suburban development near Bristol in the 1760s.[52] Nevertheless, long-standing rural residents of all social stations also co-operated to oppose the encroachment of suburban development. Village communities took these pre-emptive acts, which combined enclosure and customary rights, in odd but defensive ways, at the very time village life was becoming threatened by urban topographical expansion.

Between 1770 and 1773 in the Somerset village of Nempnett Thrubwell, in close proximity to Bristol, the resident lord of the manor, Sir Charles Kernys Tynte, and a village gentleman, Henry Hellier, drew up a set of remarkable 'articles of agreement' on the enclosure and allotment of the old common in co-operation with the village yeomen and tenants.[53] Some yeomen and squires of nearby villages were included among the agreed proprietors of Nempnett Thrubwell. All the current tenants in the village, regardless of social status, were named as proprietors in the articles and awarded right of common on designated parcels, including the waste. In 1773 a formal petition to the crown and Parliament for enclosure in the village of Ubley, Somerset, was initiated by the resident lord and lady of the manor, William and Frances Pulteney, on behalf of themselves and the residents of the manor, including the incumbent rector, all named as proprietors in the proposed act.[54] This petition, which was twenty-four printed pages in length, identified a commission of villagers to hear claims of proprietorship. Page 6 clearly stated that 'every person or persons not being proprietors of lands within the said manor and parish of Ubley neglecting or refusing to give or deliver in such claims at the said first or second meeting of the said commissioners, or any two of them, shall be totally excluded from all estate, right and interest within the said boundaries'.

The prevention of suburban practices clearly became a priority among village co-operatives. The Ubley manor articles declared 'rack rents', or short-term leases, to be void. Rack rents increased elsewhere in the eighteenth century as new land developers acquired and subdivided rural land and established terms favourable to themselves as landlords.[55] The general act at Ubley stipulated that the maintenance of existing roads through the manor was to be assigned to proprietors in the parish and that no alterations or additions in roadways would be permitted. The absentee enclosers of Brislington conducted 'exchanges'; they swapped small parcels among themselves to place contiguous plots under the control of indivvual proprietors. This was a suitable strategy for purely residential development, the intention of the investors. But, as any village farmer would have known, this suburban pattern would actively discourage farming there by violating the customary cultivation strategy designed to protect any one farmer from higly localised causes of crop failure. No such plot 'exchanges' were permitted in the village agreements. The covenant at Nempnett Thrubwell also called for a common 'oxen shut' and grazing paddock. These manoeuvres to preserve customary arrangements in the face of potential suburban encroachment were remarkable not only for the ostensibly harmonious class relations involved but for their specifically rural appeal as well.

Suburban developers were not especially interested in operating farms communally or otherwise. John Hippesley Coxe, Dickinson's collaborator in one of his early turnpike schemes, assured him that the objections they would encounter from the rural interest were 'only the general ones in husbandry, pasture, and water', areas of concern to tenants, farmers, and the managers of the larger agricultural estates, not to suburban developers.[56] There is also indirect evidence that the suburban value system, which altered patterns of land use in villages near urban areas, eventually diminished agricultural productivity. Between 1650 and 1750 England was a major exporter of agricultural produce, with grain exports reaching their peak at the end of that period. In the late eighteenth century a decline in the product of arable land was already detectable, while domestic demand increased. By the early decades of the nineteenth century, despite one good crop in 1813, England had begun to import more agricultural produce than it could export, making the imposition of protective import duties on grain a highly volatile issue.[57] At the very least, the rise of modern suburbia coincided with this dramatic shift in agricultural production. Without doubt, suburban development sowed the seeds of a new settlement pattern displaying uses of land that were questionable, and perhaps objectionable, from the rustic point of view. Many suburbanites interested in meeting their own needs still maintained small orchards and cultivated a parcel or two of land, but their strongest occupational ties were with nearby urban centres rather than with the land on which they lived.

Suburbia, a site of urban–rural convergence beginning in the mid-eighteenth century, was neither urban nor rural. It was not a centre for the manufacture and exchange of goods and services. It was not a lively location of the major institutions of learning and government. Suburbia was not an agriculturally productive use of land. The reinvention of bucolic space as a bourgeois commodity, and its appropriation for urbane forms of recreation and social display, were not the work of farmers imitating urban life. At times even the aims of enclosing gentry were consciously opposed to those of suburban developers of urban origin. The aim of suburbanites was not to insulate themselves within rural surroundings; their aim was to make their rural retreats an extension of their urban world. Those urban dwellers of means who were readily drawn to the bourgeois reinvention of the countryside not only contributed to the transformation of village settlements, they promoted the merger of urban and rural social spheres in an entirely new context.

The story of William Dyer, who wrote extensively about his movements in and around Bristol's rural environs, is illustrative.[58] Dyer was usually accompanied by any one of a number of different people in his visits to local villages and towns, so it seems safe to say that many urban dwellers of his day got about as he did. In the 1750s Dyer was an accountant and manager in a Bristol gunpowder company. He was given more and more responsibility in his job. This involved a good deal of travel, including more frequent trips to London, which he enjoyed. He hiked well beyond Bristol's rural environs. On at least one occasion he set out on foot for the cathedral city of Wells, where he visited his brother-in-law.[59] He moved about the local villages on a regular basis and in one day, travelling on horseback, he did business in Clifton, Littleton, and Nailsea, returning to St James in Bristol some time after eight o'clock that night.[60] He undertook frequent excursions into the local countryside for pleasure, to enjoy the landscape, or to look for ancient monoliths.[61] His early trips were on foot or astride a single hired or borrowed horse with another rider,[62] but eventually he enjoyed some upward mobility and good fortune of his own. In June 1762, as a guest at a friend's elaborate party, he dined across the table from the mayor of Bristol. That same month he bought his own horse, which allowed him and his wife to visit the new homes of their friends in the surrounding countryside at a moment's notice.[63]

Dyer's social interaction in the nearby villages became more frequent as many of his Bristol acquaintances – attorneys, physicians, ship's captains, and members of the clergy – took up residence in the villages of Stapleton, Shirehampton, and Clifton, not far from, or bordering directly on, the city.[64] On Sundays Dyer walked from his home in Bristol to Keynsham, Westbury, or Kingswood to attend morning church services with friends who lived in those nearby villages.[65] In 1756, when St George, formerly part of rural Gloucestershire, was absorbed by the city of Bristol, he attended the consecration of its new church and later hoped that an ordained friend of his would angle for the position there.[66] The Dyers were visited in Bristol on occasion by their friends, the Reverend and Mrs Symes, who had acquired a private chaise carriage after their short move from the city to Clifton.[67]

Clifton was among the very first villages in the vicinity of Bristol to become an extramural suburb. Urban merchants and investors had bought the manor of Clifton outright in the late seventeenth century and developed a spa there.[68] It is a measure of the importance of conscious attitudes to urban–rural interaction that the earliest suburbs in Bristol's environs appeared in lapsed manors where a rustic interest was no longer powerfully represented by resident gentry. Clifton, the attractive suburb that Dickinson recognised as so promising, became the location of closely spaced, but graciously free-standing, homes of affluent Bristol slave traders. Despite its bucolic appeal, Clifton had become more of a customer than a supplier of Bristol markets by contemporary accounts.[69] By the 1750s professionals were leaving Bristol and establishing residence in Clifton as its development spread toward the urban landscape. At some point Dyer's own brother moved to Clifton, where he died in 1764.[70]

Dyer worked for some time towards acquiring a home of his own in the developing suburbs just outside the city. He had become distraught with life in the city and was drawn to the residential areas just beyond its confines. As more and more of his friends were finding houses for themselves within a comfortable distance of Bristol, Dyer grew to see life in the city as exasperating. In December 1758 he was forced by the need of repairs to remove the windows from the parlour of his house in St James. He did not complain at all about the wintry blast, but fretted that while his windows were missing from the house he and his wife lived in 'danger of nightly depredators'.[71] He was annoyed, even horrified, by the recklessly driven waggons with which the city had become congested. In June 1758 Dyer was moved to write at length about a 'poor woman' who was crushed to death beneath a waggon on the old Bristol Bridge, where, after the rising popularity of private coaches, 'people are sometimes the greater part of an hour in getting from one end to the other'. In the following year, Dyer was nearly killed himself under the same circumstances at St Nicholas Gate.[72] It is no surprise that, not long after Dyer negotiated a salary increase for himself, he and his family moved from Bristol to the village of Littleton, Somerset.[73] The Dyers left this more remote rural home in favour of something closer to Bristol a year or so later when William established his own company. When the Dyers relocated they moved closer to Bristol but not into it. By May 1777 they too had their own chaise, which they used to travel back and forth between their home in Carolina Court, Knowle, Somerset, and Bristol, a mile or so away.

The Dyers did not simply escape to Bristol's rural environs, they contributed to a larger transformation of those environs in the second half of the eighteenth century. They had discovered that urbane sociability could be accommodated in the rural setting. For many, suburbia gratified a positive urge to live outside the confines of a city in open surroundings where residents could remain occupationally tied to a nearby urban centre. Of course, there were exceptions. Somewhat mysteriously, tailors and carpenters, who were quite numerous in seventeenth-century villages, appear to have removed themselves from the extramural scene during the period of suburban development. Cordwainers and weavers had been well represented in both settings before, as well as after, the development of extramural suburbia. Major merchants populated the new suburbs while shopkeepers and smaller merchants remained resolutely urban. On the other hand, victuallers, who moved outward from cities into those nearby villages through which the major roads and turnpikes ran, were clearly among those whose new settlement patterns contributed to suburban development.[74]

It seems beyond doubt that the evolution of England's provincial suburbs benefited many more likable Dyers than despicable Dickinsons. Although many new suburbanites were not engaged primarily in agriculture, not all early suburban growth displaced traditional farms. Suburbs developed with less resistance in agriculturally marginal areas that were attractive to people of urban origin for reasons of their own. The houses of suburban dwellers were insulated from one another by plots large enough to provide privacy, recreational space, and aesthetic possibilities. As James Jenkins saw for himself, suburbia was the relocation of affluence. Unlike most villagers, suburbanites were luxury consumers whose dwellings imitated the shapes, sizes, and specialised social arrangements of the large urban homes from which many suburbanites came. John Hewett, who set himself up as a victualler in Alveston, near the Gloucester road, some time before 1768, had in his home there paintings, mirrors, eighteen printed pictures, French brandy, and over £23 worth of coffee cups, china service, and silver for the 'dining room' and 'parlour'. Hewett extended more than £160 of credit to thirty-two different people.[75] Suburbanites, like religious dissenters, bridged and broadened social spheres. The role of late eighteenth-century suburbia in the eventual demise of guilds and old parish poor laws is difficult to determine; many suburbanites were still freemen of cities. Nevertheless, by operating legitimately in two settings, suburbanites did mediate the topographical divide and transcend the localism of corporate and parochial institutions. In suburbia the bourgeois cult of rusticity achieved an appropriation of rural space for the expression of urbane material and social values.

The transformation of villages near English provincial cities and towns in the second half of the eighteenth century anticipated a model setting as embraced by a distinctly modern set of values. These values were vindicated by their ascendance in the nineteenth and twentieth centuries.

> Advocates of the ... suburban idyll ... presented carpets of front-yard lawns, undivided by fences, as an expression of social solidarity and community, the imagined antidote to metropolitan alienation. The designation of the suburban yard as a cure for the afflictions of city life marks the greensward as a remnant of an old pastoral dream, even though its goatherds and threshers have been replaced.[76]

The development of a distinctly suburban society and culture in provincial England marked the end of the early modern period and anticipated modern suburban development in far more expansive settings. The area outside London, which underwent suburban growth in the seventeenth century, was the early exception. The development of extramural suburbia around English manufacturing centres took place even later than it did in Bristol's environs.[77] The extent to which the long-standing divisions between urban and rural society and culture persisted throughout most of the early modern urban renaissance was reflected in the delayed evolution of the extramural suburban landscape. When we picture William Dyer in his cummuter life style, and coaches clogging congested city streets and terrorising hapless pedestrians, the recognition of modern parallels seems more plausible. The resettlement of urban dwellers outside of cities, rather than the movements of rural dwellers inside them, was the modernising dynamic. The convergence of urban and rural worlds, which took place in provincial England a century or so after the urban renaissance got under way, was a development for which rustication and extraparochialism were responsible.

## NOTES

1  B. Little, *The City and County of Bristol: A Study in Atlantic Civilization* (London, 1954), p. 146.

2  J. W. Frost (ed.), *The Records and Recollections of James Jenkins 1753–1831* (Lewiston, N.Y., 1984), p. 102–3. James Jenkins (1753–1831) was a prosperous Quaker merchant who kept an extensive personal journal. I should like to thank Dr Thomas Hamm for the use of the Friends' Collection of Earlham College, including its copy of this limited edition of Jenkins's 'recollections'.

3  D. M. George, *London Life in the Eighteenth Century* (London, 1925; 3rd ed., Chicago, 1984), pp. 81 and 116–7.

4  Daniel Defoe, *A Tour through the Whole Island of Great Britain* (1724–26), ed. P. Rogers (Harmondsworth, 1971), pp. 89–90.

5  B.R.O. Probate Inventories (J. Saunders, 1727).

6  B.R.O. #9728(2), Diary of Francis Creswicke (1674). This is Creswicke's record of his tenants and holdings in the village of Bitton, Gloucestershire. See also B.R.O. AC/PL 5, Survey of a Dairy Farm in Chew Magna, Somerset (1737); B.R.O. #30120(1) Plans #232A, Survey of a Farm in the Parish of Busselton [Brislington], Somerset (*c.* 1740). For the persistence of the one-acre rural house plot in the heart of nucleated villages in the later eighteenth century, see B.R.O. AC/PL 8, Survey of sundry Fields belonging to William Brown and Matthew, esquires, in Bedminster, Somerset (1766).

7  E. P. Thompson, *Whigs and Hunters: The Origins of the Black Act* (New York, 1975).

8  B.R.O. #12154, Schedule of Southwell and Miles: Deeds of Kingsweston, Lawrence Weston, Henbury, Shirehampton (1627–1777); B.R.O. #26570, Isaac Taylor: Maps of Several Estates Belonging to Ed. Southwell, Esq., in the Tithings of Kingsweston and Lawrence Weston in the parish of Henbury and also of Shirehampton in the Parish of Westbury-on-Trym, Gloucestershire (1772).

9  L. Manley, 'From matron to monster: Tudor-Stuart London and the languages of urban description', in H. Dubrow and R. Strier (eds), *The Historical Renaissance: New Essays in Tudor and Stuart Literature and Culture* (Chicago, 1988), pp. 347–74; S. B. Ortner, 'Is female to male as nature is to culture?', in M. Z. Rosaldo and L. Lamphere (eds), *Women, Culture, and Society* (Stanford, Cal., 1974), p. 73; M. Byrd, *London Transformed: Images of the City in the Eighteenth Century* (Yale, 1978), p. 19.

10  Defoe, *A Tour through the Whole Island of Great Britain*, p. 288; Daniel Defoe, *The Complete English Tradesman* (London, 1727), II, pt. 2, p. 108. For more on the shifting of urbane attitudes to the countryside see K. Thomas, *Man and the Natural World: Changing Attitudes in England 1500–1800* (Harmondsworth, 1984), pp. 243–54.

11  J. Archer, '*Rus in urbe*: classical ideas of country and city in British town planning', *Studies in Eighteenth-Century Culture* 12 (1983), pp. 159–86; M. Girouard, *The English Town: A History of Urban Life* (New Haven, Conn., 1990), pp. 162–6 and 267–9; John Stewart, *Critical Observations on the Buildings and Improvements of London* (London, 1771), as cited in Girouard, *The English Town*, p. 166.

12  Samuel Pepys, *Diary*, ed. R. Latham (Berkeley, Cal., 1983), p. 45.

13  S. Schama, *Landscape and Memory* (New York, 1995), pp. 10–11. An early modern treatment of landscape imagery as a fantastic 'moral corrective' cited by Schama is: Henry Peacham, *Rura mihi et Silentium* (1612).

14  B.R.O. probate inventory (1685) of Anthony Lane, a mariner in St Mary Redcliffe, provides one of the earlier references to furnishings in the 'japanned' style.

15  William Chambers, *Designs of Chinese Buildings* (1757). William Gilpin is quoted in Schama, *Landscape and Memory*, p. 137.

16  John Evelyn, *Silva, or, A Discourse of Forest-Trees* (1664), cited in Schama, *Landscape and Memory*, pp. 153–62.

17  Batty Langley, *Sure Method of Improving Estates by Plantations of Oak* (1728); James

Wheeler, *The Modern Druid* (1743); Roger Fisher, *Heart of Oak: The British Bulwark* (1763); John Evelyn, *Silva* (1776 edition), all cited in Schama, *Landscape and Memory*, pp. 163–74.

18  L. White, 'The historical roots of our ecological crisis', *Science* 155 (10 March 1967), pp. 1203–7, identifies the seventh-century introduction of the harnessed plough as the watershed in the transformation of agriculture from harmonious with nature to abusive of it. For more general discussions of the impact of technology on rural ecology see C. Merchant, *Radical Ecology: The Search for a Livable World* (London, 1992), pp. 41–59; V. Ferkiss, *Nature, Technology and Society: Cultural Roots of the Current Ecological Crisis* (London, 1993); D. Rothenberg, *Hand's End: Technology and the Limits of Nature* (Berkeley, Cal., 1993).

19  B.R.O. #30120(1) and B.R.O. #AC/PL 6, Plan of Whitewoods Farm belonging to Mrs. Mary White in Norton Hawkefield, Chew Magna, and Dundry in Somerset (1752); B.R.O. #AC/PL 89(1), Plan of the parish and manor of Westerleigh, Gloucestershire (1772). For discussion of agricultural land tenure customs see M. Spufford, *Contrasting Communities: English Villagers in the Sixteenth and Seventeenth Centuries* (Cambridge, 1974), pp. 58–85, 94–104, 121–59; J. Thirsk, 'Enclosing and Engrossing', in J. Thirsk (ed.), *Agricultural Change: Policy and Practice 1500–1750* (Cambridge, 1990), pp. 54–66.

20  B.R.O. #AC/PL 5, Survey of a Dairy Farm in Chew Magna, Somerset (1737). This is a manuscript survey of the thirty-four parcels amounting to over 243 acres held by a Mr George Edwards on the estate of Buckler Weekes, Esq., and the six interspersed parcels amounting to more than twenty-four acres held by a Mr White on the same estate. The houses, it should be noted, were flanked by orchards but separated from one another by the largest arable parcels.

21  B.R.O. #AC/PL 8, A Survey of sundry Fields belonging to William Brown and Matthew Sewel, Esquires, in Bedminster (1766).

22  Langley is quoted in D. E. Allen, *The Naturalist in Britain: A Social History* (Princeton, N.J., 1994), p. 23. For more on the construed relationship between horticulture and agriculture see Thomas, *Man and the Natural World*, pp. 192–241 and 254–73; J. Thirsk, 'Agricultural innovations and their diffusion 1640–1750', in Thirsk, *Agricultural Change*, pp. 311–17; M. Leslie and T. Raylor (eds), *Culture and Cultivation in Early Modern England: Writing and the Land* (Leicester, 1992).

23  Batty Langley, *New Principles of Gardening* (London, 1728); Horace Walpole, *History of the Modern Taste in Gardening* (London, 2nd ed. 1782). These works and the concept of a 'polite kind of rudeness' are discussed in Schama, *Landscape and Memory*, pp. 538–41.

24  R. Fishman, *Bourgeois Utopias: The Rise and Fall of Suburbia* (New York, 1989) has discussed the bourgeois influence on modern suburbia during the modern period.

25  There is considerable room for debate on this point. The possibility that some cities were economic liabilities rather than assets has been raised in E. A. Wrigley, 'Parasite or stimulus? The town in a pre-industrial economy', in P. Abrams and E. A. Wrigley (eds), *Towns in Societies: Essays in Economic History and Historical Sociology* (Cambridge, 1978), pp. 295–309.

26  R. J. Brown, *The English Country Cottage* (London, 1979), pp. 37–46.

27  M. Girouard, *Life in the English Country House: A Social and Architectural History* (Harmondsworth, 1980), pp. 189–99 and 218–20.

28  A. Young, *Tour in Ireland* (1776–79). The 1892 edition, II, p. 40, is cited in George, *London Life in the Eighteenth Century*, p. 128.

29  B.R.O. P/StP&J/V/2, St Philip and Jacob: Minute Book (1723–1832), June 1774.

30  B.C.L. #B26063 SR43, Correspondence of Alexander Catcott: Letter of A. S. Catcott in Bristol to John Hutchinson in London (27 July 1733).

31  B.C.L. #B26063 SR43, Letter of Catcott to Hutchinson (23 June 1734).

32  B.C.L. #B26063 SR43, Letter of Stevens to Catcott (3 August 1751).

33  S.R.O. DD/WO/61/6, Diaries of Amos Trevelyan (1695).

34  S.R.O. Q/SR/276, Somerset Quarter Sessions (Epiphany, 1715/16), #7 and #9.

35  S.R.O. D/P/Ban./13/2/1, Banwell, Somerset Overseers Account Book (1711–38). For the rise of urbane horse racing at this very time see P. Borsay, *The English Urban Renaissance: Culture and Society in the Provincial Town 1660–1770* (Oxford, 1989), pp. 180–96 and 302–5.

36  S.R.O. DD/WHb/3087, John Walker's Travel Diary (1672–82).

37  S.R.O. DD/DN/197–198 and 201. For more on the profits of the Bristol slave trade see P. Fryer, *Staying Power: The History of Black People in Britain* (London, 1984), pp. 33–44; K. Morgan, *Bristol and the Atlantic Trade in the Eighteenth Century* (Cambridge, 1993), pp. 128–51.

38  S.R.O. DD/DN/206; DD/DN/204 and 211; DD/DN/205, 208, and 218. An inventory of Dickinson's Bristol home in 1746 is among the loose papers in S.R.O. DD/DN/203.

39  S.R.O. DD/CM/66(3).

40  S.R.O. DD/DN/230, Caleb Dickinson's Travel Diary (1740).

41  B.R.O. #247 BP210, *B. Donne's Map of the Country Eleven Miles round the City of Bristol* (1769). On ancient sites as a subject of study in popular romanticism, as opposed to the antiquarianism of Aubrey and Stukeley, see R. Hutton, *The Pagan Religions of the Ancient British Isles: Their Nature and Legacy* (Oxford, 1991), pp. 139–42 and 320; S. Piggott, The Druids (New York, 1994), pp. 123–82.

42  E. J. Climenson (ed.), *Passages from the Diaries of Mrs Lybbe Powys* (London, 1899), pp. 24–5 and 50, as cited in Girouard, *Life in the English Country House*, p. 190.

43  S.R.O. DD/DN/486, Fuller diary of a journey through the South-west from Kingswest, Gloucestershire (1776).

44  S.R.O. DD/DN/227, Scheme of proposed road near Clifton (March 1774).

45  S.R.O. Q/RDe.130, Enclosure at Brislington, Somerset, and the award of Brislington Common (1778).

46  B.R.O. #30120(1) and Bristol Plans #232A, Survey of a farm in the parish of Bussleton [Brislington] belonging to S. T. Wylde of Bristol, by W. Halfpenny (1740); B.R.O. #04713 and #26163, Plans for the Bristol Exchange and Markets by W. Halfpenny (1743).

47  S.R.O. DD/DN/203, An account of the haymaking in East Lydford (22 September 1746). Dickinson provided the labourers, most of whom were women working for 6d a day, with beer and cheese as well. But out of fifteen or so families used, only the Staceys (William and Elizabeth) were from Lydford, and it is not clear that they were Dickinson's tenants.

48 S.R.O. DD/DN/203, 209, 212, 213.

49 S.R.O. DD/DN/203, An Account of Farmer Wm. Reeves Goods (22 September 1746).

50 E. P. Thompson, 'Patrician society, plebeian culture', *Journal of Social History* 7 no. 4 (1974); *Whigs and Hunters*; 'Eighteenth-century English society: class struggle without class?' *Social History* 3 no. 2 (1978), pp. 133–65; D. Hay, 'Property, authority and the criminal law' and 'Poaching and the game laws on Cannock Chase', in D. Hay *et al.* (eds), *Albion's Fatal Tree: Crime and Society in Eighteenth-Century England* (New York, 1975).

51 B.R.O. MS #12154, Southwell and Miles: deeds of Kingsweston, Lawrence Weston, Henbury, and Shirehampton (1627–1777); B.R.O. #26570, Isaac Taylor's maps of several estates belonging to Ed. Southwell, esquire, in Gloucestershire (1772).

52 B.R.O. #AC/PL 8, A Survey of sundry Fields belonging to William Brown and Matthew Sewel, esquires, in Bedminster, [Somerset] (1766).

53 S.R.O. DD/X/HLL1/c341, Enclosure at Nempnett Thrubwell, Somerset (1770–73).

54 S.R.O. Q/RDe.62, Enclosure at Ubley, Somerset: map, act, and award (1773). The Ubley enclosure articles extended a special dispensation to the rectors of the parish allowing them to 'make leases with the consent of the bishop', using glebe lands.

55 C. Clay, 'Landlords and estate management in England 1640–1750', in C. Clay (ed.), *Rural Society: Landowners, Peasants and Labourers 1500–1750* (Cambridge, 1990), pp. 341–51.

56 S.R.O. DD/DN/210, Letter of John Hippesley Coxe to Caleb Dickinson at Kingweston (23 December 1752).

57 A. H. John, 'English agricultural improvement and grain exports 1660–1765', in D. C. Coleman and A. H. John (eds), *Trade, Government and Economy in Pre-Industrial England* (London, 1976); D. C. Coleman, *The Economy of England 1450–1750* (Oxford, 1977), pp. 121 and 177; A. Briggs, *The Age of Improvement 1783–1867* (London, 1980), pp. 201–4; M. E. Turner, 'Agricultural productivity in eighteenth-century England: further strains of speculation', *Economic History Review*, 2nd ser. 37 (1984), pp. 256–7; R. V. Jackson, 'Growth and deceleration in English agriculture 1660–1790', *Economic History Review*, 2nd ser. 38 (1985), pp. 333–51.

58 B.C.L. #20095 and #20096–7, William Dyer's Diary (1745–1801).

59 *Ibid.* (1 June 1751).

60 *Ibid.* (18 June 1762). See 31 July 1752 for an early visit to a company operation at Sea Mills just outside Bristol.

61 *Ibid.* (30 March 1752 and 23 April 1753).

62 *Ibid.* (18 May 1752), for example.

63 Dyer was riding his own horse by 18 June 1762. Six years earlier, on 3 January, he and his wife had ridden to Littleton on the back of a single horse which they had borrowed or hired.

64 *Ibid.* (18 May 1752, 9 September 1755, 3 January 1756 and 11 March 1761) provide examples.

65 *Ibid.* (28 October 1753, 5 February 1758 and 9 July 1758) provide examples.

66 *Ibid.* (6 September 1756).

67  *Ibid.* (29 July 1767).

68  Little, *The City and County of Bristol*, p. 320.

69  B.R.O. Bristol Quarter Sessions papers, bundle 4, Letter to Mr John Worrall attorney at law at Clifton near Bristol (1766).

70  B.C.L. #20095 and #20096–7, William Dyer's Diary (4 January 1764).

71  *Ibid.* (12 December 1758).

72  *Ibid.* (16 June 1758) and (6 September 1759).

73  B.C.L. #20095 and #20096–7. Dyer recorded his job change on 19 May 1767 and recorded the relocation of his family on 17 June 1767. Their new place of residence was probably Littleton, Somerset (near Glastonbury), rather than Littleton-on-Severn, Gloucestershire; on 3 September 1767 Dyer recorded that he had become eligible for the Somerset militia.

74  B.R.O. Probate Inventories. See also E. and S. George (eds), *Guide to the Probate Inventories of the Bristol Deanery of the Diocese of Bristol 1542–1804* (Bristol, 1988), occupational index.

75  B.R.O. Probate Inventories (John Hewett, 1768).

76  Schama, *Landscape and Memory*, p. 16.

77  J. R. Stilgoe, *Borderland: Origins of the American Suburb 1820–1939* (New Haven, Conn., 1988); G. R. Williams, *London in the Country: the Growth of Suburbia* (London, 1975); R. Dennis, *English Industrial Cities of the Nineteenth Century: A Social Geography* (Cambridge, 1984). For the occupational profile of Bristol and the geographical distribution of wealth in the city, indicative of the development of early suburbs in the late eighteenth century, see E. Baigent, 'Economy and society in eighteenth-century English towns: Bristol in the 1770s', in D. Denecke and G. Shaw (eds), *Urban Historical Geography: Recent Progress in Britain and Germany* (Cambridge, 1988), pp. 109–24.

# Conclusion

## Urbane and rustic England

The century or so following the Restoration is rightly associated with the so-called English urban renaissance, a widely recognised resurgence of cities and towns. Generally speaking, English cities and towns of this period enjoyed dramatic population growth, economic revitalisation, and renewed vigour as centres of conspicuous consumption, sociable recreation, and civic awareness. But villagers, even those who lived close to urban centres, were remarkably resistant to urban cultural influence during most of this period. Contrary to what we might suppose, villagers did not imitate urban trends; they preserved distinctly rustic patterns of settlement, sociability, consumption, and expression that persisted in the rural setting throughout most of the early modern period. The ties formed by direct personal interaction, material culture, and print culture maintained social spheres that were largely divided along topographical lines. Indeed, the abrupt topographical divide between provincial cities and the surrounding villages reflected a separateness of urban and rural worlds of which contemporaries themselves were explicitly aware. Moreover, this separateness complied with a normative view of community formation reinforced by laws, economic regulations, corporate institutions, religious beliefs, devotional practices, and the ubiquitous influence of the Anglican parish. In analysing the impact of urban growth on village life in early modern England we cannot fail to notice the historical grounding of locality and topographical setting as powerful bases of collective identity and consciousness.

There was very little evidence that the deliberately maintained social circles of urban and rural dwellers converged to any significant degree until nearly a century after the Restoration. Urban and rural interaction in courtship, markets, and places of work was rare, incidental, or even strained. Urban and rural dwellers exhibited different patterns of consumption and sociability. These differences were reflected in the abrupt and visible transition from one physical and domestic environment to the other. The gulf between urban and rural social practices, tastes and values was expressed in both the role and the explicit content of printed materials found in urban and rural homes. Social spheres were actively constructed, not just passively experienced. Thus the persistence of distinctly urban and rural worlds, in the face of demographic pressures, was not only the product of greater impersonal or natural forces; it was also the expression of conscious choices informed by cultural differences and affinities.

The version of the social sphere idealised in early modern England was neither especially urban nor especially rural. The ideal social sphere was formed out of life in the parish, in which spaces, resources, and ideas were all shared. That is, all people who engaged in direct personal interaction, by virtue of shared place of residence, work, recreation, and worship, should – according to the ideal – have the same material culture, conform to the same religious beliefs, and assume some shared responsibility for the material and moral well-being of their fellow parishioners. At no time or place was this ever achieved. Nevertheless, it was a powerful ideal inspired and sustained in large part by the ideology, administrative structures, and practices of the established church. The combined poor laws, settlement laws, and conformity and attendance laws following the English Reformation were the official endorsement of this ideal.[1] The ideal was buttressed by England's long history of independent civic charters, such as the one awarded Bristol in the late fourteenth century, and the Elizabethan legacy of an insular realm unified in defence of its faith and resources.

Authority figures clung to this vision of parishioners as members of a materially and culturally self-sufficient social sphere. Even near the end of the early modern period, Bristol's journalists and social commentators still embraced the ideal represented by the bees in their hive, a community in which carefully confined space, resources, and moral sensibility were shared.[2] In the 1680s Bristol's councils, constables, and mayors struggled to realise the ideal of social spheres based on both localism and religious uniformity in combination. Parish and corporation officials were mobilised to enforce attendance at parish churches and remove nonconformists from the ranks of city magistrates and parish poor alike. In 1681 Bristol's grand jury actually lodged a formal action against Sir John Knight and several aldermen for 'stigmatising and branding' the mayor and other prominent citizens 'with odious and ignominious names of papists'.[3] In Bristol, as in other cities, the official campaign against recusancy strangely included Quakerism as a target. The actual aim in purging the city of so-called recusancy was to protect Bristol's own reputation against that of rival cities within the realm and this was informed by the social ideal rather than doctrinal argument, which was conspicuously absent from the official discourse.[4] The Castle Precincts, a confined area annexed to St Peter, but effectively free of vestry authority, evolved into a refuge for nonconformists within the city. The fact that this appeared to conform to the Anglican equation of shared space and shared ideology heightened, rather than diminished, the anxiety other citizens felt about religious outsiders in their midst. In 1725 a Bristol newspaper printed the story of a notorious swindler, identified him as a Jew, and remarked that all Jews who lived in England, by virtue of their shared belief, should be held communally responsible for the frauds and debts of every other Jew within the realm.[5] Imposing the ideal of highly localised shared spaces, resources and beliefs produced divisiveness and disorder rather than communal stability.

Literate members of society may have been removed from parochial social spheres because such people relied less heavily on oral tradition and direct personal interaction for the maintenance of social contacts and the formation of shared beliefs. Rosemary O'Day has claimed, for example, that the Reformation in England wiped out 'public ceremony as a major means of transmitting knowledge and values within the community' because 'public popular culture increasingly became private popular culture, in which the printed word played a paramount role'.[6] On the other hand, it would be entirely wrong to suggest that the private access to ideas through the shared technology of literacy and print removed the educated members of society from civic ritual and other public arenas. It is clear, however, that any one of the myriad social spheres of early modern England was bound together by one or more of at least three separate, and potentially competing, cultural forms: the spatial, the material, and the intellectual.

Throughout this study an explicit effort has been made to weigh the influence of occupation, wealth, gender, and religious affiliation in the formation of social spheres and cultural ties. Although important, these factors do not provide a complete explanation for the persistence of an urban–rural gulf during the century associated with urban growth and revival. We need to look more deeply, beyond these categories, to the influence of urbane and rustic attitudes, the bases of identities linked with the topographical divide itself. It would be a mistake to assume a strict, deterministic equation between rural residence and rustic attitudes or urban residence and urbane attitudes. To do so would be to overlook the impressive geographical mobility of early modern populations and to deny the importance of conscious choice to the whole process of identity formation.

Urbane and rustic mentalities were not necessarily in hostile opposition to one another, but some of the more surprising manifestations of the urban–rural gulf must be explained in part by the persistent opposition of urbane and rustic mentalities. It has been argued elsewhere that village solidarity delayed the development of class consciousness outside the ranks of the ruling elite and the urban middle classes.[7] Despite heavy migration from countryside to city, few of the marriages which took place in Bristol united people of urban and rural origin, and the portion of Bristol marriages made up of such unions remained low. Despite the absolute rise in Bristol apprenticeships, the prosperity of the city, the advantages of skill, and the activity of urban sponsors, the representation of local villagers among Bristol's apprentices actually declined during the urban renaissance there. Rustic homes and consumers hardly imitated urban trends despite the availability of space for larger rural houses, the general superiority of rural wealth, and the ready availability of luxurious and exotic goods. Despite the widespread practice of lending, urban and rural dwellers belonged to separate credit networks and held different attitudes about the sharing and management of wealth. Despite the advent of local printing and general improvements in literacy, differences between urban and rural book ownership and use prevailed. The printed words that were disseminated locally failed to promote a regional identity; on the contrary, they fostered the mental division of the world into town and country and reinforced the notion that print was an instrument of the urban network. The religious revival of the eighteenth century, of which the rural missions and open-air sermons of Methodists were clearly evidence, can be seen as the special appeal of pastoral worship after a period of cloistered, institutionalised dogma. In short, urbane and rustic affinities informed conscious choices about the maintenance of the topographical divide in early modern England.

Urban life went through more conspicuous changes than rural life did in early modern England. Of course, from the rustic point of view, cities undergoing these dramatic changes were a visible object lesson in what to avoid. They appeared to be less effective in resisting the encroachment of strangers, a potential drain on highly localised resources. Urban problems of vagrancy, poverty, crime, crowding, polution, disease, decaying infrastructure, and corrupt officials were on a grander scale. An understanding of the rustic point of view helps to explain why villagers actively, and sometimes collectively, resisted the replication of urban–style changes in the rural setting. Early modern English villagers also resisted urban influence because they had an attachment to the rural setting itself, which they recognised as the contextual basis of the community life that sustained them. At the same time rural dwellers had in common with urban dwellers a general antipathy to strangers. Parishioners in early modern England were highly xenophobic in urban and rural communities alike. People who found themselves in an unfamiliar setting and those communities faced with encroachment were inclined to perpetuate their own distinctive and customary forms of interaction – including symbolic and ritual gestures – in order to define vigilantly the limited boundaries of their social spheres and to make outsiders conspicuously marginal.

The gap between urban and rural spheres persisted in and around provincial cities for nearly a century after the Restoration as visible and invisible boundaries between urban and rural worlds preserved distinct patterns of social interaction and cultural practice. It was not until the middle decades of the eighteenth century, when more widespread social spheres transcended the influence of corporate and communal institutions (the parish in particular) and a new suburban setting began to develop, that the urban–rural divide was significantly mediated. The observation of continuity in this specific sense is all the more fascinating in view of the fact that this period is rightly associated with significant change in other respects. The identification of rustic awareness and urbane awareness operating in the social spheres of early modern England poses a range of important questions. The interaction between provincial cities and their nearby villages during the century following 1660 shows that topographical setting belongs among occupation, wealth, gender, status, class, and religion as a powerful and historically grounded analytical category for the study of society, culture, and mentality.

## NOTES

1  See especially P. Slack, *Poverty and Policy in Tudor and Stuart England* (London, 1988); J. Pound, *Poverty and Vagrancy in Tudor England* (London, 1971); A. L. Beier, *Masterless Men: The Vagrancy Problem in England 1560–1640* (London, 1985); and, for the period leading to the Elizabethan laws, R. Houlbrooke, *Church Courts and the People during the English Reformation 1520–1570* (Oxford, 1979).

2  *The Bee and Sketchley's Weekly Advertiser* (27 October and 10 November 1777).

3  B.R.O. #04452(1), Bristol Quarter Sessions: Presentments and Convictions (1676–1700), grand jury presentment, Easter, 1681.

4  *Ibid.*, especially grand jury presentments of Easter Session, 1682.

5  *Farley's Bristol Newspaper* (4 December 1725).

6  R. O'Day, *Education and Society 1500–1800: The Social Foundations of Education in Early Modern Britain* (London, 1982), p. 16.

7  C. Calhoun, *The Question of Class Struggle: Social Foundations of Popular Radicalism during the Industrial Revolution* (Chicago, 1982).

# Bibliography

## PRINTED PRIMARY SOURCES

Amory, T., *Ministers not Lords over the Faith of Christians, but Helpers of their Joy: Preached at Lewin's Mead, Bristol, 22 May 1751*, Bristol, 1751.

Anonymous, *The Country Mouse and the City Mouse*, London, 12th ed., 1683.

— *Fables of the Female Sex*, London, 1773.

— *The History of Mother Bunch of the West, Containing many Rarities out of her Golden Closet of Curiosities*, London, early eighteenth century.

— *Leek Justified and Potatoes Downfall*, Bristol, 1754.

— *Liberty! No Placemen! No Naturalization!* Bristol, 1754.

— *The Madmen of Gotham*, London, c. 1680.

— *News! News! Very Sad News! for Jews and a Certain Clergyman*, Bristol, 1754.

— *Relief of Apprentices Wronged by their Masters*, 1687.

— *The Sackfull of News*, London, 1685.

— *Strange and Terrible Newes from Cambridge: The True Relation of the Quakers Bewitching Mary Phillips, etc.*, London, etc., 1659.

— *Vinegar and Mustard: or, Wormwood Lectures for Every Day of the Week*, London, 1686.

— *To the Worthy Freemen of Bristol: No Jews!* Bristol, 1754.

Archididascolos, C., *Union and Loyalty Recommended: Preached at the Mayor's Chapel, Bristol, 25 September 1754 by William Batt*, Bristol, 1754.

Ascham, R., *The Schoolmaster*, 1570.

Aubrey, J., *Remaines of Gentilisme and Judaisme*, 1687.

Bailey, N., *English Dictionary*, London, 1747.

Bantock, A. (ed.), *The Earlier Smyths of Ashton Court from their Letters 1545–1741*, Bristol, 1982.

— *The Later Smyths of Ashton Court from their Letters 1741–1802*, Bristol, 1984.

Barlow, E., *Barlow's Journal of his Life at Sea 1654–1703*, ed. B. Lubbock, London, 1934.

Bedford, A., *The Celebration of the King's Happy Coronation: Preached at St Mary Redcliffe Church, Bristol, 21 October 1717*, Bristol, 1717.

— *Unity, Love and Peace: Preached before the Gloucestershire Society, 2 September 1714, their Anniversary Feast Day, at St Nicholas Parish Church, Bristol*, Bristol, 1714.

Beresford, J. (ed.), *James Woodforde: The Diary of a Country Parson 1758–1802*, London, 1924–31.

Berjew, J., *Religion Essential to Civil Government: Assize Sermon Preached at the Mayor's Chapel, 2 August 1774*, Bristol, 1774.

# Bibliography

Bohun, E., *A Geographical Dictionary*, 1688.

Brent, C., *Good Man's Surpassing Worth and Glory: Preached at Christ Church, Bristol, after the Death of Edward Colston*, Bristol, 1721.

— *Honour the Lord with thy Substance: Preached before the Society of Merchants, Bristol, St Stephen's Church, 10 November 1708*, Bristol, 1708.

— *Money Essay'd; or, The True Value of it Tryed: Preached before the Society of Merchants, Bristol, 10 November 1727*, Bristol, 1728.

— *Persuasions to a Publick Spirit: Preached before the Court of Guardians of the Poor, Bristol, St Peter's Church, 13 April 1704*, Bristol, 1704.

Broughton, T., senior, *The Perfection of Christian Morality Asserted: Preached at the Parish Church of St James, Bristol, before the Subscribers of the Infirmary of the City*, Bristol, 1752.

Buller, J., *Sermon Preached before the Prisoners under Sentence of Death, in Newgate, Bristol, 24 September 1754*, Bristol, 1754.

Camplin, J., *Evidence of Christianity not Weakened by the Frailty of its Ministers: Preached at Bristol Cathedral, 29 June 1777, Occasioned by the Execution of William Dodd*, Bristol, 1777.

Castleman, J., *Sermon Preached before Subscribers to the Bristol Infirmary, in the Parish Church of St James, 13 March 1743*, Bristol, 1744.

Catcott, A. S., *Antiquity and Honourableness of the Practice of Merchandise: Preached before the Worshipful Society of Merchants, Bristol, in the Parish Church of St Stephen, 10 November 1744*, Bristol, 1744.

— *Superior and Inferior Elahim: Preached before the Corporation of Bristol at the Mayor's Chapel, 16 August 1725, the Day before Assizes*, Bristol, 2nd ed., 1742.

Catcott, J., *Sermon Preached at Bristol, 8 August 1714, on His Majesty's Inauguration*, Bristol, 1715.

Chambers, W., *Designs of Chinese Buildings*, 1757.

Chandler, S., *Sermon Preached at the Ordination of Thomas Wright, at Lewin's Mead, Bristol*, Bristol, 1759.

Cooke, E., *Voyage to the South Sea and round the World, Performed in the Years 1708–11 by the Ships 'Duke' and 'Duchess' of Bristol ... wherein an Account is given of Alexander Selkirk*, 2 vols (1712), B.C.L. Braikenridge Collection #10649–50.

Coote, E., *The English Schoolmaster*, 1596.

Crossman, S., *Sermon Preached 23 April 1680 at the Cathedral Church of Bristol before the Gentlemen of the Artillery Company Newly Raised*, London, 1680.

— *Two Sermons Preached in the Cathedral Church of Bristol, 30 January 1680 and 31 January 1680, being the Days of Publick Humiliation for the Execrable Murder of King Charles I*, London, 1681.

C.S., *Render unto Caesar the Things which are Caesar's*, Bristol, 1717.

Defoe, D., *The Complete English Tradesman*, London, 1727.

Defoe, D., *A Tour through the Whole Island of Great Britain* [1724–26], ed. P. Rogers, Harmondsworth, 1971.

Evans, C. *Hope of the Righteous Death: Preached at the New Chapel in Stapleton at the Internment of Joseph Mason*, Bristol, 1780.

— *Remembrance of Former Days: Preached at Broadmead, Bristol, 5 November 1778*, Bristol, 1778.

Evelyn, J., *Silva, or, A Discourse of Forest-Trees*, 1664.

— *Tyrannus*, 1661.

Fage, R., *A Description of the Whole World*, 1658.

Fitzherbert, J., *Booke of Husbandrie*, London, 1598.

Frost, J. W. (ed.), *The Records and Recollections of James Jenkins 1753–1831*, Lewiston, N.Y., 1984.

Gallen, T., *New Almanac*, London, 1671.

Gaskarth, J., *Sermon Preached before John, Lord Bishop of Bristol, at his Primary Visitation, 30 October 1685*, London, 1685.

Gibb, J., *Mutual Duties of Magistrates and People: Preached at St Mary Redcliffe, Bristol, 29 May 1771, before the Magistrates of Bristol*, Bristol, 1721.

Goldwin, W., *God's Judgements on a Sinful People: Preached at St Nicholas, Bristol, 8 December*, Bristol, c. 1730.

— *Light of an Exemplary Life: Preached at St Nicholas, Bristol, before a Society of Young Gentlemen Educated at the Grammar School*, Bristol, 1734.

Goreau, A. (ed.), *The Whole Duty of a Woman: Female Writers in Seventeenth-Century England*, New York, 1985.

Gough, R., *The History of Myddle* [1701], ed. D. Hey, Harmondsworth, 1981.

Gough, S., *Sermons on Effectual Calling and Practical Religion: Preached in Bristol*, Bristol, 1709.

Graham, E. (ed.), *Her own Life: Autobiographical Writings by Seventeenth-Century English-women*, London, 1989.

Hancock, E., *Pastor's Last Legacy and Counsel: A Farewell Sermon Preached at St Philip's, Bristol, 24 August 1662*, London, 1662.

Harcourt, J., *Sermon ... at the Death of Edward Colston, All Saints, Bristol*, Bristol, 1721.

Hardcastle, T., *Christian Geography and Arithmetic; or, A True Survey of the World: Being the Substance of some Sermons Preached at Bristol*, London, 1674.

Heath, G., *Spiritual Patriotism: Preached at Taylor's Hall, Bristol*, Bristol, 1778.

Heylyn, P., *Microcosmos, or, A Little Description of the Whole World*, 1621.

— *Cosmographie*, 1652.

Hole, M., *True Liberty Described and the False Pretences of Liberty Discovered, Shewing the Nature, Use, and Abuse of Christian Liberty: Preached at St Peter's Church, Bristol, 29 July 1711*, Bristol, 1711.

Horler, J., *Blessedness of Giving Superior to that of Receiving: Preached at Temple Church, Bristol, before the Annual Feast of the Wiltshire Society, 30 August 1750*, Bristol, 1750.

— *Of Clothing the Naked: Preached at St Thomas Church, Bristol, before the Wiltshire Society Annual Feast, 30 August 1739*, Bristol, 1739.

— *Works of Charity Recommended from the Common Relation we Bear to Christ: Preached at All Saints Church, Bristol, before the Wiltshire Society at their Annual Feast Held in Merchants' Hall, 21 August 1729*, Bristol, 1729.

# Bibliography

Jekyll, T., *Peace and Unity Recommended and Persuaded: Preached at Bristol, 31 January 1675*, London, 1675.

Kingston, R., *Vivant Rex: Preached at St James's Church, 25 July 1683, before the Mayor, Aldermen, Council, and Citizens of Bristol upon the Discovery of the late Treasonable, Phanatic Plot*, London, 1683.

Latham, R. C. (ed.), *Bristol Charters, 1509–1899*, Bristol Record Society 12, Bristol, 1947.

Latham, R. (ed.), *The Illustrated Pepys: Extracts from the Diary*, Berkeley, Cal., 1983.

L.W., *A Merry Dialogue between Andrew and his Sweetheart*, London, seventeenth century.

Moore, J., *Banner of Corah, Dathan, and Abairam Display'd, and their Sin Discover'd: Several Sermons Preached at Bristol*, Bristol, 1696.

Norden, J., *England: An Intended Guyde for English Travailers*, 1625.

Peacham, H., *Rura mihi et Silentium*, 1612.

Pepys, S., *Diary, 1660–69*, ed. R. Latham, Cambridge, 1978.

Pitt, M., *The English Atlas*, 1680–83.

Pope, M., *Merciful Discovery and Glorious Defeat of Perjury and Rebellion: A Thanksgiving Sermon for the Suppression of the late Unnatural Rebellion against King, Lords, and Commons Preached on the Day Appointed by the Publick Authority*, Bristol, 3rd ed., 1716.

Price, J., *Advantages of Unity Considered: Preached before the Ancient and Honourable Society of Free and Accepted Masons, in the Parish Church of St John Baptist, Bristol, 28 December 1747*, Bristol, 1748.

— *Antiquity of the Festival of St David Asserted: Preached before the Society of Ancient Britons, 1 March 1754, in the Parish Church of St James, Bristol*, Bristol, 1754.

Ray, J., *Observations Topographical, Moral and Physiological, Made on a Journey*, 1673.

Reynell, C., *Sermon Preached before the Contributors to the Bristol Infirmary, at St James, Bristol, 12 December 1738*, Bristol, 1738.

— *Two Sermons Preached before the Aldermen, Sheriffs, Mayor, and Common Council of Bristol, 5 November and 30 January 1729*, Bristol, 1729.

Reyner, K., *Knowledge of Christ and Him Crucified: Five Sermons Preached at Tucker Street, Bristol*, Bristol, 1748.

— *Select Sermons upon Practical Subjects: Preached in Bristol*, Bristol, 1745.

Rogers, W., *Cruising Voyage round the World ... 1708–1711 ... an Account of Alexander Selkirk's Living Alone for Four Years Four Months on an Island* (1712), B.C.L. #4400, Braikenridge Collection #10651–2.

Rudder, S., *A New History of Gloucestershire*, 1779.

Sheffer, J., *The History of Lapland*, Oxford, 1674.

Sheppard, W., *Of Corporations, Fraternities and Guilds*, London, 1659.

Sketchley, *Bristol Directory*, Bristol, 1775.

Society of Friends, *Epistles of the Yearly Meeting of Friends Held in London from 1681 to 1817*, London, 1817.

Standfast, R., *Sermon Preached at Christ Church, Bristol, before Sir Francis North at the Assizes Held there, 7 August 1675*, London, 1676.

Stewart, J., *Critical Observations on the Buildings and Improvements of London*, London, 1771.

Stukeley, W., *Itinerarium Curiosum*, 1724.

Taswell, W., *Expedience and Necessity of National Establishments in Religion, with Observations on that of the Church of England in Particular*, Bristol, 1763.

Thompson, J., *Joshua's Resolution to Serve the Lord: Preached at the Conclusion of the Yearly Meeting of the People Called Quakers, at Bristol, 15 May 1745*, Bristol, 1745.

Thompson, R., *Sermon Preached at the Cathedral Church, Bristol, 21 June 1685, before Henry, Duke of Beaufort, Lord Lieutenant of the City and County*, London, 1685.

Thompson, R. (ed.), *Samuel Pepys' Penny Merriments: Being a Collection of Chapbooks*, New York, 1977.

Tucker, J., *Hospitals and Infirmaries Considered as Schools of Christian Education for the Adult Poor: Preached at St James, Bristol, 18 March 1745*, Bristol, 1746.

Tryon, T., *A New Method of Educating Children*, 1695.

Vaisey, D. (ed.), *The Diary of Thomas Turner 1754–65*, Oxford, 1984.

Walpole, H., *History of the Modern Taste in Gardening*, London, 2nd ed. 1782.

Waterman, H., *Sermon Preached before the Court of Guardians of the Poor, Bristol, at St Peter's Church, 13 April 1699*, Bristol, 1699.

Wesley, John, *Free Grace: A Sermon Preached at Bristol*, Bristol, 1740–41.

Whitefield, G., *Nature and Necessity of Society: Preached at St Nicholas, Bristol*, Bristol, 1737.

Young, A., *Tour in Ireland*, 1776–79.

## SECONDARY SOURCES

Abelove, H., *The Evangelist of Desire: John Wesley and the Methodists*, Stanford, Cal., 1990.

— 'Some speculations on the history of sexual intercourse during the long eighteenth century in England', *Genders* 6 (1989), pp. 125–30.

Abrams, P., and E. A. Wrigley (eds), *Towns in Societies: Essays in Economic History and Historical Sociology*, Cambridge, 1978.

Acheson, R. J., *Radical Puritans in England 1550–1660*, London, 1990.

Adams, R., J. Arlott, *et al.*, *Book of British Villages*, London, 1980.

Alldridge, N., 'Loyalty and identity in Cheshire parishes 1540–1640', in S. J. Wright (ed.), *Parish, Church and People: Local Studies in Lay Religion 1350–1750*, London, 1988, pp. 85–124.

Allen, D. E., *The Naturalist in Britain: A Social History*, Princeton, N.J., 1994.

Amussen, S. D., *An Ordered Society: Gender and Class in Early Modern England*, Oxford, 1988.

Appleyard, D., 'Styles and methods of structuring a city', in S. and R. Kaplan (eds), *Humanscape: Environments for People*, Ann Arbor, Mich., 1982, pp. 70–81.

Archer, I., *The Pursuit of Stability: Social Relations in Elizabethan London*, Cambridge, 1991.

Archer, J., '*Rus in urbe*: classical ideas of country and city in British town planning', *Studies in Eighteenth-Century Culture* 12 (1983), pp. 159–86.

Archer, S., *Culture and Agency: The Place of Culture in Social Theory*, Cambridge, 1988.

# Bibliography

Armstrong, W. A., 'The use of information about occupation', in E. A. Wrigley (ed.), *Nineteenth-Century Society*, Cambridge, 1971, pp. 191–253.

Ashton, J. (ed.) *Chapbooks of the Eighteenth Century*, London, 1882.

Baigent, E., 'Economy and society in eighteenth-century English towns: Bristol in the 1770s', in D. Denecke and G. Shaw (eds), *Urban Historical Geography: Recent Progress in Britain and Germany*, Cambridge, 1988, pp. 109–24.

Bal, M., 'Telling objects: a narrative perspective on collecting', in J. Elsner and R. Cardinal (eds), *The Cultures of Collecting*, Cambridge, Mass., 1994, pp. 97–115.

Barker-Benfield, G. J., *The Culture of Sensibility: Sex and Society in Eighteenth-Century Britain*, Chicago, 1996.

Barley, M. W. (ed.), *The Buildings of the Countryside 1500–1750*, Cambridge, 1990.

Barnes, T. G., *Somerset 1625–40*, Cambridge, Mass., 1961.

Barry, J., 'The Cultural Life of Bristol 1640–1775', D.Phil. thesis, Oxford University, 1985.

— 'Literacy and literature in popular culture: reading and writing in historical perspective', in T. Harris (ed.), *Popular Culture in England* c. 1500–1850, New York, 1995, pp. 69–94.

— 'The parish in civic life: Bristol and its churches 1640–1750', in S. J. Wright (ed.), *Parish, Church and People: Local Studies in Lay Religion 1350–1750*, London, 1988, pp. 152–78.

— 'The politics of religion in Restoration Bristol', in T. Harris, P. Seaward, and M. Goldie (eds), *The Politics of Religion in Restoration England*, Oxford, 1990, pp. 163–89.

— 'Popular culture in seventeenth-century Bristol', in B. Reay (ed.), *Popular Culture in Seventeenth-Century England*, London, 1985, pp. 59–90.

— 'The press and the politics of culture in Bristol 1660–1775', in J. Black and J. Gregory (eds), *Culture, Politics and Society in Britain 1660–1800*, Manchester, 1991, pp. 49–81.

— 'Provincial town culture 1640–80: urbane or civic?', in J. H. Pittock and A. Wear (eds), *Interpretation and Cultural History*, London, 1991, pp. 198–234.

Barry, J., and K. Morgan (eds), *Reformation and Revival in Eighteenth-Century Bristol*, Bristol Record Society 45, Bristol, 1994.

Baudrillard, J., 'The system of collecting', in J. Elsner and R. Cardinal (eds), *The Cultures of Collecting*, Cambridge, Mass., 1994, pp. 7–24.

Baulant, M., A. Schuurman, and P. Servais (eds), *Inventaires après décès et ventes de meubles*, Louvain-la-Neuve, 1987.

Bauman, R., *Let your Words be Few: Symbolism of Speaking and Silence among the Seventeenth-Century Quakers*, Cambridge, 1983.

Beier, A. L., *Masterless Men: The Vagrancy Problem in England 1560–1640*, London, 1985.

Beier, L. M., *Sufferers and Healers: The Experience of Illness in Seventeenth-Century England*, London, 1987.

Ben-Amos, I. K., *Adolescence and Youth in Early Modern England*, New Haven, Conn., 1994.

— 'The failure to become freemen: urban apprentices in early modern England', *Social History* 16 no. 2 (1991), pp. 155–72.

— 'Women apprentices in the trades and crafts of early modern Bristol', *Continuity and Change* 6 (1991), pp. 228–38.

Benedict, P., 'Bibliothèques protestantes et catholiques à Metz au XVIIe siècle', *Annales E.S.C.* no. 2 (1985), pp. 343–70.

— 'French cities from the sixteenth century to the revolution', in P. Benedict (ed.), *Cities and Social Change in Early Modern France*, London, 1989, pp. 7–64.

— 'Towards the comparative study of the popular market for art: the ownership of paintings in seventeenth-century Metz', *Past and Present* 109 (1985), pp. 100–17.

Benedict, P. (ed.), *Cities and Social Change in Early Modern France*, London, 1989.

Bennett, G. V., 'Conflict in the church', in G. Holmes (ed.), *Britain after the Glorious Revolution 1689–1714*, London, 1969.

Berlin, M., 'Civic ceremony in early modern London', *Urban History Yearbook* (1986), pp. 15–27.

Bermingham, A., and J. Brewer (eds), *The Consumption of Culture 1600–1800: Image, Object, Text*, London, 1995.

Bingham, C., 'Seventeenth-century attitudes toward deviant sex', *Journal of Interdisciplinary History* 1 (1971), pp. 446–68.

Black, J., *The English Press in the Eighteenth Century*, Philadelphia, 1987.

Blalock, H. M., *Social Statistics*, New York, 2nd ed. 1972.

Borsay, P. '"All the town's a stage": urban ritual and ceremony 1660–1800', in P. Clark (ed.), *The Transformation of English Provincial Towns 1600–1800*, London, 1984, pp. 228–58.

— 'Culture, status, and the English urban landscape', *History* 67 no. 219 (1982), pp. 1–12.

— *The English Urban Renaissance: Culture and Society in the Provincial Town 1660–1770*, Oxford, 1989.

— 'The English urban renaissance: the development of provincial urban culture c. 1680–c. 1760', *Social History* 5 (1977), pp. 581–603.

Borsay, P. (ed.), *The Eighteenth-Century Town: A Reader in Urban History 1688–1820*, London, 1990.

Borsay, P., and A. McInnes, 'The emergence of a leisure town: or an urban renaissance?' *Past and Present* 126 (1990), pp. 189–202.

Boulton, J., *Neighbourhood and Society: A London Suburb in the Seventeenth Century*, Cambridge, 1987.

Bourne, H. R. F., *English Newspapers: Chapters in the History of Journalism 1621–1820*, New York, 1966.

Bradley, J. E., *Religion, Revolution and English Radicalism: Nonconformity in Eighteenth-Century Politics and Society*, Cambridge, 1990.

Braithwaite, W. C., *The Second Period of Quakerism*, Cambridge, 1961.

Bray, A., *Homosexuality in Renaissance England*, London, 1982, and New York, 1995.

Brewer, J., 'Theatre and counter-theatre in Georgian politics', *Radical History Review* 22 (1979–80), pp. 7–40.

Brewer, J., and R. Porter (eds), *Consumption and the World of Goods*, London, 1993.

Brewer, J., and J. Styles, (eds), *An Ungovernable People: The English and their Law in the Seventeenth and Eighteenth Centuries*, New Brunswick, N.J., 1980.

# Bibliography

Briggs, A., *The Age of Improvement 1783–1867*, London, 1980.

Brodsky Elliott, V., 'Single women in the London marriage market: age, status and mobility 1598–1619', in R. B. Outhwaite (ed.), *Marriage and Society: Studies in the History of Marriage*, London, 1981, pp. 81–100.

Brown, R. J., *The English Country Cottage*, London, 1979.

Burke, P., *Popular Culture in Early Modern Europe*, London, 1978.

— 'Popular culture in seventeenth-century London', *London Journal* 3 (1977), pp. 143–62.

Butcher, E. E. (ed.), *Bristol Corporation of the Poor 1696–1834*, Bristol Record Society 3, Bristol, 1932.

Byrd, M., *London Transformed: Images of the City in the Eighteenth Century*, New Haven, Conn., 1978.

Calhoun, C., *The Question of Class Struggle: Social Foundations of Popular Radicalism during the Industrial Revolution*, Chicago, 1982.

Capp, B., *English Almanacs 1500–1800: Astrology and the Popular Press*, Ithaca, N.Y., 1979.

— 'Popular literature', in B. Reay (ed.), *Popular Culture in Seventeenth-Century England*, London, 1985, pp. 198–243.

Chadwick, O., *Victorian Miniature*, Cambridge, 1991.

Chalklin, C. W., 'The financing of church building in the provincial towns of eighteenth-century England', in P. Clark (ed.), *The Transformation of English Provincial Towns 1600–1800*, London, 1984, pp. 284–310.

— *The Provincial Towns of Georgian England: A Study of the Building Process 1740–1820*, London, 1974.

Chalklin, C. W., and M. A. Havinden (eds), *Rural Change and Urban Growth 1500–1800*, London, 1974.

Chappell, W., *A Short History of the Printed Word*, New York, 1970.

Chartier, R., *The Cultural Uses of Print in Early Modern France*, Princeton, N.J., 1987.

— 'Culture as appropriation: popular cultural uses in early modern France', in S. Kaplan (ed.), *Understanding Popular Culture*, The Hague, 1984, pp. 229–53.

— 'Intellectual history or sociocultural history? The French trajectories', in D. LaCapra and S. L. Kaplan (eds), *Modern European Intellectual History: Reappraisals and New Perspectives*, Ithaca, N.Y., 1982, pp. 13–46.

— 'Texts, printing, readings', in L. Hunt (ed.), *The New Cultural History*, Berkeley, Cal., 1989, pp. 154–75.

Chartier, R. (ed.), *Pratiques de la lecture*, Paris, 1978.

Chartier, R., M. M. Compere, and D. Julia, *L'Education en France du XVIe au XVIIIe siècle*, Paris, 1976.

Chartres, J., and D. Hey (eds), *English Rural Society 1500–1800*, Cambridge, 1990.

Chaudhuri, K. N., *The Trading World of Asia and the East India Company 1660–1760*, Cambridge, 1978.

Cipolla, C. M., *Clocks and Culture 1300–1700*, New York, 1978.

Clark, A., *The Working Life of Women in the Seventeenth Century*, London, 1919.

Clark, J. C. D., *English Society 1688–1832: Ideology, Social Structure and Political Practice during the Ancien Regime*, Cambridge, 1985.

Clark, P., 'The civic leaders of Gloucester 1580–1800', in P. Clark (ed.), *The Transformation of English Provincial Towns 1600–1800*, London, 1984.

— *The English Alehouse: A Social History 1200–1830*, London, 1983.

— 'The migrant in Kentish towns 1580–1640', in P. Clark and P. Slack (eds), *Crisis and Order in English Towns 1500–1800*, London, 1972.

— 'Migrants in the city: the process of social adaptation in English towns 1500–1800', in P. Clark and D. Souden (eds), *Migration and Society in Early Modern England*, London, 1987, pp. 267–91.

— 'Migration in England during the late seventeenth and early eighteenth centuries', *Past and Present* 83 (1979), pp. 57–90.

— 'The ownership of books in England 1560–1640: the example of some Kentish townsfolk', in L. Stone (ed.), *Schooling and Society*, Baltimore, Md, 1976, pp. 95–111.

— '"The Ramoth-Gilead of the good": urban change and political radicalism at Gloucester 1540–1640', in P. Clark *et al.*, *The English Commonwealth 1547–1640*, Leicester, 1982.

— *Sociability and Urbanity: Clubs and Societies in the Eighteenth-Century City*, Leicester, 1986.

Clark, P. (ed.), *The Early Modern Town: A Reader*, London, 1976.

— *The Transformation of English Provincial Towns 1660–1800*, London, 1984.

Clark, P.and J., 'The social economy of Canterbury suburbs', in A. Detsicas and N. Yates (eds), *Studies in Modern Kentish History*, Maidstone, 1983.

Clark, P., and P. Slack, *English Towns in Transition 1500–1700*, Oxford, 1976.

Clark, P., and P. Slack (eds), *Crisis and Order in English Towns 1500–1700*, London, 1972.

Clark, P., and D. Souden (eds), *Migration and Society in Early Modern England*, London, 1987.

Clay, C., 'Landlords and estate management in England 1640–1750', in C. Clay (ed.), *Rural Society: Landowners, Peasants and Labourers 1500–1750*, Cambridge, 1990, pp. 246–378.

Coats, A. W., 'The relief of poverty: attitudes to labour and economic change in England 1660–1782', *International Review of Social History* 21 (1976), pp. 98–115.

Cockburn, J. S. (ed.), *Crime in England 1550–1800*, Princeton, N.J., 1977.

Coldham, P. W., 'The "spiriting" of London children to Virginia 1648–1685', *Virginia Magazine of History and Biography* 83 (1975), pp. 280–8.

Coleman, D. C., *The Economy of England 1450–1750*, London, 1977.

Colley, L., *Britons: Forging the Nation 1707–1837*, New Haven, Conn., 1992.

Corfield, P. J., *The Impact of English Towns 1700–1800*, Oxford, 1982.

— 'A provincial capital in the late seventeenth century: the case of Norwich', in P. Clark and P. Slack (eds), *Crisis and Order in English Towns 1500–1700*, London, 1972, pp. 263–310.

Corfield, P. J., and U. Priestly, 'Rooms and room use in Norwich housing 1580–1730', *Post-medieval Archaeology* 16 (1982), pp. 93–123.

Cott, N. F., *The Bonds of Womanhood: 'Woman's Sphere' in New England 1780–1835*, New Haven, Conn., 1977.

# Bibliography

Cox, J., and N., 'Valuations in probate inventories', *Local Historian* 16 no. 8 (1985), pp. 467–77.

Cragg, G. R., *The Church in the Age of Reason 1648–1789*, Harmondsworth, 1981.

Cranfield, G. A., *The Development of the Provincial Newspaper 1700–60*, Oxford, 1962.

Cressy, D., *Bonfires and Bells: National Memory and the Protestant Calendar in Elizabethan and Stuart England*, Berkeley, Cal., 1989.

— 'Education and Literacy in London and East Anglia 1580–1700', Ph.D. thesis, Cambridge University, 1972.

— 'Educational opportunity in Tudor and Stuart England', *History of Education Quarterly* 16 (1976), pp. 301–20.

— *Literacy and the Social Order*, Cambridge, 1980.

— 'Literacy in context: meaning and measurement in early modern England', in J. Brewer and R. Porter (eds), *Consumption and the World of Goods*, London, 1993, pp. 305–19.

— 'Literacy in seventeenth-century England: more evidence', *Journal of Interdisciplinary History* 8 no. 1 (1977), pp. 141–50.

Cunningham, H., 'The employment and unemployment of children in England c. 1680–1851', *Past and Present* 126 (1990), pp. 113–50.

Curry, P., *Prophecy and Power: Astrology in Early Modern England*, Cambridge, 1989.

Darnton, R., 'A bourgeois puts his world in order: the city as text', in R. Darnton, *The Great Cat Massacre and other Episodes in French Cultural History*, New York, 1984, pp. 107–43.

— *The Great Cat Massacre and other Episodes in French Cultural History*, New York, 1984.

— 'Intellectual and cultural history', in M. Kammen (ed.), *The Past before Us: Contemporary Historical Writing in the United States*, Ithaca, N.Y., 1980.

— 'La lecture rousseauiste et un lecteur "ordinaire" au XVIIIe siècle' in R. Chartier (ed.), *Pratiques de la lecture*, Paris, 1978, pp. 125–55.

— *The Literary Underground of the Old Regime*, Cambridge, Mass., 1982.

— 'The symbolic element in history', *Journal of Modern History* 58 (1986), pp. 218–34.

— 'What is the history of books?', in K. Carpenter (ed.), *Books and Society in History*, New York, 1983.

Daunton, M., 'Towns and economic growth in eighteenth-century England', in P. Abrams and E. A. Wrigley (eds), *Towns in Societies: Essays in Economic History and Historical Sociology*, Cambridge, 1978, pp. 245–78.

Davis, N. Z., 'Proverbial wisdom and popular errors', in N. Z. Davis, *Society and Culture in Early Modern France*, Stanford, Cal., 1975.

— *Society and Culture in Early Modern France*, Stanford, Cal., 1975.

Davis, R., *The Rise of the Atlantic Economies*, Ithaca, N.Y., 1973.

Davison, L., T. Hitchcock, T. Keirn, and R. B. Shoemaker (eds), *Stilling the Grumbling Hive: the Response to Social and Economic Problems in England 1689–1750*, New York, 1992.

De Krey, G. S., *A Fractured Society: The Politics of London in the First Age of Party 1688–1715*, Oxford, 1985.

De Vries, J., 'Between purchasing power and the world of goods: understanding the household economy in early modern Europe', in J. Brewer and R. Porter (eds), *Consumption and the World of Goods*, London, 1993, pp. 85–132.

— *European Urbanization 1500–1800*, Cambridge, Mass., 1984.

Denecke, D., and G. Shaw, *Urban Historical Geography: Recent Progress in Britain and Germany*, Cambridge, 1988.

Dennis, R., *English Industrial Cities of the Nineteenth Century: A Social Geography*, Cambridge, 1984.

Desan, S., 'Crowds, community and ritual in the work of E. P. Thompson and Natalie Davis', in L. Hunt (ed.), *The New Cultural History*, Berkeley, Cal., 1989, pp. 47–71.

Doran, S., and C. Durston, *Princes, Pastors and People: The Church and Religion in England 1529–1689*, London, 1991.

Drake, M., *Population and Society in Norway 1735–1865*, Cambridge, 1969.

Drake, M., and T. Barker (eds), *Population and Society in Britain 1850–1980*, New York, 1982.

Durston, C., and J. Eales (eds), *The Culture of English Puritanism 1560–1700*, New York, 1996.

Dyer, A., *The City of Worcester in the Sixteenth Century*, Leicester, 1973.

Earle, P., *The Making of the English Middle Class: Business, Society and Family Life in London, 1660–1730*, London, 1989.

Edmunds, S., 'From Schoeffer to Verard: concerning the scribes who became printers', in S. L. Hindman (ed.), *Printing the Written Word: The Social History of Books*, circa 1450–1520, Ithaca, N.Y., 1991, pp. 21–40.

Eisenstein, E., *The Printing Press as an Agent of Change: Communication and Cultural Transformation in Early Modern Europe*, Cambridge, 1980.

— *The Printing Revolution in Early Modern Europe*, Cambridge, 1983.

Ellis, J., 'A dynamic society: social relations in Newcastle-upon-Tyne 1660–1760', in P. Clark (ed.), *The Transformation of English Provincial Towns 1600–1800*, London, 1984, pp. 190–227.

Elsner, J., and R. Cardinal (eds), *The Cultures of Collecting*, Cambridge, Mass., 1994.

Eltis, D., *Economic Growth and the Ending of the Transatlantic Slave Trade*, Oxford, 1987.

Erickson, A. L., *Women and Property in Early Modern England*, London, 1993.

Estabrook, C. B., 'Bristol and the Atlantic Trade in the Eighteenth Century: a review', *Albion* 27 no. 2 (1995), pp. 312–13.

— 'In the mist of ceremony: cathedral and community in seventeenth-century Wells', in S. D. Amussen and M. A. Kishlansky (eds), *Political Culture and Cultural Politics in Early Modern England*, Manchester, 1995, pp. 133–61.

— '*Stilling the Grumbling Hive*: a review', *Albion* 25 no. 3 (1993), pp. 500–2.

Estabrook, C. B. and G. F., 'ACTUS: a solution to the problem of small samples in the analysis of two-way contingency tables', *Historical Methods* 22 (1989), pp. 5–8.

Everitt, A., 'Country, county and town: patterns of regional evolution in England', in P. Borsay (ed.), *The Eighteenth-Century Town: a Reader in English Urban History 1688–1820*, London and New York, 1990, pp. 83–115.

# Bibliography

— 'The English urban inn 1560–1760', in A. Everitt (ed.), *Perspectives in English Urban History*, London, 1973.

Everitt, A. (ed.), *Perspectives in English Urban History*, London, 1973.

Faderman, L., *Surpassing the Love of Men: Romantic Friendship and Love between Women from the Renaissance to the Present*, New York, 1981.

Fairchilds, C., 'The production and marketing of *populuxe* goods in eighteenth-century Paris', in J. Brewer and R. Porter (eds), *Consumption and the World of Goods*, London, 1993, pp. 228–48.

Feather, J., *The Provincial Book Trade in Eighteenth-Century England*, Cambridge, 1985.

Febvre, L., and H.-J. Martin, *L'Apparition du livre*, Paris, 1958.

Felsenstein, F., *Anti-Semitic Stereotypes: A Paradigm of Otherness in English Popular Culture 1660–1830*, Baltimore, Md, 1995.

Ferdinand, C. Y., 'Selling it to the provinces: news and commerce round eighteenth-century Salisbury', in J. Brewer and R. Porter (eds), *Consumption and the World of Goods*, London, 1992, pp. 393–411.

Ferkiss, V., *Nature, Technology and Society: Cultural Roots of the Current Ecological Crisis*, London, 1993.

Finlay, R., *Population and Metropolis: The Demography of London 1580–1650*, Cambridge, 1981.

Finlay, R., and A. Sharlin, 'Debate: natural decrease in early modern cities', *Past and Present* 92 (1981), pp. 169–80.

Fisch, H., *Jerusalem and Albion: The Hebraic Factor in Seventeenth-Century Literature*, New York, 1964.

Fishman, R., *Bourgeois Utopias: The Rise and Fall of Suburbia*, New York, 1989.

Fissell, M. E., 'Charity universal? Institutions and moral reform in eighteenth-century Bristol', in L. Davison, T. Hitchcock, T. Keirn, and R. B. Shoemaker (eds), *Stilling the Grumbling Hive: The Response to Social and Economic Problems in England, 1689–1750*, New York, 1992, pp. 121–44.

— *Patients, Power, and the Poor in Eighteenth-Century Bristol*, Cambridge, 1991.

— 'Readers, texts and contexts: vernacular medical works in early modern England', in R. Porter (ed.), *The Popularization of Medicine 1650–1850*, London, 1992, pp. 72–96.

Fletcher, A., *Gender, Sex and Subordination in England 1500–1800*, New Haven, Conn., 1995.

Fleury, M., and L. Henry, *Nouveau manuel de dépouillement et d'exploitation de l'état civil ancien*, Paris, 1965.

Foote, L. H., and C. L. Haines, 'Household vernacular in Concord, Massachusetts, probate inventories, 1655–1800', *Dublin Seminar for New England Folk Life Annual Proceedings* (Boston, Mass. 1983), pp. 55–69.

Friedrichs, C. R., *The Early Modern City 1450–1750*, London, 1995.

Froeschle-Chopard, M.-H., *La Religion populaire en Provence orientale au XVIIe siècle*, Paris, 1980.

Fryer, P., *Staying Power: The History of Black People in Britain*, London, 1984.

Geertz, C., 'Thick description: towards the interpretive theory of culture', in C. Geertz, *The Interpretation of Cultures*, New York, Basic Books, 1973.

George, E., and S. George (eds), *Guide to the Probate Inventories of the Bristol Deanery of the Diocese of Bristol 1542–1804*, Bristol, 1988.

George, M. D., *London Life in the Eighteenth Century*, London, 1925; 3rd ed. Chicago, 1984.

Gillis, J. R., *For Better, for Worse: British Marriages, 1600 to the Present*, New York, 1985.

Girouard, M., *The English Town: A History of Urban Life*, New Haven, Conn., 1990.

— *Life in the English Country House: A Social and Architectural History*, New Haven, Conn., 1978; repr. Harmondsworth, 1980.

Graff, H. J. (ed.), *Literacy and Social Development in the West*, Cambridge, 1981.

Grafton, A., 'The importance of being printed', *Journal of Interdisciplinary History* 11 no. 2 (1980), pp. 265–86.

Grafton, A., and A. Blair (eds), *The Transmission of Culture in Early Modern Europe*, Philadelphia, 1990.

Grassby, R., 'Personal wealth of the business community in seventeenth-century England', *Economic History Review*, 2nd ser. 23 (1970), pp. 220–34.

Greenblatt, S., *Marvelous Possessions: The Wonder of the New World*, Chicago, 1991.

Hall, K. F., *Things of Darkness: Economies of Race and Gender in Early Modern England*, Ithaca, N.Y., 1995.

Hall, P. (ed.), *Von Thunen's Isolated State*, trans. C. M. Wartenberg, London, 1966.

Halliday, P. D., 'Partisan Conflict and the Law in the English Borough Corporation 1660–1727', Ph.D. thesis, University of Chicago, 1993.

Hamlyn, H., 'Eighteenth-century circulating libraries in England', *Library*, 5th ser. 1 (1946).

Harris, M., 'London printers and newspaper production during the first half of the eighteenth century', *Printing Historical Society Journal* 12 (1977–78).

Harris, T., *London Crowds in the Reign of Charles II: Propaganda and Politics from the Restoration to the Exclusion Crisis*, Cambridge, 1987.

— *Politics under the Later Stuarts: Party Conflict in a Divided Society 1660–1715*, London, 1993.

— 'Problematising popular culture', in T. Harris (ed.), *Popular Culture in England* c. 1500–1850, New York, 1995, pp. 1–27.

— 'The problem of "popular political culture" in seventeeth-century London', *History of European Ideas* 10 (1989), pp. 43–58.

Harris, T., P. Seaward, and M. Goldie (eds), *The Politics of Religion in Restoration England*, Oxford, 1990.

Hartley, D., *Lost Country Life*, New York, 1979.

Hay, D., 'Poaching and the game laws on Cannock Chase', in D. Hay *et al.* (eds), *Albion's Fatal Tree*, New York, 1975.

— 'Property, authority and the criminal law', in D. Hay *et al.* (eds), *Albion's Fatal Tree*, New York, 1995.

Hay, D., P. Linebaugh, J. G. Rule, E. P. Thompson, and C. Winslow (eds), *Albion's Fatal Tree: Crime and Society in Eighteenth-Century England*, New York, 1975.

Heal, F., *Hospitality in Early Modern England*, Oxford, 1990.

— 'The idea of hospitality in early modern England', *Past and Present* 102 (1984), pp. 66–93.

Heal, F., and C. Holmes, *The Gentry in England and Wales 1500–1700*, Stanford, Cal., 1994.

Hellinga, L., 'Importation of books printed on the continent into England and Scotland before c. 1520', in S. L. Hindman (ed.), *Printing the Written Word: The Social History of Books* c. 1450–1520, Ithaca, N.Y., 1991, pp. 205–24.

Herlan, R. W., 'Poor relief in London during the English revolution', *Journal of British Studies* 18 (1979), pp. 30–51.

Herrup, C. B., *The Common Peace: Participation and the Criminal Law in Seventeenth-Century England*, Cambridge, 1987.

Hill, B., *Women, Work and Sexual Politics in Eighteenth-Century England*, Oxford, 1989.

Hill, C., *The English Bible and the Seventeenth-Century Revolution*, Harmondsworth, 1994.

— *Milton and the English Revolution*, Harmondsworth, 1979.

— *The World Turned Upside Down: Radical Ideas during the English Revolution*, Harmondsworth, 1975.

Hindman, S. L. (ed.), *Printing the Written Word: The Social History of Books* c. 1450–1520, Ithaca, N.Y., 1991.

Hine, T., *Populuxe*, New York, 1986.

Hitchcock, T., *English Sexualities 1700–1800* (New York, 1997).

— 'Paupers and preachers: the SPCK and the parochial workhouse movement', in L. Davison, T. Hitchcock, T. Keirn, and R. B. Shoemaker (eds), *Stilling the Grumbling Hive: The Response to Social and Economic Problems in England 1689–1750*, New York, 1992, pp. 145–66.

Hobby, E., *Virtue of Necessity: English Women's Writings 1649–88*, London, 1988.

Holderness, B. A., 'Credit in a rural community 1660–1800', *Midland History* 3 (1975), pp. 94–115.

Holman, J. R., 'Apprenticeship as a factor in migration: Bristol 1675–1726', *Transactions of the Bristol and Gloucestershire Archaeological Society* 97 (1979), pp. 85–92.

Holmes, G. S., *Augustan England: Professions, State and Society 1680–1730*, London, 1982.

Holmes, G. S. (ed.), *Britain after the Glorious Revolution 1689–1714*, London, 1969.

Horle, C. W., *The Quakers and the English Legal System 1660–88*, Philadelphia, 1988.

Horn, J., *Adapting to a New World: English Society in the Seventeenth-Century Chesapeake*, Chapel Hill, N.C., 1994.

Houlbrooke, R., *Church Courts and the People during the English Reformation 1520–1570*, Oxford, 1979.

Houston, R., 'The literacy myth? Illiteracy in Scotland 1630–1760', *Past and Present* 96 (1982), pp. 81–102.

Houston, R., and C. W. J. Withers, 'Population mobility in Scotland and Europe 1600–1900: a comparative perspective', *Annales de Démographie Historique* (1990), pp. 285–308.

Hull, S., *Chaste, Silent and Obedient: English Books for Women 1475–1640*, San Marino, Cal., 1982.

Hunt, L. (ed.), *The New Cultural History*, Berkeley, Cal., 1989.

Hunt, W., *Bristol*, London, 1895.

Hutton, R., *The Pagan Religions of the Ancient British Isles: Their Nature and Legacy*, Oxford, 1991.

— *The Restoration: A Political and Religious History of England and Wales 1658–1667*, Oxford, 1985.

— *The Rise and Fall of Merry England: The Ritual Year 1400–1700*, Oxford, 1994.

Hyde, F. E. (ed.), *Liverpool and the Mersey: An Economic History of a Port 1700–1970*, Newton Abbot, 1971.

Ingle, H. L., *First among Friends: George Fox and the Creation of Quakerism*, Oxford, 1994.

Ingram, M., *Church Courts, Sex and Marriage in England 1570–1640*, Cambridge, 1987.

— 'Communities and courts: law and order in seventeenth-century Wiltshire' in J. S. Cockburn (ed.), *Crime in England 1550–1800*, Princeton, N.J., 1977.

— 'From Reformation to toleration: popular religious cultures in England 1540–1690', in T. Harris (ed.), *Popular Culture in England c. 1500–1850*, New York, 1995, pp. 95–123.

— 'Ridings, rough music and "the reform of popular culture" in early modern England', *Past and Present* 105 (1984), pp. 79–113.

Jackson, R. V., 'Growth and deceleration in English agriculture 1660–1790', *Economic History Review*, 2nd ser. 38 (1985), pp. 333–51.

James, M. E., 'Ritual, drama and social body in the late medieval English town', *Past and Present* 98 (1983), pp. 3–29.

Jarrett, D., *England in the Age of Hogarth*, London, 1974.

John, A. H., 'English agricultural improvement and grain exports 1660–1765', in D. C. Coleman and A. H. John (eds), *Trade, Government and Economy in Pre-industrial England: Essays presented to F. J. Fisher*, London, 1976.

Jones, E., 'London in the early seventeenth century: an ecological approach', *London Journal* 6 no. 2 (1980), pp. 123–33.

Jones, E. L., S. Porter, and M. A. Turner, *A Gazetteer of English Urban Fire Disasters 1500–1900*, Norwich, 1984.

Jones, P. D., 'The Bristol Bridge riot and its antecedents: eighteenth-century perception of the crowd', *Journal of British Studies* 19 no. 2 (1980), pp. 74–92.

Jones, S. J., 'The growth of Bristol', *Transactions of British Geographers* 2 (1946), pp. 57–83.

— 'The historical geography of Bristol', *Geography* 16 (1931), pp. 180–9.

Joyce, P. (ed.), *Class*, Oxford, 1995.

Kaplan, L. J., *Thomas Chatterton: the Family Romance of the Imposter-Poet*, Berkeley, Cal., 1987.

Kaplan, S. L. (ed.), *Understanding Popular Culture: Europe from the Middle Ages to the Nineteenth Century*, Berlin, 1984.

Katz, D. S., *The Jews in the History of England 1485–1850*, Oxford, 1994.

Kaufman, P., 'The community library: a chapter in English social history', *Transactions of the American Philosophical Society* 57 no. 7 (1967).

— *Libraries and their Users*, Charlottesville, Va., 1969.

# Bibliography

Kelley, M. *Private Woman, Public Stage: Literary Domesticity in Nineteenth Century America*, Oxford, 1984.

King. P., 'Newspaper reporting, prosecution practice, and perceptions of urban crime: the Colchester crime wave of 1765', *Continuity and Change* 2 no. 3 (1987), pp. 423–54.

Kitch, M. J., 'Capital and kingdom: migration to later Stuart London', in A. L. Beier and R. Finlay (eds), *London 1500–1700: The Making of the Metropolis*, London, 1986.

Krontiris, T., *Oppositional Voices: Women as Writers and Translators of Literature in the English Renaissance*, London, 1992.

Kummer, H., 'Spacing mechanisms in social behavior', in S. and R. Kaplan (eds), *Humanscape: Environments for People*, Ann Arbor, Mich., 1982.

Kussmaul, A., *Servants in Husbandry in Early Modern England*, Cambridge, 1981.

LaCapra, D., and S. L. Kaplan, *The Cultural Uses of Print in Early Modern France*, Princeton, N.J., 1987.

Laithwaite, M., 'The buildings of Burford: a Cotswold town in the fourteenth to the nineteenth centuries', in A. Everitt (ed.), *Perspectives in English Urban History*, London, 1973, pp. 60–90.

— 'Totnes houses 1500–1800', in P. Clark (ed.), *The Transformation of English Provincial Towns 1600–1800*, London, 1984, pp. 62–98.

Landau, N., *The Justices of the Peace 1679–1760*, Berkeley, Cal., 1984.

— 'The laws of settlement and the surveillance of immigration in eighteenth-century Kent', *Continuity and Change* 3 (1988), pp. 391–420.

Lang, R. G., 'Social origins and social aspirations of Jacobean London, merchants', *Economic History Review*, 2nd ser. 27 (1974), pp. 28–47.

Large, P., 'Urban growth and agricultural change in the West Midlands during the seventeenth and eighteenth centuries', in P. Clark (ed.), *The Transformation of English Provincial Towns 1600–1800*, London, 1984, pp. 169–89.

Laslett, P., 'Clayworth and Cogenhoe', in P. Laslett (ed.), *Family Life and Illicit Love in Earlier Generations*, Cambridge, 1977, pp. 50–101.

— *The World we have Lost: England before the Industrial Age*, New York, 2nd ed. 1973.

Latimer, J., *The Annals of Bristol in the Eighteenth Century*, Bristol, 1893.

— *The Annals of Bristol in the Nineteenth Century*, Bristol, 1887–1902.

— *The Annals of Bristol in the Seventeenth Century*, Bristol, 1900.

Leslie, M., and T. Raylor (eds), *Culture and Cultivation in Early Modern England: Writing and the Land*, Leicester, 1992.

Levy, B., *Quakers and the American Family: British Settlement in the Delaware Valley*, New York, 1988.

Lewalski, B. K., *Writing Women in Jacobean England*, Cambridge, Mass., 1993.

Little, B., *The City and County of Bristol: A Study in Atlantic Civilization*, London, 1954.

Llewellin, P., and A. Saunders, *Book of British Towns*, London, 1982.

Lucas, C., *Writing for Women: The example of Women as Readers in Elizabethan Romance*, Milton Keynes, 1989.

Macfarlane, A., *Marriage and Love in England 1300–1840*, Oxford, 1986.

— 'The Regulation of Marital and Sexual Relationships in Seventeenth-Century England, with Special Reference to the County of Essex', M.Phil. thesis, University of London, 1968.

Macfarlane, A. (ed.), *The Family Life of Ralph Josselin*, Cambridge, 1970.

McGrath, P. (ed.), *Merchants and Merchandise in Seventeenth-Century Bristol*, Bristol Record Society 19, Bristol, 1955.

McInnes, A., 'The emergence of a leisure town: Shrewsbury 1660–1760', *Past and Present* 120 (1988), pp. 53–87.

McIntosh, M. K., 'Servants in the household unit in an Elizabethan English community', *Journal of Family History* 9 (1984), pp. 3–23.

McKendrick, N., 'Commercialization and the economy', in N. McKendrick *et al.* (eds), *The Birth of a Consumer Society*, Bloomington, Ind., 1982, pp. 9–194.

McKendrick, N., J. Brewer, and J. H. Plumb, *The Birth of a Consumer Society: The Commercialization of Eighteenth-Century England*, Bloomington, Ind., 1982.

McKillop, A. D., 'English circulating libraries 1725–50', *Library*, 5th ser. 1 (1934).

Malcolmson, R. W., *Popular Recreations in English Society 1700–1850*, Cambridge, 1973.

— '"A set of ungovernable people": the Kingswood colliers in the eighteenth century', in J. Brewer and J. Styles (eds), *An Ungovernable People: The English and their Law in the Seventeenth and Eighteenth Centuries*, New Brunswick, N.J., 1980, pp. 85–127.

Maltby, B., 'Easingwold marriage horizons', *Local Population Studies* 2 (1969).

Mandrou, R., *De la culture populaire aux XVIIe et XVIIIe siècles: la bibliothèque bleue de Troyes*, Paris, 1985.

Manley, L., 'From matron to monster: Tudor-Stuart London and the languages of urban description', in H. Dubrow and R. Strier (eds), *The Historical Renaissance: New Essays on Tudor and Stuart Literature and Culture*, Chicago, 1988, pp. 347–74.

Mann, J. de L., *The Cloth Industry in the West of England from 1640 to 1880*, Oxford, 1971.

Marion, M., *Les bibliothèques privées à Paris au milieu du XVIIIe siècle*, Paris, 1978.

Martin, H.-J., *Livre, pouvoirs et société à Paris au XVIIe siècle*, Geneva, 1969.

Matar, N. I., 'The idea of the restoration of the Jews in English Protestant thought 1661–1701', *Harvard Theological Review* 78 (1985), pp. 115–48.

Mayhew, G., 'Life-cycle, service and the family unit in early modern Rye', *Continuity and Change* 6 (1991), pp. 201–26.

Megroz, R. L., *The Real Robinson Crusoe*, London, 1939.

Merchant, C., *Radical Ecology: The Search for a Livable World*, London, 1992.

Michaelson, P. H., 'Women in the reading circle', *Eighteenth-Century Life* 4 (1990), pp. 59–69.

Minchinton, W. E., 'Bristol: metropolis of the west in the eighteenth century', in P. Clark (ed.), *The Early Modern Town: A Reader*, London, 1976.

— *The Trade of Bristol in the Eighteenth Century*, Bristol Record Society 20, Bristol, 1957.

Minchon, 'Table of population 1801–1901', in W. Page (ed.), *The Victoria History of the County of Somerset* II, London, 1907.

# Bibliography

Mintz, S. W., 'The changing role of food in the study of consumption', in J. Brewer and R. Porter (eds), *Consumption and the World of Goods*, London, 1993, pp. 261–73.

— *Sweetness and Power: The Place of Sugar in Modern History*, Harmondsworth, 1985.

Money, J., 'Taverns, coffee houses, and clubs: local politics and popular articulacy', *Historical Journal* 14 no. 1 (1971), pp. 15–47.

— 'Teaching in the market-place, or "*Caesar adsum jam forte: Pompey aderat*": the retailing of knowledge in provincial England during the eighteenth century" in J. Brewer and R. Porter (eds), *Consumption and the World of Goods*, London, 1993, pp. 335–77.

Moore, J. S. (ed.), *Clifton and Westbury Probate Inventories 1609–1761*, Bristol, 1981.

— *The Goods and Chattels of our Forefathers: Frampton Cotterell and District Probate Inventories 1539–1804*, Bristol, 1976.

Morgan, K., *Bristol and the Atlantic Trade in the Eighteenth Century*, Cambridge, 1993.

Mornet, D., 'Les enseignements de bibliothèques privées 1750–80', *Revue d'histoire littéraire de la France* 17 (1910), pp. 449–92.

Mortimer, R. S., 'Notes and queries', *Journal of the Friends' Historical Society* 57 no. 3 (1996), pp. 311–14.

Mueller, J., 'Troping utopia: Donne's brief for lesbianism', in J. G. Turner (ed.), *Sexuality and Gender in Early Modern Europe: Institutions, Texts, Images*, Cambridge, 1993, pp. 182–207.

Myers, R., and M. Harris (eds), *Spreading the Word: The Distribution Networks of Print 1550–1850*, Winchester, 1990.

Neuburg, V., *Chapbooks*, London, 1972.

— *The Penny Histories*, Oxford, 1968.

Neve, M., and R. Porter, 'Alexander Catcott: glory and geology', *British Journal for the History of Science* 10 (1977), pp. 37–60.

Nussbaum, F., *The Autobiographical Subject: Gender and Ideology in Eighteenth-Century England*, Baltimore, Md, 1990.

O'Day, R., *Education and Society 1500–1800: The Social Foundations of Education in Early Modern Britain*, London, 1982.

Ortner, S. B., 'Is female to male as nature is to culture?' in M. Z. Rosaldo and L. Lamphere (eds), *Women, Culture and Society*, Stanford, Cal., 1974.

Ozment, S., *When Fathers Ruled: Family Life in Reformation Europe*, Cambridge, Mass., 1983.

Page, W. (ed.), *The Victoria History of the County of Somerset*, II, London, 1911.

— *The Victoria History of the County of Gloucestershire*, II, London, 1907.

Palliser, D. M., 'Civic mentality and the environment in Tudor York', *Northern History* 18 (1982).

— 'The trade guilds of Tudor York', in P. Clark and P. Slack (eds), *Crisis and Order in English Towns 1500–1700*, London, 1972.

— *Tudor York*, Oxford, 1979.

Paradailhe-Galabrun, A., *The Birth of Intimacy: Private and Domestic Life in Early Modern Paris*, Philadelphia, 1991.

Patten, J., *English Towns 1500–1700*, Folkestone, 1978.

— *Rural–Urban Migration in Pre-industrial England*, Oxford University School of Geography Research Papers 6, Oxford, 1973.

Pearl, V., 'Change and stability in seventeenth-century London', *London Journal* 5 no. 1 (1979), pp. 3–34.

Pelling, M., 'Child health care as a social value in early modern England', *Social History of Medicine* 1 (1988), pp. 135–64.

Phythian-Adams, C., 'Ceremony and the citizen: the communal year at Coventry 1450–1550', in P. Clark and P. Slack (eds), *Crisis and Order in English Towns 1500–1700*, London, 1972, pp. 57–85.

— *Desolation of a City: Coventry and the Urban Crisis of the Later Middle Ages*, Cambridge, 1979.

Piggott, S., *The Druids*, New York, 1994.

Pittock, J. H., and A. Wear (eds), *Interpretation and Cultural History*, London, 1991.

Porter, R., *English Society in the Eighteenth Century*, Harmondsworth, 1982.

— 'The people's health in Georgian England', in T. Harris (ed.), *Popular Culture in England c. 1500–1850*, New York, 1995, pp. 124–42.

Pound, J., *Poverty and Vagrancy in Tudor England*, London, 1971.

Power, M. J., 'Shadwell: the development of a London suburb community in the seventeenth century', *London Journal* 4 (1978), pp. 29–46.

Prior, M., 'Women and the urban economy: Oxford 1500–1800', in M. Prior (ed.), *Women in English Society 1500–1800*, London, 1985, pp. 93–117.

Queniart, J., *Culture et société urbaines dans la France de l'ouest au XVIIIe siècle*, Paris, 1978.

Ralph, E., and M. Williams (eds), *The Inhabitants of Bristol in 1696*, Bristol Record Society 25, Bristol, 1968.

Rapoport, A., *The Meaning of the Built Environment: A Nonverbal Communication Approach*, London, 1982.

— *The Mutual Interaction of People and their Built Environment*, The Hague, 1976.

Rappaport, S., *Worlds within Worlds: Structures of Life in Sixteenth-Century London*, Cambridge, 1989.

Raven, J., *Judging New Wealth: Popular Publishing and Responses to Commerce in England 1750–1800*, Oxford, 1992.

Read, D., *Press and People 1790–1850: Opinion in Three English Cities*, London, 1961.

Reay, B., *The Quakers and the English Revolution*, New York, 1985.

— 'Quakerism and society', in J. McGregor and B. Reay (eds), *Radical Religion in the English Revolution*, Oxford, 1984.

— 'The social origins of early Quakerism', *Journal of Interdisciplinary History* 11 no. 1 (1980), pp. 55–72.

Reay, B. (ed.), *Popular Culture in Seventeenth-Century England*, London, 1985.

Rediker, M., *Between the Devil and the Deep Blue Sea: Merchant Seamen, Pirates, and the Anglo-American Maritime World 1700–50*, Cambridge, 1987.

# Bibliography

Reed, M., 'Economic structure and change in seventeenth-century Ipswich', in P. Clark (ed.), *Country Towns in Pre-industrial England*, Leicester, 1981, pp. 88–141.

— *The Georgian Triumph 1700–1830*, London, 1983.

Reitenbach, G., '"Maydes are simple, some men say": Thomas Campion's female persona poems', in A. M. Haselkorn and B. S. Travitsky (eds), *The Renaissance Englishwoman in Print: Counterbalancing the Canon*, Amherst, Mass., 1990, pp. 80–95.

Ripley, P., 'Poverty in Gloucester and its alleviation 1690–1740', *Transactions of the Bristol and Gloucestershire Archaeological Society* 103 (1985), pp. 185–99.

Rivers, I. (ed.), *Books and their Readers in Eighteenth-Century England*, Leicester, 1982.

Roche, D., *The People of Paris: An Essay in Popular Culture in the Eighteenth Century*, Hamburg, 1987.

Rodger, N. A. M., *The Wooden World: An Anatomy of the Georgian Navy*, Glasgow, 1990.

Rogers, N., 'Money, land and lineage: the big bourgeoisie of Hanoverian London', *Social History* 4 (1979), pp. 437–54.

— 'Popular protest in early Hanoverian London', *Past and Present* 79 (1978), pp. 76–9.

— *Whigs and Cities: Popular Politics in the Age of Walpole and Pitt*, Oxford, 1989.

Rose, J., 'Re-reading *The English Common Reader*: a preface to the history of audiences', *Journal of the History of Ideas* 53 (1992), pp. 47–70.

Rothenberg, D., *Hand's End: Technology and the Limits of Nature*, Berkeley, Cal., 1993.

Rubin, M., *Corpus Christi: The Eucharist in Late Medieval Culture*, Cambridge, 1991.

Rule, J., *The Experience of Labour in Eighteenth-Century Industry*, London, 1981.

— *The Vital Century: England's Developing Economy 1714–1815*, London, 1992.

Sacks, D. H., 'Bristol's "little businesses" 1625–41', *Past and Present* 110 (1986), pp. 69–105.

— *Trade, Society and Politics in Bristol 1500–1640*, 2 vols, New York, 1985.

— *The Widening Gate: Bristol and the Atlantic Economy 1450–1700*, Berkeley, Cal., 1991.

Schama, S., *Landscape and Memory*, New York, 1995.

Schivelbusch, W., *Tastes of Paradise: A Social History of Spices, Stimulants, and Intoxicants*, trans. D. Jacobson, New York, 1992.

Schofield, R. S., 'The measurement of literacy in pre-industrial England', in J. R. Goody (ed.), *Literacy in Traditional Societies*, Cambridge, 1968.

Scott, J. W., 'Gender: a useful category of historical analysis', *American Historical Review* 91 (1986), pp. 1053–75.

Scribner, B., 'Is a history of popular culture possible?', *History of European Ideas* 10 (1989), pp. 175–91.

Seaver, P., 'A social contract?: master against servant in the Court of Requests', *History Today* 39 (1989), pp. 50–6.

— *Wallington's World: A Puritan Artisan in Seventeenth-Century London*, Stanford, Cal., 1985.

Sennett, R., *Flesh and Stone: The Body and the City in Western Civilization*, New York, 1994.

Shammas, C., 'Changes in English and Anglo-American consumption from 1550 to 1800', in J. Brewer and R. Porter (eds), *Consumption and the World of Goods*, London, 1993, pp. 177–205.

— *The Pre-industrial Consumer in England and America*, Oxford, 1990.

Shapiro, D. J., *Probability and Certainty in the Seventeenth Century: A Study of the Relationships between Natural Science, Religion, History, Law, and Literature*, Princeton, N.J., 1983.

Sharpe, J. A., *Crime in Early Modern England 1550–1750*, London, 1984.

Sharpe, P., 'Poor children as apprentices in Colyton 1598–1830', *Continuity and Change* 6 (1991), pp. 253–69.

Shevelow, K., *Women and Print Culture: The Construction of Femininity in the Early Periodicals*, London, 1989.

Shoemaker, R. B., *Prosecution and Punishment: Petty Crime and the Law in London and Rural Middlesex* c. *1660–1725*, Cambridge, 1991.

Slack, P., *The English Poor Law 1531–1782*, Cambridge, 1995.

— *Poverty and Policy in Tudor and Stuart England*, London, 1988.

— 'Vagrants and vagrancy in England 1598–1664', *Economic History Review*, 2nd ser. 27 (1974), pp. 360–79.

Smith, A., 'Endowed schools in the diocese of Lichfield and Coventry, 1660–1699', *History of Education* 4 no. 2 (1975), pp. 5–8.

— 'Private schools and schoolmasters in the Diocese of Lichfield and Coventry 1660–99', *History of Education* 5 no. 2 (1976), pp. 117–26.

Smith, G., 'Prescribing the rules of health: self-help and advice in late eighteenth-century England', in R. Porter (ed.), *Patients and Practitioners: Lay Perceptions of Medicine in Pre-industrial Society*, Cambridge, 1985, pp. 249–82.

Smith, R. M., 'Some issues concerning families and their property in rural England 1250–1800', in R. M. Smith (ed.), *Land, Kinship and Life-Cycle*, Cambridge, 1984, pp. 1–86.

Smith, S. R., 'The ideal and reality: apprentice–master relations in seventeenth-century London', *History of Education Quarterly* 21 (1981), pp. 449–59.

— 'London apprentices as seventeenth-century adolescents', *Past and Present* 61 (1973), pp. 149–61.

— 'The social and geographical origins of London apprentices 1630–60', *Guildhall Miscellany* 4 (1973), pp. 195–206.

Smout, T. C., 'Born again at Cambuslang: new evidence on popular religion and literacy in eighteenth-century Scotland', *Past and Present* 97 (1982), pp. 114–27.

Snell, K. D. M., *Annals of the Labouring Poor: Social Change and Agrarian England 1660–1900*, Cambridge, 1985.

Snyder, H. L., 'The circulation of newspapers in the reign of Queen Anne', *Library*, 5th ser., 23 (1968).

Souden, D., 'Migrants and the population structure of later seventeenth-century provincial cities and market towns', in P. Clark (ed.), *The Transformation of English Provincial Towns 1600–1800*, London, 1984, pp. 133–68.

Spaeth, D. A., 'Common prayer? Popular observance of the Anglican liturgy in Restoration Wiltshire', in S. J. Wright (ed.), *Parish, Church and People: Local Studies in Lay Religion*

*1350–1750*, London, 1989, pp. 125–51.

— 'Parsons and Parishioners: Lay–Clerical Conflict and Popular Piety in Wiltshire Villages 1660–1740', Ph.D. thesis, Brown University, 1985.

Spufford, M., *Contrasting Communities: English Villagers in the Sixteenth and Seventeenth Centuries*, Cambridge, 1974.

— 'First steps in literacy: the reading and writing experiences of the humblest seventeenth-century spiritual autobiographers', *Social History* 4 no. 3 (1979), pp. 407–35 and in H. J. Graff (ed.), *Literacy and Social Development in the West*, Cambridge, 1981.

— *The Great Reclothing of Rural England: Petty Chapmen and their Wares in the Seventeenth Century*, London, 1984.

— 'The limitations of the probate inventory', in J. Chartres and D. Hey (eds), *English Rural Society 1500–1800*, Cambridge, 1990.

— 'Puritanism and social control?', in A. Fletcher and J. Stevenson (eds), *Order and Disorder in Early Modern England*, Cambridge, 1985, pp. 41–57.

— *Small Books and Pleasant Histories: Popular Fiction and its Readership in Seventeenth-Century England*, Cambridge, 1981.

Spufford, M. (ed.), *The World of Rural Dissenters 1520–1725*, Cambridge, 1995.

Spurr, J., 'From Puritanism to dissent 1660–1700', in C. Durston and J. Eales (eds), *The Culture of English Puritanism 1560–1700*, New York, 1996, pp. 234–65.

Staves, S., *Married Women's Separate Property in England 1660–1833*, Cambridge, Mass., 1990.

Steer, F. W., *Farm and Cottage Inventories of Mid-Essex 1635–1749*, London, 2nd ed. 1969.

Stevenson, B., 'The social and economic status of post-Restoration dissenters 1660–1725', in M. Spufford (ed.), *The World of Rural Dissenters 1520–1725*, Cambridge, 1995, pp. 332–59.

— 'The social integration of post-Restoration dissenters 1660–1725', in M. Spufford (ed.), *The World of Rural Dissenters 1520–1725*, Cambridge, 1995, pp. 360–87.

Stilgoe, J. R., *Borderland: Origins of the American Suburb 1820–1939*, New Haven, Conn., 1988.

Stone, L., *The Crisis of the Aristocracy 1558–1641* (Oxford, 1965; abridged edn, 1967).

— *The Family, Sex and Marriage in England 1500–1800*, New York, abridged ed. 1979.

— 'Literacy and education in England 1640–1900', *Past and Present* 42 (1969), pp. 69–139.

Stone, L. (ed.), *Schooling and Society*, Baltimore, Md, 1976.

Thirsk, J., 'Agricultural Innovations and their diffusion 1640–1750', in J. Thirsk (ed.), *Agricultural Change*, Cambridge, 1990, pp. 263–319.

— *The Agrarian History of England and Wales* IV, Cambridge, 1967.

— 'Enclosing and engrassing', in J. Thirsk (ed.), *Agricultural Change*, Cambridge, 1990, pp. 54–66.

— 'The horticultural revolution: a cautionary note on prices', *Journal of Interdisciplinary History* 14 no. 2 (1983), pp. 299–302.

— 'New crops and their diffusion: tobacco-growing in seventeenth-century England', in

C. W. Chalklin and M. A. Havinden (eds), *Rural Change and Urban Growth 1500–1800*, London, 1974.

Thirsk, J. (ed.), *Agricultural Change: Policy and Practice 1500–1750*, Cambridge, 1990.

Thomas, K., *Man and the Natural World: Changing Attitudes in England 1500–1800*, Harmondsworth, 1984.

— *Religion and the Decline of Magic*, New York, 1971.

Thompson, E. P., *Customs in Common*, Harmondsworth, 1993.

— 'Eighteenth-century English Society: class struggle without class?', *Social History* 3 no. 2 (1978).

— *The Making of the English Working Class*, New York, 1963.

— 'Patrician society, plebeian culture', *Journal of Social History* 7 no, 4 (1974), pp. 382–405.

— '"Rough music": le charivari anglais', *Annales E.S.C.* 27 no. 2 (1972), pp. 285–312.

— *Whigs and Hunters: The Origins of the Black Act*, New York, 1975.

Tillyard, E. M. W., *The Elizabethan World Picture*, New York, 1944.

Tittler, R., *Architecture and Power: The Town Hall and the English Urban Community* c. 1500–1640, Oxford, 1991.

Todd, B. J., 'The remarrying widow: a stereotype reconsidered', in M. Prior (ed.), *Women in English Society 1500–1800*, London, 1985, pp. 54–92.

Trumbach, R., 'The birth of the queen: sodomy and the emergence of gender equality in modern culture 1660–1750', in M. Duberman, M. Vicinus, and G. Chauncey (eds), *Hidden from History: Reclaiming the Gay and Lesbian Past*, New York, 1989, pp. 129–40.

— 'London's sodomites: homosexual behavior and Western culture in the eighteenth century', *Journal of Social History* 11 (1977), pp. 1–33.

— *Sodomy Trials*, New York, 1986.

Turner, J. G. (ed.), *Sexuality and Gender in Early Modern Europe: Institutions, Texts, Images*, Cambridge, 1993.

Turner, M. E., 'Agricultural productivity in eighteenth-century England: further strains of speculation', *Economic History Review*, 2nd ser. 37 (1984), pp. 256–7.

Underdown, D., *Fire from Heaven: Life in an English Town in the Seventeenth Century*, New Haven, Conn., 1992.

— *Revel, Riot, and Rebellion: Popular Politics and Culture in England 1603–1660*, Oxford, 1985.

— 'The taming of the scold: the enforcement of patriarchal authority in early modern England', in A. Fletcher and J. Stevenson (eds), *Order and Disorder in Early Modern England*, Cambridge, 1985, pp. 116–36.

Van Koolbergen, H., 'De materiele cultuur van Weesp en Weesperkarspel in de zeventiende en achttiende eeuw', *Volkskundig Bulletin* 9 no. 1 (1983), pp. 3–52.

Vann, R. T., *The Social Development of English Quakerism 1655–1755*, Cambridge, Mass., 1969.

Vickery, A., 'Women and the world of goods: a Lancashire consumer and her possessions 1751–81', in J. Brewer and R. Porter (eds), *Consumption and the World of Goods*, London, 1993, pp. 274–301.

# Bibliography

Von Thunen, J., *Die isolierte Staat* (1826).

Walker, R. B., 'Advertising in London newspapers 1650–1750', *Business History* 15 (1973), pp. 112–30.

Wallace, D. D., *Puritans and Predestination: Grace in English Theology 1525–1695*, Chapel Hill, N.C., 1982.

Waller, G. F., 'The Countess of Pembroke and gendered reading', in A. M. Haselkorn and B. S. Travitsky (eds), *The Renaissance Englishwoman in Print: Counterbalancing the Canon*, Amherst, Mass., 1990, pp. 327–45.

Wareing, J., 'Changes in the geographical distribution of the recruitment of apprentices to the London companies 1486–1750', *Journal of Historical Geography* 7 (1981), pp. 241–50.

Watt, T., *Cheap Print and Popular Piety 1550–1640*, Cambridge, 1991.

Watts, M., *The Dissenters: From the Reformation to the French Revolution*, Oxford, 1978.

Weatherell, C., 'The log percent (*L%*): an absolute measure of relative change', *Historical Methods* 19 (1986), pp. 25–6.

Weatherill, L., *Consumer Behaviour and Material Culture in Britain 1660–1760*, London, 1988.

— 'The meaning of consumer behaviour in late seventeenth- and early eighteenth-century England', in J. Brewer and R. Porter (eds), *Consumption and the World of Goods*, London, 1993, pp. 206–27.

— 'Patterns of Consumption in Britain *c.* 1660–1760: Problems and Sources', unpublished paper, Clark Library seminars, October 1988.

— 'A possession of one's own: women and consumer behaviour in England 1660–1740', *Journal of British Studies* 25 (1986), pp. 131–56.

White, L., 'The historical roots of our ecological crisis', *Science* 155 (10 March 1967), pp. 1203–7.

Whiting, R., *The Blind Devotion of the People: Popular Religion and the English Reformation*, Cambridge, 1989.

Wiles, R. M., *Freshest Advices: Early Provincial Newspapers in England*, Columbus, Oh., 1965.

Williams, B., *The Making of Manchester Jewry 1740–1875*, Manchester, 1976.

Williams, G. R., *London in the Country: The Growth of Suburbia*, London, 1975.

Wills, J. E., junior, 'European consumption and Asian production in the seventeenth and eighteenth centuries', in J. Brewer and R. Porter (eds), *Consumption and the World of Goods*, London, 1993, pp. 133–47.

Wiltenburg, J., *Disorderly Women and Female Power in the Street Literature of Early Modern England and Germany*, Charlottesville, Va., 1992.

Winslow, C., 'Sussex smugglers', in D. Hay *et al.* (eds), *Albion's Fatal Tree*, New York, 1975.

Woodward, D., 'The background to the Statute of Artificers: the genesis of labour policy 1558–63', *Economic History Review*, 2nd ser. 33 (1980), pp. 32–44.

Wright, S. J. (ed.), *Parish, Church and People: Local Studies in Lay Religion 1350–1750*, London, 1988.

Wrightson, K., 'Two concepts of order: justices, constables and jurymen in seventeenth-century England', in J. Brewer and J. Styles (eds), *An Ungovernable People: The English and their Law in the Seventeenth and Eighteenth Centuries*, New Brunswick, N.J., 1980, pp. 21–46.

Wrightson, K., and D. Levine, *Poverty and Piety in an English Village: Terling 1525–1700*, London, 1979.

Wrigley, E. A., *An Introduction to English Historical Demography*, London, 1966.

— 'Parasite or stimulus: the town in a pre-industrial economy', in P. Abrams and E. A. Wrigley (eds), *Towns in Societies: Essays in Economic History and Historical Sociology*, Cambridge, 1978, pp. 295–309.

— 'A simple model of London's importance in changing English society and economy 1650–1750', *Past and Present* 37 (1967), pp. 44–70.

Wrigley, E. A., and R. S. Schofield, *The Population History of England: A Reconstruction 1541–1871*, Cambridge, 1981, 2nd ed. 1989.

Yentsch, A. E., *A Chesapeake Family and their Slaves: A Study in Historical Archaeology*, Cambridge, 1994.

# Index

Note: 'n' after a page number refers to a note on that page.